I DISSENT.

Ruth Bader Ginsburg Dissents

ABU

Ruth Bader Ginsburg Dissents

FOREWORD BY LINDA GREENHOUSE

Word Cloud Classics
San Diego

Canterbury Classics
An imprint of Printers Row Publishing Group
9717 Pacific Heights Blvd, San Diego, CA 92121
www.canterburyclassicsbooks.com • mail@canterburyclassicsbooks.com

Compilation © 2022 Printers Row Publishing Group

All rights reserved. No part of this publication may be reproduced, distributed, or transmitted in any form or by any means, including photocopying, recording, or other electronic or mechanical methods, without the prior written permission of the publisher, except in the case of brief quotations embodied in critical reviews and certain other noncommercial uses permitted by copyright law.

Printers Row Publishing Group is a division of Readerlink Distribution Services, LLC.
Canterbury Classics and Word Cloud Classics are registered trademarks of Readerlink Distribution Services, LLC.

Correspondence regarding the content of this book should be sent to Canterbury Classics, Editorial Department, at the above address.

Publisher: Peter Norton • Associate Publisher: Ana Parker
Art Director: Charles McStravick
Senior Developmental Editor: April Graham
Editor: Traci Douglas
Production Team: Beno Chan, Julie Greene, Rusty von Dyl

Image credit: Rob Crandall/Shutterstock.com

Library of Congress Cataloging-in-Publication Data

Names: Ginsburg, Ruth Bader, author.
Title: Ruth Bader Ginsburg dissents / foreword by Linda Greenhouse.
Description: San Diego, CA : Word Cloud Classics, [2022] | Summary: "During
  her 27 years as an associate justice on the U.S. Supreme Court, Ruth
  Bader Ginsburg became well known for her strongly worded dissenting
  opinions against the decisions of the conservative majority. Ginsburg
  was a fierce supporter of women's rights whose personal experiences
  helped shape her into a feminist icon who employed logical,
  well-presented arguments to show that gender discrimination was harmful
  to all members of society. Ruth Bader Ginsburg Dissents includes
  majority and dissenting opinions that Ginsburg drafted during her time
  on the U.S. Supreme Court, along with briefs from her career before she
  was appointed to the court in 1993"-- Provided by publisher.
Identifiers: LCCN 2021044861 (print) | LCCN 2021044862 (ebook) | ISBN
  9781645178897 | ISBN 9781667201146 (ebook)
Subjects: LCSH: Dissenting opinions--United States. | Law--United
  States--Cases. | LCGFT: Court decisions and opinions.
Classification: LCC KF213.G56 2022 (print) | LCC KF213.G56 (ebook) | DDC
  347.73/2634--dc23/eng/20211006
LC record available at https://lccn.loc.gov/2021044861
LC ebook record available at https://lccn.loc.gov/2021044862

Printed in China

26 25 24 23 22 1 2 3 4 5

Editor's Note: The pieces in this book have been published in their original form to preserve the author's intent and style.

Contents

Foreword

"In very recent years, a new appreciation of women's place has been generated in the United States."

So wrote the young Ruth Bader Ginsburg in her first Supreme Court brief [pp. 1–44]. The case, decided unanimously in November 1971, was *Reed* v. *Reed*. It is not as well-known as *Brown* v. *Board of Education* or *Roe* v. *Wade*, but it made headlines in its day and it reverberates still. It marked the first time the Supreme Court had ever found that a government policy that discriminated on the basis of sex violated the Constitution's guarantee of equal protection. It also introduced Ruth Bader Ginsburg to the world and so, fittingly, it introduces this collection of her writings.

There are other names besides Ginsburg's on the brief, and she did not actually argue the case, which concerned a state law that automatically and arbitrarily preferred men over women to be chosen to administer the estates of people who died without naming an administrator. But Ginsburg was the author of what has come to be called the "grandmother brief" for its multifaceted argument for why, nearly two hundred years after adoption of the Fourteenth Amendment's Equal Protection Clause, sex discrimination should finally be recognized as a constitutional harm. Nearly every subsequent argument on behalf of sex equality, including the half dozen cases that Ginsburg herself argued and won during her pre-judicial career, drew on the brief's deep research and reflected its passion.

The title of this book is *Ruth Bader Ginsburg Dissents,* and, indeed, it was her powerful dissenting voice that earned her the "Notorious RBG" nickname during her final years on the Supreme Court. (She relished the nickname, bestowed on her by two young women, Irin Carmon and Shana Knizhnik, in their 2015 book, *Notorious RBG: The Life and Times of Ruth Bader Ginsburg*.) But she was, in fact, in the majority more than twice as frequently as she was in dissent. During her 27-year tenure, from her appointment by President Bill Clinton in 1993 until her death from pancreatic cancer on September 18, 2020, she wrote 115 dissenting opinions; however, she also wrote 216 majority opinions, and 87 opinions concurring with the majority. These statistics make the occasions when she felt compelled to dissent all the more interesting.

Dissent did not come naturally to this soft-spoken woman. A lecture she gave while she was a judge on the federal appeals court in Washington, D.C., described the "effective judge" as one who "speaks in a moderate and restrained voice" and who "strives to persuade and not to pontificate." Not that Ruth Bader Ginsburg ever pontificated, but what became clear over time, as new appointments turned the Supreme Court steadily to the right, was that when she was unable to persuade a majority of her colleagues, she turned her persuasive powers on audiences outside the court. By the end, she was also speaking to history.

In one of her most notable dissenting opinions, her audience was, explicitly, Congress. The case was *Ledbetter* v. *Goodyear Tire & Rubber Company* [pp. 197–215], decided in 2007. Lilly Ledbetter was the only woman in her managerial level at a Goodyear plant in Alabama. She learned only after she retired that, for years, she had been paid less than any of the men. She sued the company for pay discrimination under the Civil Rights Act's Title VII, which bars sex discrimination in the workplace. The law required a complaint to be filed within 180 days "after the alleged unlawful employment practice occurred." Ledbetter's lawyers argued that because a new act of pay discrimination occurred with each paycheck, her lawsuit was timely. A federal district court jury in Gadsden, Alabama, ruled in her favor. But by a vote of 5 to 4, the Supreme Court held that Ledbetter should have sued years earlier, when the disparity began.

Ginsburg's dissenting opinion spoke for all four dissenters. She accused the majority of ignoring "the real-world characteristics of pay discrimination," which occurs over time, shielded from the victim's knowledge by the secrecy that commonly prevents employees from learning what others are making. This was not a constitutional case, Ginsburg pointed out. It presented a simple question of statutory interpretation. Did Congress intend such a "parsimonious" reading of a law that embodied the country's commitment to equality? "The ball is in Congress's court," she wrote.

And Congress heard her. The first bill that President Barack Obama signed following his inauguration in 2009 was the Lilly Ledbetter Fair Pay Act, correcting the Supreme Court's reading of Title VII and ensuring that women would not suffer similar discrimination in the future.

Of the nine dissenting opinions collected here, it is no coincidence that seven date from the court's 2006–2007 term or later. In January 2006, Justice Sandra Day O'Connor retired, leaving Ginsburg the only woman on the Supreme Court. (She would later be joined by President Obama's two appointees, Sonia Sotomayor and Elena Kagan.) O'Connor, a moderate conservative, had for years held the center position on the court. Her replacement by Samuel Alito, an appointee of President George W. Bush, wrenched the court almost immediately to the right, a fact underscored by one of Ginsburg's dissenting opinions collected here, *Gonzales* v. *Carhart* [pp. 175–196].

This was an abortion case. At issue was the constitutionality of the federal Partial-Birth Abortion Ban Act of 2003. Congress had enacted this statute to outlaw a particular method of abortion during the second trimester of pregnancy. Anti-abortion activists had affixed the unscientific name "partial-birth abortion" to the procedure and had succeeded in prohibiting it in a number of states. In 2000, the court had ruled that a Nebraska law prohibiting the procedure was inconsistent with the precedents that protected a woman's right to abortion. Justice O'Connor was in the 5-to-4 majority that struck down the Nebraska law in *Stenberg* v. *Carhart.*

Although the federal law was essentially identical, the court upheld it. With Alito in place of O'Connor, the vote this time was 5 to 4 the other way. In her opinion for all four dissenters, Ginsburg noted pointedly that the court was now "differently composed than it was when we last considered a restrictive abortion regulation." This was a highly unusual statement for a member of the court to make. It stripped away whatever cover of legitimacy the majority hoped to place over what was, after all, not a change that was in any way legally relevant, but simply a change in personnel. The new decision, Ginsburg wrote, "is hardly faithful to our earlier invocations of 'the rule of law.'"

Of the dissenting opinions collected here, one other deserves special mention. It was Ruth Bader Ginsburg's last, issued on July 8, 2020, ten weeks before her death. In fact, when the justices heard argument in the case, Ginsburg had phoned in from her hospital bed. *Little Sisters of the Poor* v. *Pennsylvania* [pp. 339–358] concerned a policy adopted by the Trump administration to provide employers who had religious or simply "moral" objections to birth control with an exemption from the federal requirement to include contraception coverage as part of an employee health plan. It was the last of a series of cases, beginning in 2014 with *Burwell* v. *Hobby Lobby Stores* (in which Ginsburg's dissenting opinion is also printed here, pp. 305–334), that required the court to weigh the religious claims of a few against the entitlement of many to a federal benefit intended to be available to all.

The employer in this case was an order of nuns who run nursing homes for the elderly poor. They require neither their employees nor those they serve to pass a religious test. Their argument was that any connection to the government's contraception program would make them complicit in sin, even if all they had to do was simply "self-certify" that they did not want to offer contraception coverage. Under the Affordable Care Act, the insurer would then have been required to provide the coverage with no further involvement by the nuns. The court upheld the Trump policy.

Ginsburg's dissenting opinion was filled with both passion and facts. Citing the government's estimate, she noted that, as a result of the court's decision, "between 70,500 and 126,400 women would immediately lose access to no-cost contraceptive services." In her later years, Ginsburg had become increasingly concerned about the court's steady erosion of the wall between church and state. In this final opinion, she placed an unmistakable label on what had occurred: "Today, for the first time, the court casts totally aside countervailing rights and interests in its zeal to secure religious rights to the nth degree."

During the Supreme Court term following Ginsburg's death, echoes of her dissenting voice could be heard in opinions by the two women with whom she served, Sonia Sotomayor and Elena Kagan. For Justice Kagan, in particular, this was something new; in her previous ten years on the bench, she had built her dissents on meticulous logic rather than compelling rhetoric. In the 2020–2021 term, a change was evident in her dissenting opinion on *Brnovich* v. *Democratic National Committee*, a voting rights case, in which she radiated anger at the majority's weakening of a major section of the Voting Rights Act of 1965, including five references to Ginsburg's dissenting opinion from 2013 in *Shelby County* v. *Holder* [pp. 251–284].

It was also possible to hear Ginsburg's voice in Sotomayor's series of dissenting opinions during the 2020–2021 term objecting to the thirteen federal executions carried out in seven months. Referring angrily to "this expedited spree of executions" that had taken place without the court granting a single hearing, she declared "This is not justice."

And so, Ruth Bader Ginsburg's dissenting voice lives on. It is here in the pages of this volume, and it resides in those she inspired—on the bench and off—to commit themselves to make her vision of equal justice a reality.

RUTH BADER GINSBURG
DISSENTS

Brief for the Appellant in
Reed v. *Reed*
(1971)

*C*ecil and Sally Reed, a separated couple living in Idaho, both sought to be named administrator of the estate of their son, Richard, who died at nineteen without a will. Idaho law stated that "of several persons claiming and equally entitled to administer, males must be preferred to females," and Cecil was named the administrator. After numerous appeals, the case reached the United States Supreme Court.

Ruth Bader Ginsburg, then a professor of law at Rutgers University, cowrote a brief for the appellant, in which she argued that the Idaho law arbitrarily favoring men over women was unconstitutional. The Supreme Court unanimously agreed, finding that the Idaho law "cannot stand in the face of the Fourteenth Amendment's command that no State deny the equal protection of the laws to any person within its jurisdiction." The brief is an early example of Ginsburg's drive to advance gender equality.

Original footnotes have been retained but renumbered.

ARGUMENT
Introduction

By the explicit terms of Sec. 15-314 of the Idaho Code, appellant was denied the right to qualify as the administrator of her son's estate solely because of her sex. The issue in this case is whether, as appellant contends, mandatory disqualification of a woman for appointment as an administrator, whenever a man "equally entitled to administer" applies for appointment, constitutes arbitrary and unequal treatment proscribed by the fourteenth amendment to the United States Constitution.

In determining whether a state statute establishes a classification violative of the fourteenth amendment guarantee that those similarly situated shall be similarly treated, this Court has developed two standards of review. See *Developments in the Law—Equal Protection*, 82 Harv. L. Rev. 1065 (1969).

In the generality of cases a test of reasonable classification has been applied: Does the classification established by the legislature bear a reasonable and just relation to the permissible objective of the legislation? Under this general test, if the purpose of the statute is a permissible one and if the statutory classification bears the required fair relationship to that purpose, the constitutional mandate will be held satisfied. *F. S. Royster Guano Co.* v. *Virginia*, 253 U.S. 412, 415 (1920) ("But the classification must be reasonable, not arbitrary, and must rest upon some ground of difference having a fair substantial relation to the object of the legislation, so that all persons similarly circumstanced shall be treated alike.").

In two circumstances, however, a more stringent test is applied. When the legislative product affects "fundamental rights or interests," *e.g.*, *Harper* v. *Virginia Board of Elections,* 383 U.S. 663, 667, 670 (1966) (poll tax in state elections), or when the statute classifies on a basis "inherently suspect," this Court will subject the legislation to "the most rigid scrutiny." [1] Thus, a statute distinguishing on the basis of race or ancestry embodies a "suspect" or "invidious" classification and, unless supported by the most compelling affirmative justification, will not pass constitutional muster. *Graham* v. *Richardson*, —— U.S. —— June 14, 1971);

---

1 *Korematsu* v. *United States*, 323 U.S. 214, 216 (1944). Although the first case to develop the concept that classifications based on race are "suspect," *Korematsu* justified the detention of men and women solely because of their Japanese ancestry, on the basis of an espionage threat, when imminent foreign invasion was feared. With the glaring exception of *Korematsu*, "suspect" classifications have not survived this Court's rigid scrutiny. In retrospect, the extreme personal deprivation countenanced wholesale in *Korematsu* is recognized generally as having been grossly disproportionate to the national security interest at stake. See A. Girdner & A. Loftis, The Great Betrayal: The Evacuation of Japanese-Americans during World War II 16–32 (1969); B. Hosokawa, Nisei: The Quiet Americans 292–98 (1969).

McLaughlin v. *Florida*, 379 U.S. 184 (1964); *Takahashi* v. *Fish and Game Commission*, 334 U.S. 410 (1948).

It is appellant's principal position that the sex line drawn by Sec. 15-314 of the Idaho Code, mandating subordination of women to men without regard to individual capacity, creates a "suspect classification" for which no compelling justification can be shown. It is appellant's alternate position that, without regard to the suspect or invidious nature of the classification, the line drawn by the Idaho legislature, arbitrarily ranking the woman as inferior to the man by directing the probate court to take no account of the respective qualifications of the individuals involved, lacks the constitutionally required fair and reasonable relation to any legitimate state interest in providing for the efficient administration of decedents' estates.

In very recent years, a new appreciation of women's place has been generated in the United States.[2] Activated by feminists of both sexes, courts and legislatures have begun to recognize the claim of women to full membership in the class "persons" entitled to due process guarantees of life and liberty and the equal protection of the laws. But the distance to equal opportunity for women—in the face of the pervasive social, cultural and legal roots of sex-based discrimination[3]—remains considerable. In the absence of a firm constitutional foundation for equal treatment of men and women by the law, women seeking to be judged on their individual merits will continue to encounter law-sanctioned obstacles.

Currently, federal and state measures are beginning to offer

---

2 See, *e.g.*, American Women, Report of the President's Commission on the Status of Women, and seven accompanying committee reports (1963); American Women 1963–1968, Report of the Interdepartmental Committee on the Status of Women, and four accompanying Task Force Reports of the Citizens' Advisory Council (1968); Kanowitz, Women and the Law: The Unfinished Revolution (1969); A Matter of Simple Justice, Report of President's Task Force on Women's Rights and Responsibilities (1970); P. Murray, The Rights of Women, in N. Dorsen ed., The Rights of Americans: What They Are—What They Should Be 521 (1971).

3 In 1942, an incisive appraisal of the situation of women in the United States was made by the Swedish sociologist, Gunnar Myrdal, whose study was a source this Court relied on for information concerning race relations in *Brown* v. *Board of Education*, 347 U.S. 483, 494–95 n. 11 (1954). G. Myrdal, An American Dilemma 1073–78 (20th anniv. ed. 1962).

relief from discriminatory employment practices.[4] Principal measures on the national level are the Equal Pay Act of 1963,[5] Title VII of the Civil Rights Act of 1964,[6] and Executive Orders designed to eliminate discrimination against women in federal jobs and jobs under federal contracts.[7] These developments promise some protection of the equal right of men and women to pursue the employment for which individual talent and capacity best equip them. But important as these federal measures are, their coverage is limited. Even in the employment area they cover only a small percentage of the nation's employers and less than half of the labor force.[8] They provide no assistance at all in the many areas apart from employment, as in the case at bar for example, where women are relegated to second class status.

The experience of trying to root out racial discrimination in the United States has demonstrated that even when the arsenal of legislative and judicial remedies is well stocked, social and cultural institutions shaped by centuries of law-sanctioned bias

---

4 See generally 1969 Handbook on Women Workers, Women's Bureau Bulletin 294, Dept. of Labor [hereinafter Handbook].

It has long been the case that sex bias takes a greater economic toll than racial bias. For example, in 1966, the median wage or salary income of year-round, full-time workers was $7164 for white men, $4528 for nonwhite men, $4152 for white women, and $2949 for nonwhite women. Handbook at 137. In 1968 the median earnings of fully employed men workers were $7664; for fully employed women workers, median earnings were $4457. Background Facts on Women Workers in the United States, Women's Bureau, Dept. of Labor 4 (1970).

5 29 U.S.C. §206(d) (1964); see T. Murphy, Female Wage Discrimination: A Study of the Equal Pay Act 1963–1970, 39 U. Cin. L. Rev. 615 (1970).

6 42 U.S.C. §2000e (1964) ; see Developments in the Law—Title VII, 84 Harv. L. Rev. 1109, 1166–95 (1971); T. Barnard, The Conflict Between State Protective Legislation and Federal Laws Prohibiting Sex Discrimination: Is It Resolved, 17 Wayne L. Rev. 25 (1971).

7 Executive Order No. 11246, as amended by Executive Order No. 11375, 3 CFR 320 (Supp. 1967) (applicable to jobs under federal contracts); Executive Order 11478 (applicable to employment in the federal government).

8 Equal Pay Act coverage is limited to employees covered by the minimum wage provisions of the Fair Labor Standards Act. Government (federal, state, local) employees, executive, administrative and professional persons, teachers, most domestic and migrant workers are not covered. Many of the exempt industries and positions are heavily populated with female workers. See T. Murphy, supra, 39 U. Cin. L. Rev. at 619–20. Title VII excludes employers of 24 or fewer employees, private membership clubs, educational institutions and federal, state and local governments. It has been estimated that 92% of all employers, and 60% of all employees are excluded from Title VII coverage. See E . R. Larsen, 42 U.S.C. Section 1981 as a Remedy for Racial Discrimination in Employment, 4 Clearinghouse Review 572, 573 (1971) (percentages based on Department of Labor statistics).

do not crumble under the weight of legal pronouncements proscribing discrimination. Thus, just as the Equal Pay Act and Title VII have not ended discrimination against women even in the employment spheres to which they apply, sex-based discrimination will not disintegrate upon this Court's recognition that sex is a suspect classification. But without this recognition, the struggle for an end to sex-based discrimination will extend well beyond the current period in time, a period in which any functional justification for difference in treatment has ceased to exist.

Very recent history has taught us that, where racial discrimination is concerned, this Court's refusal in *Plessy* v. *Ferguson*, 163 U.S. 537 (1896), to declare the practice unconstitutional, reinforced the institutional and political foundations of racism, made it more difficult eventually to extirpate, and postponed for fifty-eight years the inevitable inauguration of a national commitment to abolish racial discrimination.

As an example of the slow awakening of the national conscience to the more subtle assignment of inferior status to women, this Court a generation ago came close to repeating the mistake of *Plessy* v. *Ferguson*. See *Goesaert* v. *Cleary*, 335 U.S. 464 (1948). Fortunately, the Court already has acknowledged a new direction, see *United States* v. *Dege*, 364 U.S. 51, 54 (1960), and the case at bar provides the opportunity clearly and affirmatively to inaugurate judicial recognition of the constitutionally imperative claim made by women for the equal rights before the law guaranteed to all persons.

In sum, appellant urges in Point I of this brief that designation of sex as a suspect classification is overdue, is the only wholly satisfactory standard for dealing with the claim in this case, and should be the starting point for assessing that claim. Nonetheless, as developed in Point II of this brief, it should be apparent that the reasonable relation test also must yield a conclusion in favor of the appellant. Surely this Court cannot give its approval to a fiduciary statute that demands preference for an idler, because he is a man, and rejects a potentially diligent administrator solely because she is a woman. In addition to the argument based on the traditional reasonable relation test, Point II formulates a modification of that test, appropriate in the event this Court, contrary to appellant's primary position, would delay recognition of sex as a suspect classification. The proposed modification would reverse the presumption of rationality when sex is implicated and, rather than requiring the party attacking a statute to show that the classification is irrational, would require the statute's proponent to prove it rational.

I.

The sex-based classification in Section 15-314 of the Idaho Code, established for a purpose unrelated to any biological difference between the sexes, is a "suspect classification" proscribed by the fourteenth amendment to the United States Constitution.

A. Sex as a Suspect Classification.

Commanding a preference for men and the subordination of women, Section 15-314 of the Idaho Code reflects a view, prevalent in the law a generation ago that, with minimal justification, the legislature could draw "a sharp line between the sexes." *Goesaert* v. *Cleary*, 335 U.S. 464, 466 (1948). Similarly, it was once settled law that differential treatment of the races was constitutionally permissible. *Plessy* v. *Ferguson*, 163 U.S. 537 (1896). Today, of course, a classification based on race, nationality or alienage is inherently "suspect" or "invidious" and this Court has required "close judicial scrutiny" of a statute or governmental action based upon such a classification. *Graham* v. *Richardson*, —— U.S. —— (June 14, 1971). The proponent of a measure creating "classifications constitutionally suspect" must establish an "overriding statutory purpose," *McLaughlin* v. *Florida*, 379 U.S. 184, 192 (1964), and bears "a very heavy burden of justification." *Loving* v. *Virginia*, 388 U.S. 1, 9 (1967).

It is only within the last half-dozen years that the light of constitutional inquiry has focused upon sex discrimination. Emerging from this fresh examination, in the context of the significant changes that have occurred in society's attitudes,[9] is a deeper appreciation of the premise underlying the "suspect classification" doctrine: although the legislature may distinguish between individuals on the basis of their ability or need, it is presumptively impermissible to distinguish on the basis of congenital and unalterable biological traits of birth over which the individual has no control and for which he or she should not be penalized. Such conditions include not only race, a matter clearly within the "suspect classification" doctrine, but include as well the sex of the individual.[10]

The kinship between race and sex discrimination has attracted increasing attention. A capsule description of the close relationship between the two appears in *Sex Discrimination and Equal Protection: Do We Need a Constitutional Amendment?*, 84 Harv. L. Rev. 1499, 1507–1508 (1971) (original footnotes retained but renumbered):

> The similarities between race and sex discrimination are indeed striking.[1] Both classifications create large, natural classes, membership in which is beyond the individual's control;[2] both are highly visible characteristics on which legislators have found it easy to draw gross, stereotypical distinctions. Historically, the legal position of black slaves was justified by analogy to the legal status of women.[3] Both slaves and wives were once subject to the all-encompassing paternalistic power of the male head of the house.[4]

9 See E. Dahlstrom ed., The Changing Roles of Men and Women (1967); A. Montagu, Man's Most Dangerous Myth 181–84 (4th ed. 1964); G. Myrdal, An American Dilemma 1073–78 (2d ed. 1962); Watson, Social Psychology: Issues and Insights 435–56 (1966); P. Murray & M. Eastwood, Jane Crow and the Law: Sex Discrimination and Title VII, 34 Geo. Wash. L. Rev. 232, 235–42 (1965).

10 See *Hernandez* v. *Texas*, 347 U.S. 475, 478 (1954) ("The Fourteenth Amendment is not directed solely against discrimination due to a 'two-class theory'—that is, based upon differences between 'white' and Negro.").

Arguments justifying different treatment for the sexes on the grounds of female inferiority, need for male protection, and happiness in their assigned roles bear a striking resemblance to the half-truths surrounding the myth of the "happy slave".[5] The historical patterns of race and sex discrimination have, in many instances, produced similar present day results. Women and blacks, for example, hold the lowest paying jobs in industry, with black men doing slightly better than white women.[6] . . .

The factual similarities between race and sex discrimination are reinforced by broader concerns. Through a process of social evolution, racial distinctions have become unacceptable. The old social consensus that race was a clear indication of inferiority has yielded to the notion that race is unrelated to ability or performance. Even allegedly rational attempts at racial classification are now generally rejected outright. The burden of showing that these attempts are based on something other than prejudice is enormous.

There are indications that sex classifications may be undergoing a similar metamorphosis in the public mind. Once thought normal, proper, and ordained in the "very nature of things," sex discrimination may soon be seen as a sham, not unlike that perpetrated in the name of racial superiority. Whatever differences may exist between the sexes, legislative judgments have frequently been based on inaccurate stereotypes of the capacities and sensibilities of women. In view of the damage that has been inflicted on individuals in the name of these "differences," any continuing distinctions should, like race, bear a heavy burden of proof. One function of the fourteenth amendment ought to be to put such broad-ranging concerns into the fundamental law of the land.[7]

1 See A. Montagu, Man's Most Dangerous Myth 181–84 (4th ed. 1964); G. Myrdal, An American Dilemma 1073–78 (2d ed. 1962).

2 See Crozier, Constitutionality of Discrimination Based on Sex, 15 Boston U.L. Rev. 723, 728 (1935). See also Report of the Committee on Civil and Political Rights to the President's Commission on the Status of Women 79 (1963).

3 G. Myrdal, *supra*, note 1 at 1073.

4 *Id.* at 1073–75.

5 See A. Montagu, *supra*, note 1 at 181.

6 See N.Y. Times, Jan. 31, 1971, § 1, at 50, col. 3.

7 *Cf.* Developments in the Law—Equal Protection, 82 Harv. L. Rev. 1065, 1174 n. 61 (1969) (as the truth of the proposition that biological differences between the sexes correlate with performance is drawn into question, all sexual classifications become more suspect).

Dr. Pauli Murray recently synopsized scholarly commentary on the same point in *The Negro Woman's Stake in the Equal Rights Amendment*, 6 Harv. Civ. Rts. Civ. Lib. Law Rev. 253, 257 (1971) (original footnotes retained but renumbered):

The relationship between sexual and racial prejudice is confirmed by contemporary scholarship.[1] The history of western culture, and particularly of ecclesiastical and English common law, suggests that the traditionally subordinate status of women provided models for the oppression of other groups. The treatment of a woman as her husband's property, as subject to his corporal punishment, as incompetent to testify under canon law, and as subject to numerous legal and social restrictions based upon sex, were precedents for the later treatment of slaves. In 1850, George Fitzhugh, one of the foremost defenders of slavery in the United States analogized it to the position of women and children.[2] And in 1944, a justice of the North Carolina Supreme Court noted "the barbarous view of the inferiority of women which manifested itself in civil and political oppression so akin to slavery that we can find no adequate word to describe her present status with men except emancipation."[3]

Race and sex are comparable classes, defined by physiological characteristics, through which status is fixed from birth. Legal and social proscriptions based upon race and sex have often been identical, and have generally implied the inherent inferiority of the proscribed class to a dominant group. Both classes have been defined by, and subordinated to, the same power group—white males.

1 See, *e.g.,* S. De Beauvoir, THE SECOND SEX 116, 297–98, 331, 714–715 (5th ed. H. Parshley trans. 1964); H. Hays, THE DANGEROUS SEX 178–79, 283 (1964); A. Montagu, MAN'S MOST DANGEROUS MYTH: THE FALLACY OF RACE, Ch. 9 (4th ed. 1964) ; G. Myrdal, AN AMERICAN DILEMMA, App. V. (1944); A. Watson, SOCIAL PSYCHOLOGY: ISSUES AND INSIGHTS, Ch. 12 (1966); Crozier, *Constitutionality of Discrimination Based on Sex,* 15 B.U.L. REV. 723, 727–28 (1935); Hacker, *Women as a Minority Group,* 30 SOCIAL FORCES 60 (1951).

2 Fitzhugh, Slavery Justified by a Southerner, in E. McKitrick, SLAVERY DEFENDED 37–38 (1963).

3 *State* v. *Emery,* 224 N.C. 581, 596, 31 S.E.2d 858, 868 (1944) (Seawell, J. dissenting).

When biological differences are not related to the activity in question,[11] sex-based discrimination clashes with contemporary notions of fair and equal treatment. No longer shackled by decisions reflecting social and economic conditions or legal and political theories of an earlier era, see *Harper* v. *Virginia Board of*

---

11 "To the degree women perform the function of motherhood, they differ from other special groups. But maternity legislation is not sex legislation; its benefits are geared to the performance of a special service much like veterans' legislation. When the law . . . regulates the conduct of women in a restrictive manner having no bearing on the maternal function, it disregards individuality and relegates an entire class to inferior status." P. Murray & M. Eastwood, Jane Crow and the Law: Sex Discrimination and Title VII, 34 Geo. Wash. L. Rev. 232, 239 (1965).

The "separate restroom" canard continues to be invoked as justification for perpetuation of "a sharp line between the sexes." *E.g.,* Amending the Constitution to Prohibit State Discrimination Based on Sex, 26 The Record of the Association of the Bar of the City of New York 77, 80 (1971). This Court's recognition of the fundamental right to personal privacy in *Griswold* v. *Connecticut,* 381 U.S. 479 (1965), indicates that separate restrooms are not in jeopardy. The basic interest shared by members of both sexes in personal privacy surely justifies, and may even require, separation of the sexes in restrooms, sleeping quarters in prisons and other public institutions, separate living quarters for male and female members of the Armed Forces, police practices by which the search of a woman can be conducted only by another woman, and the search of a man only by another man. See T. Emerson, In Support of the Equal Rights Amendment, 6 Harv. Civ. Rts. Civ. Lib. L. Rev. 225, 231–32 (1971).

Elections, 383 U.S. 663, 669–70 (1966),[12] both federal and state courts have been intensely skeptical of lines drawn or sanctioned by governmental authority on the basis of sex. Absent strong affirmative justification, these lines have not survived constitutional [*sic*] scrutiny.

A recent decision of the California Supreme Court, *Sail'er Inn, Inc. et al.* v. *Edward J. Kirby, Director, et al.,* 3 CCH Employment Practices Decisions §8222 (May 27, 1971), explicitly denominated sex a suspect classification and, consequently, held unconstitutional a California statute similar to the Michigan statute upheld by this Court in *Goesaert* v. *Cleary,* 335 U.S. 464 (1948). The California Supreme Court described the factors upon which its conclusion rested in the following terms [3 E.P.D. §8222, pp. 6756–6757 (footnotes omitted)]:

> Sex, like race and lineage, is an immutable trait, a status into which the class members are locked by the accident of birth. What differentiates sex from non-suspect statuses, such as intelligence or physical disability, and aligns it with the recognized suspect classifications is that the characteristic frequently bears no relation to ability to perform or contribute to society. (See Note: *Developments in the Law—Equal Protection, supra,* 82 Harv. L. Rev. 1065, 1173–1174.) The result is that the whole class is relegated to an inferior legal status without regard to the capabilities or characteristics of its individual members. (See *Karczewski* v. *Baltimore and Ohio Railroad Company* (1967), 274 F. Supp. 169, 179.) Where the relation between characteristic and evil to be prevented is so tenuous, courts must look closely at classifications

---

12 "In determining what lines are unconstitutionally discriminatory, we have never been confined to historic notions of equality, any more than we have restricted due process to a fixed catalogue of what was at a given time deemed to be the limits of fundamental rights [citations omitted]. Notions of what constitutes equal treatment for purposes of the Equal Protection Clause *do* change." (Emphasis in original.) See also n. 16 p. 22 *infra.*

based on that characteristic lest outdated social stereotypes result in invidious laws or practices.

Another characteristic which underlies all suspect classifications is the stigma of inferiority and second-class citizenship associated with them. (See Note: *Developments in the Law—Equal Protection, supra,* 82 Harv. L. Rev. 1065, 1125–1127.) Women, like Negroes, aliens, and the poor have historically labored under severe legal and social disabilities. Like black citizens, they were, for many years, denied the right to vote and, until recently, the right to serve on juries in many states. They are excluded from or discriminated against in employment and educational opportunities. Married women in particular have been treated as inferior persons in numerous laws relating to property and independent business ownership and the right to make contracts.

Laws which disable women from full participation in the political, business and economic arenas are often characterized as "protective" and beneficial. Those same laws applied to racial or ethnic minorities would readily be recognized as invidious and impermissible. The pedestal upon which women have been placed has all too often, upon closer inspection, been revealed as a cage. We conclude that the sexual classifications are properly treated as suspect, particularly when those classifications are made with respect to a fundamental interest such as employment.

See also *Mengelkoch* v. *Industrial Welfare Commission,* 437 F.2d 563 (9th Cir. 1971) (maximum hours law applicable to women only presents substantial federal constitutional question which must be heard and decided by three judge federal district court); *Abbott* v. *Mines,* 411 F.2d 353 (6th Cir. 1969) (holding unconstitutional exclusion of women from jury in civil case concerning cancer of male genitals); *Kirstein* v. *Rector and Visitors of University of Virginia*, 309 F. Supp. 184 (E.D. Va. 1970) (three-judge court) (women entitled to equal access with men to state university's "prestige" college);[13] *White* v. *Crook*, 251 F. Supp. 401 (M.D. Ala. 1966) (three-judge court) (Alabama's exclusion of all women from jury service violates fourteenth amendment);[14] *Cohen* v. *Chesterfield County School Board*, Civ. Action No. 678-79-R, E.D. Va. (Richmond Division), May 17, 1971 (regulation requiring female teacher to leave in the fifth month of her pregnancy violates her right to equal protection); *Seidenberg* v. *McSorleys' Old Ale House*, 317 F. Supp. 593 (S.D.N.Y. 1970), 308 F. Supp. 1253 (S.D.N.Y. 1969) (exclusion of women patrons from liquor licensed place of public accommodation violates fourteenth amendment); *Mollere* v. *Southeastern Louisiana College*, 304 F. Supp. 826 (E.D. La. 1969) (declaring unconstitutional requirement that unmarried women under 21 live in state college dormitory when no such requirement was imposed on men); *United States ex rel. Robinson* v. *York*, 281 F. Supp. 8 (D. Conn. 1968) (differential sentencing laws for men and women constitute "invidious discrimination" against women repugnant to the equal protection of the law guaranteed by the

---

13 Cf. *Williams* v. *McNair*, 316 F. Supp. 134 (D.S.C. 1970) (three-judge court), affirmed without opinion, —— U.S. —— (March 8, 1971) (females only admission policy for state supported college does not violate male students' right to equal protection where no showing was made of any feature rendering all female facility more advantageous educationally than state supported institutions to which males are admitted). *Kirstein* and *Williams* are not in conflict. Pairing the two, they reflect the opinion of distinguished academicians. See C. Jencks & D. Reisman, The Academic Revolution 298 (1968):

> . . . we do not find the arguments against women's colleges as persuasive as the arguments against men's colleges. This is a wholly contextual judgment. If America were now a matriarchy (as some paranoid men seem to fear it is becoming) we would regard women's colleges as a menace and men's colleges as a possibly justified defense.

See also Note, The Constitutionality of Sex Separation in School Desegregation Plans, 37 U. Chi. L. Rev. 296 (1970).

14 "The argument that the Fourteenth Amendment was not historically intended to require the states to make women eligible for jury service reflects a misconception of the function of the Constitution and this Court's obligation in interpreting it. The Constitution of the United States must be read as embodying general principles meant to govern society and the institutions of government as they evolve through time. It is therefore this Court's function to apply the Constitution as a living document to the legal cases and controversies of contemporary society." 251 F. Supp. at 408.

fourteenth amendment);[15] *Owen* v. *Illinois Baking Corp.*, 260 F. Supp. 820 (W.D. Mich. 1966) (wife constitutionally entitled to same right as husband to recover for loss of consortium); *Paterson Tavern & Grill Owners Ass'n* v. *Borough of Hawthorne*, 57 N.J. 180, 270 A.2d 628 (1970) (police power does not justify exclusion of women from bartender occupation); *Commonwealth* v. *Daniel*, 430 Pa. 642, 243 A.2d 400 (1968) (differential sentencing laws for men and women held unconstitutional);[16] *In re Estate of Legatos*, 1 Cal. App. 3d 657, 81 Cal. Rptr. 910 (1969) (inheritance tax on certain property when devised by husband to wife, but not when devised by wife to husband violates equal protection guarantee); *Matter of Shpritzer* v. *Lang*, 17 A.D.2d 285, 289, 234 N.Y.S.2d 285, 289 (1st Dept. 1962), *aff'd*, 13 N.Y.2d 744, 241 N.Y.S.2d 869 (1963) (exclusion of policewomen from promotional examination for sergeant would impermissibly deny constitutional rights solely because of sex); *Wilson* v. *Hacker*, 101 N.Y.S.2d 461 (Sup. Ct. 1950) (union's discrimination against female bartenders "must be condemned as a violation of the fundamental principles of American democracy").

The trend is clearly discernible. Legislative discrimination grounded on sex, for purposes unrelated to any biological difference between the sexes, ranks with legislative discrimination based on race, another condition of birth, and merits no greater judicial deference. Each exemplifies a "suspect" or "invidious" classification.[17]

---

15 Accord, *Liberti* v. *York*, 28 Conn. Supp. 9, 246 A.2d 106 (1968).

16 See also *Commonwealth* v. *Stauffer*, 214 Pa. Super. 113, 251 A.2d 718 (1969) (differential in condition of sentence—men to jail, women to penitentiary—declared unconstitutional).

17 It is not urged here that extensive compensatory treatment is needed to redress past discrimination against women. Cf. Developments in the Law—Equal Protection, 82 Harv. L. Rev. 1065, 1104–1119 (1969). *Gruenwald* v. *Gardner*, 390 F.2d 591 (2d Cir.), cert. denied, 393 U.S. 982 (1968), however, indicates that in special situations compensatory treatment may be appropriate.

Although women are not a numerical minority, the impact of sex-role stereotyping is illustrated graphically by their lack of political power. At all levels of government, few women hold elected or appointed office. See Handbook 118–26.

B. Women as a Disadvantaged Second Sex.

While the characteristics that make a classification "suspect" have not been defined explicitly by this Court, compare *Sail'er Inn* v. *Kirby, supra,* a series of cases delineates as the principal factor the presence of an unalterable identifying trait which the dominant culture views as a badge of inferiority justifying disadvantaged treatment in social, legal, economic and political contexts. Although the paradigm suspect classification is, of course, one based on race, this Court has made it plain that the doctrine is not confined to a "two-class theory." *Graham* v. *Richardson,* —— U.S. —— (June 14, 1971); *Hernandez* v. *Texas,* 347 U.S. 475, 478 (1954); *Hirabayashi* v. *United States,* 320 U.S. 81, 100 (1943); see *Takahashi* v. *Fish & Game Commission,* 334 U.S. 410 (1948); *Oyama* v. *California,* 332 U.S. 633 (1948). Rather, interpretation has been dynamic, as is appropriate to fundamental constitutional principle. *Harper* v. *Virginia Board of Elections,* 383 U.S. 663, 669–70 (1966); *White* v. *Crook,* 251 F. Supp. 401, 408 (M.D. Ala. 1966) (three-judge court).

American women have been stigmatized historically as an inferior class and are today subject to pervasive discrimination. As other groups that have been assisted toward full equality via the suspect classification doctrine, women lack political power to remedy the discriminatory treatment they are accorded in the law and in society generally. This section synopsizes attitudes toward women traditional in the United States and the principal areas in which the law limits the opportunities available to women for participation as full and equal members of society.

" 'Man's world' and 'women's place' have confronted each other since Scylla first faced Charybdis."[18] A person born female continues to be branded inferior for this congenital and unalterable condition of birth.[19] Her position in this country, at its inception, is reflected in the expression of the author of the declaration that "all men are created equal." According to Thomas

---

18 E. Janeway, Man's World Woman's Place: A Study in Social Mythology 7 (1971).

19 See C. Bird, Born Female: The High Cost of Keeping Women Down (1968).

Jefferson, women should be neither seen nor heard in society's decision-making councils:

> Were our state a pure democracy there would still
> be excluded from our deliberations women, who, to
> prevent deprivation of morals and ambiguity of issues,
> should not mix promiscuously in gatherings of men.
> Quoted in M. Gruberg, Women in American Politics
> 4 (1968).

Alexis de Tocqueville, some years later, included this observation among his commentaries on life in the young United States:

> In no country has such constant care been taken as
> in America to trace two clearly distinct lines of action
> for the two sexes, and to make them keep pace one
> with the other, but in two pathways which are always
> different. American women never manage the outward
> concerns of the family, or conduct a business, or take
> a part in political life. . . . Democracy in America, pt.
> 2 (Reeves tr. 1840), in World's Classics Series, Galaxy
> ed., p. 400 (1947).[20]

During the long debate over women's suffrage the prevailing view of the partition thought ordained by the Creator was rehearsed frequently in the press and in legislative chambers. For example, an editorial in the New York Herald in 1852 asked:

> How did women first become subject to man as she
> now is all over the world? By her nature, her sex, just
> as the negro, is and always will be, to the end of time,
> inferior to the white race, and, therefore, doomed

---

20 Cf. Ibsen's observation on the society of his day:

  A woman cannot be herself in a modern society. It is an exclusively male society with laws made by men, and with prosecutors and judges who assess female conduct from a male standpoint. Quoted in Meyer, Introduction to H. Ibsen, A Doll's House at 9 (M. Meyer transl. 1965).

to subjection; but happier than she would be in any other condition, just because it is the law of her nature. The women themselves would not have this law reversed. . . . Quoted in A. Kraditor, Up From the Pedestal: Selected Writings in the History of American Feminism 190 (1968).

And a legislator commented during an 1866 debate in Congress:

It seems to me as if the God of our race has stamped upon [the women of America] a milder, gentler nature, which not only makes them shrink from, but disqualifies them for the turmoil and battle of public life. They have a higher and holier mission. It is in retiracy [*sic*] to make the character of coming men. Their mission is at home, by their blandishments and their love to assuage the passions of men as they come in from the battle of life, and not themselves by joining in the contest to add fuel to the very flames. . . . It will be a sorry day for this country when those vestal fires of love and piety are put out. Quoted in E. Flexner, Century of Struggle 148–49 (1970 ed.), from Congressional Globe, 39 Cong., 2d Sess., Part I, p. 66.

The common law heritage, a source of pride for men, marked the wife as her husband's chattel, "something better than his dog, a little dearer than his horse."[21] Blackstone explained:

By marriage, the husband and wife are one person in law: that is, the very being or legal existence of the woman is suspended during the marriage, or at least is incorporated and consolidated into that of the husband; under whose wing, protection, and cover, she performs everything; and is therefore called in our

---

21 Alfred Lord Tennyson, Locksley Hall (1842).

law-french a *feme-covert* . . . under the protection and influence of her husband, her *baron*, or lord; and her condition during her marriage is called her *coverture*. 1 Blackstone's Commentaries on the Law of England 442 (3d ed. 1768).[22]

Prior to the Civil War, the legal status of women in the United States was comparable to that of blacks under the slave codes, albeit the white woman ranked as "chief slave of the harem."[23] Neither slaves nor married women had the legal capacity to hold property or to serve as guardians of their own children. Neither blacks nor women could hold office, serve on juries, or bring suit in their own names. Men controlled the behavior of both their slaves and their wives and had legally enforceable rights to their services without compensation. See pp. 15–19, *supra*. See also L. Kanowitz, Women and the Law: The Unfinished Revolution 5–6 (1969). As Gunnar Myrdal remarked, the parallel was not accidental, for the legal status of women and children served as the model for the legal status assigned to black slaves:

> In the earlier common law, women and children were placed under the jurisdiction of the paternal power. When a legal status had to be found for the imported Negro servants in the seventeenth century, the nearest and most natural analogy was the status of women and children. The ninth commandment—linking together

---

22 An earlier formulation of the same thesis was set out in The Lawes Resolutions of Womens Rights (London, 1632):

> Man and wife are one person, but understand in what manner. When a small brooke or little river incorporateth with Rhodanus, Humber or the Thames, the poor rivulet looseth its name, it is carried and recarried with the new associate, it beareth no sway, it possesseth nothing during coverture. A woman as soon as she is married, is called *covert*, in Latin, *nupta*, that is, *veiled*, as it were, clouded and overshadowed, she hath lost her streame. . . . To a married woman, her new self is her superior, her companion, her master. Quoted in E. Flexner, Century of Struggle 7–8 (1970 ed.).

23 Comment attributed to Dolly Madison, in H. Martineau, Society in America, Vol. 2, p. 81 (1842, 1st ed. 1837).

women, servants, mules and other property—could be invoked, as well as a great number of other passages of Holy Scripture. An American Dilemma 1073 (2d ed. 1962).

In answer to feminist protests, the legal disabilities imposed on women were rationalized at the turn of the century much as they were at an earlier age. Blackstone set the pattern:

[E]ven the disabilities which the wife lies under are for the most part intended for her protection and benefit: so great a favourite is the female sex of the laws of England. 1 Blackstone's Commentaries on the Laws of England 445 (3d ed.1768).

Grover Cleveland echoed this rationale, arguing that although women were denied the vote, the statute books were full of proof of the chivalrous concern of male legislators for the rights of women. Would Woman Suffrage Be Unwise?, 22 Ladies' Home Journal 7–8 (October 1905). Quoted in A. Kraditor, Up from the Pedestal: Selected Writings in the History of American Feminism 199–203 (1968).

American women assessed their situation from a different perspective. At the Women's Rights Convention in Seneca Falls, New York, in 1848, a declaration of women's rights was drafted which included the following sentiments:

The history of mankind is a history of repeated injuries and usurpations on the part of man toward woman, having in direct object the establishment of an absolute tyranny over her. . . .
He has compelled her to submit to laws, in the formation of which she had no voice.

* * * * *

He has taken from her all right in property, even to the wages she earns.

* * * * *

. . . .In the covenant of marriage, . . . the law gives him power to deprive her of her liberty and to administer chastisement.

* * * * *

. . . .He closes against her all the avenues to wealth and distinction which he considers most honorable to himself. . . .

* * * * *

He has endeavored, in every way that he could, to destroy her confidence in her own powers, to lessen her self-respect, and to make her willing to lead a dependent and abject life.

History of Woman Suffrage, Vol. I, at 70–75 (E. C. Stanton, S. B. Anthony & N. J. Gage eds. 1881).

Men viewing their world without rose-colored glasses would have noticed in the last century, as those who look will observe today, that no pedestal marks the place occupied by most women. At a women's rights convention in Akron, Ohio, in 1851, Sojourner Truth, an abolitionist and former slave, responded poignantly to the taunts of clergymen who maintained that women held a favored position and were too weak to vote:

The man over there says women need to be helped into carriages and lifted over ditches, and to have the best place everywhere. Nobody ever helps me into carriages or over puddles, or gives me the best place—and ain't I a woman?

Look at my arm! I have ploughed and planted and gathered into barns, and no man could head me—and ain't I a woman? I could work as much and eat as

much as a man—when I could get it—and bear the
lash as well! And ain't I a woman? I have born thirteen
children, and seen most of 'em sold into slavery, and
when I cried out with my mother's grief, none but
Jesus heard me—and ain't I a woman? E. Flexner,
Century of Struggle 90–91 (1970 ed.).

Of course, the legal status of women has improved since the
nineteenth century. The Married Women's Property Acts, passed
in the middle of the nineteenth century, opened the door to
a measure of economic independence for married women. See
L. Kanowitz, Women and the Law: The Unfinished Revolution
40–41 (1969). The nineteenth amendment gave women the
vote in 1920, after almost three-quarters of a century of struggle.[24] But woman's place as subordinate to man is still reflected
in many statutes regulating diverse aspects of life. A small sample
of those statutes is contained in the Appendix, *infra*, pp. 69–88.
Some of the areas in which women receive less favored treatment
than men are summarized below.

1. Male as head of household

It remains the general rule that a wife's domicile follows that
of her husband. The Idaho provision is typical:

The husband is the head of the family. He may choose
any reasonable place or mode of living and the wife
must conform thereto. Idaho Code sec. 32-902
(1947).

Thus the law subordinates a woman's work and home preference to her husband's. If the two are in fact living apart, the
attribution of husband's domicile to wife may nullify her right
to vote, to run for public office, or to serve as administrator of

---

24 See E. Flexner, Century of Struggle (1970 ed.); W. O'Neill, Everyone Was Brave: The
Rise and Fall of Feminism in America (1969); L. Noun, Strong-Minded Women (1969).

an estate.[25] A 1968 survey of the laws of all of the states revealed only five that permit a married woman to establish a separate domicile for all purposes, eight that permit a separate domicile for eligibility for public office, six that permit a separate domicile for jury service, eight that recognize a separate domicile for probate, nine that permit a separate domicile for taxation, and eighteen that permit a separate domicile for voting. Report of the Task Force on Family Law and Policy to the Citizens' Advisory Council on the Status of Women 47–49 (1968).

The social custom in the United States that upon marriage a woman takes her husband's surname, and ceases to be known by her maiden name, is supported by laws and decisions that deal harshly with a woman who seeks to retain her separate identity. See Kanowitz, Women and the Law: The Unfinished Revolution 41–46 (1969). For example, in *Bacon* v. *Boston Elevated Ry.*, 256 Mass. 30, 152 N.E. 35 (1926), a married woman who retained her car registration in her maiden name was declared a "nuisance on the highway" and therefore barred from maintaining an action for injuries occasioned when her car was struck by a train. A federal decision of the same order is *In re Kayaloff*, 9 F. Supp. 176 (S.D.N.Y. 1934), holding that a married woman should not be granted a naturalization certificate in her maiden name, although in her career as a musician she was well-known by that name. For voting purposes the married woman, but not the married man, may be required to indicate marital status. N.J.S.A. 19:31-3(b)(1) (married woman shall prefix her name by the word "Mrs.", single women, by the word "Miss"). Cf. *Rago* v. *Lipsky*, 327 Ill. App. 63, 63 N.E.2d 642 (1945) (lawyer admitted to practice in state and federal courts and United States Supreme Court in her maiden name denied the right to register to vote in that name).

The common law system of separate ownership of property by each spouse, effective in most states, fails to accord adequate recognition to the contribution to the family made by a wife who

25 *E.g.*, Idaho Code sec.15-317(1).

works only in the home. By accepting a "woman's place" and relieving her husband of the burdens of child and home care, she foregoes the opportunity to acquire earnings and property of her own. In community property states, in which marriage is regarded in theory as an economic partnership, management and control generally vest exclusively in the husband. See Report of the Task Force on Family Law and Policy to the Citizens' Advisory Council on the Status of Women 16 (1968); President's Commission on the Status of Women, Report of the Committee on Civil and Political Rights 16 (1963) (recommending complete reappraisal of the law governing matrimonial property in all jurisdictions).[26] And although Married Women's Property Acts were passed over a century ago, numerous anachronistic limitations on the contractual capacity of women survive. See L. Kanowitz, Women and the Law: The Unfinished Revolution 55–69 (1969).

2. Women and the role of motherhood

The traditional division within the home—father decides, mother nurtures—is reinforced by diverse provisions of state law. For example, several retain general statutes reflecting the common law rule that father is sole guardian of the children. See Appendix, *infra* pp. 74–76. More particularized provisions include the Washington rule that father, not mother, is qualified to sue for the wrongful death of a legitimate child. Wash. Code sec. 4.24.010. In Idaho, the father presumptively may make a testamentary guardianship appointment for a child, while the mother may do so only if the father is dead or incapable of consent. Idaho Code sec. 15-1812.

If the parents separate, mother generally gets custody preference when the child is of tender years. But if the child is older, and needs preparation for the world, preference may go to father. *E.g.,* Mont. Rev. Code Ann. sec. 91-4515 (1947).

---

26 Enlightened by the matrimonial property systems effective in the Scandinavian countries, Texas had amended its law to provide for joint management of community property. Texas Rev. Civ. Stats. art. 4621. But cf. *Perez* v. *Campbell*, 421 F.2d 619 (9th Cir. 1970), reversed, 401 U.S. —— (1971).

Most states permit girls to marry without parental consent at an earlier age than boys.[27] The differential, generally three years, reflects two presumptions: (1) the married state is the only proper goal of womanhood; (2) men need more time to prepare for bigger, better and more useful pursuits. L. Kanowitz, Women and the Law: The Unfinished Revolution 11 (1969).

3. Women and criminal law

As of 1970, women served on juries on the same basis as men in only 28 states. See note 50, *infra*. Differential treatment for women in the remaining states takes a variety of forms. Some states automatically exempt women on the basis of their sex alone; others exempt women, but not men, who have child care responsibilities; and some exempt women based on the nature of the proceeding or inadequate courthouse facilities. See L. Kanowitz, Women and the Law: The Unfinished Revolution 28–31 (1969).

In most states, only a woman can be prosecuted as a "prostitute" and only her conduct, not her male partner's, is criminal. L. Kanowitz, *supra* at 16–18; G. Mueller, Legal Regulations of Sexual Conduct 50 (1961).

Special treatment of female juvenile offenders is another example of the double standard in operation. In New York, for example, a child can be declared a "person in need of supervision"[28] for acts that would be non-criminal if committed by an adult. New York Family Court Act sec. 712(b). While there may be sound reasons for this special category for juveniles, there can be no constitutional justification for New York's treatment of young women as "persons in need of supervision" until age 18, while boys are subject to the statute only until age 16. In addition to the age differential, the statute discriminates against girls in a manner less apparent but no less real. A charge

---

27 See Table on State Marriage Laws as of December 1, 1969, in Hearings on S.J. Res. 61, Subcommittee on Constitutional Amendments of the Senate Committee on the Judiciary, 91st Cong., 2d Sess. 728 (1970).

28 A person who is a "habitual truant . . . incorrigible, ungovernable or habitually disobedient and beyond the lawful control of parent or other lawful authority."

of ungovernability against a girl occurs most frequently as a promiscuity-control device. A study of 1500 cases decided by a New York juvenile court judge revealed that he "refused to treat any form of sexual behavior on the part of boys, even the most bizarre forms, as warranting more than probationary status. The Judge, however, regarded girls as the cause of sexual deviation in boys in all cases of coition involving an adolescent couple and refused to hear the complaints of the girl and her family; the girl was regarded as a prostitute." Reiss, Sex Offenses: The Marginal Status of the Adolescent, 25 Law and Contemporary Problems 310, 316 (1960).

While a very young woman is considered dangerous for her sexuality, in adult life she is considered far less passionate than the adult man. At least this appears to be the view of states that allow the defense of "passion killing" only to the wronged husband. Texas Penal Code 1220; Utah Code sec. 76-30-10 (4).

4. Women and employment

Current tax law presents a significant disincentive to the woman who contemplates combining a career with marriage and a family. If a wife's earnings approach those of her husband, the Internal Revenue Code counsels divorce, for the couple will retain more if they live together without benefit of a marriage license. See B. Richards, Single v. Married Income Tax Returns under the Tax Reform Act of 1969, 48 Taxes 301 (1970). And if a father or mother goes off to work as a divorcee, he or she may be entitled to a child care deduction regardless of income. For a married pair, both working, however, the deduction is available only if joint adjusted gross income of the couple remains close to the subsistence level. Internal Revenue Code sec. 214. See A Matter of Simple Justice: Report of the President's Task Force on Women's Rights and Responsibilities 15 (1970). Moreover, the size of the deduction ($600) renders it of scant assistance even to the few who qualify for it.[29]

---

29 For a person who works 40 hours a week, 50 weeks a year, and spends an hour each work

Despite the tax disincentive, married women are entering the labor force in increasing numbers. In the two decades between 1947 and 1967, the percentage of women in the labor force increased by 70%, from an average of 24% to an average of 41%. Married women constitute a majority of full-time women workers. Report of the Task Force on Labor Standards to the Citizens' Advisory Council on the Status of Women 6–7 (1968). This development is particularly remarkable in view of the deplorable shortage of child care facilities. During World War II, when women workers were essential to the economy, provision was made for the care of some 1,600,000 children. By 1967, although more women were in the labor force, only 200,000 children were accommodated. Dept. of Health, Education and Welfare Children's Bureau, Childcare Arrangements for the Nation's Working Mothers 1 (1969). Although the dire need for commitment of substantial resources to development of childcare facilities is beginning to be appreciated,[30] progress has been slow. For example, in New York City, day care services may not be provided for children under the age of two. New York City Health Code, sec. 47.07(a)(1).[31] Moreover, an explanatory note to this section states:

[I]t is recognized that as an ultimate goal, it is not desirable to permit children under three years of age in a day care service, and many services now have a policy of not admitting such children. . . .

In April 1971, 42.7% of all women sixteen years of age or older were in the labor force[32] as compared to 28.9% in March

---

day traveling to and from the place of employment, the $600 amount represents a deduction of less than 30¢ an hour for baby sitting expenses.

30 *E.g.,* S. 1512, currently before the Senate Committee on Labor and Public Welfare; H.R. 6748, currently before the House Committee on Education and Labor.

31 Art. 53 of the New York City Health Code authorizes day care of no more than two children under the age of two in a private household. Certificates of approval for such private household care may be issued only to a woman. Sec. 53.07 (d).

32 Dept. of Labor Bureau of Labor Statistics: Employment and Earnings, May 1971 at 34–35.

1940.[33] But wage statistics are indicative of the pervasive sex discrimination still characteristic of the labor market. The wage or salary income for full-time year-round women workers dropped from 63.9% of male workers' salaries in 1956 to 58.2% in 1968.[34]

The disparity in earnings is often discounted by men who accept the myth that women are secondary workers seeking employment only to enjoy some consumer luxuries. But in fact, almost 60% of all employed women work in order to provide primary support of themselves or others or to supplement the incomes of husbands who earn under $5,915 a year.[35]

Within occupational categories, women are paid less for the same jobs. For example, in 1968 the median salary for all scientists was $13,200. For women scientists, the median salary was $10,000.[36] The median wage for a full-time male factory worker in 1968 was $6,738. His female counterpart earned only $3,991.[37] Differences in work experience, job tenure and training do not account for these large gaps. Cf. McNally, Patterns of Female Labor Force Activity, Industrial Relations 204 (May 1968).

Women at work remain heavily concentrated in a small number of sex-stereotyped occupations. In 1968, about one-quarter of all employed women worked in only five occupations: secretary-stenographer, household worker, bookkeeper, elementary school teacher, and waitress. Over a third of all employed women held clerical jobs; 70% of all clerical positions were filled by women.[38] Two-thirds of the female labor force would have to change jobs to achieve an occupational distribution corresponding to that of men. Indeed, the index of occupational segregation

---

33 Handbook 10.

34 Dept. of Labor, Women's Bureau: Fact Sheet on the Earnings Gap 1 (Feb. 1970) [hereinafter Fact Sheet on the Earnings Gap].

35 Dept. of Labor, Women's Bureau: Why Women Work 1 (Jan. 1970).

36 Fact Sheet on the Earnings Gap 2.

37 *Ibid.*

38 Handbook 87–103.

by sex is approximately the same now as it was in 1900. See E. Gross, Plus ça change . . . ? The Sexual Structure of Occupations Over Time, 16 Social Problems 198, 202 (Fall 1968).

Beyond doubt, the status of women in the labor force is separate and unequal. The consequence for the nation is severe: almost two-thirds of this country's adult poor are women. See A Matter of Simple Justice: Report of the President's Task Force on Women's Rights and Responsibilities 24 (1970). Compare *id.* at 21:

> Without any question, the growing number of families on Aid to Families with Dependent Children is related to the increase in unemployed young women. For many . . . the inability to find a job means . . . having a child to get on welfare. Potential husbands do not earn enough to support an unemployed wife.
>
> The stability of the low-income family depends as much on training women for employment as it does on training men . . .
>
> The task force expects welfare rolls will continue to rise unless society takes more seriously the needs of disadvantaged girls and young women.

While this brief survey offers merely a sample of the legal and economic realities of woman's inferior status, it should suffice to indicate a compelling need for correction. Strict scrutiny of classifications disadvantaging the "submissive majority,"[39] the "majority" so sparsely represented in legislative and policy-making chambers, should speed the day when emancipated men accept Mill's thesis:

> That the principle which regulates the existing social relations between the two sexes—the legal

---

39 F. Seidenberg, The Submissive Majority: Modern Trends in the Law Concerning Women's Rights, 55 Cornell L. Rev. 262 (1970).

subordination of one sex to other—is wrong in
itself, and now one of the chief hindrances to human
improvement; and that it ought to be replaced by a
principle of perfect equality, admitting no power or
privilege on the one side, nor disability on the other.
John Stuart Mill, The Subjection of Women (1869)[40]

C. Muller, Goesaert and Hoyt.

Three decisions of this Court bear particularly close examination for the support they appear to give those who urge
perpetuation of the treatment of women as less than full persons
within the meaning of the Constitution: *Muller* v. *Oregon*, 208
U.S. 412 (1908); *Goesaert* v. *Cleary*, 335 U.S. 464 (1948); *Hoyt*
v. *Florida*, 368 U.S. 57 (1961).

A landmark decision of this Court responding to turn of the
century conditions when women labored long into the night
in sweatshop operations,[41] *Muller* v. *Oregon*, 208 U.S. 412
(1908),[42] has been misinterpreted by some as an impediment to
appellant's position. Recently, in a perceptive opinion, the Court
of Appeals for the Ninth Circuit focused on the different societal climate and legal setting in which *Muller* was decided, and
demonstrated that the equal protection issue presented here was
not at all involved in that case. *Mengelkoch* v. *Industrial Welfare
Commission*, 437 F.2d 563 (9th Cir. 1971).

The issue in *Muller* was the constitutionality of a state statute
prohibiting employment of women "in any mechanical establishment, factory, or laundry" for more than ten hours a day.
Muller, a laundry owner, was prosecuted for violating the statute and was convicted. Muller contended in this Court that the

---

40 In World's Classics Series, Three Essays by J. S. Mill 427 (1966).

41 For historical perspective, see E. Baker, Protective Labor Legislation 101, 149-277,
444–456 (1925); E. Flexner, Century of Struggle: The Women's Rights Movement in the
United States 203–15 (1970 ed.).

42 *Muller* was followed in several cases presented in much the same societal climate and
legal setting: *West Coast Hotel Co.* v. *Parrish*, 300 U.S. 379 (1937); *Radice* v. *New York*, 264
U.S. 292 (1924); *Bosley* v. *McLaughlin*, 236 U.S. 385 (1915) ; *Miller* v. *Wilson*, 236 U.S. 373
(1915); *Riley* v. *Massachusetts*, 232 U.S. 671 (1914).

statute abridged freedom of contract in violation of the four-teenth amendment, that it was class legislation, and that it was an invalid exercise of the police power because it lacked a reasonable relation to public health, safety or welfare. 208 U.S. at 417–18. He relied principally upon *Lochner* v. *New York*, 198 U.S. 45 (1905), which had struck down only three years earlier a state statute limiting employment (of men as well as women) in bakeries to ten hours each day and sixty hours each week.

To distinguish *Lochner*, the Court was required to rely upon differences in the station occupied by men and women in the society of that day. Interwoven in the opinion are two themes: (1) recognition of the intolerable exploitation of women workers ("in the struggle for subsistence she is not an equal competitor with her brother" (208 U.S. at 422)); (2) concern for the health of the sex believed to be weaker in physical structure but assigned the role of bearing the future generation ("the physical well-being of woman becomes an object of public interest and care in order to preserve the strength and vigor of the race" (208 U.S. at 421)). Accepting as historic fact man's domination of woman, the Court stressed that women must "rest upon and look to [man] for protection" and, somewhat inconsistently, that she requires aid of the law "to protect her from the greed as well as the passion of man." 208 U.S. at 422.

Putting *Muller* in its proper place, the Ninth Circuit, in *Mengelkoch* v. *Industrial Welfare Commission*, 437 F.2d 563 (1971), presented three reasons for its lack of precedential value in a case such as the one at bar.

First, it was the *Muller* Court's task to determine "whether the state, in exerting its police power to the end of establishing maximum hours of labor for women, acted with the wisdom which, in those days, it was thought was required by the Due Process Clause. That kind of inquiry is no longer made by the federal courts. *Ferguson* v. *Skrupa*, 372 U.S. 726, 730 (1963)." 437 F.2d at 567.

Second, in *Mengelkoch*, as in *Muller*, a state statute limiting hours of work for women only was challenged on constitutional grounds, but the basis of the challenge, and the identity of the challenger put the two cases at opposite poles. As the Ninth Circuit explained:

> In our case, the constitutional attack against a state statute is mounted, not by an employer, but by an employee. The employee, Velma Mengelkoch, unlike the employer in *Muller*, does not question the state's police power to legislate in the field of hours of labor. Unlike *Muller*, she invokes the Equal Protection Clause, and she does so not to preserve the right of employers to employ women for long hours, but to overcome what she regards as a system which discriminates in favor of male employees and against female employees. In *Muller*, the statute was upheld in part because it was thought to be a necessary way of safeguarding women's competitive position. Here the statute is attacked on the ground that it gives male employees an unfair economic advantage over females. 437 F.2d at 567.

Here, as in *Mengelkoch*, the challenger is a woman and she invokes the equal protection clause to shield her against discrimination. Of course, the second point made by the Ninth Circuit in *Mengelkoch* applies with even greater force to the case at bar. Perhaps the California legislature, decades ago when it originally enacted the legislation at issue in *Mengelkoch*, was motivated by an intent to protect women against "the greed as well as the passion of man."[43] The Idaho statute here at issue lacks even that ostensible justification. It was not designed to protect women.

---

43 *Muller* v. *Oregon*, 208 U.S. 412, 422 (1908). But see E. Baker, Protective Labor Legislation 101, 444–56 (1925); M. Wade, ed., Writings of Margaret Fuller 124 (1941): As the friend of the Negro assumes that one man cannot by right hold another in bondage, so would the friend of Woman assume that Man cannot by right lay even well-meant restrictions on Woman.

On the contrary, it is explicit in its deliberate subordination of women to men for expediency's sake.

Third, the *Muller* Court, unprepared to overrule *Lochner* barely three years after it was decided, had to place men and women in different categories in order to escape its prior holding. As the Ninth Circuit pointed out, "the right of states to prescribe maximum hours of labor by employees, including male employees, has been recognized since at least *Bunting* v. *Oregon*, 243 U.S. 426 (1917)." 437 F.2d at 567. And in 1940, in *United States* v. *Darby*, 312 U.S. 100, this Court completely repudiated the reasoning responsible for the *Lochner* decision. Thus, the critical issue in *Muller*—whether half a loaf would be allowed to state legislatures after the full loaf was denied by the Court—long ago lost all vitality.

In sum, *Muller* was a product of social conditions and constitutional theory peculiar to an earlier era in this nation's history. It is entirely irrelevant to the issue presented here, whether sex-based classifications are "suspect." The wholly different constitutional perspective, the difference in the nature of the claims, and the magnitude of the disparity between present day social and cultural norms and those prevailing at the time of *Muller*, require the conclusion that *Muller* has no bearing at all on the issue at bar.

While *Muller* reflects the law in mid-passage from *Lochner* to *Darby*, *Goesaert* v. *Cleary*, 335 U.S. 464 (1948) hardly exemplifies a first step toward enlightened change. It was retrogressive in its day and is intolerable a generation later. Unlike *Muller*, *Goesaert* was not intended to assist women "in the struggle for subsistence" or to safeguard women's competitive position. The statute at issue in *Goesaert*, although it allowed women to serve as waitresses in taverns, barred them from the more lucrative employment of bartender. In contrast to the protective motive apparently present in *Muller*, the actual motivation behind the statute in *Goesaert* was said by the appellant to be "an unchivalrous desire of male bartenders to try to monopolize the calling."

335 U.S. at 467. E. Baker, Protective Labor Legislation 444–56 (1925).

The majority opinion in *Goesaert* reflects an antiquarian male attitude towards women—man as provider, man as protector, man as guardian of female morality. While the attitude is antiquarian, unfortunately it is still indulged even by persons who would regard as anathema attribution of inferiority to racial or religious groups. But however much some men may wish to preserve Victorian notions about woman's relation to man, and the "proper" role of women in society, the law cannot provide support for obsolete male prejudices or translate them into statutes that enforce sex-based discrimination.

Although recognizing that society had advanced beyond the Victorian age, Mr. Justice Frankfurter stated for the *Goesaert* majority, "The Constitution does not require legislatures to reflect sociological insight, or shifting social standards, any more than it requires them to keep abreast of the latest scientific standards." 335 U.S. at 466. But only six years later, this Court explicitly relied upon "sociological insight" and contemporary "social standards" in declaring racial segregation unconstitutional. *Brown* v. *Board of Education*, 347 U.S. 483, 489 n. 4, 493, 494–95 n. 11 (1954).[44]

Perhaps the *Brown* decision led Mr. Justice Frankfurter to reconsider the position he expressed in *Goesaert*. In any event, in 1960, he refused to rely on "ancient doctrine" concerning the status of women. In *United States* v. *Dege*, 364 U.S. 51 (1960), he buried the historic common law notion that husband and wife are legally one person. Writing for the Court, he declared, "we . . . do not allow ourselves to be obfuscated by medieval views regarding the legal status of women and the common law's reflection of them." 364 U.S. at 52. Precedent from an earlier age was appraised by Mr. Justice Frankfurter as expressing a view

---

44 Had the *Goesaert* majority taken a less static view of the Constitution as it relates to women's rights, it might have used the occasion, much as the *Brown* court did, to clear away old debris. *E.g.*, *Bradwell* v. *Illinois*, 83 U.S. 130 (1872) (equal protection clause does not preclude a state from barring women from the practice of law).

of womanhood "offensive to the ethos of our society." 364 U.S. at 53. Sounding the death-knell as well of *Goesaert's* disregard of "sociological insight or shifting social standards," he quoted Mr. Justice Holmes and applied the quoted wisdom to the case before him:

> "It is revolting to have no better reason for a rule of law than that so it was laid down in the time of Henry IV. It is still more revolting if the grounds upon which it was laid down have vanished long since, and the rule simply persists from blind imitation of the past." Holmes, Collected Legal Papers, 187 (1920), reprinting The Path of the Law, 10 Harv. L. Rev. 457, 469 (1897).

For this Court now to act on Hawkins's formulation of the medieval view that husband and wife "are esteemed but as one Person in Law, and are presumed to have but one Will" would indeed be "blind imitation of the past." It would require us to disregard the vast changes in the status of woman—the extension of her rights and correlative duties—whereby a wife's legal submission to her husband has been wholly wiped out, not only in the English-speaking world generally but emphatically so in this country. 364 U.S. at 53–54. Unfortunately, Mr. Justice Frankfurter's observation in *Dege* does not correspond to contemporary reality. As this case and the statutes set out in the Appendix, *infra*, illustrate, the law-sanctioned subordination of wife to husband, mother to father, woman to man, is not yet extinguished in this country.

A federal court deciding a closely related issue, and two state courts deciding the identical issue, found scant difficulty in dispatching *Goesaert*.

In *Seidenberg* v. *McSorleys' Old Ale House*, 317 F. Supp. 593 (S.D.N.Y. 1970), Judge Mansfield declared a tavern owner's exclusion of women patrons inconsistent with the fourteenth amendment. In answer to the argument that *Goesaert* was controlling, he stated:

> Nor do we find any merit in the argument that the
> presence of women in bars gives rise to "moral and
> social problems" against which McSorleys' can reasonably protect itself by excluding women from the
> premises. Social mores have not stood still since that
> argument was used in 1948 to convince a 6-3 majority
> of the Supreme Court that women might rationally
> be prohibited from working as bartenders unless
> they were wives or daughters of male owners of the
> premises. 317 F. Supp. at 606.

In *Paterson Tavern & Grill Owners Ass'n* v. *Borough of Hawthorne*, 57 N.J. 180, 270 A.2d 628 (1970), the New Jersey Supreme Court considered a local ordinance which, like the statute in *Goesaert*, denied women the right to tavern employment behind the bar. Indicative of the change in social norms to which Judge Mansfield referred in *Seidenberg* v. *McSorleys' Old Ale House*, the New Jersey case presented this interesting difference in party line-up: The plaintiffs were a male tavern owner who wished the freedom to select a woman bartender, and an association of tavern owners. The New Jersey Supreme Court ruled that in the light of current customs and mores, "the municipal restriction against female bartending may no longer fairly be viewed as a necessary and reasonable exercise of the police power." 57 N.J. at 186, 270 A.2d at 631. It concluded, reminiscent of this Court's expressions in *United States* v. *Dege*:

> While the law may look to the past for the lessons it
> teaches, it must be geared to the present and towards
> the future if it is to serve the people in just and proper
> fashion. In the current climate the law may not tolerate

blanket municipal bartending exclusions grounded solely on sex. 57 N.J. at 189, 270 A.2d at 633.

Finally, the California Supreme Court in *Sail'er Inn Inc.* v. *Kirby, supra* at p. 6758, said of *Goesaert*: "Although *Goesaert* has not been overruled, its holding has been the subject of academic critisism [*sic*] . . . and its sweeping statement that the states are not constitutionally precluded from 'drawing a sharp line between the sexes' has come under increasing limitation."

In sum, *Goesaert's* sanction of "a sharp line between the sexes" and its "blind imitation of the past" have rendered it a burden and an embarrassment to state and federal courts; enlightened jurists politely discard it as precedent, refusing "to be obfuscated by medieval views regarding the legal status of women." It should be plain that no one would now mourn its formal burial.

Hoyt v. *Florida*, 368 U.S. 57 (1961), completes the trilogy of cases invoked most frequently to justify second class status for women. In *Hoyt*, this Court sustained a Florida statute limiting jury service by women to those who registered with the court a desire to be placed on the jury list.[45] That case, although it harks back to the stereotyped view of women rejected in *United States* v. *Dege*, 364 U.S. 51 (1960), is readily distinguishable. Unlike the situation now before the Court, in which a woman's disqualification is mandated whenever a male contender appears, in *Hoyt*, the Court "found no substantial evidence whatever in this record that Florida has arbitrarily undertaken to exclude women from jury service." 368 U.S. at 69. Underscoring the point, the three concurring Justices stated their inability to find "from this record that Florida is not making a good faith effort to have women perform jury duty without discrimination on the ground of sex." 368 U.S. at 69.

---

45 Despite the *Hoyt* decision, the Florida statute was amended to call women for jury service on the same basis as men; the statute now limits its special female exemptions to pregnant women and women with children under the age of eighteen who affirmatively request exemptions. Fla. Stat. Ann. §40.01, as amended, Laws 1967, c. 67-154, §1.

While the *Hoyt* holding offers no support at all for a statute of the Idaho Code sec. 15-314 genre, in which discrimination on the ground of sex is undisguised, this Court included language in the opinion that has been turned against women who seek to realize their full potential as individual human beings:

> Despite the enlightened emancipation of women from the restrictions and protections of bygone years, and their entry into many parts of community life formerly considered to be reserved to men, *woman is still regarded as the center of home and family life*. We cannot say that it is constitutionally impermissible for a State, acting in pursuit of the general welfare, to conclude that a woman should be relieved from the civic duty of jury service unless she herself determines that such service is consistent with her own special responsibilities. 368 U.S. at 61–62. (Emphasis supplied.)

While an image of woman, first and predominantly as keeper of the hearth, might have been expected from jurists writing at the turn of the century, it is disquieting to find the antiquated stereotype repeated so late in the day. Even in times past, when the absence of family planning and effective birth-control devices restricted options for most women, many by choice or fortune did not play the role of mother-wife. Today, of course, scientific developments have placed the choice and timing of parenthood within the realm of individual decision. Even for those who suspend or curtail economic activity to care for offspring, the period devoted to child-rearing is limited. In these days of longevity, most women, for the larger part of their lives, are not preoccupied with child care functions.[46]

---

46 "Women today live 25 years longer than they did at the turn of the century; half of today's women are married by the time they are 21; and the average mother has her last child enter school when she is 30. When her youngest child enters school today's mother has 40 years of life yet ahead. The challenge to women to use those years in fulfilling ways, and

The brief reversion to stereotype in the *Hoyt* opinion has had unfortunate consequences. For example, in a 1970 decision a New York trial court rejected the challenge of a female plaintiff to a jury system with automatic exemption for women. As a result of this exemption, women constituted less than twenty percent of the available jury pool. In his published opinion, the judge relied on *Hoyt* to explain to the complainant that she was "in the wrong forum." Less chivalrous than this Court, but more accurately reflecting the impact of the stereotype, the judge stated that plaintiff's "lament" should be addressed to her sisters who prefer "cleaning and cooking, rearing of children and television soap operas, bridge and canasta, the beauty parlor and shopping, to becoming embroiled in plaintiff's problems. . . ." *DeKosenko* v. *Brandt*, 313 N.Y.S. 2d 827, 830 (Sup. Ct. 1970). Nothing was said of the likelihood that many men would find other pursuits preferable to jury service were they offered automatic exemption.

Although *Hoyt* no doubt has impeded full recognition throughout the country that jury duty is a responsibility shared equally by all citizens, male and female alike,[47] the majority of states either treat women and men on the same basis, or relieve women only when family duties in the particular case require exemption.[48] For example recognizing the contemporary reality that among today's young parents, child care functions are often shared, the New Jersey statute provides exemption for any "person" who has

---

society's need for mature judgment and talent have never been greater." California Women, Report of the Advisory Commission on the Status of Women 5 (1971).

47 See *Alexander* v. *Louisiana*, 255 La. 941, 233 So. 2d 891 (1970), cert. granted, March 1, 1971.

48 The Library of Congress Legislative Reference Service, American Law Division, reported to the Senate on June 10, 1970, the results of a search of the laws of the fifty states concerning women as jurors on state juries. At the time of the survey, 26 states provided no female exemptions and two states exempted all "persons" responsible for the care of children. The remaining states displayed a range of female exemptions, from the Ohio provision exempting nurses and nuns (Page's Ohio Rev. Code Ann. §2313.34) to the Louisiana provision excluding all women who do not file with the court clerk a written declaration of desire to be subject to jury service (L.S.A. R.S. 13:3055). Hearings on S. J. Res. 61 before the Subcommittee on Constitutional Amendments of the Senate Committee on the Judiciary, 91st Cong., 2d Sess. 725–27 (1970).

the actual physical care and custody of a minor child. N.J.S.A. 2A:69-1, 2(g). See also Rev. Codes of Montana §93-1304(12) (exemption for "person" caring directly for one or more children).

D. The Discrimination Against Women Mandated by Sec. 15-314 Is Not Justified by Any Compelling State Interest.

If, as appellant urges, sex-based classification is declared "suspect," this Court must next consider whether a compelling state interest justifies the discrimination embodied in Sec. 15-314 of the Idaho Code.

Section 15-314 is the direct descendant of Sec. 52 of the Idaho Probate Practice Act adopted by the First Territorial Legislature in 1864. The current provision incorporates the language of its 1864 predecessor without change. S.L. 1864, sec. 53, p. 335; Rev. Stats. 1887, sec. 5352; Idaho Code Ann. 1901, vol. 3, sec. 4042. Idaho does not publish legislative committee reports or debate proceedings; consequently, no legislative history is available. Indeed, no source for discovering legislative intent exists apart from the decisions by the courts below in this case, the only Idaho case directly in point.[49]

The Supreme Court of Idaho justified the statute in these terms:

> By I.C. §15-314, the legislature eliminated [an area] of controversy, *i.e.,* if both a man and woman of the same class seek letters of administration, the male would be entitled over the female. . . . This provision of the statute is neither an illogical nor arbitrary method devised by the legislature to resolve an issue that would otherwise require a hearing as to the relative merits as to which of the two or more petitioning relatives should be appointed.

---

49 Section 15-314 has been cited in *Miller* v. *Lewiston Nat'l Bank*, 18 Idaho 124, 108 Pac. 901 (1910); *Miller* v. *Mitcham*, 21 Idaho 741, 123 Pac. 941 (1912); *Chandler* v. *Probate Court*, 26 Idaho 173, 141 Pac. 635 (1914). None of these cases dealt with the issue at bar.

> Philosophically it can be argued with some
> degree of logic that the provisions of I.C. 15-314
> do discriminate against women on the basis of sex.
> However, nature itself has established the distinction
> and this statute is not designed to discriminate but
> is only designed to alleviate the problem of holding
> hearings by the court to determine eligibility to
> administer. . . . (A. 21a).

> It is our opinion that the state has a legitimate
> interest in promoting the prompt administration of
> estates and that the statute in question promotes this
> interest by curtailing litigation over the appointment
> of administrators. . . . (A. 23a).

Thus, the Idaho Supreme Court explained as a time and decision saving device its tolerance of a patent legislative discrimination against women. The decision below contrasts dramatically with decisions on kindred matters rendered by the West German Federal Constitutional Court, a high court created with the model of the United States Supreme Court in close view. In a leading case, several wives and mothers challenged under the equal protection principle of the post–World War II West German Constitution, provisions of the German Civil Code (Bürgerliches Gesetzbuch §§1628, 1629 par. 1) declaring "if parents are unable to agree, father decides," and mandating preference to the father as representative of the child. Both Code provisions were declared unconstitutional. BVerfGE 10, 59 (July 29, 1959). While the Idaho Supreme Court was content to rely on considerations of expediency and the legislature's evident conclusion "that in general men are better qualified to act as administrators than are women," the West German Federal Constitutional Court focused on the superior norm. The differences in life styles alleged to exist, and the interest in saving time and sparing court facilities, it declared, are hardly so decisive as to override the fundamental constitutional guarantee of equal protection. The Court expressly rejected the notion that the legislature may introduce discriminations "of women, Jews, members of some political party or religious association" under "reasonable" circumstances. In a subsequent case concerning preference to sons over daughters in agrarian inheritance law, the West German Federal Constitutional Court relegated to the scrap heap of history legal distinctions based on the assumption that men are better equipped than women to manage property. BVerfGE 15, 337 (March 20, 1963).[50]

No doubt promotion of expeditious administration of estates and curtailment of litigation are bona fide state interests. But it is equally plain that the end of expediency cannot be served by unconstitutional means. Surely this Court would find offensive to the Constitution, to "the ethos of our society," and to common sense a fiduciary selection statute that preferred whites to blacks or Christians to Jews. A statute preferring men to women should fare no better. If sex is a "suspect classification," a state interest in avoiding a hearing cannot justify rank discrimination against a person, solely on the ground that she is a female.

Convenience, simplicity and curtailment of litigation, while grand virtues in the administration of public affairs, do not supersede the fundamental right of individuals to even-handed application of governmental action. Thus, such obviously convenient state measures as restricting the ballot to "two old, established parties" (*Williams* v. *Rhodes*, 393 U.S. 23 (1968)), and denying welfare payments to persons with less than a year's residency in the state (*Shapiro* v. *Thompson*, 394 U.S. 618

---

50 Cf. United Nations Charter preamble, Art. 1, para. 3 (calling for respect for human rights and fundamental freedoms for all persons without distinction as to race, sex, language or religion). For a progress report indicating a pace more rapid than that of the United States, see The Status of Women in Sweden: Report to the United Nations (1968). See also The Emancipation of Man, address by Mr. Olof Palme, Swedish Prime Minister, at the Women's National Democratic Club, Washington, D.C., June 8, 1970: The public opinion is nowadays so well informed that if a politician should declare that the woman ought to have a different role than the man and that it is natural that she devotes more time to the children he would be regarded to be of the Stone Age.

(1969)), did not survive this Court's scrutiny under the equal protection clause.

Williams v. *Rhodes* and *Shapiro* v. *Thompson* involved justifications more substantial than expedition. Yet the several reasons offered by the states in those cases, even in combination, were found insufficient to overcome the heavy burden required by this Court.

In *Shapiro* v. *Thompson*, the state sought to justify its one-year waiting period on seven grounds: (1) as a protective device to preserve the fiscal integrity of the state public assistance programs (394 U.S. at 627); (2) to discourage the influx of poor families in need of assistance (394 U.S. at 629); (3) to discourage the influx of indigents who would enter the state solely to obtain larger benefits (394 U.S. at 631); (4) to facilitate planning of the welfare budget; (5) to provide an objective test of residency; (6) to minimize the opportunity for recipients fraudulently to receive payments from more than one jurisdiction; (7) to encourage early entry of new residents into the labor force. 394 U.S. at 634.

In *Williams* v. *Rhodes*, the state asserted that its restrictive election legislation (1) promoted a two-party system in order to encourage compromise and political stability (393 U.S. at 31–32), (2) avoided election of plurality candidates (393 U.S. at 32), (3) allowed those who disagree with the major parties and their policies "a choice of leadership as well as issues" (393 U.S. at 32), and (4) avoided confronting voters with a choice so confusing that the popular will could be frustrated (393 U.S. at 33).

While any of these reasons might be considered "rational," this Court concluded that, even taken together, they were not "compelling." In contrast to the relatively serious reasons asserted to save the Connecticut, Pennsylvania and District of Columbia statutes in *Shapiro* v. *Thompson*, and the Ohio law in *Williams* v. *Rhodes*, the justification advanced here by the Idaho Supreme Court—administrative convenience—falls far short of a "compelling" state interest when appraised in light of the interest of the class against which the statute discriminates—an interest in treatment as full human personalities.[51] As this Court said in *Williams* v. *Illinois*, 399 U.S. 235, 245 (1970), "the constitutional imperatives of the Equal Protection Clause must have priority over the comfortable convenience of the status quo."

Moreover, even the vaunted convenience afforded by Idaho Code sec. 15-314 is largely illusory. Hearings are avoided only in those cases where an eligible female applicant is challenged by an equally eligible male applicant. But if, for example, four sisters individually sought letters of administration,[52] the court would have to hold a hearing to select an administrator; if three brothers and one sister each sought appointment, the court would have to hold a hearing—even though the female applicant would be eliminated from the competition. In any situation in which two or more applicants of the same sex from a class of equal eligibles separately seek letters of administration, a hearing must be held so that the court may issue letters of administration "to the party best entitled thereto." Idaho Code sec. 15-323.

The fact that not all women are denied the right to a hearing or presumed less than competent to administer an estate highlights the invidious discrimination inherent in the statute. A woman may compete on terms of equality whenever her challenger is another woman. If no male equally eligible opposes, the woman will be appointed. Through this device of law-mandated subordination of "equally entitled" women to men, the dominant

---

51 The convenience argument, with more significant consequences to the fisc than are present in this case, was appropriately dispatched in *Mollere* v. *Southeastern Louisiana College*, 304 F. Supp. 826 (E.D. La. 1969) (declaring unconstitutional requirement that unmarried women under 21 live in state college dormitory when no such requirement was imposed on men) and *In re Estate of Legatos*, 1 Cal. App. 3d 657, 81 Cal. Rptr. 910 (1969) (inheritance tax on certain property when devised by husband to wife, but not when devised by wife to husband, violates equal protection).

52 Idaho Code sec. 15-315 permits the appointment of joint administrators, an expedient measure fully consistent with constitutional principle.

male society, exercising its political power,[53] has secured women's place as the second sex.

II.

The statutory classification based on the sex of the applicant established in Section 15-314 of the Idaho Code is arbitrary and capricious and bears no rational relationship to a legitimate legislative purpose.

If the Court concludes that sex is not a suspect classification, appellant urges application of an intermediate test. Attributable in part to decisions of this Court, see pp. 41–53 *supra*, women continue to receive disadvantaged treatment by the law. In answer to the compelling claim of women for recognition by the law as full human personalities, this Court, at the very least, should reverse the presumption of a statute's rationality when the statute accords a preference to males. Rather than require the party attacking the statute to show that the classification is irrational, the Court should require the statute's proponent to prove it rational.

Yet, the discrimination embodied in section 15-314 of the Idaho Code is so patently visible that the statute is readily assailable under the less stringent reasonable-relationship test. The mandatory preference to males lacks the constitutionally required fair and substantial relation to a permissible legislative purpose

---

53 Although women were granted the vote over fifty years ago, the legacy of their disenfranchisement is still apparent. Elected or appointed office in this country remains, with sparse exceptions, a male preserve. See Handbook 118–26.

For the levity with which even the judiciary treats women's lack of representation, see *State* v. *Hunter*, 208 Ore. 282, 287–88, 300 P.2d 455, 457–58 (1956):

> We believe that we are justified in taking judicial notice of the fact that the membership of the legislative assembly which enacted this statute was predominantly masculine. That fact is important in determining what the legislature might have had in mind with respect to this particular statute. . . . It seems to us that its purpose, although somewhat selfish in nature, stands out in the statute like a sore thumb. . . . [I]s it any wonder that the legislative assembly took advantage of the police power of the state in its decision to halt this ever-increasing feminine encroachment upon what for ages had been considered strictly as manly arts and privileges?

At the time Idaho Code section 15-314 was originally enacted, 1864, women in Idaho lacked the right to vote for members of the legislature.

and therefore must be held to violate the equal protection clause.[54] *F. S. Royster Gitano Co.* v. *Virginia*, 253 U.S. 412, 415 (1920); *Gulf, Colorado & S. F. Ry.* v. *Ellis*, 165 U.S. 150, 155 (1897).

The Idaho Supreme Court held the sex-based classification of section 15-314 reasonable on the ground that "the legislature when it enacted this statute evidently concluded that in general men are better qualified to act as an administrator than are women." Conceding that "there are doubtless particular instances in which [the legislature's evident conclusion] is incorrect," the Idaho Supreme Court was "not prepared to say that [the conclusion] is so completely without a basis in fact as to be irrational and arbitrary" (A. 22a).[55]

Declaring that "nature itself has established the distinction," (A. 21a), the Idaho Supreme Court seemingly justified the discrimination challenged here by finding it "rational" to assume the mental inferiority of women to men. This assumption, particularized in the judgment that "men are better qualified to act as an administrator than are women" demands swift condemnation of this Court. In the Idaho District Court, where the argument was made in terms of the supposed greater "business experience" of men, Judge Donaldson responded, "The Court feels that this statement has no basis in fact in this modern age

---

54 Contrast with the wholly irrational discrimination embodied in section 15-314 of the Idaho Code, the Louisiana succession statute upheld by this Court in *Labine* v. *Vincent*, 401 U.S. —— (1971). Finding that it was permissible for the Louisiana legislature to distinguish for inheritance purposes between legitimate and illegitimate children, the Justice who cast the deciding vote stressed the different quality of the male parent's relation to legitimate and illegitimate children: "[I]t is surely entirely reasonable for the Louisiana legislature to provide that a man who has entered into a marital relationship thereby undertakes obligations to any resulting offspring beyond those which he owes to the products of a casual liaison. . . ." (Harlan, J., concurring opinion.) By parity of reasoning, it is surely entirely unreasonable for Idaho to provide that a female person who bears the very same relationship to the decedent as does a male person ranks, automatically, as the inferior human being.

55 The Idaho Supreme Court observed that "other courts construing similar provisions have also held that the preference is mandatory" (A. 19a–20a). To support this observation, it cited a solitary 1901 California case, *In re Coan's Estate*, 132 Cal. 401, 64 P. 691. That case is no longer law. California long ago repealed its male preference provision. See California Probate Law SPCS. 422, 423. If the Idaho Supreme Court wished to determine California's present view, it might have consulted *In re Estate of Legatos*, 1 Cal. App. 3d 657, 81 Cal. Rptr. 910 (1969) (inheritance tax on certain property when devised by husband to wife, but not when devised by wife to husband, violates equal protection).

and society" (A. 14a), and promptly declared section 15-314 unconstitutional. At a time when assumptions concerning the physical inferiority of women no longer go unquestioned,[56] the Court surely cannot countenance distinctions based on totally unfounded assumptions of differences in mental capacity, or "experience" relevant to the office of administrator.[57]

Despite the massive discrimination that women still face in the job market, their participation in the business world is increasing dramatically. In 1969, 30,512,000 women over the age of sixteen were at work, and comprised 37.8% of all workers.[58] The comparable figures thirty years ago were 13,783,000 and 25.4%.[59] About 42% of all women over the age of sixteen work full-time the year round.[60] In 1969, 58.9% of all married women living with husbands worked.[61] The Department of Labor has projected that by 1980 there will be 37,000,000 working women, twice as many as there were in 1950, and that for the first time there will be as many female professionals and technical workers as female blue-collar workers.[62]

56 See, *e.g., Weeks* v. *Southern Bell Telephone & Telegraph Co.*, 408 F.2d 228 (5th Cir. 1969); *Bowe* v. *Colgate-Palmolive Co.*, 416 F.2d 711 (7th Cir. 1969); *Rosenfeld* v. *Southern Pacific Co.*, —— F.2d —— (9th Cir. 1971); *Cheatwood* v. *South Central Bell Telephone & Telegraph Co.*, 303 F. Supp. 754 (M.D. Ala. 1969); *Richards* v. *Griffith Rubber Mills*, 300 F. Supp. 338 (D. Ore. 1969); Note, The Mandate of Title VII of the Civil Rights Act of 1964: To Treat Women as Individuals, 59 Georgetown L. Rev. 221 (1970).

57 While the office of administrator may not constitute "employment" within the meaning of federal and state anti-discrimination laws, it does require work and carries a fee. It would be strange indeed if state appointments of fiduciary officers were exempt from the standards of nondiscrimination declared national policy and imposed on private employers. See *Schattman* v. *Texas Employment Commission*, Civ. Action A-70-CA.-75, W.D. Texas (Austin Division), order denying motion for relief from judgment, April 16, 1971 ("Private employers can hardly be expected to comply voluntarily with the law when the state . . . operates in open disregard of the national policy of nondiscrimination.").

58 Dept. of Labor, Women's Bureau: Background Facts on Women Workers in the United States 5 (1970) [hereinafter Background Facts].

59 Handbook 10.

60 Handbook 3.

61 Background Facts 8. The Labor Department reported that in 1970, four out of every 10 husbands in the United States had wives who were employed. The ratio of working wives compared with an overall figure of 3 out of 10 a decade ago. See New York Times, January 31, 1971, p. 45.

62 See New York Times, November 11, 1970, p. 32, col. 1 (report of Secretary of Labor James D. Hodgson news conference presenting major conclusions of Department of Labor Study, "United States Manpower in the Nineteen-Seventies").

A similar trend is apparent in education. In 1967, women comprised 40.5% of the undergraduate student population in four year institutions of higher learning and 29.7% of the graduate population.[63] In the same year, women earned 40.3% of the bachelor's degrees, 34.7% of the master's degrees, and 11.9% of the doctorate degrees.[64] Close to 3,000,000 women were enrolled in institutions of higher learning in 1967, representing a 10% increase over 1966 and a 53% increase over 1963.[65]

In April, 1971, 4,500,000 women were employed as professional or technical workers compared to 6,706,000 men; 1,440,000 women were employed as managers, officials or proprietors, compared to 7,150,000 men.[66] In 1968, 10,000 women worked as accountants, 20% of the total; 12,500 were employed as bank officers, 10% of the total; 8,100 were employed as lawyers, 3% of the total; 6,500 worked as mathematicians, 10% of the total; and 7,650 were engaged as statisticians, 33% of the total.[67]

In 1970, 2,226 women passed the federal service management intern examination, 38% of the total.[68] Women employed by the federal government as category III employees in 1969 included 5,481 in accounting and budget, 12% of the total; 5,621 in legal and law-related areas, 23% of the total; 6,686 in business and industry, 14% of the total.[69] As of April 1971, 13,000 women were serving as officers in the Armed Forces.[70]

63 Handbook 188.

64 *Id.* at 191. On obstacles confronting women in academic life and measures proposed at one institution "to create a climate in which prejudice against women, or apathy toward their presence . . . will be hard to maintain," see Report of the Committee on the Status of Women in the Faculty of Arts and Sciences (Harvard University 1971).

65 *Id.* at 187.

66 Dept. of Labor, Bureau of Labor Statistics: Employment and Earnings 44 (May 1971). Cf. M. Hennig, What happens on the way up, The MBA 8–10 (March, 1971).

67 Dept. of Labor, Bureau of Labor Statistics: Occupational Outlook Handbook Bulletin No. 1650, pp. 28, 789, 230, 127, 129 (1970–71 ed.).

68 Civil Service Commission, Bureau of Recruiting and Examining, Program Development Division (unpublished data).

69 Civil Service Commission, Bureau of Manpower Information Systems: Study of Employment of Women in the Federal Government 137, 141 (1969).

70 Office of the Assistant Secretary of Defense, Manpower and Reserve Affairs (unpublished data).

Any legislative judgment that "men are better qualified to act as an administrator than are women" is simply untenable in view of these statistics, revealing what the Department of Labor describes as "a major change in American life style."[71] Moreover, although the Idaho Supreme Court did not provide any enlightenment on the specific functions an administrator performs for which "men are better qualified," the standard responsibilities are evident: receiving payments from creditors, paying out debts, paying state and federal taxes if any, preserving the assets of the estate, and finally paying out the net estate to the lawful heirs. Except for the occasional millionaire who dies intestate, the responsibilities are hardly onerous. They can be handled satisfactorily by most people who have completed secondary school education.[72]

Moreover, the extent to which "business experience" is needed for performance of the duties of an administrator is questionable. The Idaho Code, like most statutes relating to administration, confers very limited authority upon the administrator and empowers the court to supervise the estate closely during the entire period of administration. Thus the administrator must hire an appraiser for the estate. Idaho Code sec. 15-401, 402. No claims can be allowed without court approval. Idaho Code sec. 15-607. Distribution of the estate is strictly prescribed. Idaho Code sec. 15-1301–15-1308. Furthermore, the criteria for disqualification of an administrator set out in Idaho Code sec. 15-317 provide no support whatever for treating "business experience" as a characteristic of the competent executor. Any resident above the age of majority who has not been convicted of an infamous crime, and who is not mentally defective, a drunk, a wastrel, a spendthrift, or a cheat, is presumptively competent.[73]

---

71 See New York Times, November 11, 1970, p. 32, col. 3.

72 As of March 1968, apart from those who went on to higher education, 38.2% of the female population had completed four years of high school while only 30.6% of the male population were high school graduates. Handbook 178.

73 The primary criterion reflected in the Idaho statutes is not worldly experience but the degree of kinship to the decedent. Preference is given to the person with the greatest interest

In any event, it is not unlikely that more women than men have the kind of "business experience" most relevant to the duties of an administrator. Women who do not work outside the home often handle most if not all the financial affairs of their family unit. Managerial responsibility, including the settlement of accounts and the preservation of property, is a central part of their daily occupation. As preparation for the duties of an administrator, experience in household management surely is not inferior to experience in such typically male occupations as truck driver, construction worker, factory worker, or farm laborer.[74] Finally, as developed in the preceding section (*supra*, pp. 53–58), Idaho's interest in prompt administration of estates and curtailment of litigation is barely served by section 15-314. The male preference system operates in relatively few cases. In most situations in which more than one applicant from a class of equal eligibles separately seek letters of administration, hearings must be held. Indeed, and quite appropriately, the Idaho Code invites hearings by providing that "any person interested" may challenge the competency of the administrator. Idaho Code 15-322.[75]

To eliminate women who share an eligibility category with a man, when there is no basis in fact to assume that women are less competent to administer than are men, is patently unreasonable and constitutionally impermissible. A woman's right to equal treatment may not be sacrificed to expediency.

---

in the estate on the reasonable assumption that he or she will be motivated to preserve the property with due care during the period of administration.

74 If the Idaho legislature was in fact motivated by the misguided assumption that men are better qualified than women to administer an estate, the scheme it adopted would delight Lewis Carroll. Within a family unit, the death most likely to occur first is the father's. But when husband predeceases wife, Idaho Code sec. 15-312 provides that in appointing an administrator, first priority goes to the widow.

75 Recently, this Court reasserted the fundamental principle that "a State must afford to all individuals a meaningful opportunity to be heard." *Boddie* v. *Connecticut*, 401 U.S. —— (1971).

CONCLUSION

For the reasons stated above, the decision of the Idaho Supreme Court should be reversed and Sec. 15-314 should be declared unconstitutional.

Respectfully submitted,

MELVIN L. WULF
American Civil Liberties Union Foundation
156 Fifth Avenue New York, N. Y. 10010

ALLEN R. DERR
817 West Franklin Street
Boise, Idaho 83701

RUTH BADER GINSBURG
Rutgers Law School
180 University Avenue
Newark, New Jersey

PAULI MURRAY
504 Beacon Street
Boston, Mass. 02115

DOROTHY KENYON
433 W. 21st Street
New York, N. Y. 10011

Attorneys for Appellant[76]

---

76 Attorneys for Appellant gratefully acknowledge the invaluable assistance provided in preparation of this brief by Ms. Ann Freedman, J.D., Yale Law School, 1971; Ms. Janice Goodman, J.D., New York University School of Law, 1971; Professor Eva Hanna Hanks, Rutgers Law School (Newark); Ms. Mary Kelly, J.D., New York University School of Law, 1971; Ms. Diane Riegelman, 3rd year student, Rutgers Law School (Newark).

Brief for the Appellant in
Craig v. *Boren*, 429 U.S. 190
(1976)

*A*n Oklahoma law allowed the sale of "nonintoxicating" 3.2-percent beer to females between the ages of 18 and 21, but not to males. Curtis Craig, a male under the age of 21, and Carolyn Whitener, a licensed beer vendor, challenged the law on the basis that it violated the Fourteenth Amendment's Equal Protection Clause.

At the time the case reached the U.S. Supreme Court, Ruth Bader Ginsburg was counsel to the American Civil Liberty Union's Women's Rights Project, and stepped in to assist Craig's legal team, famously quipping that she was "Delighted to see the Supreme Court is interested in beer drinkers." Her involvement could have been seen as her asserting that men's equality was as important to her as women's equality: on its surface, the Oklahoma law was discriminatory against men. However, her amicus curiae brief—a document filed by someone who is not involved in the case but who has an interest in the legal question at hand—thoroughly explained that the Oklahoma law relied on outdated stereotypes about the differences between men and women, and stereotyping women favorably does not constitute fair and equal treatment of the sexes. In a 7-2 decision, the Court struck down the Oklahoma law, finding its gender-based classifications to be unconstitutional.

Original footnotes have been retained but renumbered.

ARGUMENT

I.

Oklahoma's sex/age classification to determine qualification for association with 3.2 beer pigeonholes impermissibly on the basis of gender in violation of the fourteenth amendment's equal protection principle.

A. *This Court's precedent condemns legislative classification based on overbroad generalization about "the way women (or men) are."*

Since *Reed* v. *Reed*, 404 U.S. 71 (1971), this Court has instructed consistently that gender-based legislative classification, premised on overbroad generalization concerning the behavior, proclivities and preferences of the two sexes, cannot be tolerated under the Constitution. *Stanley* v. *Illinois*, 405 U.S. 645 (1972); *Frontiero* v. *Richardson*, 411 U.S. 677 (1973); *Taylor* v. *Louisiana*, 419 U.S. 522 (1975); *Weinberger* v. *Wiesenfeld*, 420 U.S. 636 (1975); *Stanton* v. *Stanton*, 421 U.S. 7 (1975). The decision below rests exclusively upon such overbroad generalization. That decision, and the gender line it upholds, merit this Court's decisive disapprobation.

Recognizing that it is no longer in vogue to rely on the "demonstrated facts of life"[1] to justify gender lines in the law, appellees offered statistics which, they asserted, tended to show that 18–20 year old males "drive more, drink more, and commit more alcohol related offenses."[2] Even if the highly questionable statistical presentation[3] served to prove the proposition asserted by appellees, that proposition does not suffice to justify the sex/

---

1 *Lamb* v. *Brown*, 456 F.2d 18, at 20 (10th Cir. 1972).

2 Transcript of Proceedings before the United States District Court for the Western District of Oklahoma, *Walker* v. *Hall*, May 20, 1974 [hereafter cited as Transcript] at 5 (Appendix at 43) (opening statement of Oklahoma Assistant Attorney General). As the court below repeatedly noted, Oklahoma's statistical presentation indicated that males 21 and over "drive more, drink more and commit more alcohol related offenses" than males in the 18–20 age range. See 399 F. Supp. at 1309, 1311 n. 5.

3 See pp. 25–34, *infra*.

age classification here at issue. Indeed, had proof of the quality presented below satisfied the demands of the equal protection principle, the gender lines this Court has so firmly rejected would have remained on the books.

For example, in *Reed*, the proposition that men have more business experience than women was not without empirical support. In *Frontiero* and in *Wiesenfeld*, the statistics tendered by the Government to document men's nondependency, and their labor-market orientation,[4] were far more impressive than the concededly infirm data[5] relied upon in the case at bar. In short, the essence of this Court's decisions condemning laws drawing "a sharp line between the sexes"[6] escaped appellees and the court below: neither unsubstantiated stereotypes nor generalized factual data suffice to justify pigeonholing by gender; a legislature may not place all males in one pigeonhole, all females in another, based on assumed or documented notions about "the way women or men are."

The sole *post-Reed* cases in which this Court has countenanced classification based on "gender as such"[7] involved legislation justified as compensating women for past and present economic disadvantage. *Schlesinger* v. *Ballard*, 419 U.S. 498 (1975); *Kahn* v. *Shevin*, 416 U.S. 351 (1974). But Oklahoma's action cannot be rationalized on the ground that nowadays, females may be favored, but not disfavored by the law. For surely the concept "compensatory" or "rectificatory" gender classification[8] does not encompass the solace 3.2 beer might provide to young women already exposed to society's double standards or about to encounter an inhospitable job market.

4 *E.g.,* to demonstrate men's independence and work force participation, appellees in *Frontiero* presented census data showing that in 1971, "97.7 percent of married men between the ages of 25 and 44, whose wives were present, were in the civilian labor force." Brief for the Appellees at 9 n. 6, *Frontiero* v. *Richardson, supra.*

5 See 399 F. Supp. at 1311 & n. 4; Transcript at 37–38 (Appendix 66–67) (Assistant Attorney General concedes traffic death and injury statistics (Exhibit 5) do not indicate level of intoxication, if any, and are not "specifically on point"); pp. 29–30, *infra.*

6 The phrase appears in this Court's discredited decision in *Goesaert* v. *Cleary,* 335 U.S. 464, 466 (1948); see pp. 19–20, *infra.*

7 See *Geduldig* v. *Aiello,* 417 U.S. 484, at 496 n. 20 (1974).

8 Cf. *Frontiero* v. *Richardson, supra,* 411 U.S. at 689 n. 22.

B. *Sex/age lines in the law cannot be justified on any basis—"compelling state interest, or rational basis, or something in between."*

In *Stanton* v. *Stanton*, *supra*, this Court held that Utah's sex/age line, drawn for child support purposes, could not survive careful review, whatever the appropriate test, "compelling state interest, or rational basis, or something in between." 421 U.S. at 1.7. The Court noted that male/female age of majority differentials have become museum pieces in most states. 421 U.S. at 15. Appellees have not pointed to, nor has our investigation disclosed any state other than Oklahoma that today maintains a sex/age line for "nonintoxicating" 3.2 beer, or even "intoxicating" alcoholic beverage sales.[9] Nor has investigation revealed any state other than Oklahoma that today draws a gender line to determine who may work in a place where alcoholic ("intoxicating" or "nonintoxicating") beverages are sold.

The three-judge court hearing in the instant case occurred on May 20, 1974. The decision was filed almost a year later, on May 17, 1975. This Court's decision in *Stanton* was issued on April 15, 1975. It may be that the court below did not sufficiently consider or reflect upon *Stanton* when it voted to uphold Oklahoma's singular 3.2 beer law. While the three-judge court opinion purports not to rely on "old notions" but to rest upon a statistical revelation of sex-linked proclivities, census data provides numerical support of the same quality for the assumptions operative in *Stanton*. If statistics show that young men "drive more" and "drink more," they also show young women marry and relinquish education earlier. Yet surely factual data on the "nesting" proclivity of women[10] would not have persuaded a majority of this Court to uphold Utah's differential.

In sum, the Utah decision in *Stanton* and the decision below

---

9 Appellees introduced Exhibits (7 and 8) concerning experience in two other states, Minnesota and Michigan. Significantly, legislators in those states did not conceive of a sex/age line as a rational response to a traffic safety problem.

10 See Transcript at 71 (Appendix at 91).

ultimately rely on the very same notion—that gross categorization by gender is legitimate legislative action. Indeed, the transcript of the three-judge court hearing[11] strongly suggests that a familiar assumption, not fully articulated in the opinion, influenced the decision—namely, that it is "safe" to allow young women to drink 3.2 beer because young women are (usually) more "mature" than young men, and are (inclined to be) passive, unassertive, "settled," while young men are (generally) boys at heart, (apt to be) adventurous, daring, even reckless. But whether or not the court below wholly discarded "old notions" about the earlier maturation of females, the Oklahoma legislature may have had precisely those notions in mind when it allowed females, but not males, to purchase 3.2 beer and work in 3.2 beer parlors at 18.[12] The hypothesis that the legislature responded to "the common myth" that "women mature faster than men" is at least as plausible as any *post-Stanton* hypothesis defenders of the 3.2 beer sex/age differential might conceive.

The ruling below, in short, is a curiosity. It conflicts with *Stanton* and virtually every other recent adjudication concerning sex/age differentials in the law. See, *e.g., Lamb* v. *Brown*, 456 F.2d 18 (10th Cir. 1972); *Matter of Patricia A.*, 31 N.Y.2d 83, 335 N.Y.S.2d 33, 286 N.E. 2d 432 (1972); *Tang* v. *Ping*, 209 N.W. 2d 624 (N. Dak. 1973); *Harrigfeld* v. *District Court*, 95 Idaho 540, 511 P.2d 822 (1973); *Phelps* v. *Bing*, 58 Ill.2d 32, 316 N.E.2d 775 (1974).

C. *Gender-based discrimination in laws regulating the sale and consumption of alcohol is wholly without support in currently viable precedent.*

This case involves more than an impermissible sex/age differential. It also involves the lore relating to women and liquor—a

---

11 See Transcript at 68–78, 95–97 (Appendix at 89–96, 109–111).

12 See Transcript 68–70 (Appendix at 89–91). Indeed, the first hypothesis tendered by the state officials as to the legislative rationale was "[t]hat there is a difference in the ages of maturity between males and females, with males maturing at an older age." Motion to Dismiss at 7 (Appendix at 19).

combination that has fascinated lawmen for generations. The legislation at issue is a manifestation, with a bizarre twist, of the erstwhile propensity of legislatures to prescribe the conditions under which women and alcohol may mix. In recent years, however, outside Oklahoma, such legislation has been relegated to history's scrap heap. As the Court of Appeals for the First Circuit said of once traditional judicial essays in this area, "the authority of those precedents . . . has waned with the metamorphosis of the attitudes which fed them. What was then gallantry now appears Victorian condescension or even misogyny, and this cultural evolution is now reflected in the Constitution." *Women's Liberation Union of Rhode Island* v. *Israel*, 512 F.2d 106, 109 (1st Cir. 1975).

The case at bar apart, this decade's precedent unequivocally rejects discrimination between men and women in laws regulating the sale and consumption of alcohol. See *Women's Liberation Union of Rhode Island* v. *Israel, supra*; *White* v. *Fleming*, 522 F.2d 730 (7th Cir. 1975); *Daugherty* v. *Daley*, 370 F. Supp. 338 (N.D. Ill. 1974) (three-judge court); *Commonwealth* v. *Burke*, 481 S.W.2d 52 (Ky. 1972); *Sail'er Inn, Inc.* v. *Kirby*, 5 Cal. 3d 1, 485 P.2d 529 (1971); *Paterson Tavern Grill Owners Ass'n* v. *Hawthorne*, 57 N.J. 180, 270 A.2d 628 (1970). In both result and reasoning, the judgment below is an isolated retrogression, packaged in an opinion that jousts with conflicting decisions but ultimately fails to offer a single supporting authority.

Only by wishing away current precedent and reaching back more than a quarter of a century to *Goesaert* v. *Cleary*, 335 U.S. 464 (1948), can Oklahoma conjure up support for a gender-based differential in the context of liquor regulation. Once formidable authority for "a sharp line between the sexes," *Goesaert* is today an embarrassment reflecting male/female role delineation "offensive to the ethos of our society." *United States* v. *Dege*, 364 U.S. 51, at 53 (1960). *Goesaert* appears conspicuously in briefs tendered below by the state officials. But significantly, the three-judge court avoided citation to *Goesaert*, tied as that decision so plainly is to "old notions" and "archaic or overbroad generalizations." See 399 F. Supp. at 1313.

The statute in *Goesaert*, prohibiting employment of women as bartenders, was rationalized as protecting females and the public against "moral and social problems." 335 U.S. at 466. But suspicion lurked that "the real impulse behind [the] legislation was an unchivalrous desire of male bartenders to . . . monopolize the calling." 335 U.S. at 467.[13] In the instant case too, the purported rationale is protection, ironically, protection of males and the public against the vulnerabilities of the dominant sex. But the acknowledged basis for the once pervasive 18 female/21 male age of majority differential[14] suggests another perspective. Is it not probable that Oklahoma's legislators had in view likely coupling at the beer parlor—the 21 year old male paired with a female two or three years his junior?

It bears emphasis that no legislative history informed the conjecture of the court below as to the lawmaker's design. Post hoc attempts to hypothesize an appropriate rationale, though once routinely accepted where gender lines were at issue, are no longer immune from close scrutiny. Cf. *Weinberger* v. *Wiesenfeld*, *supra*, 420 U.S. at 648 n. 16. Moreover, no legislative design has been advanced that would even remotely satisfy the constitutional requirement that, at the least, gender-based classification must be "reasonable, not arbitrary, and must rest upon some ground of difference having a fair and substantial relation to the object of the legislation . . . ." *Reed* v. *Reed*, *supra*, 404 U.S. at 76. For gender is no more rational or less arbitrary a criterion upon which to base liquor or traffic safety laws than is religion or national origin?[15] If ethnic identification were the criterion, however buttressed by proof of drinking proclivities and

---

13 See "Bartending Must Revert to Bartenders, Says the G.E.B.," in Catering Industry Employee (April 12, 1946 pp. 4–5), extracted in Babcock, Freedman, Norton & Ross, Sex Discrimination and the Law 280 (1975).

14 See L. Kanowitz, Women and the Law 10–13 (1969); Davidson, Ginsburg & Kay, Sex-Based Discrimination 119–123 (1974).

15 See note 26, *infra*.

preferences, the state officials would "concede error."[16] Their willingness and the three-judge court's readiness to accept the gender line as unobjectionable warrant prompt correction by this Court.

In sum, the instant case provides an opportunity for this Court explicitly to overrule *Goesaert*, a decision universally criticized in commentary,[17] politely discarded by enlightened jurists, overdue for formal burial. Cf. *Taylor* v. *Louisiana*, 419 U.S. 522 (1975), overruling *Hoyt* v. *Florida*, 368 U.S. 57 (1961). Another opportunity seems unlikely in view of the singularity of Oklahoma's gender line and the illegality of the *Goesaert* classification, as well as the one in 37 Okla. Stat. §243 (18–20 year old females, but not 18–20 year old males may be employed in places where 3.2 beer is sold for on-premises consumption), under Title VII of the Civil Rights Act of 1964, 42 U.S.C. §2000e, and state law analogs. See *Sail'er Inn, Inc.* v. *Kirby, supra*; *Rosenfeld* v. *Southern Pacific Co.*, 444 F.2d 1219 (9th Cir. 1971).

D. *Laws such as 37 Okla. Stat. §§ 241, 243, 245 shore up artificial barriers to realization by men and women of their full human potential and retard society's progress toward equal opportunity, free from gender-based discrimination.*

Oklahoma's sex/age 3.2 beer line may appear at first glance a sport, a ridiculous distinction.[18] In comparison to other business vying for this Court's attention, 37 Okla. Stat. §§241, 243, 245 might be viewed as supplying comic relief. Yet if this Oklahoma legislative action is not checked, if the overbroad generalizations

---

16 See Transcript at 79 (Appendix at 97–98).

17 See, *e.g.*, L. Kanowitz, Women and the Law 33–34 (1969); Johnston, Jr. & Knapp, Sex Discrimination by Law: A Study in Judicial Perspective, 46 N.Y.U.L. Rev. 675, 682–92 (1971).

18 See Editorial, Tulsa Daily World, January 13, 1975, at 8-A: Oklahoma's ridiculous beer law has finally made the big time; it's gone all the way up to the U.S. Supreme Court.

. . . .

For years it has been argued that this is a stupid distinction that, if it ever did have a justification, it was long outdated. It is worse than obsolete; it is laughable . . . .

Let us hope the Justices dispose of it quickly, putting it quietly out of its misery.

tendered in its support are allowed to stand as proof adequate to justify a gender-based criterion, then this Court will have turned back the clock to the day when "anything goes" was the approach to line drawing by gender. For any defender of a gender line, with a modicum of sophistication, could avoid express reliance on "old notions" and, instead, invoke statistics to "demonstrate the facts of life."[19] But this Court's recent precedent should stand as a bulwark against "the imposition of special disabilities upon the member's [sic] of a particular sex because of their sex." *Frontiero* v. *Richardson, supra,* 411 U.S. at 686. For "[w]here the relation between characteristic and evil to be prevented" is as "tenuous" as it is here, "courts must look closely at that characteristic lest outdated social stereotypes result in invidious laws or practices." *Sail'er Inn, Inc.* v. *Kirby, supra,* 5 Cal. 3d at 18, 485 P.2d at 540.

On its face, Oklahoma's 3.2 beer differential accords young women a liberty withheld from young men. Upon deeper inspection, however, the discrimination is revealed as simply another manifestation of traditional attitudes and prejudices about the expected behavior and roles of the two sexes in our society, part of the myriad signals and messages that daily underscore the notion of men as society's active members, women as men's quiescent companions, members of the "other" or second sex. S. de Beauvoir, Second Sex (1949); see E. Maccoby & C. Jacklin, Psychology of Sex Differences (1974); W. Chafe, The American Woman (1972); Broverman, Vogel, Broverman, Clarkson & Rosencrantz, Sex-Role Stereotypes: A Current Appraisal, 28 J. Social Issues 59 (1972).

Laws such as 37 Okla. Stat. §§241, 243, 245 serve only to shore up artificial barriers to full realization by men and women of their human potential, and to retard progress toward equal opportunity, free from gender-based discrimination. Ultimately harmful to women by casting the weight of the state on the side of traditional notions concerning woman's behavior and her relation to man, such laws have no place in a nation preparing to celebrate a 200-year commitment to equal justice under law.

19 Cf. *Lamb* v. *Brown*, 456 F.2d 18, at 20 (10th Cir. 1972).

II.

The twenty-first amendment does not insulate from close scrutiny Oklahoma's separation of 3.2 beer purchasers along gender lines.

As a "main reason" for its decision, the court below proffered, "the statutes in question concern the regulation of alcoholic beverages—an area where the State's police powers are strengthened by the Twenty-first Amendment." 399 F. Supp. at 1307. Ambivalent, if not schizophrenic on this point, the court also asserted, the twenty-first amendment "does not call for the use of a less stringent equal protection standard than would otherwise apply," "the standards of review [the Equal Protection Clause] mandates are not relaxed." 399 F. Supp. at 1307–1308.

Beyond question, Oklahoma has broad authority to require effectively the sale and service of alcoholic beverages. But the twenty-first amendment is not a talisman insulating from careful review legislative resort to gross classification by gender. This has been the clear understanding of federal and state jurists attentive to this Court's precedent in the current decade. See, *e.g., Women's Liberation Union of Rhode Island* v. *Israel*, 512 F.2d 106 (1st Cir. 1975); *White* v. *Fleming*, 522 F.2d 730 (7th Cir. 1975); *Daugherty* v. *Daley*, 370 F. Supp. 338 (N.D. Ill. 1974) (three-judge court); cf. *Commonwealth* v. *Burke*, 481 S.W.2d 52 (Ky. 1972); *Sail'er Inn, Inc.* v. *Kirby*, 5 Cal. 3d 1, 485 P.2d 529 (1971); *Paterson Tavern & Grill Owners Ass'n.* v. *Hawthorne*, 57 N.J. 180, 270 A.2d 628 (1975).[20] Just as drinking preferences and proclivities associated with a particular ethnic group or social class would be perceived as an unfair and insubstantial basis for a beverage sale or service prohibition directed to that group or class (see Transcript at 79, Appendix at 97–98) so a gender-based[21] classification should be

---

20 As to the precedential value of *Goesaert* v. *Cleary*, 335 U.S. 464 (1948), see pp. 19–21. For an account of *pre-Reed* judicial performance, see Johnston, Jr. & Knapp, Sex Discrimination by Law: A Study in Judicial Perspective, 46 N.Y.U.L. Rev. 675, 682–92, 702–708 (1971).

21 The "facts of life" the state officials sought to demonstrate, cf. *Lamb* v. *Brown*, 456 F.2d 18, at 20 (10th Cir. 1972), might have been demonstrated more dramatically with respect to

recognized as an inappropriate, invidious means to the legislative end of rational regulation in the public interest.

Several times in the course of its opinion, the court below found "reinforcement" in this Court's decision in *California* v. *LaRue*, 409 U.S. 109 (1972). *LaRue* upheld state regulations prohibiting nude dancing and explicit sexual acts in establishments licensed to sell liquor by the drink. But whatever support the twenty-first amendment provides for state action explicitly and precisely directed to the commingling of live sex and liquor,[22] that brand of "sex" is not the issue in the case at bar.[23]

III.
The statistical proof on which the court below relied fails to establish that the hypothesized legislative objective (protection of young men and the public, particularly on the road) is fairly, substantially or sensibly served by a 3.2 beer sex/age line.

Evidence "entirely in the form of statistics," embodied in eight exhibits, was the sole proof presented by the state officials.

---

ethnic and religious groups. Yet surely the long-recognized and well-documented ethnic and religious differences in drinking habits and problems would not justify legislation using ethnic identification or religion as the criterion for a 3.2 beer or any other beverage regulation. See, *e.g.*, Wechsler, Thum, Demone & Kasey, Religious-Ethnic Differences in Alcohol Consumption, 11 J. of Health & Social Behavior 21 (1969); Wechsler, Thum, Demone & Dwinnell, Social Characteristics and BAC Level, 33 Quarterly Journal of Studies on Alcohol 132, 143–44 (1972) (Jews and Italian Catholics consistently manifest the lowest frequencies of positive BAC readings, highest frequencies occur among native-born, Canadian, and Irish Catholics; in the 16–25 age groups, native-born Catholics had the highest proportion with positive BACs (19% in the study reported), Jews and Italian Catholics, the lowest (5%)). Among adolescents, conspicuous differences appear as well. See Williams, Brehm, Cavanaugh, Moore & Eckerman, Final Report of Research Triangle Institute Center for the Study of Adolescent Drinking Behavior, Attitudes and Correlates 7 (National Institute on Alcohol Abuse and Alcoholism, U.S. Department of Health, Education, and Welfare, April 1975) (reporting percentage of adolescent heavy drinkers by ethnic group as follows: Black, 5.7%; White 10.7%; American Indian, 16.5%). See also Kandel, Single & Kessler, The Epidemiology of Drug Use Among New York State High School Students, 66 Am. J. Pub. Health 43, Table 2 (Jan. 1976).

22 See Comments, 1975 Wis. L. Rev. 161; 24 Syr. L. Rev. 1131 (1973).

23 For impressionable minds, the word "sex" may conjure up images of the kind this Court has left to "contemporary community standards." See *Paris Adult Theater I* v. *Slaton*, 413 U.S. 49 (1973). Gender, the grammar book term generally used in this brief, has a neutral, clinical tone that may ward off distracting associations.

(Transcript at 5, Appendix at 43.) As developed herein at pp. 13–23, *supra*, even if this proof did the service claimed for it, *i.e.*, even if the proof established that, in general, males within the 18–20 age group "drive more, drink more and commit more alcohol-related offenses" (Transcript at 5, Appendix at 43), such gross generalizations do not provide license for line drawing by gender. In this section, it will be demonstrated that the state officials' presentation does not do the service claimed for it. Further, the presentation falls far short of establishing a fair and substantial relationship between the hypothesized legislative end (traffic safety) and the statutory criterion employed (a sex/age 3.2 beer line).

A. *Oklahoma arrest statistics.*

State officials' Exhibits 1 and 2 (described in 399 F. Supp. at 1309, excerpts reproduced in 399 F. Supp. at 1314–1315) present certain arrest statistics for 1) Oklahoma, covering the last four months of 1973, and 2) Oklahoma City, covering the year 1973.[24] These exhibits show that, for the time periods covered, male arrests for "driving under the influence" and "drunkenness" substantially exceeded female arrests for those offenses.[25] But that is all they show. Unadorned arrest statistics hardly constitute proof that "driving under the influence" and "drunkenness" in the population of 18–20 year olds occur peculiarly in males. Among glaring deficiencies in the attempt to associate alcohol-related offenses with young men and 3.2 beer drinking: no evidence whatever was offered as to dispositions or convictions, bare arrests alone are recited;[26] no indication is offered of the

24 These statistics post-dated the 1972 legislative action here at issue. There is no indication that statistics of any kind informed or influenced the legislative judgment that 18–20 year old males, but not 18–20 year old females, were vulnerable to the hazards of 3.2 beer. See 399 F. Supp. at 1311 n. 6.

25 Both State and City figures show that male involvement increases with age, *i.e.*, the percentage of female arrests is highest in the 18–20 age range, while the percentage of male arrests is considerably higher at 21 and over than it is at 18. See 399 F. Supp. at 1309.

26 Because it would have been burdensome to do so, Oklahoma law enforcement officers did "not even attempt to keep dispositions as to age groups." Transcript at 26–27 (Appendix at 59). Cf. Transcript at 9 (Appendix at 46–47).

number of male and female *individuals* arrested; not a single arrest is attributed to 3.2 beer drinking; no attempt is made to grapple with the "chivalry factor," *i.e.*, the documented reality that for the very same behavior, the male may be arrested, while the female is escorted home, perhaps with a fatherly warning.

As to the inference of offense from arrest, this Court said in *Schware* v. *Board of Bar Examiners*, 353 U.S. 232, 241 (1957), "The mere fact that a man has been arrested has very little, if any, probative value in showing that he has engaged in any misconduct. An arrest shows nothing more than that someone probably suspected the person apprehended of an offense." See also *Gregory* v. *Litton Systems, Inc.*, 316 F. Supp. 401 (C.D. Calif. 1970) (because of general societal practices, use of arrest records in hiring decisions discriminates on race grounds); *Menard* v. *Mitchell*, 328 F. Supp. 718, at 724 (D.D.C. 1971), *rev'd on other grounds*, 498 F.2d 1017 (D.C. Cir. 1974) ("[O]nly a conviction carries legal significance as to a person's involvement in criminal behavior."); McCormick, Evidence §43 at 85 (Cleary ed. 1972).

Moreover, even as arrest indications the statistics are opaque: they do not account for multiple arrests. Forty-seven arrests of eighteen-year-old males in Oklahoma City could mean 47 different young men were arrested, or one young man was arrested 47 times, or something in between. In short, the arrest figures do not even negate the possibility that the disproportion is attributable to multiple arrests on the male side, rather than to marked disparity in the number of males and females arrested. Additionally, the arrest statistics demonstrate no relationship between the alleged offense and drinking 3.2 beer, the prohibition which the statistics purport to support. In view of the relative potencies of the beverages, arrestees' alcohol association, if any, might more likely involve 100-proof vodka than "nonintoxicating" 3.2 beer.

Furthermore, Exhibits 1 and 2 tell a familiar story. National arrest statistics for all age groups and most offenses reflect a similar pattern. For example, in 1964, while the sex ratio varied considerably by type of offense, the average arrest ratio of males to females was 7.5 to 1. See Reckless & Kay, The Female Offender 4 (1967). See also Nagel & Weitzman, Women as Litigants, 23 Hastings L. J. 171 (1971). Viewed in this light, Oklahoma's arrest figures almost certainly suggest more about the conduct and attitudes of the state's police officers than they do about the 3.2 beer drinking habits of young men and women. For prime among factors identified as relevant to the underinvolvement of women in officially-acted-upon crime is the "chivalry factor," *i.e.*, men's willingness to cover up women's crimes, and the unwillingness of the public and law enforcement officers to hold women accountable for criminal activity. Reckless & Kay, *supra*, at 13.[27]

B. *Oklahoma traffic death and injury statistics.*

State officials' Exhibits 4 and 5 indicate the number of persons killed and injured in 1972 and 1973 Oklahoma motor vehicle traffic collisions. Youths 17–21 are overrepresented in these statistics; for all age groups, the number of males exceeds the number of females.[28] Although presumably introduced to illustrate the "evil" the legislature sought to prevent, as the state officials themselves acknowledged, these Exhibits are not "specifically on point" (Transcript at 37, Appendix at 67), for they supply no indication whatever of alcohol involvement in collisions.[29] (Transcript at 36, Appendix at 66.) Indeed, closer

---

27 Paternalism in the criminal justice system and stereotypical views on women's nature do not always operate benignly in women's favor. See, *e.g.*, *New Jersey* v. *Chambers*, 63 N.J. 287, 307 A.2d 78 (1973); Nagel & Weitzman, *supra*; Note, The Sexual Segregation of American Prisons, 82 Yale L. J. 1229 (1973).

28 However, if state officials' Exhibit 3 is any guide to relative male/female road use, then the 17–21 female death rate is about the same as the male rate, while the 17–21 female injury rate is substantially higher than the male rate. *I.e.*, the 1972 roadside survey population reported in Exhibit 3 was 78% male, 22% female. 399 F. Supp. at 1309. Females accounted for 23% of traffic deaths in the 17–21 age group that year, and 40% of traffic injuries. 399 F. Supp. at 1320 (Exhibit 4).

29 For all these Exhibits reveal (pedestrian, passenger and driver death and injuries are lumped together in the portions of the Exhibits excerpted by the court below, 399 F. Supp. at 1320–1321), all collision victims may have been free from fault, and all persons responsible for the deaths and injuries may have been 18–20 female 3.2 beer drinkers.

examination of the state officials' Exhibits should have demonstrated that overrepresentation of young persons in collisions is *not* occasioned by alcohol use:

> If younger drivers were involved in more collisions than older drivers because of the excessive use of alcohol, it would be expected that: (a) young drivers would show a higher frequency of driving-after-drinking than older drivers; and (b) that young drivers would have a worse collision-involvement index among all drivers, whether they had been drinking or not, than among alcohol-free drivers. *A comparison of Tables 7 and 8 shows that this is not true.* (Emphasis supplied.)

Proceedings of the Joint Conference on Alcohol Abuse and Alcoholism, February 21–23, 1972, Defendants' (state officials') Exhibit 8 at 120, 124 (Appendix at 213–214). In short, Oklahoma's age- but not alcohol-correlated collision statistics suggest a relationship between accidents and driving experience. They might well support a compulsory driver-training law, but they provide no basis for a 3.2 beer sex/age classification.

C. *National, Minnesota and Michigan statistics and reports.*

Exhibit 6 (Appendix at 182–184) is an FBI report showing an increase nationwide in arrests for "driving under the influence." It reveals no convictions, shows nothing about 3.2 beer drinking and does not present any sex/age breakdown for 18–20 year olds. Exhibit 7 (Appendix at 185–207), a Minnesota Department of Public Safety report, was introduced to show "Oklahoma statistics are at least in line with statistics in other states." (Transcript at 41, Appendix at 70.) Minnesota maintains no sex/age line for 3.2 beer or, indeed, any other beverage. Exhibit 8 (Appendix at 208–226), a federally-sponsored conference report, was introduced for its reference to a Michigan study. A portion of the Michigan study is quoted in the opinion below. 399 F. Supp. at 1310. Michigan maintains no sex/age line for 3.2 beer or, indeed, any other beverage. As already noted,[30] the Michigan report, in a passage skipped over by the court below, explains that younger drivers are not involved in more collisions than older drivers because of the excessive use of alcohol.

The remaining item in appellees' proof, state officials' Exhibit 3, figures in the opinion below as the *pièce de résistance*. This Exhibit summarizes the results of a voluntary roadside survey of drivers in selected locations in Oklahoma City during the post-work hours 6:00 p.m. to 10:00 p.m. and 11:00 p.m. to 3:00 a.m. in August of 1972 and 1973. Drivers were asked: 1) Do you drink? 2) If you do, what is your drink preference (beer,[31] wine, liquor)? 3) Did you drink in the last two hours? Survey participants were tested for Blood Alcohol Concentrations (BACs). No inquiry was made as to 3.2 beer drinking. The survey provides no answers at all to the questions: 1) Did the drivers who stated a preference for beer prefer "nonintoxicating" 3.2 beer over other alcohol beverages? 2) Did any driver consume 3.2 beer within the two hours preceding the survey? 3) Had any driver who registered a positive BAC imbibed 3.2 beer? Whatever limited purpose the survey may have been designed to serve,[32] Exhibit 3 is highly questionable as an indicator of the gender make-up of Oklahoma's driving population, and as a predictor of gender-based differences in conduct related to

---

30 See p. 29, *supra*.

31 The court below incorrectly reports that in 1972, 84% of the under-20 males surveyed, and 77% of the under-20 females stated that their drink preference was beer, 399 F. Supp. at 1309. Taking into account nondrinkers in the survey population, 58.8% of the under-20 males and 52.9% of the under-20 females preferred beer.

32 No testimony was offered as to the purpose of the survey. No basis was laid for any inference that the small male sample (243 males under-20 in 1972, 238 in 1973) and minimal female sample (70 females under-20 in 1972, 68 in 1973) displayed characteristics that may be generalized to the under-20 Oklahoma driving population. In addition to the small size of the under-20 survey population, a numerical discrepancy, unexplained in the Exhibit or Transcript, casts further doubt on the survey's utility: the survey reports 243 as the total number of under-20 males interviewed in 1972, but the BAC columns for that group account in numbers and percentages for 253 males. Further, one-third of the "minor" male population covered by Okla. Stat. §§241, 243, 245 (20-year olds) ranks as adults in the survey.

drinking and driving. The exhibit provides no elucidation of any kind as to conduct related to drinking 3.2 beer and driving.

Males accounted for 52.9% of Oklahoma's driving population in 1972, and 52.5% in 1973. U.S. Department of Transportation, Federal Highway Administration, Drivers Licenses—1972 and 1973.[33] The sample of drivers interviewed for the Oklahoma City survey was 77.8% male in 1972 and 76.8% male in 1973. Similar disproportions appear in the sample of drivers in the 18–20 age range. Although it is reasonable to anticipate more drinking in nighttime hours, it may well be that a daytime hours survey would produce a higher percentage of female drivers and a significantly different distribution in the positive BAC columns.[34] Considering the small size of the survey population, any unprovided for difference in male/female drinking/driving habits, such as time of day, yielding even a very few more women on the road with positive BACs, would drastically alter the female percentages and, in turn, the comparison with the male group. For example, the court below observed: "Of those drivers under 20 [in the 1972 survey] who had a BAC of greater than .01%, 29.7% of the males and 14.3% of the females had a BAC equal to, or greater than, .05%." 399 F. Supp. at 1309. Restating these figures in terms of the total under-20 survey group, 4.35% of the males and 1.43% of the females had a BAC equal to, or greater than .05%. Should a change from nighttime to daytime survey add two more females to the .05% BAC category, the female percentage (4.29%) would nearly match the male's.

In addition, far from supporting distinctive treatment of young men, the survey suggests that age may be more relevant to

---

33 Drivers Licenses—1972, Table DL-1A, p. 6 (18–20 drivers at Table DL-21, Sheet 4); Drivers Licenses—1973, Table DL-1A, p. 8 (18–20 drivers at Table DL-21, p. 14). The most recently published national licensed drivers statistics, covering the year 1974, show these figures for Oklahoma: total licensed drivers, 1,711,805 (52.21% male); 18 year old drivers, 45,565 (53.29% male); 19 year old drivers, 46,155 (53.03% male); 20 year old drivers, 45,191 (52.81% male). U.S. Department of Transportation, Drivers Licenses—1974, Table DL-21, Sheet 4.

34 Since the survey occurred after work hours and in a city, the sample does not reflect daytime suburban housewife drinking/driving behavior for 18–20 year olds or any other age group. Further, the sample included drivers of "pickup trucks and an occasional motorcycle," drivers more likely to be male. See Exhibit 3, cover letter.

the drinking behavior of female drivers. For example, in 1972, the percentages of under-20 males and females who answered yes to the question, "Do you drink," are in the same range: 70.4% for males, 68.6% for females. But when young people are compared with their elders (persons 20 and over), young women stand out as the group distinctive in attraction to alcohol: 76.8% of the older men, but only 57.7% of the older women reported themselves as drinkers.

In sum, the state officials have utterly failed to demonstrate that the supposed legislative objective (protection of young men and the public from weaknesses male flesh is heir to) is fairly, substantially and sensibly served by a 3.2 beer sex/age line. On the contrary, the gender criterion retained in 37 Okla. Stat. §§241, 243, 245 is a paradoxical remnant of the day when sharp lines between the sexes were routinely drawn by the legislature, and just as routinely upheld by the judiciary.

CONCLUSION

For the reasons stated above, the decision of the District Court for the Western District of Oklahoma should be reversed and the gender line drawn in 37 Okla. Stat. §§241, 243 and 245 should be declared unconstitutional.

Adarand Constructors, Inc. v. Peña, 515 U.S. 200 (1995)

Dissenting Opinion

*I*n 1989, Mountain Gravel and Construction in Colorado sought a subcontractor to do work for a highway project funded by the U.S. Department of Transportation. Adarand Constructors, Inc., was the lowest bidder for job; however, Mountain Gravel awarded the bid to Gonzalez Construction instead. Mountain Gravel's federal contract—like most federal government contracts at the time—included financial incentives for using businesss run by "socially and economically disadvantaged individuals include[ing] Black Americans, Hispanic Americans, Native Americans, Asian Pacific Americans, and other minorities." Gonzalez Construction was certified as one such business, and Adarand Constructors, Inc., was not. In federal court, Adarand maintained that the Department of Transportation's subcontracting incentives were unconstitutional; after losing that case, Adarand appealed to the Supreme Court.

The question before the Court was whether the presumption of disadvantage, and the ensuing favorable treatment, based on race alone is a violation of the Fifth Amendment's Due Process Clause. With a 5-4 majority opinion written by Justice Sandra Day O'Connor, the Court sided with Adarand, stating that racial classifications must pass strict scrutiny review—meaning they "must serve a compelling government interest, and must be narrowly tailored to further that interest"—and arguing that race in and of itself is not a sufficient condition for presuming "disadvantage." In her dissent, Justice Ginsburg argued that the Due Process

Clause should ensure policies that will advance true equality for race and gender groups that have been traditionally marginalized.

ADARAND CONSTRUCTORS INC.
v.
PEÑA, SECRETARY OF TRANSPORTATION, ET AL.
CERTIORARI TO THE UNITED STATES COURT OF APPEALS FOR THE TENTH CIRCUIT
[June 12, 1995]

JUSTICE GINSBURG, with whom JUSTICE BREYER joins, dissenting.

For the reasons stated by Justice Souter, and in view of the attention the political branches are currently giving the matter of affirmative action, I see no compelling cause for the intervention the Court has made in this case. I further agree with Justice Stevens that, in this area, large deference is owed by the Judiciary to "Congress' institutional competence and constitutional authority to overcome historic racial subjugation." *Ante*, at 253 (Stevens, J., dissenting); see *ante*, at 254–255.[1] I write separately to underscore not the differences the several opinions in this case display, but the considerable field of agreement—the common understandings and concerns—revealed in opinions that together speak for a majority of the Court.

I

The statutes and regulations at issue, as the Court indicates, were adopted by the political branches in response to an "unfortunate reality": "[t]he unhappy persistence of both the practice and the lingering effects of racial discrimination against minority groups in this country." *Ante*, at 237 (lead opinion). The United

---

1 On congressional authority to enforce the equal protection principle, see, *e.g.*, *Heart of Atlanta Motel, Inc.* v. *United States*, 379 U.S. 241, 286 (1964) (Douglas, J., concurring) (recognizing Congress' authority, under § 5 of the Fourteenth Amendment, to "pu[t] an end to all obstructionist strategies and allo[w] every person—whatever his race, creed, or color—to patronize all places of public accommodation without discrimination whether he travels interstate or intrastate."); *id.*, at 291, 293 (Goldberg, J., concurring) ("primary purpose of the Civil Rights Act of 1964 . . . is the vindication of human dignity"; "Congress clearly had authority under both § 5 of the Fourteenth Amendment and the Commerce Clause" to enact the law); G. Gunther, Constitutional Law 147–151 (12th ed. 1991).

States suffers from those lingering effects because, for most of our Nation's history, the idea that "we are just one race," *ante*, at 239 (Scalia, J., concurring in part and concurring in judgment), was not embraced. For generations, our lawmakers and judges were unprepared to say that there is in this land no superior race, no race inferior to any other. In *Plessy* v. *Ferguson*, 163 U.S. 537 (1896), not only did this Court endorse the oppressive practice of race segregation, but even Justice Harlan, the advocate of a "color-blind" Constitution, stated:

> "The white race deems itself to be the dominant race in
> this country. And so it is, in prestige, in achievements,
> in education, in wealth and in power. So, I doubt not,
> it will continue to be for all time, if it remains true
> to its great heritage and holds fast to the principles of
> constitutional liberty." *Id.*, at 559 (dissenting opinion).

Not until *Loving* v. *Virginia*, 388 U.S. 1 (1967), which held unconstitutional Virginia's ban on interracial marriages, could one say with security that the Constitution and this Court would abide no measure "designed to maintain White Supremacy." *Id.*, at 11.[2]

The divisions in this difficult case should not obscure the Court's recognition of the persistence of racial inequality and a majority's acknowledgment of Congress' authority to act affirmatively, not only to end discrimination, but also to counteract discrimination's lingering effects. *Ante*, at 237 (lead opinion); see also *ante*, at 269–270 (Souter, J., dissenting). Those effects, reflective of a system of racial caste only recently ended, are

---

2 The Court, in 1955 and 1956, refused to rule on the constitutionality of antimiscegenation laws; it twice declined to accept appeals from the decree on which the Virginia Supreme Court of Appeals relied in *Loving*. See *Naim* v. *Naim*, 197 Va. 80, 87 S. E. 2d 749, vacated and remanded, 350 U.S. 891 (1955), reinstated and aff'd, 197 Va. 734, 90 S. E. 2d 849, appeal dism'd, 350 U.S. 985 (1956). *Naim* expressed the state court's view of the legislative purpose served by the Virginia law: "to preserve the racial integrity of [Virginia's] citizens"; to prevent "the corruption of blood," "a mongrel breed of citizens," and "the obliteration of racial pride." 197 Va., at 90, 87 S. E. 2d, at 756.

evident in our workplaces, markets, and neighborhoods. Job applicants with identical résumés, qualifications, and interview styles still experience different receptions, depending on their race.[3] White and African-American consumers still encounter different deals.[4] People of color looking for housing still face discriminatory treatment by landlords, real estate agents, and mortgage lenders.[5] Minority entrepreneurs sometimes fail to gain contracts though they are the low bidders, and they are sometimes refused work even after winning contracts.[6] Bias both conscious and unconscious, reflecting traditional and unexamined habits of thought,[7] keeps up barriers that must come down if equal opportunity and nondiscrimination are ever genuinely to become this country's law and practice.

Given this history and its practical consequences, Congress

3 See, e.g., H. Cross, G. Kennedy, J. Mell, & W. Zimmermann, Employer Hiring Practices: Differential Treatment of Hispanic and Anglo Job Seekers 42 (Urban Institute Report 90–4, 1990) (e.g., Anglo applicants sent out by investigators received 52% more job offers than matched Hispanics); M. Turner, M. Fix, & R. Struyk, Opportunities Denied, Opportunities Diminished: Racial Discrimination in Hiring xi (Urban Institute Report 91–9, 1991) ("In one out of five audits, the white applicant was able to advance farther through the hiring process than his black counterpart. In one out of eight audits, the white was offered a job although his equally qualified black partner was not. In contrast, black auditors advanced farther than their white counterparts only 7 percent of the time, and received job offers while their white partners did not in 5 percent of the audits.").

4 See, e.g., Ayres, Fair Driving: Gender and Race Discrimination in Retail Car Negotiations, 104 Harv. L. Rev. 817, 821–822, 819, 828 (1991) ("blacks and women simply cannot buy the same car for the same price as can white men using identical bargaining strategies"; the final offers given white female testers reflected 40 percent higher markups than those given white male testers; final offer markups for black male testers were twice as high, and for black female testers three times as high as for white male testers).

5 See, e.g., A Common Destiny: Blacks and American Society 50 (G. Jaynes & R. Williams eds. 1989) ("[I]n many metropolitan areas one-quarter to one-half of all [housing] inquiries by blacks are met by clearly discriminatory responses."); M. Turner, R. Struyk, & J. Yinger, U.S. Dept. of Housing and Urban Development, Housing Discrimination Study: Synthesis i–vii (Sept. 1991) (1989 audit study of housing searches in 25 metropolitan areas; over half of African-American and Hispanic testers seeking to rent or buy experienced some form of unfavorable treatment compared to paired white testers); Leahy, Are Racial Factors Important for the Allocation of Mortgage Money?, 44 Am. J. Econ. & Soc. 185, 193 (1985) (controlling for socioeconomic factors, and concluding that "even when neighborhoods appear to be similar on every major mortgage-lending criterion except race, mortgage-lending outcomes are still unequal").

6 See, e.g., Associated General Contractors v. Coalition for Economic Equity, 950 F. 2d 1401, 1415 (CA9 1991) (detailing examples in San Francisco).

7 Cf. Wygant v. Jackson Bd. of Ed., 476 U.S. 267, 318 (1986) (STEVENS, J., dissenting); Califano v. Goldfarb, 430 U.S. 199, 222–223 (1977) (STEVENS, J., concurring in judgment).

surely can conclude that a carefully designed affirmative action program may help to realize, finally, the "equal protection of the laws" the Fourteenth Amendment has promised since 1868.[8]

II

The lead opinion uses one term, "strict scrutiny," to describe the standard of judicial review for all governmental classifications by race. *Ante*, at 235–237. But that opinion's elaboration strongly suggests that the strict standard announced is indeed "fatal" for classifications burdening groups that have suffered discrimination in our society. That seems to me, and, I believe, to the Court, the enduring lesson one should draw from *Korematsu* v. *United States*, 323 U.S. 214 (1944); for in that case, scrutiny the Court described as "most rigid," *id.*, at 216, nonetheless yielded a pass for an odious, gravely injurious racial classification. See *ante*, at 214–215 (lead opinion). A *Korematsu*-type classification, as I read the opinions in this case, will never again survive scrutiny: Such a classification, history and precedent instruct, properly ranks as prohibited.

For a classification made to hasten the day when "we are just one race," *ante*, at 239 (Scalia, J., concurring in part and concurring in judgment), however, the lead opinion has dispelled the notion that "strict scrutiny" is " 'fatal in fact.' " *Ante*, at 237 (quoting *Fullilove* v. *Klutznick*, 448 U.S. 448, 519 (1980) (Marshall, J., concurring in judgment)). Properly, a majority of the Court calls for review that is searching, in order to ferret out classifications in reality malign, but masquerading as benign. See *ante*, at 228–229 (lead opinion). The Court's once lax review of sex-based classifications demonstrates the need for such suspicion. See, *e.g.*, *Hoyt* v. *Florida*, 368 U.S. 57, 60 (1961) (upholding

---

8 On the differences between laws designed to benefit a historically disfavored group and laws designed to burden such a group, see, *e.g.*, Carter, When Victims Happen To Be Black, 97 Yale L. J. 420, 433–434 (1988) ("[W]hatever the source of racism, to count it the same as racialism, to say that two centuries of struggle for the most basic of civil rights have been mostly about freedom from racial categorization rather than freedom from racial oppression, is to trivialize the lives and deaths of those who have suffered under racism. To pretend . . . that the issue presented in *Bakke* was the same as the issue in *Brown* is to pretend that history never happened and that the present doesn't exist.").

women's "privilege" of automatic exemption from jury service); *Goesaert* v. *Cleary*, 335 U.S. 464 (1948) (upholding Michigan law barring women from employment as bartenders); see also Johnston & Knapp, Sex Discrimination by Law: A Study in Judicial Perspective, 46 N. Y. U. L. Rev. 675 (1971). Today's decision thus usefully reiterates that the purpose of strict scrutiny "is precisely to distinguish legitimate from illegitimate uses of race in governmental decision making," *ante*, at 228 (lead opinion), "to 'differentiate between' permissible and impermissible governmental use of race," *ibid.*, to distinguish " 'between a "No Trespassing" sign and a welcome mat,' " *ante*, at 229.

Close review also is in order for this further reason. As Justice Souter points out, *ante*, at 270 (dissenting opinion), and as this very case shows, some members of the historically favored race can be hurt by catchup mechanisms designed to cope with the lingering effects of entrenched racial subjugation. Court review can ensure that preferences are not so large as to trammel unduly upon the opportunities of others or interfere too harshly with legitimate expectations of persons in once-preferred groups. See, *e.g.*, *Bridgeport Guardians, Inc.* v. *Bridgeport Civil Service Comm'n*, 482 F. 2d 1333, 1341 (CA2 1973).

* * *

While I would not disturb the programs challenged in this case, and would leave their improvement to the political branches, I see today's decision as one that allows our precedent to evolve, still to be informed by and responsive to changing conditions.

United States v. Virginia, 518 U.S. 515 (1996)

Majority Opinion

*T*he Virginia Military Institute (VMI) was an all-male higher-education institution with a longstanding reputation as an exceptional leadership school. The United States sued Virginia and VMI, claiming that VMI's exclusion of females violated the Fourteenth Amendment's Equal Protection Clause. Virginia countered by proposing that instead of admitting women to VMI, the commonwealth create the Virginia Women's Institute for Leadership (VWIL) exclusively for women, which the Fourth Circuit court found acceptable.

When the United States appealed to the U.S. Supreme Court, the question before the justices was whether the creation of a women-only institution billed as comparable to the existing male-only institution satisfied the Equal Protection Clause. The Court found 7-1 that it did not. Justice Ginsburg's majority opinion, clearly and forcefully explained, not only outlines the Court's position, but also contains shades of the staunch anti-sexism positions she so frequently adopted as a lawyer prior to her time on the court.

UNITED STATES

v.

VIRGINIA ET AL.
CERTIORARI TO THE UNITED STATES COURT OF APPEALS FOR THE FOURTH CIRCUIT

[June 26, 1996]

JUSTICE GINSBURG DELIVERED THE OPINION OF THE COURT.

Virginia's public institutions of higher learning include an incomparable military college, Virginia Military Institute (VMI). The United States maintains that the Constitution's equal protection guarantee precludes Virginia from reserving exclusively to men the unique educational opportunities VMI affords. We agree.

I

Founded in 1839, VMI is today the sole single-sex school among Virginia's 15 public institutions of higher learning. VMI's distinctive mission is to produce "citizen-soldiers," men prepared for leadership in civilian life and in military service. VMI pursues this mission through pervasive training of a kind not available anywhere else in Virginia. Assigning prime place to character development, VMI uses an "adversative method" modeled on English public schools and once characteristic of military instruction. VMI constantly endeavors to instill physical and mental discipline in its cadets and impart to them a strong moral code. The school's graduates leave VMI with heightened comprehension of their capacity to deal with duress and stress, and a large sense of accomplishment for completing the hazardous course.

VMI has notably succeeded in its mission to produce leaders; among its alumni are military generals, Members of Congress, and business executives. The school's alumni overwhelmingly perceive that their VMI training helped them to realize their personal goals. VMI's endowment reflects the loyalty of its graduates; VMI has the largest per-student endowment of all public undergraduate institutions in the Nation.

Neither the goal of producing citizen-soldiers nor VMI's implementing methodology is inherently unsuitable to women. And the school's impressive record in producing leaders has made admission desirable to some women. Nevertheless, Virginia has elected to preserve exclusively for men the advantages and opportunities a VMI education affords.

II
A

From its establishment in 1839 as one of the Nation's first state military colleges, see 1839 Va. Acts, ch. 20, VMI has remained financially supported by Virginia and "subject to the control of the [Virginia] General Assembly," Va. Code Ann. § 23–92 (1993). First southern college to teach engineering and industrial chemistry, see H. Wise, Drawing Out the Man: The VMI Story 13 (1978) (The VMI Story), VMI once provided teachers for the Commonwealth's schools, see 1842 Va. Acts, ch. 24, § 2 (requiring every cadet to teach in one of the Commonwealth's schools for a 2-year period).[1] Civil War strife threatened the school's vitality, but a resourceful superintendent regained legislative support by highlighting "VMI's great potential[,] through its technical know-how," to advance Virginia's postwar recovery. The VMI Story 47.

VMI today enrolls about 1,300 men as cadets.[2] Its academic offerings in the liberal arts, sciences, and engineering are also available at other public colleges and universities in Virginia. But VMI's mission is special. It is the mission of the school

---

1 During the Civil War, school teaching became a field dominated by women. See A. Scott, The Southern Lady: From Pedestal to Politics,1830–1930, p. 82 (1970).

2 Historically, most of Virginia's public colleges and universities were single sex; by the mid-1970's, however, all except VMI had become coeducational. 766 F. Supp. 1407, 1418–1419 (WD Va. 1991). For example, Virginia's legislature incorporated Farmville Female Seminary Association in 1839, the year VMI opened. 1839 Va. Acts, ch. 167. Originally providing instruction in "English, Latin, Greek, French, and piano" in a "home atmosphere," R. Sprague, Longwood College: A History 7–8, 15(1989) (Longwood College), Farmville Female Seminary became a public institution in 1884 with a mission to train "white female teachers for public schools," 1884 Va. Acts, ch. 311. The school became Longwood College in 1949, Longwood College 136, and introduced coeducation in 1976, *id.*, at 133.

" 'to produce educated and honorable men, prepared for the varied work of civil life, imbued with love of learning, confident in the functions and attitudes of leadership, possessing a high sense of public service, advocates of the American democracy and free enterprise system, and ready as citizen-soldiers to defend their country in time of national peril.' " 766 F. Supp. 1407, 1425 (WD Va. 1991) (quoting Mission Study Committee of the VMI Board of Visitors, Report, May 16, 1986).

In contrast to the federal service academies, institutions maintained "to prepare cadets for career service in the armed forces," VMI's program "is directed at preparation for both military and civilian life"; "[o]nly about 15% of VMI cadets enter career military service." 766 F. Supp., at 1432.

VMI produces its "citizen-soldiers" through "an adversative, or doubting, model of education" which features "[p]hysical rigor, mental stress, absolute equality of treatment, absence of privacy, minute regulation of behavior, and indoctrination in desirable values." *Id.*, at 1421. As one Commandant of Cadets described it, the adversative method " 'dissects the young student,' " and makes him aware of his " 'limits and capabilities,' " so that he knows " 'how far he can go with his anger, . . . how much he can take under stress, . . . exactly what he can do when he is physically exhausted.' " *Id.*, at 1421–1422 (quoting Col. N. Bissell).

VMI cadets live in spartan barracks where surveillance is constant and privacy nonexistent; they wear uniforms, eat together in the mess hall, and regularly participate in drills. *Id.*, at 1424, 1432. Entering students are incessantly exposed to the rat line, "an extreme form of the adversative model," comparable in intensity to Marine Corps boot camp. *Id.*, at 1422. Tormenting and punishing, the rat line bonds new cadets to their fellow sufferers and, when they have completed the 7-month experience, to their former tormentors. *Ibid.*

VMI's "adversative model" is further characterized by a hierarchical "class system" of privileges and responsibilities, a "dyke system" for assigning a senior class mentor to each entering class "rat," and a stringently enforced "honor code," which prescribes that a cadet " 'does not lie, cheat, steal nor tolerate those who do.' " *Id.*, at 1422–1423.

VMI attracts some applicants because of its reputation as an extraordinarily challenging military school, and "because its alumni are exceptionally close to the school." *Id.*, at 1421. "[W]omen have no opportunity anywhere to gain the benefits of [the system of education at VMI]." *Ibid.*

B

In 1990, prompted by a complaint filed with the Attorney General by a female high-school student seeking admission to VMI, the United States sued the Commonwealth of Virginia and VMI, alleging that VMI's exclusively male admission policy violated the Equal Protection Clause of the Fourteenth Amendment. *Id.*, at 1408.[3] Trial of the action consumed six days and involved an array of expert witnesses on each side. *Ibid.*

In the two years preceding the lawsuit, the District Court noted, VMI had received inquiries from 347 women, but had responded to none of them. *Id.*, at 1436. "[S]ome women, at least," the court said, "would want to attend the school if they had the opportunity." *Id.*, at 1414. The court further recognized that, with recruitment, VMI could "achieve at least 10% female enrollment"—"a sufficient 'critical mass' to provide the female cadets with a positive educational experience." *Id.*, at 1437–1438. And it was also established that "some women are capable of all of the individual activities required of VMI cadets." *Id.*, at 1412. In addition, experts agreed that if VMI admitted women, "the VMI ROTC experience would become a better training program from the perspective of the armed forces, because it would provide training in dealing with a mixed-gender army." *Id.*, at 1441.

---

3 The District Court allowed the VMI Foundation and the VMI Alumni Association to intervene as defendants. 766 F. Supp., at 1408.

The District Court ruled in favor of VMI, however, and rejected the equal protection challenge pressed by the United States. That court correctly recognized that *Mississippi Univ. for Women* v. *Hogan*, 458 U.S. 718 (1982), was the closest guide. 766 F. Supp., at 1410. There, this Court underscored that a party seeking to uphold government action based on sex must establish an "exceedingly persuasive justification" for the classification. *Mississippi Univ. for Women*, 458 U.S., at 724 (internal quotation marks omitted). To succeed, the defender of the challenged action must show "at least that the classification serves important governmental objectives and that the discriminatory means employed are substantially related to the achievement of those objectives." *Ibid.* (internal quotation marks omitted).

The District Court reasoned that education in "a single-gender environment, be it male or female," yields substantial benefits. 766 F. Supp., at 1415. VMI's school for men brought diversity to an otherwise coeducational Virginia system, and that diversity was "enhanced by VMI's unique method of instruction." *Ibid.* If single-gender education for males ranks as an important governmental objective, it becomes obvious, the District Court concluded, that the *only* means of achieving the objective "is to exclude women from the all-male institution—VMI." *Ibid.*

"Women are [indeed] denied a unique educational opportunity that is available only at VMI," the District Court acknowledged. *Id.*, at 1432. But "[VMI's] single-sex status would be lost, and some aspects of the [school's] distinctive method would be altered," if women were admitted, *id.*, at 1413: "Allowance for personal privacy would have to be made," *id.*, at 1412; "[p]hysical education requirements would have to be altered, at least for the women," *id.*, at 1413; the adversative environment could not survive unmodified, *id.*, at 1412–1413. Thus, "sufficient constitutional justification" had been shown, the District Court held, "for continuing [VMI's] single-sex policy." *Id.*, at 1413.

The Court of Appeals for the Fourth Circuit disagreed and

vacated the District Court's judgment. The appellate court held: "The Commonwealth of Virginia has not . . . advanced any state policy by which it can justify its determination, under an announced policy of diversity, to afford VMI's unique type of program to men and not to women." 976 F. 2d 890, 892 (1992).

The appeals court greeted with skepticism Virginia's assertion that it offers single-sex education at VMI as a facet of the Commonwealth's overarching and undisputed policy to advance "autonomy and diversity." The court underscored Virginia's non-discrimination commitment: " '[I]t is extremely important that [colleges and universities] deal with faculty, staff, and students *without regard to sex, race, or ethnic origin.*' " *Id.*, at 899 (quoting 1990 Report of the Virginia Commission on the University of the 21st Century). "That statement," the Court of Appeals said, "is the only explicit one that we have found in the record in which the Commonwealth has expressed itself with respect to gender distinctions." 976 F. 2d, at 899. Furthermore, the appeals court observed, in urging "diversity" to justify an all-male VMI, the Commonwealth had supplied "no explanation for the movement away from [single-sex education] in Virginia by public colleges and universities." *Ibid.* In short, the court concluded, "[a] policy of diversity which aims to provide an array of educational opportunities, including single-gender institutions, must do more than favor one gender." *Ibid.*

The parties agreed that "*some* women can meet the physical standards now imposed on men," *id.*, at 896, and the court was satisfied that "neither the goal of producing citizen soldiers nor VMI's implementing methodology is inherently unsuitable to women," *id.*, at 899. The Court of Appeals, however, accepted the District Court's finding that "at least these three aspects of VMI's program—physical training, the absence of privacy, and the adversarial approach—would be materially affected by coeducation." *Id.*, at 896–897. Remanding the case, the appeals court assigned to Virginia, in the first instance, responsibility for selecting a remedial course. The court suggested these options for the Commonwealth: Admit women to VMI; establish parallel institutions or programs; or abandon state support, leaving VMI free to pursue its policies as a private institution. *Id.*, at 900. In May 1993, this Court denied certiorari. See 508 U.S. 946; see also *ibid.* (opinion of Scalia, J., noting the interlocutory posture of the litigation).

C

In response to the Fourth Circuit's ruling, Virginia proposed a parallel program for women: Virginia Women's Institute for Leadership (VWIL). The 4-year, state-sponsored undergraduate program would be located at Mary Baldwin College, a private liberal arts school for women, and would be open, initially, to about 25 to 30 students. Although VWIL would share VMI's mission—to produce "citizen-soldiers"—the VWIL program would differ, as does Mary Baldwin College, from VMI in academic offerings, methods of education, and financial resources. See 852 F. Supp. 471, 476–477 (WD Va. 1994).

The average combined SAT score of entrants at Mary Baldwin is about 100 points lower than the score for VMI freshmen. See *id.*, at 501. Mary Baldwin's faculty holds "significantly fewer Ph. D.'s than the faculty at VMI," *id.*, at 502, and receives significantly lower salaries, see Tr. 158 (testimony of James Lott, Dean of Mary Baldwin College), reprinted in 2 App. in Nos. 94–1667 and 94–1717 (CA4) (hereinafter Tr.). While VMI offers degrees in liberal arts, the sciences, and engineering, Mary Baldwin, at the time of trial, offered only bachelor of arts degrees. See 852 F. Supp., at 503. A VWIL student seeking to earn an engineering degree could gain one, without public support, by attending Washington University in St. Louis, Missouri, for two years, paying the required private tuition. See *ibid.*

Experts in educating women at the college level composed the Task Force charged with designing the VWIL program; Task Force members were drawn from Mary Baldwin's own faculty and staff. *Id.*, at 476. Training its attention on methods of instruction appropriate for "most women," the Task Force determined that a military model would be "wholly inappropriate" for VWIL. *Ibid.*; see 44 F. 3d 1229,1233 (CA4 1995).

VWIL students would participate in ROTC programs and a newly established, "largely ceremonial" Virginia Corps of Cadets, *id.*, at 1234, but the VWIL House would not have a military format, 852 F. Supp., at 477, and VWIL would not require its students to eat meals together or to wear uniforms during the school day, *id.*, at 495. In lieu of VMI's adversative method, the VWIL Task Force favored "a cooperative method which reinforces self-esteem." *Id.*, at 476. In addition to the standard bachelor of arts program offered at Mary Baldwin, VWIL students would take courses in leadership, complete an off-campus leadership externship, participate in community service projects, and assist in arranging a speaker series. See 44 F. 3d, at 1234.

Virginia represented that it will provide equal financial support for in-state VWIL students and VMI cadets, 852 F. Supp., at 483, and the VMI Foundation agreed to supply a $5.4625 million endowment for the VWIL program, *id.*, at 499. Mary Baldwin's own endowment is about $19 million; VMI's is $131 million. *Id.*, at 503. Mary Baldwin will add $35 million to its endowment based on future commitments; VMI will add $220 million. *Ibid.* The VMI Alumni Association has developed a network of employers interested in hiring VMI graduates. The Association has agreed to open its network to VWIL graduates, *id.*, at 499, but those graduates will not have the advantage afforded by a VMI degree.

D

Virginia returned to the District Court seeking approval of its proposed remedial plan, and the court decided the plan met the requirements of the Equal Protection Clause. *Id.*, at 473. The District Court again acknowledged evidentiary support for these determinations: "[T]he VMI methodology could be used to educate women and, in fact, some women . . . may prefer the VMI methodology to the VWIL methodology." *Id.*, at 481. But the "controlling legal principles," the District Court decided, "do not require the Commonwealth to provide a mirror image VMI for women." *Ibid.* The court anticipated that the two schools would "achieve substantially similar outcomes." *Ibid.* It concluded: "If VMI marches to the beat of a drum, then Mary Baldwin marches to the melody of a fife and when the march is over, both will have arrived at the same destination." *Id.*, at 484.

A divided Court of Appeals affirmed the District Court's judgment. 44 F. 3d 1229 (CA4 1995). This time, the appellate court determined to give "greater scrutiny to the selection of means than to the [Commonwealth's] proffered objective." *Id.*, at 1236. The official objective or purpose, the court said, should be reviewed deferentially. *Ibid.* Respect for the "legislative will," the court reasoned, meant that the judiciary should take a "cautious approach," inquiring into the "legitima[cy]" of the governmental objective and refusing approval for any purpose revealed to be "pernicious." *Ibid.*

"[P]roviding the option of a single-gender college education may be considered a legitimate and important aspect of a public system of higher education," the appeals court observed, *id.*, at 1238; that objective, the court added, is "not pernicious," *id.*, at 1239. Moreover, the court continued, the adversative method vital to a VMI education "has never been tolerated in a sexually heterogeneous environment." *Ibid.* The method itself "was not designed to exclude women," the court noted, but women could not be accommodated in the VMI program, the court believed, for female participation in VMI's adversative training "would destroy . . . any sense of decency that still permeates the relationship between the sexes." *Ibid.*

Having determined, deferentially, the legitimacy of Virginia's purpose, the court considered the question of means. Exclusion of "men at Mary Baldwin College and women at VMI," the court said, was essential to Virginia's purpose, for without such exclusion, the Commonwealth could not "accomplish [its] objective of providing single-gender education." *Ibid.*

The court recognized that, as it analyzed the case, means

merged into end, and the merger risked "bypass[ing] any equal protection scrutiny." *Id.*, at 1237. The court therefore added another inquiry, a decisive test it called "substantive comparability." *Ibid.* The key question, the court said, was whether men at VMI and women at VWIL would obtain "substantively comparable benefits at their institution or through other means offered by the [S]tate." *Ibid.* Although the appeals court recognized that the VWIL degree "lacks the historical benefit and prestige" of a VMI degree, it nevertheless found the educational opportunities at the two schools "sufficiently comparable." *Id.*, at 1241.

Senior Circuit Judge Phillips dissented. The court, in his judgment, had not held Virginia to the burden of showing an "'exceedingly persuasive [justification]'" for the Commonwealth's action. *Id.*, at 1247 (quoting *Mississippi Univ. for Women*, 458 U.S., at 724). In Judge Phillips' view, the court had accepted "rationalizations compelled by the exigencies of this litigation," and had not confronted the Commonwealth's "actual overriding purpose." 44 F. 3d, at 1247. That purpose, Judge Phillips said, was clear from the historical record; it was "not to create a new type of educational opportunity for women, . . . nor to further diversify the Commonwealth's higher education system[,] . . . but [was]simply . . . to allow VMI to continue to exclude women in order to preserve its historic character and mission." *Ibid.*

Judge Phillips suggested that the Commonwealth would satisfy the Constitution's equal protection requirement if it "simultaneously opened single-gender undergraduate institutions having substantially comparable curricular and extracurricular programs, funding, physical plant, administration and support services, and faculty and library resources." *Id.*, at 1250. But he thought it evident that the proposed VWIL program, in comparison to VMI, fell "far short . . . from providing substantially equal tangible and intangible educational benefits to men and women." *Ibid.*

The Fourth Circuit denied rehearing en banc. 52 F. 3d 90 (1995). Circuit Judge Motz, joined by Circuit Judges Hall,

Murnaghan, and Michael, filed a dissenting opinion.[4] Judge Motz agreed with Judge Phillips that Virginia had not shown an "'exceedingly persuasive justification'" for the disparate opportunities the Commonwealth supported. *Id.*, at 92 (quoting *Mississippi Univ. for Women*, 458 U.S., at 724). She asked: "[H]ow can a degree from a yet to be implemented supplemental program at Mary Baldwin be held 'substantively comparable' to a degree from a venerable Virginia military institution that was established more than 150 years ago?" 52 F. 3d, at 93. "Women need not be guaranteed equal 'results,'" Judge Motz said, "but the Equal Protection Clause does require equal opportunity . . . [and] that opportunity is being denied here." *Ibid.*

III

The cross-petitions in this suit present two ultimate issues. First, does Virginia's exclusion of women from the educational opportunities provided by VMI—extraordinary opportunities for military training and civilian leadership development—deny to women "capable of all of the individual activities required of VMI cadets," 766 F. Supp., at 1412, the equal protection of the laws guaranteed by the Fourteenth Amendment? Second, if VMI's "unique" situation, *id.*, at 1413—as Virginia's sole single-sex public institution of higher education—offends the Constitution's equal protection principle, what is the remedial requirement?

IV

We note, once again, the core instruction of this Court's path-marking decisions in *J. E. B.* v. *Alabama ex rel. T. B.*, 511 U.S. 127, 136–137, and n. 6 (1994), and *Mississippi Univ. for Women*, 458 U.S., at 724 (internal quotation marks omitted): Parties who seek to defend gender-based government action must demonstrate an "exceedingly persuasive justification" for that action.

Today's skeptical scrutiny of official action denying rights or

---

4 Six judges voted to rehear the case en banc, four voted against rehearing, and three were recused. The Fourth Circuit's local Rule permits rehearing en banc only on the vote of a majority of the Circuit's judges in regular active service (currently 13) without regard to recusals. See 52 F. 3d, at 91, and n. 1.

opportunities based on sex responds to volumes of history. As a plurality of this Court acknowledged a generation ago, "our Nation has had a long and unfortunate history of sex discrimination." *Frontiero* v. *Richardson*, 411 U.S. 677, 684 (1973). Through a century plus three decades and more of that history, women did not count among voters composing "We the People";[5] not until 1920 did women gain a constitutional right to the franchise. *Id.*, at 685. And for a half century thereafter, it remained the prevailing doctrine that government, both federal and state, could withhold from women opportunities accorded men so long as any "basis in reason" could be conceived for the discrimination. See, *e.g.*, *Goesaert* v. *Cleary*, 335 U.S. 464, 467 (1948) (rejecting challenge of female tavern owner and her daughter to Michigan law denying bartender licenses to females—except for wives and daughters of male tavern owners; Court would not "give ear" to the contention that "an unchivalrous desire of male bartenders to . . . monopolize the calling" prompted the legislation).

In 1971, for the first time in our Nation's history, this Court ruled in favor of a woman who complained that her State had denied her the equal protection of its laws. *Reed* v. *Reed*, 404 U.S. 71, 73 (holding unconstitutional Idaho Code prescription that, among " 'several persons claiming and equally entitled to administer [a decedent's estate], males must be preferred to females' "). Since *Reed*, the Court has repeatedly recognized that neither federal nor state government acts compatibly with the equal protection principle when a law or official policy denies to women, simply because they are women, full citizenship stature—equal opportunity to aspire, achieve, participate in and contribute to society based on their individual talents and capacities. See, *e.g.*, *Kirchberg* v. *Feenstra*, 450 U.S. 455, 462–463

---

5 As Thomas Jefferson stated the view prevailing when the Constitution was new:

"Were our State a pure democracy . . . there would yet be excluded from their deliberations . . . [w]omen, who, to prevent depravation of morals and ambiguity of issue, could not mix promiscuously in the public meetings of men." Letter from Thomas Jefferson to Samuel Kercheval (Sept. 5, 1816), in 10 Writings of Thomas Jefferson 45–46, n. 1 (P. Ford ed. 1899).

(1981) (affirming invalidity of Louisiana law that made husband "head and master" of property jointly owned with his wife, giving him unilateral right to dispose of such property without his wife's consent); *Stanton* v. *Stanton*, 421 U.S. 7 (1975) (invalidating Utah requirement that parents support boys until age 21, girls only until age 18).

Without equating gender classifications, for all purposes, to classifications based on race or national origin,[6] the Court, in post-*Reed* decisions, has carefully inspected official action that closes a door or denies opportunity to women (or to men). See *J. E. B.*, 511 U.S., at 152 (KENNEDY, J., concurring in judgment) (case law evolving since 1971 "reveal[s] a strong presumption that gender classifications are invalid"). To summarize the Court's current directions for cases of official classification based on gender: Focusing on the differential treatment or denial of opportunity for which relief is sought, the reviewing court must determine whether the proffered justification is "exceedingly persuasive." The burden of justification is demanding and it rests entirely on the State. See *Mississippi Univ. for Women*, 458 U.S., at 724. The State must show "at least that the [challenged] classification serves 'important governmental objectives and that the discriminatory means employed' are 'substantially related to the achievement of those objectives.'" *Ibid.* (quoting *Wengler* v. *Druggists Mut. Ins. Co.*, 446 U.S. 142, 150 (1980)). The justification must be genuine, not hypothesized or invented *post hoc* in response to litigation. And it must not rely on overbroad generalizations about the different talents, capacities, or preferences of males and females. See *Weinberger* v. *Wiesenfeld*, 420 U.S. 636, 643, 648 (1975); *Califano* v. *Goldfarb*, 430 U.S. 199, 223–224 (1977) (STEVENS, J., concurring in judgment).

The heightened review standard our precedent establishes does not make sex a proscribed classification. Supposed "inherent

---

6 The Court has thus far reserved most stringent judicial scrutiny for classifications based on race or national origin, but last Term observed that strict scrutiny of such classifications is not inevitably "fatal in fact." *Adarand Constructors, Inc.* v. *Peña*, 515 U.S. 200, 237 (1995) (internal quotation marks omitted).

differences" are no longer accepted as a ground for race or national origin classifications. See *Loving* v. *Virginia*, 388 U.S. 1 (1967). Physical differences between men and women, however, are enduring: "[T]he two sexes are not fungible; a community made up exclusively of one [sex] is different from a community composed of both." *Ballard* v. *United States*, 329 U.S. 187, 193 (1946).

"Inherent differences" between men and women, we have come to appreciate, remain cause for celebration, but not for denigration of the members of either sex or for artificial constraints on an individual's opportunity. Sex classifications may be used to compensate women "for particular economic disabilities [they have] suffered," *Califano* v. *Webster*, 430 U.S. 313, 320 (1977) *(per curiam)*, to "promot[e] equal employment opportunity," see *California Fed. Sav. & Loan Assn.* v. *Guerra*, 479 U.S. 272, 289 (1987), to advance full development of the talent and capacities of our Nation's people.[7] But such classifications may not be used, as they once were, see *Goesaert*, 335 U.S., at 467, to create or perpetuate the legal, social, and economic inferiority of women.

Measuring the record in this case against the review standard just described, we conclude that Virginia has shown no "exceedingly persuasive justification" for excluding all women from the citizen-soldier training afforded by VMI. We therefore affirm the Fourth Circuit's initial judgment, which held that Virginia had violated the Fourteenth Amendment's Equal Protection Clause.

---

7 Several *amici* have urged that diversity in educational opportunities is an altogether appropriate governmental pursuit and that single-sex schools can contribute importantly to such diversity. Indeed, it is the mission of some single-sex schools "to dissipate, rather than perpetuate, traditional gender classifications." See Brief for Twenty-six Private Women's Colleges as *Amici Curiae* 5. We do not question the Commonwealth's prerogative evenhandedly to support diverse educational opportunities. We address specifically and only an educational opportunity recognized by the District Court and the Court of Appeals as "unique," see 766 F. Supp., at 1413, 1432; 976 F. 2d, at 892, an opportunity available only at Virginia's premier military institute, the Commonwealth's sole single-sex public university or college. Cf. *Mississippi Univ. for Women* v. *Hogan*, 458 U.S. 718, 720, n. 1 (1982) ("Mississippi maintains no other single-sex public university or college. Thus, we are not faced with the question of whether States can provide 'separate but equal' undergraduate institutions for males and females.").

Because the remedy proffered by Virginia—the Mary Baldwin VWIL program—does not cure the constitutional violation, *i.e.*, it does not provide equal opportunity, we reverse the Fourth Circuit's final judgment in this case.

V

The Fourth Circuit initially held that Virginia had advanced no state policy by which it could justify, under equal protection principles, its determination "to afford VMI's unique type of program to men and not to women." 976 F. 2d, at 892. Virginia challenges that "liability" ruling and asserts two justifications in defense of VMI's exclusion of women. First, the Commonwealth contends, "single-sex education provides important educational benefits," Brief for Cross-Petitioners 20, and the option of single-sex education contributes to "diversity in educational approaches," *id.*, at 25. Second, the Commonwealth argues, "the unique VMI method of character development and leadership training," the school's adversative approach, would have to be modified were VMI to admit women. *Id.*, at 33–36 (internal quotation marks omitted). We consider these two justifications in turn.

A

Single-sex education affords pedagogical benefits to at least some students, Virginia emphasizes, and that reality is uncontested in this litigation.[8] Similarly, it is not disputed that diversity among public educational institutions can serve the public good. But Virginia has not shown that VMI was established, or has been maintained, with a view to diversifying, by its categorical exclusion of women, educational opportunities within the

---

8 On this point, the dissent sees fire where there is no flame. See *post*, at 596–598, 598–600. "Both men and women can benefit from a single-sex education," the District Court recognized, although "the beneficial effects" of such education, the court added, apparently "are stronger among women than among men." 766 F. Supp., at 1414. The United States does not challenge that recognition. Cf. C. Jencks & D. Riesman, The Academic Revolution 297–298 (1968):

"The pluralistic argument for preserving all-male colleges is uncomfortably similar to the pluralistic argument for preserving all-white colleges . . . . The all-male college would be relatively easy to defend if it emerged from a world in which women were established as fully equal to men. But it does not. It is therefore likely to be a witting or unwitting device for preserving tacit assumptions of male superiority—assumptions for which women must eventually pay."

Commonwealth. In cases of this genre, our precedent instructs that "benign" justifications proffered in defense of categorical exclusions will not be accepted automatically; a tenable justification must describe actual state purposes, not rationalizations for actions in fact differently grounded. See Wiesenfeld, 420 U.S., at 648, and n. 16 ("mere recitation of a benign [or] compensatory purpose" does not block "inquiry into the actual purposes" of government-maintained gender-based classifications); *Goldfarb*, 430 U.S., at 212–213 (rejecting government-proffered purposes after "inquiry into the actual purposes" (internal quotation marks omitted)).

Mississippi Univ. for Women is immediately in point. There the State asserted, in justification of its exclusion of men from a nursing school, that it was engaging in "educational affirmative action" by "compensat[ing] for discrimination against women." 458 U.S., at 727. Undertaking a "searching analysis," *id.*, at 728, the Court found no close resemblance between "the alleged objective" and "the actual purpose underlying the discriminatory classification," *id.*, at 730. Pursuing a similar inquiry here, we reach the same conclusion.

Neither recent nor distant history bears out Virginia's alleged pursuit of diversity through single-sex educational options. In 1839, when the Commonwealth established VMI, a range of educational opportunities for men and women was scarcely contemplated. Higher education at the time was considered dangerous for women;[9] reflecting widely held views about women's

---

9 Dr. Edward H. Clarke of Harvard Medical School, whose influential book, Sex in Education, went through 17 editions, was perhaps the most well-known speaker from the medical community opposing higher education for women. He maintained that the physiological effects of hard study and academic competition with boys would interfere with the development of girls' reproductive organs. See E. Clarke, Sex in Education 38–39, 62–63 (1873); *id.*, at 127 ("identical education of the two sexes is a crime before God and humanity, that physiology protests against, and that experience weeps over"); see also H. Maudsley, Sex in Mind and in Education 17 (1874) ("It is not that girls have not ambition, nor that they fail generally to run the intellectual race [in coeducational settings], but it is asserted that they do it at a cost to their strength and health which entails life-long suffering, and even incapacitates them for the adequate performance of the natural functions of their sex."); C. Meigs, Females and Their Diseases 350 (1848) (after five or six weeks of "mental and educational discipline," a healthy woman would "lose . . . the habit of menstruation" and suffer numerous ills as a result of depriving her body for the sake of her mind).

proper place, the Nation's first universities and colleges—for example, Harvard in Massachusetts, William and Mary in Virginia—admitted only men. See E. Farello, A History of the Education of Women in the United States 163 (1970). VMI was not at all novel in this respect: In admitting no women, VMI followed the lead of the Commonwealth's flagship school, the University of Virginia, founded in 1819.

"[N]o struggle for the admission of women to a state university," a historian has recounted, "was longer drawn out, or developed more bitterness, than that at the University of Virginia." 2 T. Woody, A History of Women's Education in the United States 254 (1929) (History of Women's Education). In 1879, the State Senate resolved to look into the possibility of higher education for women, recognizing that Virginia " 'has never, at any period of her history,' " provided for the higher education of her daughters, though she " 'has liberally provided for the higher education of her sons.' " *Ibid.* (quoting 10 Educ. J. Va. 212 (1879)). Despite this recognition, no new opportunities were instantly open to women.[10]

Virginia eventually provided for several women's seminaries and colleges. Farmville Female Seminary became a public institution in 1884. See *supra*, at 521, n. 2. Two women's schools, Mary Washington College and James Madison University, were founded in 1908; another, Radford University, was founded in 1910. 766 F. Supp., at 1418–1419. By the mid-1970's, all four schools had become coeducational. *Ibid.*

Debate concerning women's admission as undergraduates at the main university continued well past the century's midpoint. Familiar arguments were rehearsed. If women were admitted, it was feared, they "would encroach on the rights of men; there would be new problems of government, perhaps scandals; the old honor system would have to be changed; standards would be

---

10 Virginia's Superintendent of Public Instruction dismissed the coeducational idea as " 'repugnant to the prejudices of the people' " and proposed a female college similar in quality to Girton, Smith, or Vassar. 2 History of Women's Education 254 (quoting Dept. of Interior, 1 Report of Commissioner of Education, H. R. Doc. No. 5, 58th Cong., 2d Sess., 438 (1904)).

lowered to those of other coeducational schools; and the glorious reputation of the university, as a school for men, would be trailed in the dust." 2 History of Women's Education 255.

Ultimately, in 1970, "the most prestigious institution of higher education in Virginia," the University of Virginia, introduced coeducation and, in 1972, began to admit women on an equal basis with men. See *Kirstein* v. *Rector and Visitors of Univ. of Virginia*, 309 F. Supp. 184, 186 (ED Va. 1970). A three-judge Federal District Court confirmed: "Virginia may not now deny to women, on the basis of sex, educational opportunities at the Charlottesville campus that are not afforded in other institutions operated by the [S]tate." *Id.*, at 187.

Virginia describes the current absence of public single-sex higher education for women as "an historical anomaly." Brief for Cross-Petitioners 30. But the historical record indicates action more deliberate than anomalous: First, protection of women against higher education; next, schools for women far from equal in resources and stature to schools for men; finally, conversion of the separate schools to coeducation. The state legislature, prior to the advent of this controversy, had repealed "[a]ll Virginia statutes requiring individual institutions to admit only men or women." 766 F. Supp., at 1419. And in 1990, an official commission, "legislatively established to chart the future goals of higher education in Virginia," reaffirmed the policy " 'of affording broad access' while maintaining 'autonomy and diversity.' " 976 F. 2d, at 898–899 (quoting Report of the Virginia Commission on the University of the 21st Century). Significantly, the commission reported:

> " 'Because colleges and universities provide
> opportunities for students to develop values and learn
> from role models, it is extremely important that they
> deal with faculty, staff, and students without regard
> to sex, race, or ethnic origin.' " *Id.*, at 899 (emphasis
> supplied by Court of Appeals deleted).

This statement, the Court of Appeals observed, "is the only explicit one that we have found in the record in which the Commonwealth has expressed itself with respect to gender distinctions." *Ibid.*

Our 1982 decision in *Mississippi Univ. for Women* prompted VMI to reexamine its male-only admission policy. See 766 F. Supp., at 1427–1428. Virginia relies on that reexamination as a legitimate basis for maintaining VMI's single-sex character. See Reply Brief for Cross-Petitioners 6. A Mission Study Committee, appointed by the VMI Board of Visitors, studied the problem from October 1983 until May 1986, and in that month counseled against "change of VMI status as a single-sex college." See 766 F. Supp., at 1429 (internal quotation marks omitted). Whatever internal purpose the Mission Study Committee served—and however well meaning the framers of the report—we can hardly extract from that effort any commonwealth policy evenhandedly to advance diverse educational options. As the District Court observed, the Committee's analysis "primarily focuse[d] on anticipated difficulties in attracting females to VMI," and the report, overall, supplied "very little indication of how th[e] conclusion was reached." *Ibid.*

In sum, we find no persuasive evidence in this record that VMI's male-only admission policy "is in furtherance of a state policy of 'diversity.'" See 976 F. 2d, at 899. No such policy, the Fourth Circuit observed, can be discerned from the movement of all other public colleges and universities in Virginia away from single-sex education. See *ibid.* That court also questioned "how one institution with autonomy, but with no authority over any other state institution, can give effect to a state policy of diversity among institutions." *Ibid.* A purpose genuinely to advance an array of educational options, as the Court of Appeals recognized, is not served by VMI's historic and constant plan—a plan to "affor[d] a unique educational benefit only to males." *Ibid.* However "liberally" this plan serves the Commonwealth's sons, it makes no provision whatever for her daughters. That is not *equal* protection.

B

Virginia next argues that VMI's adversative method of training provides educational benefits that cannot be made available, unmodified, to women. Alterations to accommodate women would necessarily be "radical," so "drastic," Virginia asserts, as to transform, indeed "destroy," VMI's program. See Brief for Cross-Petitioners 34–36. Neither sex would be favored by the transformation, Virginia maintains: Men would be deprived of the unique opportunity currently available to them; women would not gain that opportunity because their participation would "eliminat[e] the very aspects of [the] program that distinguish [VMI] from . . . other institutions of higher education in Virginia." *Id.*, at 34.

The District Court forecast from expert witness testimony, and the Court of Appeals accepted, that coeducation would materially affect "at least these three aspects of VMI's program— physical training, the absence of privacy, and the adversative approach." 976 F. 2d, at 896–897. And it is uncontested that women's admission would require accommodations, primarily in arranging housing assignments and physical training programs for female cadets. See Brief for Cross-Respondent 11, 29–30. It is also undisputed, however, that "the VMI methodology could be used to educate women." 852 F. Supp., at 481. The District Court even allowed that some women may prefer it to the methodology a women's college might pursue. See *ibid.* "[S]ome women, at least, would want to attend [VMI] if they had the opportunity," the District Court recognized, 766 F. Supp., at 1414, and "some women," the expert testimony established, "are capable of all of the individual activities required of VMI cadets," *id.*, at 1412. The parties, furthermore, agree that "some women can meet the physical standards [VMI] now impose[s] on men." 976 F. 2d, at 896. In sum, as the Court of Appeals stated, "neither the goal of producing citizen soldiers," VMI's *raison d'être*, "nor VMI's implementing methodology is inherently unsuitable to women." *Id.*, at 899.

In support of its initial judgment for Virginia, a judgment rejecting all equal protection objections presented by the United States, the District Court made "findings" on "gender-based developmental differences." 766 F. Supp., at 1434–1435. These "findings" restate the opinions of Virginia's expert witnesses, opinions about typically male or typically female "tendencies." *Id.*, at 1434. For example, "[m]ales tend to need an atmosphere of adversativeness," while "[f]emales tend to thrive in a cooperative atmosphere." *Ibid.* "I'm not saying that some women don't do well under [the] adversative model," VMI's expert on educational institutions testified, "undoubtedly there are some [women] who do"; but educational experiences must be designed "around the rule," this expert maintained, and not "around the exception." *Ibid.* (internal quotation marks omitted).

The United States does not challenge any expert witness estimation on average capacities or preferences of men and women. Instead, the United States emphasizes that time and again since this Court's turning point decision in *Reed* v. *Reed*, 404 U.S. 71 (1971), we have cautioned reviewing courts to take a "hard look" at generalizations or "tendencies" of the kind pressed by Virginia, and relied upon by the District Court. See O'Connor, Portia's Progress, 66 N. Y. U. L. Rev. 1546, 1551 (1991). State actors controlling gates to opportunity, we have instructed, may not exclude qualified individuals based on "fixed notions concerning the roles and abilities of males and females." *Mississippi Univ. for Women*, 458 U.S., at 725; see *J. E. B.*, 511 U.S., at 139, n. 11 (equal protection principles, as applied to gender classifications, mean state actors may not rely on "overbroad" generalizations to make "judgments about people that are likely to . . . perpetuate historical patterns of discrimination").

It may be assumed, for purposes of this decision, that most women would not choose VMI's adversative method. As Fourth Circuit Judge Motz observed, however, in her dissent from the Court of Appeals' denial of rehearing en banc, it is also probable that "many men would not want to be educated in such an environment." 52 F. 3d, at 93. (On that point, even our dissenting colleague might agree.) Education, to be sure, is not a "one size fits all" business. The issue, however, is not whether "women—or men—should be forced to attend VMI"; rather, the question is whether the Commonwealth can constitutionally deny to women who have the will and capacity, the training and attendant opportunities that VMI uniquely affords. *Ibid.*

The notion that admission of women would downgrade VMI's stature, destroy the adversative system and, with it, even the school,[11] is a judgment hardly proved,[12] a prediction hardly different from other "self-fulfilling prophec[ies]," see *Mississippi Univ. for Women*, 458 U.S., at 730, once routinely used to deny rights or opportunities. When women first sought admission to the bar and access to legal education, concerns of the same order were expressed. For example, in 1876, the Court of Common Pleas of Hennepin County, Minnesota, explained why women were thought ineligible for the practice of law. Women train and educate the young, the court said, which

---

11 See *post*, at 566, 598–599, 603. Forecasts of the same kind were made regarding admission of women to the federal military academies. See, *e.g.,* Hearings on H. R. 9832 et al. before Subcommittee No. 2 of the House Committee on Armed Services, 93d Cong., 2d Sess., 137 (1975) (statement of Lt. Gen. A. P. Clark, Superintendent of U.S. Air Force Academy) ("It is my considered judgment that the introduction of female cadets will inevitably erode this vital atmosphere."); *id.,* at 165 (statement of Hon. H. H. Callaway, Secretary of the Army) ("Admitting women to West Point would irrevocably change the Academy. . . . The Spartan atmosphere—which is so important to producing the final product—would surely be diluted, and would in all probability disappear.").

12 See 766 F. Supp., at 1413 (describing testimony of expert witness David Riesman: "[I]f VMI were to admit women, it would eventually find it necessary to drop the adversative system altogether, and adopt a system that provides more nurturing and support for the students."). Such judgments have attended, and impeded, women's progress toward full citizenship stature throughout our Nation's history. Speaking in 1879 in support of higher education for females, for example, Virginia State Senator C. T. Smith of Nelson recounted that legislation proposed to protect the property rights of women had encountered resistance. 10 Educ. J. Va. 213 (1879). A Senator opposing the measures objected that "there [was] no formal call for the [legislation]," and "depicted in burning eloquence the terrible consequences such laws would produce." *Ibid.* The legislation passed, and a year or so later, its sponsor, C. T. Smith, reported that "not one of [the forecast "terrible consequences"] has or ever will happen, even unto the sounding of Gabriel's trumpet." *Ibid.* See also *supra,* at 537–538.

"forbids that they shall bestow that time (early
and late) and labor, so essential in attaining to the
eminence to which the true lawyer should ever aspire.
It cannot therefore be said that the opposition of
courts to the admission of females to practice . . . is
to any extent the outgrowth of . . . 'old fogyism[.]'
. . . [I]t arises rather from a comprehension of the
magnitude of the responsibilities connected with the
successful practice of law, and a desire to *grade up* the
profession." In re Application of Martha Angle Dorsett
to Be Admitted to Practice as Attorney and Counselor
at Law (Minn. C. P. Hennepin Cty., 1876), in The
Syllabi, Oct. 21, 1876, pp. 5, 6 (emphasis added).

A like fear, according to a 1925 report, accounted for Columbia
Law School's resistance to women's admission, although

"[t]he faculty . . . never maintained that women could
not master legal learning. . . . No, its argument has
been . . . more practical. If women were admitted to
the Columbia Law School, [the faculty] said, then the
choicer, more manly and red-blooded graduates of
our great universities would go to the Harvard Law
School!" The Nation, Feb. 18, 1925, p. 173.

Medical faculties similarly resisted men and women as
partners in the study of medicine. See R. Morantz-Sanchez,
Sympathy and Science: Women Physicians in American Medicine 51–54, 250 (1985); see also M. Walsh, "Doctors Wanted:
No Women Need Apply" 121–122 (1977) (quoting E. Clarke,
Medical Education of Women, 4 Boston Med. & Surg. J. 345,
346 (1869) (" 'God forbid that I should ever see men and
women aiding each other to display with the scalpel the secrets
of the reproductive system. . . . ' ")); cf. *supra*, at 536–537, n. 9.
More recently, women seeking careers in policing encountered

resistance based on fears that their presence would "undermine male solidarity," see F. Heidensohn, Women in Control? 201 (1992); deprive male partners of adequate assistance, see *id.*, at 184–185; and lead to sexual misconduct, see C. Milton et al., Women in Policing 32–33 (1974). Field studies did not confirm these fears. See Heidensohn, *supra*, at 92–93; P. Bloch & D. Anderson, Policewomen on Patrol: Final Report (1974).

Women's successful entry into the federal military academies,[13] and their participation in the Nation's military forces,[14] indicate that Virginia's fears for the future of VMI may not be solidly grounded.[15] The Commonwealth's justification for excluding all women from "citizen-soldier" training for which some are qualified, in any event, cannot rank as "exceedingly persuasive," as we have explained and applied that standard.

Virginia and VMI trained their argument on "means" rather than "end," and thus misperceived our precedent. Single-sex education at VMI serves an "important governmental objective," they maintained, and exclusion of women is not only "substantially related," it is essential to that objective. By this notably circular argument, the "straightforward" test *Mississippi Univ. for Women* described, see 458 U.S., at 724–725, was bent and bowed.

The Commonwealth's misunderstanding and, in turn, the

---

13 Women cadets have graduated at the top of their class at every federal military academy. See Brief for Lieutenant Colonel Rhonda Cornum et al. as *Amici Curiae* 11, n. 25; cf. Defense Advisory Committee on Women in the Services, Report on the Integration and Performance of Women at West Point 64 (1992).

14 Brief for Lieutenant Colonel Rhonda Cornum, *supra*, at 5–9 (reporting the vital contributions and courageous performance of women in the military); see Mintz, President Nominates 1st Woman to Rank of Three-Star General, Washington Post, Mar. 27, 1996, p. A19, col. 1 (announcing President's nomination of Marine Corps Major General Carol Mutter to rank of Lieutenant General; Mutter will head corps manpower and planning); Tousignant, A New Era for the Old Guard, Washington Post, Mar. 23, 1996, p. C1, col. 2 (reporting admission of Sergeant Heather Johnsen to elite Infantry unit that keeps round-the-clock vigil at Tomb of the Unknowns in Arlington National Cemetery).

15 Inclusion of women in settings where, traditionally, they were not wanted inevitably entails a period of adjustment. As one West Point cadet squad leader recounted: "[T]he classes of '78 and '79 see the women as women, but the classes of '80 and '81 see them as classmates." U.S. Military Academy, A. Vitters, Report of Admission of Women (Project Athena II) 84 (1978) (internal quotation marks omitted).

District Court's, is apparent from VMI's mission: to produce "citizen-soldiers," individuals

> " 'imbued with love of learning, confident in the
> functions and attitudes of leadership, possessing a
> high sense of public service, advocates of the American
> democracy and free enterprise system, and ready . . . to
> defend their country in time of national peril.' " 766 F.
> Supp., at 1425 (quoting Mission Study Committee of
> the VMI Board of Visitors, Report, May 16, 1986).

Surely that goal is great enough to accommodate women, who today count as citizens in our American democracy equal in stature to men. Just as surely, the Commonwealth's great goal is not substantially advanced by women's categorical exclusion, in total disregard of their individual merit, from the Commonwealth's premier "citizen-soldier" corps.[16] Virginia, in sum, "has fallen far short of establishing the 'exceedingly persuasive justification,' " *Mississippi Univ. for Women*, 458 U.S., at 731, that must be the solid base for any gender-defined classification.

VI

In the second phase of the litigation, Virginia presented its remedial plan—maintain VMI as a male-only college and create VWIL as a separate program for women. The plan met District Court approval. The Fourth Circuit, in turn, deferentially reviewed the Commonwealth's proposal and decided that the two single-sex programs directly served Virginia's reasserted purposes: single-gender education, and "achieving the results of an adversative method in a military environment." See 44 F. 3d,

---

16 VMI has successfully managed another notable change. The school admitted its first African-American cadets in 1968. See The VMI Story 347–349 (students no longer sing "Dixie," salute the Confederate flag or the tomb of General Robert E. Lee at ceremonies and sports events). As the District Court noted, VMI established a program on "retention of black cadets" designed to offer academic and social-cultural support to "minority members of a dominantly white and tradition-oriented student body." 766 F. Supp., at 1436–1437. The school maintains a "special recruitment program for blacks" which, the District Court found, "has had little, if any, effect on VMI's method of accomplishing its mission." *Id.*, at 1437.

at 1236, 1239. Inspecting the VMI and VWIL educational programs to determine whether they "afford[ed] to both genders benefits comparable in substance, [if] not in form and detail," *id.*, at 1240, the Court of Appeals concluded that Virginia had arranged for men and women opportunities "sufficiently comparable" to survive equal protection evaluation, *id.*, at 1240–1241. The United States challenges this "remedial" ruling as pervasively misguided.

A

A remedial decree, this Court has said, must closely fit the constitutional violation; it must be shaped to place persons unconstitutionally denied an opportunity or advantage in "the position they would have occupied in the absence of [discrimination]." See *Milliken* v. *Bradley*, 433 U.S. 267, 280 (1977) (internal quotation marks omitted). The constitutional violation in this suit is the categorical exclusion of women from an extraordinary educational opportunity afforded men. A proper remedy for an unconstitutional exclusion, we have explained, aims to "eliminate [so far as possible] the discriminatory effects of the past" and to "bar like discrimination in the future." *Louisiana* v. *United States*, 380 U.S. 145, 154 (1965).

Virginia chose not to eliminate, but to leave untouched, VMI's exclusionary policy. For women only, however, Virginia proposed a separate program, different in kind from VMI and unequal in tangible and intangible facilities.[17] Having violated the Constitution's equal protection requirement, Virginia was obliged to show that its remedial proposal "directly address[ed]

---

17 As earlier observed, see *supra*, at 529, Judge Phillips, in dissent, measured Virginia's plan against a paradigm arrangement, one that "could survive equal protection scrutiny": single-sex schools with "substantially comparable curricular and extra-curricular programs, funding, physical plant, administration and support services, . . . faculty[,] and library resources." 44 F. 3d 1229, 1250 (CA4 1995). Cf. *Bray* v. *Lee*, 337 F. Supp. 934 (Mass. 1972) (holding inconsistent with the Equal Protection Clause admission of males to Boston's Boys Latin School with a test score of 120 or higher (up to a top score of 200) while requiring a score, on the same test, of at least 133 for admission of females to Girls Latin School, but not ordering coeducation). Measuring VMI/VWIL against the paradigm, Judge Phillips said, "reveals how far short the [Virginia] plan falls from providing substantially equal tangible and intangible educational benefits to men and women." 44 F. 3d, at 1250.

and relate[d] to" the violation, see *Milliken*, 433 U.S., at 282, *i.e.*, the equal protection denied to women ready, willing, and able to benefit from educational opportunities of the kind VMI offers. Virginia described VWIL as a "parallel program," and asserted that VWIL shares VMI's mission of producing "citizen-soldiers" and VMI's goals of providing "education, military training, mental and physical discipline, character . . . and leadership development." Brief for Respondents 24 (internal quotation marks omitted). If the VWIL program could not "eliminate the discriminatory effects of the past," could it at least "bar like discrimination in the future"? See *Louisiana*, 380 U.S., at 154. A comparison of the programs said to be "parallel" informs our answer. In exposing the character of, and differences in, the VMI and VWIL programs, we recapitulate facts earlier presented. See *supra*, at 520–523, 526–527.

VWIL affords women no opportunity to experience the rigorous military training for which VMI is famed. See 766 F. Supp., at 1413–1414 ("No other school in Virginia or in the United States, public or private, offers the same kind of rigorous military training as is available at VMI."); *id.*, at 1421 (VMI "is known to be the most challenging military school in the United States"). Instead, the VWIL program "deemphasize[s]" military education, 44 F. 3d, at 1234, and uses a "cooperative method" of education "which reinforces self-esteem," 852 F. Supp., at 476.

VWIL students participate in ROTC and a "largely ceremonial" Virginia Corps of Cadets, see 44 F. 3d, at 1234, but Virginia deliberately did not make VWIL a military institute. The VWIL House is not a military-style residence and VWIL students need not live together throughout the 4-year program, eat meals together, or wear uniforms during the schoolday. See 852 F. Supp., at 477, 495. VWIL students thus do not experience the "barracks" life "crucial to the VMI experience," the spartan living arrangements designed to foster an "egalitarian ethic." See 766 F. Supp., at 1423–1424. "[T]he most important aspects of the VMI educational experience occur in the barracks," the District Court found, *id.*, at 1423, yet Virginia deemed that core experience nonessential, indeed inappropriate, for training its female citizen-soldiers.

VWIL students receive their "leadership training " in seminars, externships, and speaker series, see 852 F. Supp., at 477, episodes and encounters lacking the "[p]hysical rigor, mental stress, . . . minute regulation of behavior, and indoctrination in desirable values" made hallmarks of VMI's citizen-soldier training, see 766 F. Supp., at 1421.[18] Kept away from the pressures, hazards, and psychological bonding characteristic of VMI's adversative training, see *id.*, at 1422, VWIL students will not know the "feeling of tremendous accomplishment" commonly experienced by VMI's successful cadets, *id.*, at 1426.

Virginia maintains that these methodological differences are "justified pedagogically," based on "important differences between men and women in learning and developmental needs," "psychological and sociological differences" Virginia describes as "real" and "not stereotypes." Brief for Respondents 28 (internal quotation marks omitted). The Task Force charged with developing the leadership program for women, drawn from the staff and faculty at Mary Baldwin College, "determined that a military model and, especially VMI's adversative method, would be wholly inappropriate for educating and training *most women*." 852 F. Supp., at 476 (emphasis added). See also 44 F. 3d, at 1233–1234 (noting Task Force conclusion that, while "some women would be suited to and interested in [a VMI-style experience]," VMI's adversative method "would not be effective for *women as a group*" (emphasis added)). The Commonwealth embraced the Task Force view, as did expert witnesses who testified for Virginia. See 852 F. Supp., at 480–481.

As earlier stated, see *supra*, at 541–542, generalizations about "the way women are," estimates of what is appropriate for *most*

---

18 Both programs include an honor system. Students at VMI are expelled forthwith for honor code violations, see 766 F. Supp., at 1423; the system for VWIL students, see 852 F. Supp., at 496–497, is less severe, see Tr. 414–415 (testimony of Mary Baldwin College President Cynthia Tyson).

women, no longer justify denying opportunity to women whose talent and capacity place them outside the average description. Notably, Virginia never asserted that VMI's method of education suits *most men*. It is also revealing that Virginia accounted for its failure to make the VWIL experience "the entirely militaristic experience of VMI" on the ground that VWIL "is planned for women who do not necessarily expect to pursue military careers." 852 F. Supp., at 478. By that reasoning, VMI's "entirely militaristic" program would be inappropriate for men in general or as a group, for "[o]nly about 15% of VMI cadets enter career military service." See 766 F. Supp., at 1432.

In contrast to the generalizations about women on which Virginia rests, we note again these dispositive realities: VMI's "implementing methodology" is not "inherently unsuitable to women," 976 F. 2d, at 899; "some women . . . do well under [the] adversarial model," 766 F. Supp., at 1434 (internal quotation marks omitted); "some women, at least, would want to attend [VMI] if they had the opportunity," *id.*, at 1414; "some women are capable of all of the individual activities required of VMI cadets," *id.*, at 1412, and "can meet the physical standards [VMI] now impose[s] on men," 976 F. 2d, at 896. It is on behalf of these women that the United States has instituted this suit, and it is for them that a remedy must be crafted,[19] a remedy that will end their exclusion from a state-supplied educational opportunity for which they are fit, a decree that will "bar like discrimination in the future." *Louisiana*, 380 U.S., at 154.

---

19 Admitting women to VMI would undoubtedly require alterations necessary to afford members of each sex privacy from the other sex in living arrangements, and to adjust aspects of the physical training programs. See Brief for Petitioner 27–29; cf. note following 10 U. S. C. § 4342 (academic and other standards for women admitted to the Military, Naval, and Air Force Academies "shall be the same as those required for male individuals, except for those minimum essential adjustments in such standards required because of physiological differences between male and female individuals"). Experience shows such adjustments are manageable. See U.S. Military Academy, A. Vitters, N. Kinzer, & J. Adams, Report of Admission of Women (Project Athena I–IV) (1977–1980) (4-year longitudinal study of the admission of women to West Point); Defense Advisory Committee on Women in the Services, Report on the Integration and Performance of Women at West Point 17–18 (1992).

B

In myriad respects other than military training, VWIL does not qualify as VMI's equal. VWIL's student body, faculty, course offerings, and facilities hardly match VMI's. Nor can the VWIL graduate anticipate the benefits associated with VMI's 157-year history, the school's prestige, and its influential alumni network.

Mary Baldwin College, whose degree VWIL students will gain, enrolls first-year women with an average combined SAT score about 100 points lower than the average score for VMI freshmen. 852 F. Supp., at 501. The Mary Baldwin faculty holds "significantly fewer Ph.D.'s," *id.*, at 502, and receives substantially lower salaries, see Tr. 158 (testimony of James Lott, Dean of Mary Baldwin College), than the faculty at VMI.

Mary Baldwin does not offer a VWIL student the range of curricular choices available to a VMI cadet. VMI awards baccalaureate degrees in liberal arts, biology, chemistry, civil engineering, electrical and computer engineering, and mechanical engineering. See 852 F. Supp., at 503; Virginia Military Institute: More than an Education 11 (Govt. exh. 75, lodged with Clerk of this Court). VWIL students attend a school that "does not have a math and science focus," 852 F. Supp., at 503; they cannot take at Mary Baldwin any courses in engineering or the advanced math and physics courses VMI offers, see *id.*, at 477.

For physical training, Mary Baldwin has "two multi-purpose fields" and "[o]ne gymnasium." *Id.*, at 503. VMI has "an NCAA competition level indoor track and field facility; a number of multi-purpose fields; baseball, soccer and lacrosse fields; an obstacle course; large boxing, wrestling and martial arts facilities; an 11-laps-to-the-mile indoor running course; an indoor pool; indoor and outdoor rifle ranges; and a football stadium that also contains a practice field and outdoor track." *Ibid.*

Although Virginia has represented that it will provide equal financial support for in-state VWIL students and VMI cadets, *id.*, at 483, and the VMI Foundation has agreed to endow VWIL with $5.4625 million, *id.*, at 499, the difference between the two schools' financial reserves is pronounced. Mary Baldwin's endowment, currently about $19 million, will gain an additional $35 million based on future commitments; VMI's current endowment, $131 million—the largest public college per-student endowment in the Nation—will gain $220 million. *Id.*, at 503.

The VWIL student does not graduate with the advantage of a VMI degree. Her diploma does not unite her with the legions of VMI "graduates [who] have distinguished themselves" in military and civilian life. See 976 F. 2d, at 892–893. "[VMI] alumni are exceptionally close to the school," and that closeness accounts, in part, for VMI's success in attracting applicants. See 766 F. Supp., at 1421. A VWIL graduate cannot assume that the "network of business owners, corporations, VMI graduates and non-graduate employers . . . interested in hiring VMI graduates," 852 F. Supp., at 499, will be equally responsive to her search for employment, see 44 F. 3d, at 1250 (Phillips, J., dissenting) ("the powerful political and economic ties of the VMI alumni network cannot be expected to open" for graduates of the fledgling VWIL program).

Virginia, in sum, while maintaining VMI for men only, has failed to provide any "comparable single-gender women's institution." *Id.*, at 1241. Instead, the Commonwealth has created a VWIL program fairly appraised as a "pale shadow" of VMI in terms of the range of curricular choices and faculty stature, funding, prestige, alumni support and influence. See *id.*, at 1250 (Phillips, J., dissenting).

Virginia's VWIL solution is reminiscent of the remedy Texas proposed 50 years ago, in response to a state trial court's 1946 ruling that, given the equal protection guarantee, African-Americans could not be denied a legal education at a state facility. See *Sweatt* v. *Painter*, 339 U.S. 629 (1950). Reluctant to admit African-Americans to its flagship University of Texas Law School, the State set up a separate school for Heman Sweatt and other black law students. *Id.*, at 632. As originally opened, the new school had no independent faculty or library, and it lacked accreditation. *Id.*, at 633. Nevertheless, the state trial and appellate courts were satisfied that the new school offered Sweatt opportunities for the study of law "substantially equivalent to those offered by the State to white students at the University of Texas." *Id.*, at 632 (internal quotation marks omitted).

Before this Court considered the case, the new school had gained "a faculty of five full-time professors; a student body of 23; a library of some 16,500 volumes serviced by a full-time staff; a practice court and legal aid association; and one alumnus who ha[d] become a member of the Texas Bar." *Id.*, at 633. This Court contrasted resources at the new school with those at the school from which Sweatt had been excluded. The University of Texas Law School had a full-time faculty of 16, a student body of 850, a library containing over 65,000 volumes, scholarship funds, a law review, and moot court facilities. *Id.*, at 632–633. More important than the tangible features, the Court emphasized, are "those qualities which are incapable of objective measurement but which make for greatness" in a school, including "reputation of the faculty, experience of the administration, position and influence of the alumni, standing in the community, traditions and prestige." *Id.*, at 634. Facing the marked differences reported in the *Sweatt* opinion, the Court unanimously ruled that Texas had not shown "substantial equality in the [separate] educational opportunities" the State offered. *Id.*, at 633. Accordingly, the Court held, the Equal Protection Clause required Texas to admit African-Americans to the University of Texas Law School. *Id.*, at 636. In line with *Sweatt*, we rule here that Virginia has not shown substantial equality in the separate educational opportunities the Commonwealth supports at VWIL and VMI.

C

When Virginia tendered its VWIL plan, the Fourth Circuit did not inquire whether the proposed remedy, approved by the District Court, placed women denied the VMI advantage in "the position they would have occupied in the absence of [discrimination]." *Milliken*, 433 U.S., at 280 (internal quotation marks omitted). Instead, the Court of Appeals considered whether the Commonwealth could provide, with fidelity to the equal protection principle, separate and unequal educational programs for men and women.

The Fourth Circuit acknowledged that "the VWIL degree from Mary Baldwin College lacks the historical benefit and prestige of a degree from VMI." 44 F. 3d, at 1241. The Court of Appeals further observed that VMI is "an ongoing and successful institution with a long history," and there remains no "comparable single-gender women's institution." *Ibid.* Nevertheless, the appeals court declared the substantially different and significantly unequal VWIL program satisfactory. The court reached that result by revising the applicable standard of review. The Fourth Circuit displaced the standard developed in our precedent, see *supra*, at 532–534, and substituted a standard of its own invention.

We have earlier described the deferential review in which the Court of Appeals engaged, see *supra*, at 528–529, a brand of review inconsistent with the more exacting standard our precedent requires, see *supra*, at 532–534. Quoting in part from *Mississippi Univ. for Women*, the Court of Appeals candidly described its own analysis as one capable of checking a legislative purpose ranked as "pernicious," but generally according "deference to [the] legislative will." 44 F. 3d, at 1235, 1236. Recognizing that it had extracted from our decisions a test yielding "little or no scrutiny of the effect of a classification directed at [single-gender education]," the Court of Appeals devised another test, a "substantive comparability" inquiry, *id.*, at 1237, and proceeded to find that new test satisfied, *id.*, at 1241.

The Fourth Circuit plainly erred in exposing Virginia's VWIL plan to a deferential analysis, for "all gender-based classifications today" warrant "heightened scrutiny." See *J. E. B.*, 511 U.S., at 136. Valuable as VWIL may prove for students who seek the program offered, Virginia's remedy affords no cure at all for the opportunities and advantages withheld from women who want a

VMI education and can make the grade. See *supra*, at 549–554.[20] In sum, Virginia's remedy does not match the constitutional violation; the Commonwealth has shown no "exceedingly persuasive justification" for withholding from women qualified for the experience premier training of the kind VMI affords.

VII

A generation ago, "the authorities controlling Virginia higher education," despite long established tradition, agreed "to innovate and favorably entertain[ed] the [then] relatively new idea that there must be no discrimination by sex in offering educational opportunity." *Kirstein*, 309 F. Supp., at 186. Commencing in 1970, Virginia opened to women "educational opportunities at the Charlottesville campus that [were] not afforded in other [state-operated] institutions." *Id.*, at 187; see *supra*, at 538. A federal court approved the Commonwealth's innovation, emphasizing that the University of Virginia "offer[ed] courses of instruction . . . not available elsewhere." 309 F. Supp., at 187. The court further noted: "[T]here exists at Charlottesville a 'prestige' factor [not paralleled in] other Virginia educational institutions." *Ibid.*

---

20 Virginia's prime concern, it appears, is that "plac[ing] men and women into the adversarial relationship inherent in the VMI program . . . would destroy, at least for that period of the adversarial training, any sense of decency that still permeates the relationship between the sexes." 44 F. 3d, at 1239; see *supra*, at 540–546. It is an ancient and familiar fear. Compare *In re Lavinia Goodell*, 39 Wis. 232, 246 (1875) (denying female applicant's motion for admission to the bar of its court, Wisconsin Supreme Court explained: "Discussions are habitually necessary in courts of justice, which are unfit for female ears. The habitual presence of women at these would tend to relax the public sense of decency and propriety."), with Levine, Closing Comments, 6 Law & Inequality 41 (1988) (presentation at Eighth Circuit Judicial Conference, Colorado Springs, Colo., July 17, 1987) (footnotes omitted):

"Plato questioned whether women should be afforded equal opportunity to become guardians, those elite Rulers of Platonic society. Ironically, in that most undemocratic system of government, the Republic, women's native ability to serve as guardians was not seriously questioned. The concern was over the wrestling and exercise class in which all candidates for guardianship had to participate, for rigorous physical and mental training were prerequisites to attain the exalted status of guardian. And in accord with Greek custom, those exercise classes were conducted in the nude. Plato concluded that their virtue would clothe the women's nakedness and that Platonic society would not thereby be deprived of the talent of qualified citizens for reasons of mere gender."

For Plato's full text on the equality of women, see 2 The Dialogues of Plato 302–312 (B. Jowett transl., 4th ed. 1953). Virginia, not bound to ancient Greek custom in its "rigorous physical and mental training" programs, could more readily make the accommodations necessary to draw on "the talent of [all] qualified citizens." Cf. *supra*, at 550–551, n. 19.

VMI, too, offers an educational opportunity no other Virginia institution provides, and the school's "prestige"—associated with its success in developing "citizen-soldiers"—is unequaled. Virginia has closed this facility to its daughters and, instead, has devised for them a "parallel program," with a faculty less impressively credentialed and less well paid, more limited course offerings, fewer opportunities for military training and for scientific specialization. Cf. *Sweatt*, 339 U.S., at 633. VMI, beyond question, "possesses to a far greater degree" than the VWIL program "those qualities which are incapable of objective measurement but which make for greatness in a . . . school," including "position and influence of the alumni, standing in the community, traditions and prestige." *Id.*, at 634. Women seeking and fit for a VMI-quality education cannot be offered anything less, under the Commonwealth's obligation to afford them genuinely equal protection.

A prime part of the history of our Constitution, historian Richard Morris recounted, is the story of the extension of constitutional rights and protections to people once ignored or excluded.[21] VMI's story continued as our comprehension of "We the People" expanded. See *supra*, at 532, n. 6.

There is no reason to believe that the admission of women capable of all the activities required of VMI cadets would destroy the Institute rather than enhance its capacity to serve the "more perfect Union."

* * *

For the reasons stated, the initial judgment of the Court of Appeals, 976 F. 2d 890 (CA4 1992), is affirmed, the final

---

21 R. Morris, The Forging of the Union, 1781–1789, p. 193 (1987); see *id.*, at 191, setting out letter to a friend from Massachusetts patriot (later second President) John Adams, on the subject of qualifications for voting in his home State:

"[I]t is dangerous to open so fruitful a source of controversy and altercation as would be opened by attempting to alter the qualifications of voters; there will be no end of it. New claims will arise; women will demand a vote; lads from twelve to twenty-one will think their rights not enough attended to; and every man who has not a farthing, will demand an equal voice with any other, in all acts of state. It tends to confound and destroy all distinctions, and prostrate all ranks to one common level." Letter from John Adams to James Sullivan (May 26, 1776), in 9 Works of John Adams 378 (C. Adams ed. 1854).

judgment of the Court of Appeals, 44 F. 3d 1229 (CA4 1995), is reversed, and the case is remanded for further proceedings consistent with this opinion.

It is so ordered.

Friends of the Earth, Inc. v. Laidlaw Environmental Services (TOC), Inc., 528 U.S. 167 (2000)

Majority Opinion

L *aidlaw Environmental Services, Inc., operated a wastewater treatment plant along South Carolina's North Tyger River, into which they repeatedly dumped mercury in excess of the amount allowed by their National Pollutant Discharge Elimination System (NPDES) permit. Local residents, banding together as the group Friends of the Earth (FOE), filed a citizen suit against Laidlaw and sought injunctive relief and civil penalties.*

By the time the case reached the Supreme Court, Laidlaw had ceased operations at the plant, which they argued made the case moot; they also believed FOE lacked standing to bring a lawsuit because its members could not prove they were personally and actually harmed by the activity. In a 7-2 majority authored by Justice Ginsburg, the Court held that "a defendant's voluntary cessation of allegedly unlawful conduct ordinarily does not suffice to moot a case," and also found that FOE did have standing to bring suit.

FRIENDS OF THE EARTH, INC., ET AL.
v.
LAIDLAW ENVIRONMENTAL SERVICES (TOC), INC.
CERTIORARI TO THE UNITED STATES
COURT OF APPEALS FOR
THE FOURTH CIRCUIT
[January 12, 2000]

Justice Ginsburg delivered the opinion of the Court.

This case presents an important question concerning the operation of the citizen-suit provisions of the Clean Water Act. Congress authorized the federal district courts to entertain Clean Water Act suits initiated by "a person or persons having an interest which is or may be adversely affected." 33 U. S. C. §§ 1365(a), (g). To impel future compliance with the Act, a district court may prescribe injunctive relief in such a suit; additionally or alternatively, the court may impose civil penalties payable to the United States Treasury. § 1365(a). In the Clean Water Act citizen suit now before us, the District Court determined that injunctive relief was inappropriate because the defendant, after the institution of the litigation, achieved substantial compliance with the terms of its discharge permit. 956 F. Supp. 588, 611 (SC 1997). The court did, however, assess a civil penalty of $405,800. *Id.*, at 610. The "total deterrent effect" of the penalty would be adequate to forestall future violations, the court reasoned, taking into account that the defendant "will be required to reimburse plaintiffs for a significant amount of legal fees and has, itself, incurred significant legal expenses." *Id.*, at 610–611.

The Court of Appeals vacated the District Court's order. 149 F. 3d 303 (CA4 1998). The case became moot, the appellate court declared, once the defendant fully complied with the terms of its permit and the plaintiff failed to appeal the denial of equitable relief. "[C]ivil penalties payable to the government," the Court of Appeals stated, "would not redress any injury Plaintiffs have suffered." *Id.*, at 307. Nor were attorneys' fees in order, the Court of Appeals noted, because absent relief on the merits, plaintiffs could not qualify as prevailing parties. *Id.*, at 307, n. 5.

We reverse the judgment of the Court of Appeals. The appellate court erred in concluding that a citizen suitor's claim for civil penalties must be dismissed as moot when the defendant, albeit after commencement of the litigation, has come into compliance. In directing dismissal of the suit on grounds of mootness, the Court of Appeals incorrectly conflated our case law on initial standing to bring suit, see, *e.g.*, *Steel Co.* v. *Citizens for Better Environment*, 523 U.S. 83 (1998), with our case law on postcommencement mootness, see, *e.g.*, *City of Mesquite* v. *Aladdin's Castle, Inc.*, 455 U.S. 283 (1982). A defendant's voluntary cessation of allegedly unlawful conduct ordinarily does not suffice to moot a case. The Court of Appeals also misperceived the remedial potential of civil penalties. Such penalties may serve, as an alternative to an injunction, to deter future violations and thereby redress the injuries that prompted a citizen suitor to commence litigation.

I

A

In 1972, Congress enacted the Clean Water Act (Act), also known as the Federal Water Pollution Control Act, 86 Stat. 816, as amended, 33 U. S. C. § 1251 *et seq.* Section 402 of the Act, 33 U. S. C. § 1342, provides for the issuance, by the Administrator of the Environmental Protection Agency (EPA) or by authorized States, of National Pollutant Discharge Elimination System (NPDES) permits. NPDES permits impose limitations on the discharge of pollutants, and establish related monitoring and reporting requirements, in order to improve the cleanliness and safety of the Nation's waters. Noncompliance with a permit constitutes a violation of the Act. § 1342(h).

Under § 505(a) of the Act, a suit to enforce any limitation in an NPDES permit may be brought by any "citizen," defined as "a person or persons having an interest which is or may be adversely affected." 33 U. S. C. §§ 1365(a), (g). Sixty days before initiating a citizen suit, however, the would-be plaintiff must give notice of the alleged violation to the EPA, the State in which the alleged violation occurred, and the alleged violator. § 1365(b)(1) (A). "[T]he purpose of notice to the alleged violator is to give it an opportunity to bring itself into complete compliance with the Act and thus . . . render unnecessary a citizen suit." *Gwaltney of Smithfield, Ltd.* v. *Chesapeake Bay Foundation, Inc.*, 484 U.S. 49, 60 (1987). Accordingly, we have held that citizens lack statutory standing under § 505(a) to sue for violations that have ceased by the time the complaint is filed. *Id.*, at 56–63. The Act also bars a citizen from suing if the EPA or the State has already commenced, and is "diligently prosecuting," an enforcement action. 33 U. S. C. § 1365(b)(1)(B).

The Act authorizes district courts in citizen-suit proceedings to enter injunctions and to assess civil penalties, which are payable to the United States Treasury. § 1365(a). In determining the amount of any civil penalty, the district court must take into account "the seriousness of the violation or violations, the economic benefit (if any) resulting from the violation, any history of such violations, any good-faith efforts to comply with the applicable requirements, the economic impact of the penalty on the violator, and such other matters as justice may require." § 1319(d). In addition, the court "may award costs of litigation (including reasonable attorney and expert witness fees) to any prevailing or substantially prevailing party, whenever the court determines such award is appropriate." § 1365(d).

B

In 1986, defendant-respondent Laidlaw Environmental Services (TOC), Inc., bought a hazardous waste incinerator facility in Roebuck, South Carolina, that included a waste-water treatment plant. (The company has since changed its name to Safety-Kleen (Roebuck), Inc., but for simplicity we will refer to it as "Laidlaw" throughout.) Shortly after Laidlaw acquired the facility, the South Carolina Department of Health and Environmental

Control (DHEC), acting under 33 U. S. C. § 1342(a)(1), granted Laidlaw an NPDES permit authorizing the company to discharge treated water into the North Tyger River. The permit, which became effective on January 1, 1987, placed limits on Laidlaw's discharge of several pollutants into the river, including—of particular relevance to this case—mercury, an extremely toxic pollutant. The permit also regulated the flow, temperature, toxicity, and pH of the effluent from the facility, and imposed monitoring and reporting obligations.

Once it received its permit, Laidlaw began to discharge various pollutants into the waterway; repeatedly, Laidlaw's discharges exceeded the limits set by the permit. In particular, despite experimenting with several technological fixes, Laidlaw consistently failed to meet the permit's stringent 1.3 ppb (parts per billion) daily average limit on mercury discharges. The District Court later found that Laidlaw had violated the mercury limits on 489 occasions between 1987 and 1995. 956 F. Supp., at 613–621.

On April 10, 1992, plaintiff-petitioners Friends of the Earth (FOE) and Citizens Local Environmental Action Network, Inc. (CLEAN) (referred to collectively in this opinion, together with later joined plaintiff-petitioner Sierra Club, as "FOE") took the preliminary step necessary to the institution of litigation. They sent a letter to Laidlaw notifying the company of their intention to file a citizen suit against it under § 505(a) of the Act after the expiration of the requisite 60-day notice period, *i.e.*, on or after June 10, 1992. Laidlaw's lawyer then contacted DHEC to ask whether DHEC would consider filing a lawsuit against Laidlaw. The District Court later found that Laidlaw's reason for requesting that DHEC file a lawsuit against it was to bar FOE's proposed citizen suit through the operation of 33 U. S. C. § 1365(b)(1)(B). 890 F. Supp. 470, 478 (SC 1995). DHEC agreed to file a lawsuit against Laidlaw; the company's lawyer then drafted the complaint for DHEC and paid the filing fee. On June 9, 1992, the last day before FOE's 60-day notice period expired, DHEC and Laidlaw reached a settlement requiring Laidlaw to pay $100,000 in civil penalties and to make "'every effort'" to comply with its permit obligations. *Id.*, at 479–481.

On June 12, 1992, FOE filed this citizen suit against Laidlaw under § 505(a) of the Act, alleging noncompliance with the NPDES permit and seeking declaratory and injunctive relief and an award of civil penalties. Laidlaw moved for summary judgment on the ground that FOE had failed to present evidence demonstrating injury in fact, and therefore lacked Article III standing to bring the lawsuit. Record, Doc. No. 43. In opposition to this motion, FOE submitted affidavits and deposition testimony from members of the plaintiff organizations. Record, Doc. No. 71 (Exhs. 41–51). The record before the District Court also included affidavits from the organizations' members submitted by FOE in support of an earlier motion for preliminary injunctive relief. Record, Doc. No. 21 (Exhs. 5–10). After examining this evidence, the District Court denied Laidlaw's summary judgment motion, finding—albeit "by the very slimmest of margins"—that FOE had standing to bring the suit. App. in No. 97–1246 (CA4), pp. 207–208 (Tr. of Hearing 39–40 (June 30, 1993)).

Laidlaw also moved to dismiss the action on the ground that the citizen suit was barred under 33 U. S. C. § 1365(b)(1)(B) by DHEC's prior action against the company. The United States, appearing as *amicus curiae*, joined FOE in opposing the motion. After an extensive analysis of the Laidlaw-DHEC settlement and the circumstances under which it was reached, the District Court held that DHEC's action against Laidlaw had not been "diligently prosecuted"; consequently, the court allowed FOE's citizen suit to proceed. 890 F. Supp., at 499.[1] The record indicates that after FOE initiated the suit, but before the District

---

1 The District Court noted that "Laidlaw drafted the state-court complaint and settlement agreement, filed the lawsuit against itself, and paid the filing fee." 890 F. Supp., at 489. Further, "the settlement agreement between DHEC and Laidlaw was entered into with unusual haste, without giving the Plaintiffs the opportunity to intervene." *Ibid.* The court found "most persuasive" the fact that "in imposing the civil penalty of $100,000 against Laidlaw, DHEC failed to recover, or even to calculate, the economic benefit that Laidlaw received by not complying with its permit." *Id.*, at 491.

Court rendered judgment, Laidlaw violated the mercury discharge limitation in its permit 13 times. 956 F. Supp., at 621. The District Court also found that Laidlaw had committed 13 monitoring and 10 reporting violations during this period. *Id.*, at 601. The last recorded mercury discharge violation occurred in January 1995, long after the complaint was filed but about two years before judgment was rendered. *Id.*, at 621.

On January 22, 1997, the District Court issued its judgment. 956 F. Supp. 588 (SC). It found that Laidlaw had gained a total economic benefit of $1,092,581 as a result of its extended period of noncompliance with the mercury discharge limit in its permit. *Id.*, at 603. The court concluded, however, that a civil penalty of $405,800 was adequate in light of the guiding factors listed in 33 U. S. C. § 1319(d). 956 F. Supp., at 610. In particular, the District Court stated that the lesser penalty was appropriate taking into account the judgment's "total deterrent effect." In reaching this determination, the court "considered that Laidlaw will be required to reimburse plaintiffs for a significant amount of legal fees." *Id.*, at 610–611. The court declined to grant FOE's request for injunctive relief, stating that an injunction was inappropriate because "Laidlaw has been in substantial compliance with all parameters in its NPDES permit since at least August 1992." *Id.*, at 611.

FOE appealed the District Court's civil penalty judgment, arguing that the penalty was inadequate, but did not appeal the denial of declaratory or injunctive relief. Laidlaw cross-appealed, arguing, among other things, that FOE lacked standing to bring the suit and that DHEC's action qualified as a diligent prosecution precluding FOE's litigation. The United States continued to participate as *amicus curiae* in support of FOE.

On July 16, 1998, the Court of Appeals for the Fourth Circuit issued its judgment. 149 F. 3d 303. The Court of Appeals assumed without deciding that FOE initially had standing to bring the action, *id.*, at 306, n. 3, but went on to hold that the case had become moot. The appellate court stated, first, that the elements of Article III standing—injury, causation, and redressability—must persist at every stage of review, or else the action becomes moot. *Id.*, at 306. Citing our decision in *Steel Co.*, the Court of Appeals reasoned that the case had become moot because "the only remedy currently available to [FOE]— civil penalties payable to the government—would not redress any injury [FOE has] suffered." 149 F. 3d, at 306–307. The court therefore vacated the District Court's order and remanded with instructions to dismiss the action. In a footnote, the Court of Appeals added that FOE's "failure to obtain relief on the merits of [its] claims precludes any recovery of attorneys' fees or other litigation costs because such an award is available only to a 'prevailing or substantially prevailing party.'" *Id.*, at 307, n. 5 (quoting 33 U. S. C. § 1365(d)).

According to Laidlaw, after the Court of Appeals issued its decision but before this Court granted certiorari, the entire incinerator facility in Roebuck was permanently closed, dismantled, and put up for sale, and all discharges from the facility permanently ceased. Respondent's Suggestion of Mootness 3.

We granted certiorari, 525 U.S. 1176 (1999), to resolve the inconsistency between the Fourth Circuit's decision in this case and the decisions of several other Courts of Appeals, which have held that a defendant's compliance with its permit after the commencement of litigation does not moot claims for civil penalties under the Act. See, *e.g., Atlantic States Legal Foundation, Inc.* v. *Stroh Die Casting Co.*, 116 F. 3d 814, 820 (CA7), cert. denied, 522 U.S. 981 (1997); *Natural Resources Defense Council, Inc.* v. *Texaco Rfg. And Mktg., Inc.*, 2 F. 3d 493, 503–504 (CA3 1993); *Atlantic States Legal Foundation, Inc.* v. *Pan American Tanning Corp.*, 993 F. 2d 1017, 1020–1021 (CA2 1993); *Atlantic States Legal Foundation, Inc.* v. *Tyson Foods, Inc.*, 897 F. 2d 1128, 1135–1136 (CA11 1990).

II

A

The Constitution's case-or-controversy limitation on federal judicial authority, Art. III, § 2, underpins both our standing and our mootness jurisprudence, but the two inquiries differ in respects critical to the proper resolution of this case, so we address them separately. Because the Court of Appeals was persuaded that the case had become moot and so held, it simply assumed without deciding that FOE had initial standing. See *Arizonans for Official English* v. *Arizona*, 520 U.S. 43, 66–67 (1997) (court may assume without deciding that standing exists in order to analyze mootness). But because we hold that the Court of Appeals erred in declaring the case moot, we have an obligation to assure ourselves that FOE had Article III standing at the outset of the litigation. We therefore address the question of standing before turning to mootness.

In *Lujan* v. *Defenders of Wildlife*, 504 U.S. 555, 560–561 (1992), we held that, to satisfy Article III's standing requirements, a plaintiff must show (1) it has suffered an "injury in fact" that is (a) concrete and particularized and (b) actual or imminent, not conjectural or hypothetical; (2) the injury is fairly traceable to the challenged action of the defendant; and (3) it is likely, as opposed to merely speculative, that the injury will be redressed by a favorable decision. An association has standing to bring suit on behalf of its members when its members would otherwise have standing to sue in their own right, the interests at stake are germane to the organization's purpose, and neither the claim asserted nor the relief requested requires the participation of individual members in the lawsuit. *Hunt* v. *Washington State Apple Advertising Comm'n*, 432 U.S. 333, 343 (1977).

Laidlaw contends first that FOE lacked standing from the outset even to seek injunctive relief, because the plaintiff organizations failed to show that any of their members had sustained or faced the threat of any "injury in fact" from Laidlaw's activities. In support of this contention Laidlaw points to the District Court's finding, made in the course of setting the penalty amount, that there had been "no demonstrated proof of harm to the environment" from Laidlaw's mercury discharge violations.

956 F. Supp., at 602; see also *ibid.* ("[T]he NPDES permit violations at issue in this citizen suit did not result in any health risk or environmental harm.").

The relevant showing for purposes of Article III standing, however, is not injury to the environment but injury to the plaintiff. To insist upon the former rather than the latter as part of the standing inquiry (as the dissent in essence does, *post*, at 199–200) is to raise the standing hurdle higher than the necessary showing for success on the merits in an action alleging noncompliance with an NPDES permit. Focusing properly on injury to the plaintiff, the District Court found that FOE had demonstrated sufficient injury to establish standing. App. in No. 97–1246 (CA4), at 207–208 (Tr. Of Hearing 39–40). For example, FOE member Kenneth Lee Curtis averred in affidavits that he lived a half-mile from Laidlaw's facility; that he occasionally drove over the North Tyger River, and that it looked and smelled polluted; and that he would like to fish, camp, swim, and picnic in and near the river between 3 and 15 miles downstream from the facility, as he did when he was a teenager, but would not do so because he was concerned that the water was polluted by Laidlaw's discharges. Record, Doc. No. 71 (Exhs. 41, 42). Curtis reaffirmed these statements in extensive deposition testimony. For example, he testified that he would like to fish in the river at a specific spot he used as a boy, but that he would not do so now because of his concerns about Laidlaw's discharges. *Ibid.* (Exh. 43, at 52–53; Exh. 44, at 33).

Other members presented evidence to similar effect. CLEAN member Angela Patterson attested that she lived two miles from the facility; that before Laidlaw operated the facility, she picnicked, walked, birdwatched, and waded in and along the North Tyger River because of the natural beauty of the area; that she no longer engaged in these activities in or near the river because she was concerned about harmful effects from discharged pollutants; and that she and her husband would like to purchase a home near the river but did not intend to do so, in part because of Laidlaw's discharges. Record, Doc. No. 21 (Exh. 10). CLEAN member Judy Pruitt averred that she lived one-quarter mile from Laidlaw's facility and would like to fish, hike, and picnic along the North Tyger River, but has refrained from those activities because of the discharges. *Ibid.* (Exh. 7). FOE member Linda Moore attested that she lived 20 miles from Roebuck, and would use the North Tyger River south of Roebuck and the land surrounding it for recreational purposes were she not concerned that the water contained harmful pollutants. Record, Doc. No. 71 (Exhs. 45, 46). In her deposition, Moore testified at length that she would hike, picnic, camp, swim, boat, and drive near or in the river were it not for her concerns about illegal discharges. *Ibid.* (Exh. 48, at 29, 36–37, 62–63, 72). CLEAN member Gail Lee attested that her home, which is near Laidlaw's facility, had a lower value than similar homes located farther from the facility, and that she believed the pollutant discharges accounted for some of the discrepancy. Record, Doc. No. 21 (Exh. 9). Sierra Club member Norman Sharp averred that he had canoed approximately 40 miles downstream of the Laidlaw facility and would like to canoe in the North Tyger River closer to Laidlaw's discharge point, but did not do so because he was concerned that the water contained harmful pollutants. *Ibid.* (Exh. 8).

These sworn statements, as the District Court determined, adequately documented injury in fact. We have held that environmental plaintiffs adequately allege injury in fact when they aver that they use the affected area and are persons "for whom the aesthetic and recreational values of the area will be lessened" by the challenged activity. *Sierra Club* v. *Morton*, 405 U.S. 727, 735 (1972). See also *Defenders of Wildlife*, 504 U.S., at 562–563 ("Of course, the desire to use or observe an animal species, even for purely esthetic purposes, is undeniably a cognizable interest for purposes of standing.").

Our decision in *Lujan* v. *National Wildlife Federation*, 497 U.S. 871 (1990), is not to the contrary. In that case an environmental organization assailed the Bureau of Land Management's "land withdrawal review program," a program covering millions of acres, alleging that the program illegally opened up public lands to mining activities. The defendants moved for summary judgment, challenging the plaintiff organization's standing to initiate the action under the Administrative Procedure Act, 5 U. S. C. § 702. We held that the plaintiff could not survive the summary judgment motion merely by offering "averments which state only that one of [the organization's] members uses unspecified portions of an immense tract of territory, on some portions of which mining activity has occurred or probably will occur by virtue of the governmental action." 497 U.S., at 889.

In contrast, the affidavits and testimony presented by FOE in this case assert that Laidlaw's discharges, and the affiant members' reasonable concerns about the effects of those discharges, directly affected those affiants' recreational, aesthetic, and economic interests. These submissions present dispositively more than the mere "general averments" and "conclusory allegations" found inadequate in *National Wildlife Federation. Id.*, at 888. Nor can the affiants' conditional statements—that they would use the nearby North Tyger River for recreation if Laidlaw were not discharging pollutants into it—be equated with the speculative "'some day' intentions" to visit endangered species halfway around the world that we held insufficient to show injury in fact in *Defenders of Wildlife.* 504 U.S., at 564.

Los Angeles v. *Lyons*, 461 U.S. 95 (1983), relied on by the dissent, *post*, at 199, does not weigh against standing in this case. In *Lyons*, we held that a plaintiff lacked standing to seek an injunction against the enforcement of a police chokehold policy because he could not credibly allege that he faced a realistic threat from the policy. 461 U.S., at 107, n. 7. In the footnote from *Lyons* cited by the dissent, we noted that "[t]he reasonableness of Lyons' fear is dependent upon the likelihood of a recurrence of the allegedly unlawful conduct," and that his "subjective apprehensions" that such a recurrence would even take place were not enough to support standing. *Id.*, at 108, n. 8. Here, in contrast, it is undisputed that Laidlaw's unlawful conduct—discharging pollutants in excess of permit limits—was occurring at the time the complaint was filed. Under *Lyons*, then, the only "subjective" issue here is "[t]he reasonableness of [the] fear" that led the affiants to respond to that concededly ongoing conduct by refraining from use of the North Tyger River and surrounding areas. Unlike the dissent, *post*, at 200, we see nothing "improbable" about the proposition that a company's continuous and pervasive illegal discharges of pollutants into a river would cause nearby residents to curtail their recreational use of that waterway and would subject them to other economic and aesthetic harms. The proposition is entirely reasonable, the District Court found it was true in this case, and that is enough for injury in fact.

Laidlaw argues next that even if FOE had standing to seek injunctive relief, it lacked standing to seek civil penalties. Here the asserted defect is not injury but redressability. Civil penalties offer no redress to private plaintiffs, Laidlaw argues, because they are paid to the Government, and therefore a citizen plaintiff can never have standing to seek them.

Laidlaw is right to insist that a plaintiff must demonstrate standing separately for each form of relief sought. See, *e.g.*, *Lyons*, 461 U.S., at 109 (notwithstanding the fact that plaintiff had standing to pursue damages, he lacked standing to pursue injunctive relief); see also *Lewis* v. *Casey*, 518 U.S. 343, 358, n. 6 (1996) ("[S]tanding is not dispensed in gross."). But it is wrong to maintain that citizen plaintiffs facing ongoing violations never have standing to seek civil penalties.

We have recognized on numerous occasions that "all civil penalties have some deterrent effect." *Hudson* v. *United States*, 522 U.S. 93, 102 (1997); see also, *e.g.*, *Department of Revenue of Mont.* v. *Kurth Ranch*, 511 U.S. 767, 778 (1994). More specifically, Congress has found that civil penalties in Clean Water Act cases do more than promote immediate compliance by limiting the defendant's economic incentive to delay its attainment of permit limits; they also deter future violations. This congressional determination warrants judicial attention and respect. "The legislative history of the Act reveals that Congress wanted the district court to consider the need for retribution and deterrence, in addition to restitution, when it imposed civil penalties. . . . [The district court may] seek to deter future violations by basing the penalty on its economic impact." *Tull* v. *United States*, 481 U.S. 412, 422–423 (1987).

It can scarcely be doubted that, for a plaintiff who is injured or faces the threat of future injury due to illegal conduct ongoing at the time of suit, a sanction that effectively abates that conduct and prevents its recurrence provides a form of redress. Civil penalties can fit that description. To the extent that they encourage defendants to discontinue current violations and deter them from committing future ones, they afford redress to citizen plaintiffs who are injured or threatened with injury as a consequence of ongoing unlawful conduct.

The dissent argues that it is the availability rather than the imposition of civil penalties that deters any particular polluter from continuing to pollute. *Post*, at 207–208. This argument misses the mark in two ways. First, it overlooks the interdependence of the availability and the imposition; a threat has no deterrent value unless it is credible that it will be carried out. Second, it is reasonable for Congress to conclude that an actual award of civil penalties does in fact bring with it a significant quantum of deterrence over and above what is achieved by the mere prospect of such penalties. A would-be polluter may or may not be dissuaded by the existence of a remedy on the books, but a defendant once hit in its pocketbook will surely think twice before polluting again.[2]

---

2 The dissent suggests that there was little deterrent work for civil penalties to do in this case because the lawsuit brought against Laidlaw by DHEC had already pushed the level of deterrence to "near the top of the graph." *Post*, at 208. This suggestion ignores the District Court's specific finding that the penalty agreed to by Laidlaw and DHEC was far too low to remove Laidlaw's economic benefit from noncompliance, and thus was inadequate to deter future violations. 890 F. Supp. 470, 491–494, 497–498 (SC 1995). And it begins to look especially farfetched when one recalls that Laidlaw itself prompted the DHEC lawsuit, paid the filing fee, and drafted the complaint. See *supra*, at 176–177, 178, n. 1.

We recognize that there may be a point at which the deterrent effect of a claim for civil penalties becomes so insubstantial or so remote that it cannot support citizen standing. The fact that this vanishing point is not easy to ascertain does not detract from the deterrent power of such penalties in the ordinary case. Justice Frankfurter's observations for the Court, made in a different context nearly 60 years ago, hold true here as well:

> "How to effectuate policy—the adaptation of means to legitimately sought ends—is one of the most intractable of legislative problems. Whether proscribed conduct is to be deterred by *qui tam* action or triple damages or injunction, or by criminal prosecution, or merely by defense to actions in contract, or by some, or all, of these remedies in combination, is a matter within the legislature's range of choice. Judgment on the deterrent effect of the various weapons in the armory of the law can lay little claim to scientific basis." *Tigner* v. *Texas*, 310 U.S. 141, 148 (1940).[3]

In this case we need not explore the outer limits of the principle that civil penalties provide sufficient deterrence to support redressability. Here, the civil penalties sought by FOE carried with them a deterrent effect that made it likely, as opposed to merely speculative, that the penalties would redress FOE's injuries by abating current violations and preventing future ones—as the District Court reasonably found when it assessed a penalty of $405,800. 956 F. Supp., at 610–611.

Laidlaw contends that the reasoning of our decision in *Steel Co.* directs the conclusion that citizen plaintiffs have no standing to seek civil penalties under the Act. We disagree. *Steel Co.* established that citizen suitors lack standing to seek civil penalties for violations that have abated by the time of suit. 523 U.S.,

---

3 In *Tigner* the Court rejected an equal protection challenge to a statutory provision exempting agricultural producers from the reach of the Texas antitrust laws.

at 106–107. We specifically noted in that case that there was no allegation in the complaint of any continuing or imminent violation, and that no basis for such an allegation appeared to exist. *Id.*, at 108; see also *Gwaltney*, 484 U.S., at 59 ("the harm sought to be addressed by the citizen suit lies in the present or the future, not in the past"). In short, *Steel Co.* held that private plaintiffs, unlike the Federal Government, may not sue to assess penalties for wholly past violations, but our decision in that case did not reach the issue of standing to seek penalties for violations that are ongoing at the time of the complaint and that could continue into the future if undeterred.[4]

B

Satisfied that FOE had standing under Article III to bring this action, we turn to the question of mootness.

The only conceivable basis for a finding of mootness in this case is Laidlaw's voluntary conduct—either its achievement by August 1992 of substantial compliance with its NPDES permit or its more recent shutdown of the Roebuck facility. It is well

---

4 In insisting that the redressability requirement is not met, the dissent relies heavily on *Linda R. S. v. Richard D.,* 410 U.S. 614 (1973). That reliance is sorely misplaced. In *Linda R. S.,* the mother of an out-of-wedlock child filed suit to force a district attorney to bring a criminal prosecution against the absentee father for failure to pay child support. *Id.,* at 616. In finding that the mother lacked standing to seek this extraordinary remedy, the Court drew attention to "the special status of criminal prosecutions in our system," *id.,* at 619, and carefully limited its holding to the "unique context of a challenge to [the nonenforcement of] a criminal statute," *id.,* at 617. Furthermore, as to redressability, the relief sought in *Linda R. S.*—a prosecution which, if successful, would automatically land the delinquent father in jail for a fixed term, *id.,* at 618, with predictably negative effects on his earning power—would scarcely remedy the plaintiff 's lack of child support payments. In this regard, the Court contrasted "the civil contempt model whereby the defendant 'keeps the keys to the jail in his own pocket' and may be released whenever he complies with his legal obligations." *Ibid.* The dissent's contention, *post,* at 204, that "precisely the same situation exists here" as in *Linda R. S.* is, to say the least, extravagant.

Putting aside its mistaken reliance on *Linda R. S.,* the dissent's broader charge that citizen suits for civil penalties under the Act carry "grave implications for democratic governance," *post,* at 202, seems to us overdrawn. Certainly the Federal Executive Branch does not share the dissent's view that such suits dissipate its authority to enforce the law. In fact, the Department of Justice has endorsed this citizen suit from the outset, submitting *amicus* briefs in support of FOE in the District Court, the Court of Appeals, and this Court. See *supra,* at 177, 179. As we have already noted, *supra,* at 175, the Federal Government retains the power to foreclose a citizen suit by undertaking its own action. 33 U. S. C. § 1365(b)(1)(B). And if the Executive Branch opposes a particular citizen suit, the statute allows the Administrator of the EPA to "intervene as a matter of right" and bring the Government's views to the attention of the court. § 1365(c)(2).

settled that "a defendant's voluntary cessation of a challenged practice does not deprive a federal court of its power to determine the legality of the practice." *City of Mesquite*, 455 U.S., at 289. "[I]f it did, the courts would be compelled to leave '[t]he defendant . . . free to return to his old ways.'" *Id.*, at 289, n. 10 (citing *United States* v. *W. T. Grant Co.*, 345 U.S. 629, 632 (1953)). In accordance with this principle, the standard we have announced for determining whether a case has been mooted by the defendant's voluntary conduct is stringent: "A case might become moot if subsequent events made it absolutely clear that the allegedly wrongful behavior could not reasonably be expected to recur." *United States* v. *Concentrated Phosphate Export Assn., Inc.*, 393 U.S. 199, 203 (1968). The "heavy burden of persua[ding]" the court that the challenged conduct cannot reasonably be expected to start up again lies with the party asserting mootness. *Ibid.*

The Court of Appeals justified its mootness disposition by reference to *Steel Co.*, which held that citizen plaintiffs lack standing to seek civil penalties for wholly past violations. In relying on *Steel Co.*, the Court of Appeals confused mootness with standing. The confusion is understandable, given this Court's repeated statements that the doctrine of mootness can be described as "the doctrine of standing set in a time frame: The requisite personal interest that must exist at the commencement of the litigation (standing) must continue throughout its existence (mootness)." *Arizonans for Official English*, 520 U.S., at 68, n. 22 (quoting *United States Parole Comm'n* v. *Geraghty*, 445 U.S. 388, 397 (1980), in turn quoting Monaghan, Constitutional Adjudication: The Who and When, 82 Yale L. J. 1363, 1384 (1973)) (internal quotation marks omitted).

Careful reflection on the long-recognized exceptions to mootness, however, reveals that the description of mootness as "standing set in a time frame" is not comprehensive. As just noted, a defendant claiming that its voluntary compliance moots a case bears the formidable burden of showing that it is absolutely clear the allegedly wrongful behavior could not reasonably be expected to recur. *Concentrated Phosphate Export Assn.*, 393 U.S., at 203. By contrast, in a lawsuit brought to force compliance, it is the plaintiff's burden to establish standing by demonstrating that, if unchecked by the litigation, the defendant's allegedly wrongful behavior will likely occur or continue, and that the "threatened injury [is] certainly impending." *Whitmore* v. *Arkansas*, 495 U.S. 149, 158 (1990) (citations and internal quotation marks omitted). Thus, in *Lyons*, as already noted, we held that a plaintiff lacked initial standing to seek an injunction against the enforcement of a police chokehold policy because he could not credibly allege that he faced a realistic threat arising from the policy. 461 U.S., at 105–110. Elsewhere in the opinion, however, we noted that a citywide moratorium on police chokeholds—an action that surely diminished the already slim likelihood that any particular individual would be choked by police—would not have mooted an otherwise valid claim for injunctive relief, because the moratorium by its terms was not permanent. *Id.*, at 101. The plain lesson of these cases is that there are circumstances in which the prospect that a defendant will engage in (or resume) harmful conduct may be too speculative to support standing, but not too speculative to overcome mootness.

Furthermore, if mootness were simply "standing set in a time frame," the exception to mootness that arises when the defendant's allegedly unlawful activity is "capable of repetition, yet evading review," could not exist. When, for example, a mentally disabled patient files a lawsuit challenging her confinement in a segregated institution, her postcomplaint transfer to a community-based program will not moot the action, *Olmstead* v. *L. C.*, 527 U.S. 581, 594, n. 6 (1999), despite the fact that she would have lacked initial standing had she filed the complaint after the transfer. Standing admits of no similar exception; if a plaintiff lacks standing at the time the action commences, the fact that the dispute is capable of repetition yet evading review will not entitle the complainant to a federal judicial forum. See *Steel Co.*, 523 U.S., at 109 ("'the mootness exception for disputes capable of repetition yet evading review . . . will not revive a dispute which became moot before the action commenced'") (quoting *Renne* v. *Geary*, 501 U.S. 312, 320 (1991)).

We acknowledged the distinction between mootness and standing most recently in *Steel Co.*:

> "The United States . . . argues that the injunctive relief does constitute remediation because 'there is a presumption of [future] injury when the defendant has voluntarily ceased its illegal activity in response to litigation,' even if that occurs before a complaint is filed. . . . This makes a sword out of a shield. The 'presumption' the Government refers to has been applied to refute the assertion of mootness by a defendant who, when sued in a complaint that alleges present or threatened injury, ceases the complained-of activity. . . . It is an immense and unacceptable stretch to call the presumption into service as a substitute for the allegation of present or threatened injury upon which initial standing must be based." 523 U.S., at 109.

Standing doctrine functions to ensure, among other things, that the scarce resources of the federal courts are devoted to those disputes in which the parties have a concrete stake. In contrast, by the time mootness is an issue, the case has been brought and litigated, often (as here) for years. To abandon the case at an advanced stage may prove more wasteful than frugal. This argument from sunk costs[5] does not license courts to retain jurisdiction over cases in which one or both of the parties plainly lack a continuing interest, as when the parties have settled or a plaintiff pursuing a nonsurviving claim has died. See, *e.g.*, *DeFunis* v.

---

5 Of course we mean sunk costs to the judicial system, not to the litigants. *Lewis* v. *Continental Bank Corp.*, 494 U.S. 472 (1990) (cited by the dissent, *post*, at 213), dealt with the latter, noting that courts should use caution to avoid carrying forward a moot case solely to vindicate a plaintiff's interest in recovering attorneys' fees.

Odegaard, 416 U.S. 312 (1974) (*per curiam*) (non-class-action challenge to constitutionality of law school admissions process mooted when plaintiff, admitted pursuant to preliminary injunction, neared graduation and defendant law school conceded that, as a matter of ordinary school policy, plaintiff would be allowed to finish his final term); *Arizonans*, 520 U.S., at 67 (non-class-action challenge to state constitutional amendment declaring English the official language of the State became moot when plaintiff, a state employee who sought to use her bilingual skills, left state employment). But the argument surely highlights an important difference between the two doctrines. See generally *Honig* v. *Doe*, 484 U.S. 305, 329–332 (1988) (Rehnquist, C. J., concurring).

In its brief, Laidlaw appears to argue that, regardless of the effect of Laidlaw's compliance, FOE doomed its own civil penalty claim to mootness by failing to appeal the District Court's denial of injunctive relief. Brief for Respondent 14–17. This argument misconceives the statutory scheme. Under § 1365(a), the district court has discretion to determine which form of relief is best suited, in the particular case, to abate current violations and deter future ones. "[A] federal judge sitting as chancellor is not mechanically obligated to grant an injunction for every violation of law." *Weinberger* v. *Romero-Barcelo*, 456 U.S. 305, 313 (1982). Denial of injunctive relief does not necessarily mean that the district court has concluded there is no prospect of future violations for civil penalties to deter. Indeed, it meant no such thing in this case. The District Court denied injunctive relief, but expressly based its award of civil penalties on the need for deterrence. See 956 F. Supp., at 610–611. As the dissent notes, *post*, at 205, federal courts should aim to ensure " 'the framing of relief no broader than required by the precise facts.' " *Schlesinger* v. *Reservists Comm. to Stop the War*, 418 U.S. 208, 222 (1974). In accordance with this aim, a district court in a Clean Water Act citizen suit properly may conclude that an injunction would be an excessively intrusive remedy, because it could entail continuing superintendence of the permit holder's activities by a federal court—a process burdensome to court and permit holder alike. See *City of Mesquite*, 455 U.S., at 289 (although the defendant's voluntary cessation of the challenged practice does not moot the case, "[s]uch abandonment is an important factor bearing on the question whether a court should exercise its power to enjoin the defendant from renewing the practice").

Laidlaw also asserts, in a supplemental suggestion of mootness, that the closure of its Roebuck facility, which took place after the Court of Appeals issued its decision, mooted the case. The facility closure, like Laidlaw's earlier achievement of substantial compliance with its permit requirements, might moot the case, but—we once more reiterate—only if one or the other of these events made it absolutely clear that Laidlaw's permit violations could not reasonably be expected to recur. *Concentrated Phosphate Export Assn.*, 393 U.S., at 203. The effect of both Laidlaw's compliance and the facility closure on the prospect of future violations is a disputed factual matter. FOE points out, for example—and Laidlaw does not appear to contest—that Laidlaw retains its NPDES permit. These issues have not been aired in the lower courts; they remain open for consideration on remand.[6]

C

FOE argues that it is entitled to attorneys' fees on the theory that a plaintiff can be a "prevailing party" for purposes of 33 U. S. C. § 1365(d) if it was the "catalyst" that triggered a favorable outcome. In the decision under review, the Court of Appeals noted that its Circuit precedent construed our decision in *Farrar* v. *Hobby*, 506 U.S. 103 (1992), to require rejection of that theory. 149 F. 3d, at 307, n. 5 (citing S–1 & S–2 v. State Bd. of Ed. of N. C., 21 F. 3d 49, 51(CA4 1994) (en banc)). Cf.

---

6 We note that it is far from clear that vacatur of the District Court's judgment would be the appropriate response to a finding of mootness on appeal brought about by the voluntary conduct of the party that lost in the District Court. See *U.S. Bancorp Mortgage Co.* v. *Bonner Mall Partnership*, 513 U.S. 18 (1994) (mootness attributable to a voluntary act of a nonprevailing party ordinarily does not justify vacatur of a judgment under review); see also *Walling* v. *James V. Reuter, Inc.*, 321 U.S. 671 (1944).

Foreman v. *Dallas County*, 193 F. 3d 314, 320 (CA5 1999) (stating, in dicta, that "[a]fter *Farrar* . . . the continuing validity of the catalyst theory is in serious doubt").

Farrar acknowledged that a civil rights plaintiff awarded nominal damages may be a "prevailing party" under 42 U. S. C. § 1988. 506 U.S., at 112. The case involved no catalytic effect. Recognizing that the issue was not presented for this Court's decision in *Farrar*, several Courts of Appeals have expressly concluded that *Farrar* did not repudiate the catalyst theory. See *Marbley* v. *Bane*, 57 F. 3d 224, 234 (CA2 1995); *Baumgartner* v. *Harrisburg Housing Authority*, 21 F. 3d 541, 546–550 (CA3 1994); *Zinn* v. *Shalala*, 35 F. 3d 273, 276 (CA7 1994); *Little Rock School Dist.* v. *Pulaski County Special Sch. Dist., #1*, 17 F. 3d 260, 263, n. 2 (CA8 1994); *Kilgour* v. *Pasadena*, 53 F. 3d 1007, 1010 (CA9 1995); *Beard* v. *Teska*, 31 F. 3d 942, 951–952 (CA10 1994); *Morris* v. *West Palm Beach*, 194 F. 3d 1203, 1207 (CA11 1999). Other Courts of Appeals have likewise continued to apply the catalyst theory notwithstanding *Farrar*. *Paris* v. *United States Dept. of Housing and Urban Development*, 988 F. 2d 236, 238 (CA1 1993); *Citizens Against Tax Waste* v. *Westerville City School*, 985 F. 2d 255, 257 (CA6 1993).

It would be premature, however, for us to address the continuing validity of the catalyst theory in the context of this case. The District Court, in an order separate from the one in which it imposed civil penalties against Laidlaw, stayed the time for a petition for attorneys' fees until the time for appeal had expired or, if either party appealed, until the appeal was resolved. See 149 F. 3d, at 305 (describing order staying time for attorneys' fees petition). In the opinion accompanying its order on penalties, the District Court stated only that "this court has considered that Laidlaw will be required to reimburse plaintiffs for a significant amount of legal fees," and referred to "potential fee awards." 956 F. Supp., at 610–611. Thus, when the Court of Appeals addressed the availability of counsel fees in this case, no order was before it either denying or awarding fees. It is for the District Court, not this Court, to address in the first instance any request for reimbursement of costs, including fees.

* * *

For the reasons stated, the judgment of the United States Court of Appeals for the Fourth Circuit is reversed, and the case is remanded for further proceedings consistent with this opinion.

It is so ordered.

Olmstead v. L. C.,
527 U.S. 581
(1999)

Majority Opinion

Two Georgia women, both diagnosed with schizophrenia and other psychological disorders, were being held in psychiatric isolation despite their desire to move into a community treatment setting (a move sanctioned by medical professionals treating them). The women argued that their disorders were disabilities, and were qualified for protection under the 1990 Americans with Disabilities Act (ADA). However, the move was blocked by Tommy Olmstead, the Commissioner of Georgia's Department of Human Resources, who claimed that a move to a community setting was financially prohibitive and would require a fundamental change in their treatment programs.

The Court found, in a 6-3 decision, that financial constraints were not an excuse for states to refuse to comply with the ADA. Justice Ginsburg's majority opinion outlined the Court's belief that the women's being held in isolation against their wishes was "properly regarded as discrimination based on disability."

OLMSTEAD, COMMISSIONER, GEORGIA
DEPARTMENT OF HUMAN RESOURCES, ET AL.
v.
L. C. BY ZIMRING, GUARDIAN AD LITEM
AND NEXT FRIEND, ET AL.
[June 22, 1999]

JUSTICE GINSBURG announced the judgment of the Court and delivered the opinion of the Court with respect to Parts I, II, and III–A, and an opinion with respect to Part III–B, in which JUSTICE O'CONNOR, JUSTICE SOUTER, and JUSTICE BREYER join.

This case concerns the proper construction of the antidiscrimination provision contained in the public services portion (Title II) of the Americans with Disabilities Act of 1990 (ADA), 104 Stat. 337, 42 U. S. C. § 12132. Specifically, we confront the question whether the proscription of discrimination may require placement of persons with mental disabilities in community settings rather than in institutions. The answer, we hold, is a qualified yes. Such action is in order when the State's treatment professionals have determined that community placement is appropriate, the transfer from institutional care to a less restrictive setting is not opposed by the affected individual, and the placement can be reasonably accommodated, taking into account the resources available to the State and the needs of others with mental disabilities. In so ruling, we affirm the decision of the Eleventh Circuit in substantial part. We remand the case, however, for further consideration of the appropriate relief, given the range of facilities the State maintains for the care and treatment of persons with diverse mental disabilities, and its obligation to administer services with an even hand.

I

This case, as it comes to us, presents no constitutional question. The complaints filed by plaintiffs-respondents L. C. and E. W. did include such an issue; L. C. and E. W. alleged that defendants-petitioners, Georgia health care officials, failed to afford them minimally adequate care and freedom from undue restraint, in violation of their rights under the Due Process Clause of the Fourteenth Amendment. See Complaint ¶¶ 87–91; Intervenor's Complaint ¶¶ 30–34. But neither the District Court nor the Court of Appeals reached those Fourteenth Amendment claims. See Civ. No. 1:95–cv–1210–MHS (ND Ga., Mar. 26, 1997), pp. 5–6, 11–13, App. to Pet. for Cert. 34a–35a, 40a–41a; 138 F. 3d 893, 895, and n. 3 (CA11 1998). Instead, the courts below resolved the case solely on statutory grounds. Our review is similarly confined. Cf. *Cleburne* v. *Cleburne Living Center, Inc.*, 473 U.S. 432, 450 (1985) (Texas city's requirement of special use permit for operation of group home for mentally retarded, when other care and multiple-dwelling facilities were freely permitted, lacked rational basis and therefore violated Equal Protection Clause of Fourteenth Amendment). Mindful that it is a statute we are construing, we set out first the legislative and regulatory prescriptions on which the case turns.

In the opening provisions of the ADA, Congress stated findings applicable to the statute in all its parts. Most relevant to this case, Congress determined that

> "(2) historically, society has tended to isolate and segregate individuals with disabilities, and, despite some improvements, such forms of discrimination against individuals with disabilities continue to be a serious and pervasive social problem;
> "(3) discrimination against individuals with disabilities persists in such critical areas as . . . institutionalization . . . ;
>
> . . . . .
>
> "(5) individuals with disabilities continually encounter various forms of discrimination, including outright intentional exclusion, . . . failure to make modifications

> to existing facilities and practices, . . . [and]
> segregation. . . ." 42 U. S. C. §§ 12101(a)(2), (3), (5).[1]

Congress then set forth prohibitions against discrimination in employment (Title I, §§ 12111–12117), public services furnished by governmental entities (Title II, §§ 12131–12165), and public accommodations provided by private entities (Title III, §§ 12181–12189). The statute as a whole is intended "to provide a clear and comprehensive national mandate for the elimination of discrimination against individuals with disabilities." § 12101(b)(1).[2]

This case concerns Title II, the public services portion of the ADA.[3] The provision of Title II centrally at issue reads:

> "Subject to the provisions of this subchapter, no
> qualified individual with a disability shall, by reason
> of such disability, be excluded from participation in
> or be denied the benefits of the services, programs,
> or activities of a public entity, or be subjected to
> discrimination by any such entity." § 201, as set forth
> in 42 U. S. C. § 12132.

Title II's definition section states that "public entity" includes

---

1 The ADA, enacted in 1990, is the Federal Government's most recent and extensive endeavor to address discrimination against persons with disabilities. Earlier legislative efforts included the Rehabilitation Act of 1973, 87 Stat. 355, 29 U. S. C. § 701 *et seq.* (1976 ed.), and the Developmentally Disabled Assistance and Bill of Rights Act, 89 Stat. 486, 42 U. S. C. § 6001 *et seq.* (1976 ed.), enacted in 1975. In the ADA, Congress for the first time referred expressly to "segregation" of persons with disabilities as a "for[m] of discrimination," and to discrimination that persists in the area of "institutionalization." §§ 12101(a)(2), (3), (5).

2 The ADA defines "disability," "with respect to an individual," as

"(A) a physical or mental impairment that substantially limits one or more of the major life activities of such individual;

"(B) a record of such an impairment; or

"(C) being regarded as having such an impairment." § 12102(2).

There is no dispute that L. C. and E. W. are disabled within the meaning of the ADA.

3 In addition to the provisions set out in Part A governing public services generally, see §§ 12131–12134, Title II contains in Part B a host of provisions governing public transportation services, see §§ 12141–12165.

"any State or local government," and "any department, agency, [or] special purpose district." §§ 12131(1)(A),(B). The same section defines "qualified individual with a disability" as

"an individual with a disability who, with or without reasonable modifications to rules, policies, or practices, the removal of architectural, communication, or transportation barriers, or the provision of auxiliary aids and services, meets the essential eligibility requirements for the receipt of services or the participation in programs or activities provided by a public entity." § 12131(2).

On redress for violations of § 12132's discrimination prohibition, Congress referred to remedies available under § 505 of the Rehabilitation Act of 1973, 92 Stat. 2982, 29 U. S. C. § 794a. See § 203, as set forth in 42 U. S. C. § 12133 ("The remedies, procedures, and rights set forth in [§ 505 of the Rehabilitation Act] shall be the remedies, procedures, and rights this subchapter provides to any person alleging discrimination on the basis of disability in violation of section 12132 of this title.").[4]

Congress instructed the Attorney General to issue regulations implementing provisions of Title II, including § 12132's discrimination proscription. See § 204, as set forth in § 12134(a) ("[T]he Attorney General shall promulgate regulations in an accessible format that implement this part.").[5] The Attorney

---

4 Section 505 of the Rehabilitation Act incorporates the remedies, rights, and procedures set forth in Title VI of the Civil Rights Act of 1964 for violations of § 504 of the Rehabilitation Act. See 29 U. S. C. § 794a(a)(2). Title VI, in turn, directs each federal department authorized to extend financial assistance to any department or agency of a State to issue rules and regulations consistent with achievement of the objectives of the statute authorizing financial assistance. See 78 Stat. 252, 42 U. S. C. § 2000d–1. Compliance with such requirements may be effected by the termination or denial of federal funds, or "by any other means authorized by law." *Ibid.* Remedies both at law and in equity are available for violations of the statute. See § 2000d–7(a)(2).

5 Congress directed the Secretary of Transportation to issue regulations implementing the portion of Title II concerning public transportation. See 42 U. S. C. §§ 12143(b), 12149, 12164. As stated in the regulations, a person alleging discrimination on the basis of disability in violation of Title II may seek to enforce its provisions by commencing a private lawsuit, or

General's regulations, Congress further directed, "shall be consistent with this chapter and with the coordination regulations . . . applicable to recipients of Federal financial assistance under [§ 504 of the Rehabilitation Act]." § 204, as set forth in 42 U. S. C. § 12134(b). One of the § 504 regulations requires recipients of federal funds to "administer programs and activities in the most integrated setting appropriate to the needs of qualified handicapped persons." 28 CFR § 41.51(d) (1998).

As Congress instructed, the Attorney General issued Title II regulations, see 28 CFR pt. 35 (1998), including one modeled on the § 504 regulation just quoted; called the "integration regulation," it reads:

> "A public entity shall administer services, programs,
> and activities in the most integrated setting appropriate
> to the needs of qualified individuals with disabilities."
> 28 CFR § 35.130(d) (1998).

The preamble to the Attorney General's Title II regulations defines "the most integrated setting appropriate to the needs of qualified individuals with disabilities" to mean "a setting that enables individuals with disabilities to interact with non-disabled persons to the fullest extent possible." 28 CFR pt. 35, App.

---

by filing a complaint with (a) a federal agency that provides funding to the public entity that is the subject of the complaint, (b) the Department of Justice for referral to an appropriate agency, or (c) one of eight federal agencies responsible for investigating complaints arising under Title II: the Department of Agriculture, the Department of Education, the Department of Health and Human Services, the Department of Housing and Urban Development, the Department of the Interior, the Department of Justice, the Department of Labor, and the Department of Transportation. See 28 CFR §§ 35.170(c), 35.172(b), 35.190(b) (1998).

The ADA contains several other provisions allocating regulatory and enforcement responsibility. Congress instructed the Equal Employment Opportunity Commission (EEOC) to issue regulations implementing Title I, see 42 U. S. C. § 12116; the EEOC, the Attorney General, and persons alleging discrimination on the basis of disability in violation of Title I may enforce its provisions, see § 12117(a). Congress similarly instructed the Secretary of Transportation and the Attorney General to issue regulations implementing provisions of Title III, see §§ 12186(a)(1), (b); the Attorney General and persons alleging discrimination on the basis of disability in violation of Title III may enforce its provisions, see §§ 12188(a)(1), (b). Each federal agency responsible for ADA implementation may render technical assistance to affected individuals and institutions with respect to provisions of the ADA for which the agency has responsibility. See § 12206(c)(1).

A, p. 450 (1998). Another regulation requires public entities to "make reasonable modifications" to avoid "discrimination on the basis of disability," unless those modifications would entail a "fundamenta[l] alter[ation]"; called here the "reasonable-modifications regulation," it provides:

> "A public entity shall make reasonable modifications in policies, practices, or procedures when the modifications are necessary to avoid discrimination on the basis of disability, unless the public entity can demonstrate that making the modifications would fundamentally alter the nature of the service, program, or activity." 28 CFR § 35.130(b)(7) (1998).

We recite these regulations with the caveat that we do not here determine their validity. While the parties differ on the proper construction and enforcement of the regulations, we do not understand petitioners to challenge the regulatory formulations themselves as outside the congressional authorization. See Brief for Petitioners 16–17, 36, 40–41; Reply Brief 15–16 (challenging the Attorney General's interpretation of the integration regulation).

II

With the key legislative provisions in full view, we summarize the facts underlying this dispute. Respondents L. C. and E. W. are mentally retarded women; L. C. has also been diagnosed with schizophrenia, and E. W. with a personality disorder. Both women have a history of treatment in institutional settings. In May 1992, L. C. was voluntarily admitted to Georgia Regional Hospital at Atlanta (GRH), where she was confined for treatment in a psychiatric unit. By May 1993, her psychiatric condition had stabilized, and L. C.'s treatment team at GRH agreed that her needs could be met appropriately in one of the community-based programs the State supported. Despite this evaluation, L. C. remained institutionalized until February

1996, when the State placed her in a community-based treatment program.

E. W. was voluntarily admitted to GRH in February 1995; like L. C., E. W. was confined for treatment in a psychiatric unit. In March 1995, GRH sought to discharge E. W. to a homeless shelter, but abandoned that plan after her attorney filed an administrative complaint. By 1996, E. W.'s treating psychiatrist concluded that she could be treated appropriately in a community-based setting. She nonetheless remained institutionalized until a few months after the District Court issued its judgment in this case in 1997.

In May 1995, when she was still institutionalized at GRH, L. C. filed suit in the United States District Court for the Northern District of Georgia, challenging her continued confinement in a segregated environment. Her complaint invoked 42 U. S. C. § 1983 and provisions of the ADA, §§ 12131–12134, and named as defendants, now petitioners, the Commissioner of the Georgia Department of Human Resources, the Superintendent of GRH, and the Executive Director of the Fulton County Regional Board (collectively, the State). L. C. alleged that the State's failure to place her in a community-based program, once her treating professionals determined that such placement was appropriate, violated, *inter alia*, Title II of the ADA. L. C.'s pleading requested, among other things, that the State place her in a community care residential program, and that she receive treatment with the ultimate goal of integrating her into the mainstream of society. E. W. intervened in the action, stating an identical claim.[6]

The District Court granted partial summary judgment in favor of L. C. and E. W. See App. to Pet. for Cert. 31a–42a.

---

6 L. C. and E. W. are currently receiving treatment in community-based programs. Nevertheless, the case is not moot. As the District Court and Court of Appeals explained, in view of the multiple institutional placements L. C. and E. W. have experienced, the controversy they brought to court is "capable of repetition, yet evading review." No. 1:95–cv–1210–MHS (ND Ga., Mar. 26, 1997), p. 6, App. to Pet. for Cert. 35a (internal quotation marks omitted); see 138 F. 3d 893, 895, n. 2 (CA11 1998) (citing *Honig* v. *Doe*, 484 U. S. 305, 318–323 (1988), and *Vitek* v. *Jones*, 445 U. S. 480, 486–487 (1980)).

The court held that the State's failure to place L. C. and E. W. in an appropriate community-based treatment program violated Title II of the ADA. See *id.*, at 39a, 41a. In so ruling, the court rejected the State's argument that inadequate funding, not discrimination against L. C. and E. W. "by reason of" their disabilities, accounted for their retention at GRH. Under Title II, the court concluded, "unnecessary institutional segregation of the disabled constitutes discrimination *per se*, which cannot be justified by a lack of funding." *Id.*, at 37a.

In addition to contending that L. C. and E. W. had not shown discrimination "by reason of [their] disabilit[ies]," the State resisted court intervention on the ground that requiring immediate transfers in cases of this order would "fundamentally alter" the State's activity. The State reasserted that it was already using all available funds to provide services to other persons with disabilities. See *id.*, at 38a. Rejecting the State's "fundamental alteration" defense, the court observed that existing state programs provided community-based treatment of the kind for which L. C. and E. W. qualified, and that the State could "provide services to plaintiffs in the community at considerably *less* cost than is required to maintain them in an institution." *Id.*, at 39a.

The Court of Appeals for the Eleventh Circuit affirmed the judgment of the District Court, but remanded for reassessment of the State's cost-based defense. See 138 F. 3d, at 905. As the appeals court read the statute and regulations: When "a disabled individual's treating professionals find that a community-based placement is appropriate for that individual, the ADA imposes a duty to provide treatment in a community setting—the most integrated setting appropriate to that patient's needs"; "[w]here there is no such finding [by the treating professionals], nothing in the ADA requires the deinstitutionalization of th[e] patient." *Id.*, at 902.

The Court of Appeals recognized that the State's duty to provide integrated services "is not absolute"; under the Attorney

General's Title II regulation, "reasonable modifications" were required of the State, but fundamental alterations were not demanded. *Id.*, at 904. The appeals court thought it clear, however, that "Congress wanted to permit a cost defense only in the most limited of circumstances." *Id.*, at 902. In conclusion, the court stated that a cost justification would fail "[u]nless the State can prove that requiring it to [expend additional funds in order to provide L. C. and E. W. with integrated services] would be so unreasonable given the demands of the State's mental health budget that it would fundamentally alter the service [the State] provides." *Id.*, at 905. Because it appeared that the District Court had entirely ruled out a "lack of funding " justification, see App. to Pet. for Cert. 37a, the appeals court remanded, repeating that the District Court should consider, among other things, "whether the additional expenditures necessary to treat L. C. and E. W. in community-based care would be unreasonable given the demands of the State's mental health budget."138 F. 3d, at 905.[7]

We granted certiorari in view of the importance of the question presented to the States and affected individuals. See 525 U.S. 1054 (1998).[8]

III

Endeavoring to carry out Congress' instruction to issue regulations implementing Title II, the Attorney General, in the integration and reasonable-modifications regulations, see *supra*, at 591–592, made two key determinations. The first concerned the scope of the ADA's discrimination proscription, 42 U. S. C. § 12132; the second concerned the obligation of the States to

---

7 After this Court granted certiorari, the District Court issued a decision on remand rejecting the State's fundamental-alteration defense. See 1:95–cv–1210–MHS (ND Ga., Jan. 29, 1999), p. 1. The court concluded that the annual cost to the State of providing community-based treatment to L. C. and E. W. was not unreasonable in relation to the State's overall mental health budget. See *id.*, at 5. In reaching that judgment, the District Court first declared "irrelevant" the potential impact of its decision beyond L. C. and E. W. 1:95–cv–1210-MHS (ND Ga., Oct. 20, 1998), p. 3, App. 177. The District Court's decision on remand is now pending appeal before the Eleventh Circuit.

8 Twenty-two States and the Territory of Guam joined a brief urging that certiorari be granted. Ten of those States joined a brief in support of petitioners on the merits.

counter discrimination. As to the first, the Attorney General concluded that unjustified placement or retention of persons in institutions, severely limiting their exposure to the outside community, constitutes a form of discrimination based on disability prohibited by Title II. See 28 CFR § 35.130(d) (1998) ("A public entity shall administer services . . . in the most integrated setting appropriate to the needs of qualified individuals with disabilities."); Brief for United States as *Amicus Curiae* in *Helen L.* v. *DiDario*, No. 94–1243 (CA3 1994), pp. 8, 15–16 (unnecessary segregation of persons with disabilities constitutes a form of discrimination prohibited by the ADA and the integration regulation). Regarding the States' obligation to avoid unjustified isolation of individuals with disabilities, the Attorney General provided that States could resist modifications that "would fundamentally alter the nature of the service, program, or activity." 28 CFR § 35.130(b)(7) (1998).

The Court of Appeals essentially upheld the Attorney General's construction of the ADA. As just recounted, see *supra*, at 595–596, the appeals court ruled that the unjustified institutionalization of persons with mental disabilities violated Title II; the court then remanded with instructions to measure the cost of caring for L. C. and E. W. in a community-based facility against the State's mental health budget.

We affirm the Court of Appeals' decision in substantial part. Unjustified isolation, we hold, is properly regarded as discrimination based on disability. But we recognize, as well, the States' need to maintain a range of facilities for the care and treatment of persons with diverse mental disabilities, and the States' obligation to administer services with an even hand. Accordingly, we further hold that the Court of Appeals' remand instruction was unduly restrictive. In evaluating a State's fundamental-alteration defense, the District Court must consider, in view of the resources available to the State, not only the cost of providing community-based care to the litigants, but also the range of services the State provides others with mental disabilities, and the State's obligation to mete out those services equitably.

A

We examine first whether, as the Eleventh Circuit held, undue institutionalization qualifies as discrimination "by reason of . . . disability." The Department of Justice has consistently advocated that it does.[9] Because the Department is the agency directed by Congress to issue regulations implementing Title II, see *supra*, at 591–592, its views warrant respect. We need not inquire whether the degree of deference described in *Chevron U. S. A. Inc.* v. *Natural Resources Defense Council, Inc.*, 467 U.S. 837, 844 (1984), is in order; "[i]t is enough to observe that the well-reasoned views of the agencies implementing a statute 'constitute a body of experience and informed judgment to which courts and litigants may properly resort for guidance.'" *Bragdon* v. *Abbott*, 524 U.S. 624, 642 (1998) (quoting *Skidmore* v. *Swift & Co.*, 323 U.S. 134, 139–140 (1944)).

The State argues that L. C. and E. W. encountered no discrimination "by reason of" their disabilities because they were not denied community placement on account of those disabilities. See Brief for Petitioners 20. Nor were they subjected to "discrimination," the State contends, because "'discrimination' necessarily requires uneven treatment of similarly situated individuals," and L. C. and E. W. had identified no comparison class, *i.e.*, no similarly situated individuals given preferential treatment. *Id.*, at 21. We are satisfied that Congress had a more

---

9 See Brief for United States in *Halderman* v. *Pennhurst State School and Hospital*, Nos. 78–1490, 78–1564, 78–1602 (CA3 1978), p. 45 ("[I]nstitutionalization result[ing] in separation of mentally retarded persons for no permissible reason . . . is 'discrimination,' and a violation of Section 504 [of the Rehabilitation Act] if it is supported by federal funds."); Brief for United States in *Halderman* v. *Pennhurst State School and Hospital*, Nos. 78–1490, 78–1564, 78–1602 (CA3 1981), p. 27 ("Pennsylvania violates Section 504 by indiscriminately subjecting handicapped persons to [an institution] without first making an individual reasoned professional judgment as to the appropriate placement for each such person among all available alternatives."); Brief for United States as *Amicus Curiae* in *Helen L.* v. *DiDario*, No. 94–1243 (CA3 1994), p. 7 ("Both the Section 504 coordination regulations and the rest of the ADA make clear that the unnecessary segregation of individuals with disabilities in the provision of public services is itself a form of discrimination within the meaning of those statutes."); *id.*, at 8–16.

comprehensive view of the concept of discrimination advanced in the ADA.[10]

The ADA stepped up earlier measures to secure opportunities for people with developmental disabilities to enjoy the benefits of community living. The Developmentally Disabled Assistance and Bill of Rights Act, a 1975 measure, stated in aspirational terms that "[t]he treatment, services, and habilitation for a person with developmental disabilities . . . *should be* provided in the setting that is least restrictive of the person's personal liberty." 89 Stat. 502, 42 U. S. C. § 6010(2) (1976 ed.) (emphasis added); see also *Pennhurst State School and Hospital* v. *Halderman*, 451 U.S. 1, 24 (1981) (concluding that the § 6010 provisions "were intended to be hortatory, not mandatory"). In a related legislative endeavor, the Rehabilitation Act of 1973, Congress used mandatory language to proscribe discrimination against persons with disabilities. See 87 Stat. 394, as amended, 29 U. S. C. § 794 (1976 ed.) ("No otherwise qualified individual with a disability in the United States . . . *shall*, solely by reason of her or his disability, be excluded from the participation in, be denied the benefits of, or be subjected to discrimination under any program or activity receiving Federal financial assistance." (Emphasis added.)) Ultimately, in the ADA, enacted in 1990, Congress not only required all

---

10 The dissent is driven by the notion that "this Court has never endorsed an interpretation of the term 'discrimination' that encompassed disparate treatment among members of the *same* protected class," *post*, at 616 (opinion of THOMAS, J.), that "[o]ur decisions construing various statutory prohibitions against 'discrimination' have not wavered from this path," *post*, at 616, and that "a plaintiff cannot prove 'discrimination' by demonstrating that one member of a particular protected group has been favored over another member of that same group," *post*, at 618. The dissent is incorrect as a matter of precedent and logic. See *O'Connor* v. *Consolidated Coin Caterers Corp.*, 517 U.S. 308, 312 (1996) (The Age Discrimination in Employment Act of 1967 "does not ban discrimination against employees because they are aged 40 or older; it bans discrimination against employees because of their age, but limits the protected class to those who are 40 or older. The fact that one person in the protected class has lost out to another person in the protected class is thus irrelevant, so long as he has lost out because of his age."); cf. *Oncale* v. *Sundowner Offshore Services, Inc.*, 523 U.S. 75, 76 (1998) ("[W]orkplace harassment can violate Title VII's prohibition against 'discriminat[ion] . . . because of . . . sex,' 42 U. S. C. § 2000e–2(a)(1), when the harasser and the harassed employee are of the same sex."); *Jefferies* v. *Harris County Community Action Assn.*, 615 F. 2d 1025, 1032 (CA5 1980) ("[D]iscrimination against black females can exist even in the absence of discrimination against black men or white women.").

public entities to refrain from discrimination, see 42 U. S. C. § 12132; additionally, in findings applicable to the entire statute, Congress explicitly identified unjustified "segregation" of persons with disabilities as a "for[m] of discrimination." See § 12101(a)(2) ("historically, society has tended to isolate and segregate individuals with disabilities, and, despite some improvements, such forms of discrimination against individuals with disabilities continue to be a serious and pervasive social problem"); § 12101(a)(5) ("individuals with disabilities continually encounter various forms of discrimination, including . . . segregation").[11]

Recognition that unjustified institutional isolation of persons with disabilities is a form of discrimination reflects two evident judgments. First, institutional placement of persons who can handle and benefit from community settings perpetuates unwarranted assumptions that persons so isolated are incapable or unworthy of participating in community life. Cf. *Allen* v. *Wright*, 468 U.S. 737, 755 (1984) ("There can be no doubt that [stigmatizing injury often caused by racial discrimination] is one of the most serious consequences of discriminatory government action."); *Los Angeles Dept. of Water and Power* v. *Manhart*, 435 U.S. 702, 707, n. 13 (1978) (" 'In forbidding employers to discriminate against individuals because of their sex, Congress intended to strike at the entire spectrum of disparate treatment of men and women resulting from sex stereotypes.' " (quoting *Sprogis* v. *United Air Lines, Inc.*, 444 F. 2d 1194, 1198 (CA7 1971)). Second, confinement in an institution severely diminishes the everyday life activities of individuals, including family relations, social contacts, work options, economic independence, educational advancement, and cultural enrichment. See Brief for American Psychiatric Association et al. as *Amici Curiae* 20–22. Dissimilar treatment correspondingly exists in this key

---

11 Unlike the ADA, § 504 of the Rehabilitation Act contains no express recognition that isolation or segregation of persons with disabilities is a form of discrimination. Section 504's discrimination proscription, a single sentence attached to vocational rehabilitation legislation, has yielded divergent court interpretations. See Brief for United States as *Amicus Curiae* 23–25.

respect: In order to receive needed medical services, persons with mental disabilities must, because of those disabilities, relinquish participation in community life they could enjoy given reasonable accommodations, while persons without mental disabilities can receive the medical services they need without similar sacrifice. See Brief for United States as *Amicus Curiae* 6–7, 17.

The State urges that, whatever Congress may have stated as its findings in the ADA, the Medicaid statute "reflected a congressional policy preference for treatment in the institution over treatment in the community." Brief for Petitioners 31. The State correctly used the past tense. Since 1981, Medicaid has provided funding for state-run home and community-based care through a waiver program. See 95 Stat. 812–813, as amended, 42 U. S. C. § 1396n(c); Brief for United States as *Amicus Curiae* 20–21.[12] Indeed, the United States points out that the Department of Health and Human Services (HHS) "has a policy of encouraging States to take advantage of the waiver program, and often approves more waiver slots than a State ultimately uses." *Id.*, at 25–26 (further observing that, by 1996, "HHS approved up to 2109 waiver slots for Georgia, but Georgia used only 700").

We emphasize that nothing in the ADA or its implementing regulations condones termination of institutional settings for persons unable to handle or benefit from community settings. Title II provides only that "qualified individual[s]with a disability" may not "be subjected to discrimination." 42 U. S. C. § 12132. "Qualified individuals," the ADA further explains, are persons with disabilities who, "with or without reasonable modifications to rules, policies, or practices, . . . mee[t] the essential eligibility requirements for the receipt of services or the participation in programs or activities provided by a public entity." § 12131(2).

Consistent with these provisions, the State generally may

---

12 The waiver program provides Medicaid reimbursement to States for the provision of community-based services to individuals who would otherwise require institutional care, upon a showing that the average annual cost of such services is not more than the annual cost of institutional services. See § 1396n(c).

rely on the reasonable assessments of its own professionals in determining whether an individual "meets the essential eligibility requirements" for habilitation in a community-based program. Absent such qualification, it would be inappropriate to remove a patient from the more restrictive setting. See 28 CFR § 35.130(d) (1998) (public entity shall administer services and programs in "the most integrated setting *appropriate* to the needs of qualified individuals with disabilities" (emphasis added)); cf. *School Bd. of Nassau Cty.* v. *Arline*, 480 U.S. 273, 288 (1987) ("[C]ourts normally should defer to the reasonable medical judgments of public health officials.").[13] Nor is there any federal requirement that community-based treatment be imposed on patients who do not desire it. See 28 CFR § 35.130(e)(1) (1998) ("Nothing in this part shall be construed to require an individual with a disability to accept an accommodation . . . which such individual chooses not to accept."); 28 CFR pt. 35, App. A, p. 450 (1998) ("[P]ersons with disabilities must be provided the option of declining to accept a particular accommodation."). In this case, however, there is no genuine dispute concerning the status of L. C. and E. W. as individuals "qualified" for noninstitutional care: The State's own professionals determined that community-based treatment would be appropriate for L. C. and E. W., and neither woman opposed such treatment. See *supra*, at 593.[14]

B

The State's responsibility, once it provides community-based treatment to qualified persons with disabilities, is not boundless. The reasonable-modifications regulation speaks of "reasonable

---

13 Georgia law also expresses a preference for treatment in the most integrated setting appropriate. See Ga. Code Ann. § 37–4–121 (1995) ("It is the policy of the state that the least restrictive alternative placement be secured for every client at every stage of his habilitation. It shall be the duty of the facility to assist the client in securing placement in noninstitutional community facilities and programs.").

14 We do not in this opinion hold that the ADA imposes on the States a "standard of care" for whatever medical services they render, or that the ADA requires States to "provide a certain level of benefits to individuals with disabilities." Cf. *post*, at 623, 624 (THOMAS, J., dissenting). We do hold, however, that States must adhere to the ADA's nondiscrimination requirement with regard to the services they in fact provide.

modifications" to avoid discrimination, and allows States to resist modifications that entail a "fundamenta[l] alter[ation]" of the States' services and programs. 28 CFR § 35.130(b)(7) (1998). The Court of Appeals construed this regulation to permit a cost-based defense "only in the most limited of circumstances," 138 F. 3d, at 902, and remanded to the District Court to consider, among other things, "whether the additional expenditures necessary to treat L. C. and E. W. in community-based care would be unreasonable given the demands of the State's mental health budget," *id.*, at 905.

The Court of Appeals' construction of the reasonable-modifications regulation is unacceptable for it would leave the State virtually defenseless once it is shown that the plaintiff is qualified for the service or program she seeks. If the expense entailed in placing one or two people in a community-based treatment program is properly measured for reasonableness against the State's entire mental health budget, it is unlikely that a State, relying on the fundamental-alteration defense, could ever prevail. See Tr. of Oral Arg. 27 (State's attorney argues that Court of Appeals' understanding of the fundamental-alteration defense, as expressed in its order to the District Court, "will always preclude the State from a meaningful defense"); cf. Brief for Petitioners 37–38 (Court of Appeals' remand order "mistakenly asks the district court to examine [the fundamental-alteration] defense based on the cost of providing community care to just two individuals, not all Georgia citizens who desire community care"); 1:95–cv–1210–MHS (ND Ga., Oct. 20, 1998), p. 3, App. 177 (District Court, on remand, declares the impact of its decision beyond L. C. and E. W. "irrelevant"). Sensibly construed, the fundamental-alteration component of the reasonable-modifications regulation would allow the State to show that, in the allocation of available resources, immediate relief for the plaintiffs would be inequitable, given the responsibility the State has undertaken for the care and treatment of a large and diverse population of persons with mental disabilities.

When it granted summary judgment for plaintiffs in this case, the District Court compared the cost of caring for the plaintiffs in a community-based setting with the cost of caring for them in an institution. That simple comparison showed that community placements cost less than institutional confinements. See App. to Pet. for Cert. 39a. As the United States recognizes, however, a comparison so simple overlooks costs the State cannot avoid; most notably, a "State . . . may experience increased overall expenses by funding community placements without being able to take advantage of the savings associated with the closure of institutions." Brief for United States as *Amicus Curiae* 21.[15]

As already observed, see *supra*, at 601–602, the ADA is not reasonably read to impel States to phase out institutions, placing patients in need of close care at risk. Cf. *post*, at 610 (KENNEDY, J., concurring in judgment). Nor is it the ADA's mission to drive States to move institutionalized patients into an inappropriate setting, such as a homeless shelter, a placement the State proposed, then retracted, for E. W. See *supra*, at 593. Some individuals, like L. C. and E. W. in prior years, may need institutional care from time to time "to stabilize acute psychiatric symptoms." App. 98 (affidavit of Dr. Richard L. Elliott); see 138 F. 3d, at 903 ("[T]here may be times [when] a patient can be treated in the community, and others whe[n] an institutional placement is necessary."); Reply Brief 19 (placement in a community-based treatment program does not mean the State will no longer need to retain hospital accommodations for the person so placed). For other individuals, no placement outside the institution may ever be appropriate. See Brief for American Psychiatric Association et al. as *Amici Curiae* 22–23 ("Some individuals, whether mentally retarded or mentally ill, are not prepared at particular times—perhaps in the short run, perhaps

---

15 Even if States eventually were able to close some institutions in response to an increase in the number of community placements, the States would still incur the cost of running partially full institutions in the interim. See Brief for United States as *Amicus Curiae* 21.

in the long run—for the risks and exposure of the less protective environment of community settings"; for these persons, "institutional settings are needed and must remain available."); Brief for Voice of the Retarded et al. as *Amici Curiae* 11 ("Each disabled person is entitled to treatment in the most integrated setting possible for that person—recognizing that, on a case-by-case basis, that setting may be in an institution."); *Youngberg* v. *Romeo*, 457 U.S. 307, 327 (1982) (Blackmun, J., concurring) ("For many mentally retarded people, the difference between the capacity to do things for themselves within an institution and total dependence on the institution for all of their needs is as much liberty as they ever will know.").

To maintain a range of facilities and to administer services with an even hand, the State must have more leeway than the courts below understood the fundamental-alteration defense to allow. If, for example, the State were to demonstrate that it had a comprehensive, effectively working plan for placing qualified persons with mental disabilities in less restrictive settings, and a waiting list that moved at a reasonable pace not controlled by the State's endeavors to keep its institutions fully populated, the reasonable-modifications standard would be met. See Tr. of Oral Arg. 5 (State's attorney urges that, "by asking [a] person to wait a short time until a community bed is available, Georgia does not exclude [that] person by reason of disability, neither does Georgia discriminate against her by reason of disability"); see also *id.*, at 25 ("[I]t is reasonable for the State to ask someone to wait until a community placement is available."). In such circumstances, a court would have no warrant effectively to order displacement of persons at the top of the community-based treatment waiting list by individuals lower down who commenced civil actions.[16]

---

16 We reject the Court of Appeals' construction of the reasonable-modifications regulation for another reason. The Attorney General's Title II regulations, Congress ordered, "shall be consistent with" the regulations in part 41 of Title 28 of the Code of Federal Regulations implementing § 504 of the Rehabilitation Act. 42 U. S. C. § 12134(b). The § 504 regulation upon which the reasonable-modifications regulation is based provides now, as it did at the time the ADA was enacted:

"A recipient shall make reasonable accommodation to the known physical or mental

* * *

For the reasons stated, we conclude that, under Title II of the ADA, States are required to provide community-based treatment for persons with mental disabilities when the State's treatment professionals determine that such placement is appropriate, the affected persons do not oppose such treatment, and the placement can be reasonably accommodated, taking into account the resources available to the State and the needs of others with mental disabilities. The judgment of the Eleventh Circuit is therefore affirmed in part and vacated in part, and the case is remanded for further proceedings.

It is so ordered.

---

limitations of an otherwise qualified handicapped applicant or employee unless the recipient can demonstrate that the accommodation would impose an undue hardship on the operation of its program." 28 CFR § 41.53 (1990 and 1998 eds.).

While the part 41 regulations do not define "undue hardship," other § 504 regulations make clear that the "undue hardship" inquiry requires not simply an assessment of the cost of the accommodation in relation to the recipient's overall budget, but a "case-by-case analysis weighing factors that include: (1) [t]he overall size of the recipient's program with respect to number of employees, number and type of facilities, and size of budget; (2) [t]he type of the recipient's operation, including the composition and structure of the recipient's workforce; and (3) [t]he nature and cost of the accommodation needed." 28 CFR § 42.511(c) (1998); see 45 CFR § 84.12(c) (1998) (same).

Under the Court of Appeals' restrictive reading, the reasonable-modifications regulation would impose a standard substantially more difficult for the State to meet than the "undue burden" standard imposed by the corresponding § 504 regulation.

Bush v. Gore, 531 U.S. 98 (2000)

Dissenting Opinion

*B*y *the wee hours of the morning on November 8, 2000, there was still no clear winner of the presidential election held the prior day; the outcome hinged on which candidate—George W. Bush or Al Gore—had won the state of Florida. But the confusing nature of Florida's ballot system made it difficult to determine a winner with any certainty. Numerous recounts ensued, with the Florida Supreme Court eventually intervening to demand statewide manual recounts.*

On December 9, the issue came before the U.S. Supreme Court. There were two legal matters at hand: had the Florida Supreme Court violated Article II Section 1 Clause 2 of the Constitution by making new election law? And did the manual recounts violate the Equal Protection and Due Process Clauses of the Constitution because there were no consistent standards being used to judge ballots across all of Florida's counties and precincts? The justices decided 7–2 on the unconstitutionality of the former matter, and 5–4 on the unconstitutionality of the latter. Justice Ginsburg was in the minority on both issues—and as evidence of just how strongly she disagreed, she ended her dissent with her now-famous "I dissent," rather than the traditional "I respectfully dissent."

SUPREME COURT OF THE UNITED STATES
BUSH ET AL.
v.
GORE ET AL.

CERTIORARI TO THE SUPREME COURT OF FLORIDA
[December 12, 2000]

JUSTICE GINSBURG, with whom JUSTICE STEVENS joins, and with whom JUSTICE SOUTER and JUSTICE BREYER join as to Part I, dissenting.

I

THE CHIEF JUSTICE acknowledges that provisions of Florida's Election Code "may well admit of more than one interpretation." *Ante*, at 114 (concurring opinion). But instead of respecting the state high court's province to say what the State's Election Code means, THE CHIEF JUSTICE maintains that Florida's Supreme Court has veered so far from the ordinary practice of judicial review that what it did cannot properly be called judging. My colleagues have offered a reasonable construction of Florida's law. Their construction coincides with the view of one of Florida's seven Supreme Court justices. *Gore* v. *Harris*, 772 So. 2d 1243, 1264–1270 (Fla. 2000) (Wells, C. J., dissenting); *Palm Beach County Canvassing Bd.* v. *Harris*, 772 So. 2d 1273, 1291–1292 (Fla. 2000) (on remand) (confirming, 6 to 1, the construction of Florida law advanced in *Gore*). I might join THE CHIEF JUSTICE were it my commission to interpret Florida law. But disagreement with the Florida court's interpretation of its own State's law does not warrant the conclusion that the justices of that court have legislated. There is no cause here to believe that the members of Florida's high court have done less than "their mortal best to discharge their oath of office," *Sumner* v. *Mata*, 449 U.S. 539, 549 (1981), and no cause to upset their reasoned interpretation of Florida law.

This Court more than occasionally affirms statutory, and

even constitutional, interpretations with which it disagrees. For example, when reviewing challenges to administrative agencies' interpretations of laws they implement, we defer to the agencies unless their interpretation violates "the unambiguously expressed intent of Congress." *Chevron U.S.A. Inc. v. Natural Resources Defense Council, Inc.*, 467 U.S. 837, 843 (1984). We do so in the face of the declaration in Article I of the United States Constitution that "All legislative Powers herein granted shall be vested in a Congress of the United States." Surely the Constitution does not call upon us to pay more respect to a federal administrative agency's construction of federal law than to a state high court's interpretation of its own State's law. And not uncommonly, we let stand state-court interpretations of *federal* law with which we might disagree. Notably, in the habeas context, the Court adheres to the view that "there is 'no intrinsic reason why the fact that a man is a federal judge should make him more competent, or conscientious, or learned with respect to [federal law] than his neighbor in the state courthouse.'" *Stone* v. *Powell*, 428 U.S. 465, 494, n. 35 (1976) (quoting Bator, Finality in Criminal Law and Federal Habeas Corpus for State Prisoners, 76 Harv. L. Rev. 441, 509 (1963)); see *O'Dell* v. *Netherland*, 521 U.S. 151, 156 (1997) ("[T]he *Teague* doctrine validates reasonable, good-faith interpretations of existing precedents made by state courts even though they are shown to be contrary to later decisions.") (citing *Butler* v. *McKellar*, 494 U.S. 407, 414 (1990)); O'Connor, Trends in the Relationship Between the Federal and State Courts from the Perspective of a State Court Judge, 22 Wm. & Mary L. Rev. 801, 813 (1981) ("There is no reason to assume that state court judges cannot and will not provide a 'hospitable forum' in litigating federal constitutional questions.").

No doubt there are cases in which the proper application of federal law may hinge on interpretations of state law. Unavoidably, this Court must sometimes examine state law in order to protect federal rights. But we have dealt with such cases ever mindful of the full measure of respect we owe to interpretations of state law by a State's highest court. In the Contract Clause case, *General Motors Corp.* v. *Romein*, 503 U.S. 181 (1992), for example, we said that although "ultimately we are bound to decide for ourselves whether a contract was made," the Court "accord[s] respectful consideration and great weight to the views of the State's highest court." *Id.*, at 187 (citing *Indiana ex rel. Anderson* v. *Brand*, 303 U.S. 95, 100 (1938)). And in *Central Union Telephone Co.* v. *Edwardsville*, 269 U.S. 190 (1925), we upheld the Illinois Supreme Court's interpretation of a state waiver rule, even though that interpretation resulted in the forfeiture of federal constitutional rights. Refusing to supplant Illinois law with a federal definition of waiver, we explained that the state court's declaration "should bind us unless so unfair or unreasonable in its application to those asserting a federal right as to obstruct it." *Id.*, at 195.[1]

In deferring to state courts on matters of state law, we appropriately recognize that this Court acts as an "'outside[r]' lacking the common exposure to local law which comes from sitting in the jurisdiction." *Lehman Brothers* v. *Schein*, 416 U.S. 386, 391 (1974). That recognition has sometimes prompted us to resolve doubts about the meaning of state law by certifying issues to a State's highest court, even when federal rights are at stake. Cf. *Arizonans for Official English* v. *Arizona*, 520 U.S. 43,

---

1 See also *Lucas* v. *South Carolina Coastal Council*, 505 U.S. 1003, 1032, n. 18 (1992) (South Carolina could defend a regulatory taking "if an *objectively reasonable application* of relevant precedents [by its courts] would exclude . . . beneficial uses in the circumstances in which the land is presently found"); *Bishop* v. *Wood*, 426 U.S. 341, 344–345 (1976) (deciding whether North Carolina had created a property interest cognizable under the Due Process Clause by reference to state law as interpreted by the North Carolina Supreme Court). Similarly, in *Gurley* v. *Rhoden*, 421 U.S. 200 (1975), a gasoline retailer claimed that due process entitled him to deduct a state gasoline excise tax in computing the amount of his sales subject to a state sales tax, on the grounds that the legal incidence of the excise tax fell on his customers and that he acted merely as a collector of the tax. The Mississippi Supreme Court held that the legal incidence of the excise tax fell on petitioner. Observing that "a State's highest court is the final judicial arbiter of the meaning of state statutes," we said that "[w]hen a state court has made its own definitive determination as to the operating incidence, . . . [w]e give this finding great weight in determining the natural effect of a statute, and if it is consistent with the statute's reasonable interpretation it will be deemed conclusive." *Id.*, at 208 (citing *American Oil Co.* v. *Neill*, 380 U.S. 451, 455–456 (1965)).

79 (1997) ("Warnings against premature adjudication of constitutional questions bear heightened attention when a federal court is asked to invalidate a State's law, for the federal tribunal risks friction-generating error when it endeavors to construe a novel state Act not yet reviewed by the State's highest court."). Notwithstanding our authority to decide issues of state law underlying federal claims, we have used the certification device to afford state high courts an opportunity to inform us on matters of their own State's law because such restraint "helps build a cooperative judicial federalism." *Lehman Brothers*, 416 U.S., at 391.

Just last Term, in *Fiore* v. *White*, 528 U.S. 23 (1999), we took advantage of Pennsylvania's certification procedure. In that case, a state prisoner brought a federal habeas action claiming that the State had failed to prove an essential element of his charged offense in violation of the Due Process Clause. *Id.*, at 25–26. Instead of resolving the state-law question on which the federal claim depended, we certified the question to the Pennsylvania Supreme Court for that court to "help determine the proper state-law predicate for our determination of the federal constitutional questions raised." *Id.*, at 29; *id.*, at 28 (asking the Pennsylvania Supreme Court whether its recent interpretation of the statute under which Fiore was convicted "was always the statute's meaning, even at the time of Fiore's trial"). THE CHIEF JUSTICE's willingness to *reverse* the Florida Supreme Court's interpretation of Florida law in this case is at least in tension with our reluctance in *Fiore* even to interpret Pennsylvania law before seeking instruction from the Pennsylvania Supreme Court. I would have thought the "cautious approach" we counsel when federal courts address matters of state law, *Arizonans*, 520 U.S., at 77, and our commitment to "build[ing] cooperative judicial federalism," *Lehman Brothers*, 416 U.S., at 391, demanded greater restraint.

Rarely has this Court rejected outright an interpretation of state law by a state high court. *Fairfax's Devisee* v. *Hunter's Lessee*,

7 Cranch 603 (1813), *NAACP* v. *Alabama ex rel. Patterson*, 357 U.S. 449 (1958), and *Bouie* v. *City of Columbia*, 378 U.S. 347 (1964), cited by THE CHIEF JUSTICE, are three such rare instances. See *ante*, at 114–115, and n. 1. But those cases are embedded in historical contexts hardly comparable to the situation here. *Fairfax's Devisee*, which held that the Virginia Court of Appeals had misconstrued its own forfeiture laws to deprive a British subject of lands secured to him by federal treaties, occurred amidst vociferous States' rights attacks on the Marshall Court. G. Gunther & K. Sullivan, Constitutional Law 61–62 (13th ed. 1997). The Virginia court refused to obey this Court's *Fairfax's Devisee* mandate to enter judgment for the British subject's successor in interest. That refusal led to the Court's pathmarking decision in *Martin* v. *Hunter's Lessee*, 1 Wheat. 304 (1816). *Patterson*, a case decided three months after *Cooper* v. *Aaron*, 358 U.S. 1 (1958), in the face of Southern resistance to the civil rights movement, held that the Alabama Supreme Court had irregularly applied its own procedural rules to deny review of a contempt order against the NAACP arising from its refusal to disclose membership lists. We said that "our jurisdiction is not defeated if the nonfederal ground relied on by the state court is 'without any fair or substantial support.'" 357 U.S., at 455 (quoting *Ward* v. *Board of Commr's of Love Cty.*, 253 U.S. 17, 22 (1920)). *Bouie*, stemming from a lunch counter "sit-in" at the height of the civil rights movement, held that the South Carolina Supreme Court's construction of its trespass laws—criminalizing conduct not covered by the text of an otherwise clear statute— was "unforeseeable" and thus violated due process when applied retroactively to the petitioners. 378 U.S., at 350, 354.

THE CHIEF JUSTICE's casual citation of these cases might lead one to believe they are part of a larger collection of cases in which we said that the Constitution impelled us to train a skeptical eye on a state court's portrayal of state law. But one would be hard pressed, I think, to find additional cases that fit the mold. As JUSTICE BREYER convincingly explains, see *post*, at 149–152 (dissenting opinion), this case involves nothing close to the kind of recalcitrance by a state high court that warrants extraordinary action by this Court. The Florida Supreme Court concluded that counting every legal vote was the overriding concern of the Florida Legislature when it enacted the State's Election Code. The court surely should not be bracketed with state high courts of the Jim Crow South.

THE CHIEF JUSTICE says that Article II, by providing that state legislatures shall direct the manner of appointing electors, authorizes federal superintendence over the relationship between state courts and state legislatures, and licenses a departure from the usual deference we give to state-court interpretations of state law. *Ante*, at 115 (concurring opinion) ("To attach definitive weight to the pronouncement of a state court, when the very question at issue is whether the court has actually departed from the statutory meaning, would be to abdicate our responsibility to enforce the explicit requirements of Article II."). The Framers of our Constitution, however, understood that in a republican government, the judiciary would construe the legislature's enactments. See U.S. Const., Art. III; The Federalist No. 78 (A. Hamilton). In light of the constitutional guarantee to States of a "Republican Form of Government," U.S. Const., Art. IV, § 4, Article II can hardly be read to invite this Court to disrupt a State's republican regime. Yet THE CHIEF JUSTICE today would reach out to do just that. By holding that Article II requires our revision of a state court's construction of state laws in order to protect one organ of the State from another, THE CHIEF JUSTICE contradicts the basic principle that a State may organize itself as it sees fit. See, *e.g.*, *Gregory* v. *Ashcroft*, 501 U.S. 452, 460 (1991) ("Through the structure of its government, and the character of those who exercise government authority, a State defines itself as a sovereign."); *Highland Farms Dairy, Inc.* v. *Agnew*, 300 U.S. 608, 612 (1937) ("How power shall be distributed by a state among its governmental organs is commonly, if not always, a question for the state itself.").[2] Article II does not call for the scrutiny undertaken by this Court.

The extraordinary setting of this case has obscured the ordinary principle that dictates its proper resolution: Federal courts defer to a state high court's interpretations of the State's own law. This principle reflects the core of federalism, on which all agree. "The Framers split the atom of sovereignty. It was the genius of their idea that our citizens would have two political capacities, one state and one federal, each protected from incursion by the other." *Saenz* v. *Roe*, 526 U.S. 489, 504, n. 17 (1999) (citing *U.S. Term Limits, Inc.* v. *Thornton*, 514 U.S. 779, 838 (1995) (KENNEDY, J., concurring)). THE CHIEF JUSTICE's solicitude for the Florida Legislature comes at the expense of the more fundamental solicitude we owe to the legislature's sovereign. U.S. Const., Art. II, § 1, cl. 2 ("Each *State* shall appoint, in such Manner as the Legislature *thereof* may direct," the electors for President and Vice President (emphasis added)); *ante*, at 123–124 (STEVENS, J., dissenting).[3] Were the other Members of this Court as mindful as they generally are of our system of dual sovereignty, they would affirm the judgment of the Florida Supreme Court.

II

I agree with JUSTICE STEVENS that petitioners have not presented a substantial equal protection claim. Ideally, perfection would be the appropriate standard for judging the recount. But we live in an imperfect world, one in which thousands of

---

2 Even in the rare case in which a State's "manner" of making and construing laws might implicate a structural constraint, Congress, not this Court, is likely the proper governmental entity to enforce that constraint. See U.S. Const., Amdt. 12; 3 U. S. C. §§ 1–15; cf. *Ohio ex rel. Davis* v. *Hildebrant*, 241 U.S. 565, 569 (1916) (treating as a nonjusticiable political question whether use of a referendum to override a congressional districting plan enacted by the state legislature violates Art. I, § 4); *Luther* v. *Borden*, 7 How. 1, 42 (1849).

3 "[B]ecause the Framers recognized that state power and identity were essential parts of the federal balance, see The Federalist No. 39, the Constitution is solicitous of the prerogatives of the States, even in an otherwise sovereign federal province. The Constitution . . . grants States certain powers over the times, places, and manner of federal elections (subject to congressional revision), Art. I, § 4, cl.1 . . . , and allows States to appoint electors for the President, Art. II, § 1, cl. 2." *U.S. Term Limits, Inc.* v. *Thornton*, 514 U.S. 779, 841–842 (1995) (KENNEDY, J., concurring).

votes have not been counted. I cannot agree that the recount adopted by the Florida court, flawed as it may be, would yield a result any less fair or precise than the certification that preceded that recount. See, *e.g.*, *McDonald* v. *Board of Election Comm'rs of Chicago*, 394 U.S. 802, 809 (1969) (even in the context of the right to vote, the State is permitted to reform "one step at a time") (citing *Williamson* v. *Lee Optical of Okla., Inc.*, 348 U.S. 483, 489 (1955)).

Even if there were an equal protection violation, I would agree with JUSTICE STEVENS, JUSTICE SOUTER, and JUSTICE BREYER that the Court's concern about the December 12 date, *ante*, at 110–111, is misplaced. Time is short in part because of the Court's entry of a stay on December 9, several hours after an able circuit judge in Leon County had begun to superintend the recount process. More fundamentally, the Court's reluctance to let the recount go forward—despite its suggestion that "[t]he search for intent can be confined by specific rules designed to ensure uniform treatment," *ante*, at 106—ultimately turns on its own judgment about the practical realities of implementing a recount, not the judgment of those much closer to the process.

Equally important, as JUSTICE BREYER explains, *post*, at 155 (dissenting opinion), the December 12 date for bringing Florida's electoral votes into 3 U. S. C. § 5's safe harbor lacks the significance the Court assigns it. Were that date to pass, Florida would still be entitled to deliver electoral votes Congress must count unless both Houses find that the votes "ha[d] not been . . . regularly given." 3 U. S. C. § 15. The statute identifies other significant dates. See, *e.g.*, § 7 (specifying December 18 as the date electors "shall meet and give their votes"); § 12 (specifying "the fourth Wednesday in December"—this year, December 27—as the date on which Congress, if it has not received a State's electoral votes, shall request the state secretary of state to send a certified return immediately). But none of these dates has ultimate significance in light of Congress' detailed provisions for determining, on "the sixth day of January," the validity of electoral votes. § 15.

The Court assumes that time will not permit "orderly judicial review of any disputed matters that might arise." *Ante*, at 110. But no one has doubted the good faith and diligence with which Florida election officials, attorneys for all sides of this controversy, and the courts of law have performed their duties. Notably, the Florida Supreme Court has produced two substantial opinions within 29 hours of oral argument. In sum, the Court's conclusion that a constitutionally adequate recount is impractical is a prophecy the Court's own judgment will not allow to be tested. Such an untested prophecy should not decide the Presidency of the United States.

I dissent.

Gratz v. Bollinger, 539 U.S. 244 (2003)

Dissenting Opinion

*T*he University of Michigan included race among the factors it considered for undergraduate admissions, using a "points" system assigning extra points to applicants considered to be members of "underrepresented minorities." Jennifer Gratz and Patrick Hamacher, both white and both denied admission to the school despite being otherwise qualified. They argued that the university's admissions procedures discriminated against certain racial and ethnic groups.

The Court had to determine whether the racial preferences used by the University of Michigan's Office of Undergraduate Admissions violated the Equal Protection Clause of the Fourteenth Amendment and Title VI of the 1964 Civil Rights Act. Chief Justice William H. Rehnquist, writing on behalf of a 6-3 majority, determined that yes, the school was in violation. Justice Ginsburg, in a separate dissent, argued the policies did not violate the Equal Protection Clause because there was no evidence they attempted to limit enrollment of any particular race.

GRATZ ET AL.

v.

BOLLINGER ET AL.
CERTIORARI BEFORE JUDGMENT TO THE UNITED
STATES COURT OF APPEALS FOR THE SIXTH
CIRCUIT
[June 23, 2003]

JUSTICE GINSBURG, with whom JUSTICE SOUTER joins, dissenting. JUSTICE BREYER joins Part I of this opinion.

I

Educational institutions, the Court acknowledges, are not barred from any and all consideration of race when making admissions decisions. *Ante*, at 268; see *Grutter* v. *Bollinger*, *post*, at 326–333. But the Court once again maintains that the same standard of review controls judicial inspection of all official race classifications. *Ante*, at 270 (quoting *Adarand Constructors, Inc.* v. *Peña*, 515 U.S. 200, 224 (1995); *Richmond* v. *J. A. Croson Co.*, 488 U.S. 469, 494 (1989) (plurality opinion)). This insistence on "consistency," *Adarand*, 515 U.S., at 224, would be fitting were our Nation free of the vestiges of rank discrimination long reinforced by law, see *id.*, at 274–276, and n. 8 (GINSBURG, J., dissenting). But we are not far distant from an overtly discriminatory past, and the effects of centuries of law-sanctioned inequality remain painfully evident in our communities and schools.

In the wake "of a system of racial caste only recently ended," *id.*, at 273 (GINSBURG, J., dissenting), large disparities endure. Unemployment,[1] poverty,[2] and access to health care[3] vary disproportionately by race. Neighborhoods and schools remain racially divided.[4] African-American and Hispanic children are

---

1 See, *e.g.*, U.S. Dept. of Commerce, Bureau of Census, Statistical Abstract of the United States: 2002, p. 368 (2002) (Table 562) (hereinafter Statistical Abstract) (unemployment rate among whites was 3.7% in 1999, 3.5% in 2000, and 4.2% in 2001; during those years, the unemployment rate among African-Americans was 8.0%, 7.6%, and 8.7%, respectively; among Hispanics, 6.4%, 5.7%, and 6.6%).

2 See, *e.g.*, U.S. Dept of Commerce, Bureau of Census, Poverty in the United States: 2000, p. 291 (2001) (Table A) (In 2000, 7.5% of non-Hispanic whites, 22.1% of African-Americans, 10.8% of Asian-Americans, and 21.2% of Hispanics were living in poverty.); S. Staveteig & A. Wigton, Racial and Ethnic Disparities: Key Findings from the National Survey of America's Families 1 (Urban Institute Report B–5, Feb. 2000) ("Blacks, Hispanics, and Native Americans . . . each have poverty rates almost twice as high as Asians and almost three times as high as whites.").

3 See, *e.g.*, U.S. Dept. of Commerce, Bureau of Census, Health Insurance Coverage: 2000, p. 391 (2001) (Table A) (In 2000, 9.7% of non-Hispanic whites were without health insurance, as compared to 18.5% of African-Americans, 18.0% of Asian-Americans, and 32.0% of Hispanics.); Waidmann & Rajan, Race and Ethnic Disparities in Health Care Access and Utilization: An Examination of State Variation, 57 Med. Care Res. and Rev. 55, 56 (2000) ("On average, Latinos and African Americans have both worse health and worse access to effective health care than do non-Hispanic whites . . . .").

4 See, *e.g.*, U.S. Dept. of Commerce, Bureau of Census, Racial and Ethnic Residential Segregation in the United States: 1980–2000 (2002) (documenting residential segregation); E. Frankenberg, C. Lee, & G. Orfield, A Multiracial Society with Segregated Schools: Are

all too often educated in poverty-stricken and underperforming institutions.[5] Adult African-Americans and Hispanics generally earn less than whites with equivalent levels of education.[6] Equally credentialed job applicants receive different receptions depending on their race.[7] Irrational prejudice is still encountered in real estate markets[8] and consumer transactions.[9] "Bias both conscious and unconscious, reflecting traditional and unexamined habits of thought, keeps up barriers that must come down if equal opportunity and nondiscrimination are ever genuinely to become this country's law and practice." *Id.*, at 274 (GINSBURG, J., dissenting); see generally Krieger, Civil Rights Perestroika:

We Losing the Dream? 4 (Jan. 2003), http://www.civilrightsproject.harvard.edu/research/reseg03/AreWeLosingtheDream.pdf (all Internet materials as visited June 2, 2003, and available in Clerk of Court's case file) ("[W]hites are the most segregated group in the nation's public schools; they attend schools, on average, where eighty percent of the student body is white."); *id.*, at 28 ("[A]lmost three-fourths of black and Latino students attend schools that are predominantly minority . . . . More than one in six black children attend a school that is 99–100% minority . . . . One in nine Latino students attend virtually all minority schools.").

5 See, *e.g.*, Ryan, Schools, Race, and Money, 109 Yale L. J. 249, 273–274 (1999) ("Urban public schools are attended primarily by African-American and Hispanic students"; students who attend such schools are disproportionately poor, score poorly on standardized tests, and are far more likely to drop out than students who attend nonurban schools.).

6 See, *e.g.*, Statistical Abstract 140 (Table 211).

7 See, *e.g.*, Holzer, Career Advancement Prospects and Strategies for Low-Wage Minority Workers, in Low-Wage Workers in the New Economy 228 (R. Kazis & M. Miller eds. 2001) ("[I]n studies that have sent matched pairs of minority and white applicants with apparently equal credentials to apply for jobs, whites routinely get more interviews and job offers than either black or Hispanic applicants."); M. Bertrand & S. Mullainathan, Are Emily and Brendan More Employable than Lakisha and Jamal?: A Field Experiment on Labor Market Discrimination (Nov. 18, 2002), http://gsb.uchicago.edu/pdf/bertrand.pdf; Mincy, The Urban Institute Audit Studies: Their Research and Policy Context, in Clear and Convincing Evidence: Measurement of Discrimination in America 165–186 (M. Fix & R. Struyk eds. 1993).

8 See, *e.g.*, M. Turner et al., Discrimination in Metropolitan Housing Markets: National Results from Phase I HDS 2000, pp. i, iii (Nov. 2002), http://www.huduser.org/Publications/pdf/Phase1_Report.pdf (paired testing in which "two individuals—one minority and the other white—pose as otherwise identical homeseekers, and visit real estate or rental agents to inquire about the availability of advertised housing units" revealed that "discrimination still persists in both rental and sales markets of large metropolitan areas nationwide"); M. Turner & F. Skidmore, Mortgage Lending Discrimination: A Review of Existing Evidence 2 (1999) (existing research evidence shows that minority homebuyers in the United States "face discrimination from mortgage lending institutions.").

9 See, *e.g.*, Ayres, Further Evidence of Discrimination in New Car Negotiations and Estimates of its Cause, 94 Mich. L. Rev. 109, 109–110 (1995) (study in which 38 testers negotiated the purchase of more than 400 automobiles confirmed earlier finding "that dealers systematically offer lower prices to white males than to other tester types").

Intergroup Relations After Affirmative Action, 86 Calif. L. Rev. 1251, 1276–1291 (1998).

The Constitution instructs all who act for the government that they may not "deny to any person . . . the equal protection of the laws." Amdt. 14, § 1. In implementing this equality instruction, as I see it, government decisionmakers may properly distinguish between policies of exclusion and inclusion. See *Wygant* v. *Jackson Bd. of Ed.*, 476 U.S. 267, 316 (1986) (STEVENS, J., dissenting). Actions designed to burden groups long denied full citizenship stature are not sensibly ranked with measures taken to hasten the day when entrenched discrimination and its after-effects have been extirpated. See Carter, When Victims Happen To Be Black, 97 Yale L. J. 420, 433–434 (1988) ("[T]o say that two centuries of struggle for the most basic of civil rights have been mostly about freedom from racial categorization rather than freedom from racial oppressio[n] is to trivialize the lives and deaths of those who have suffered under racism. To pretend . . . that the issue presented in [*Regents of Univ. of Cal.* v. *Bakke*, 438 U.S. 265 (1978)] was the same as the issue in [*Brown* v. *Board of Education*, 347 U.S. 483 (1954)] is to pretend that history never happened and that the present doesn't exist.").

Our jurisprudence ranks race a "suspect" category, "not because [race] is inevitably an impermissible classification, but because it is one which usually, to our national shame, has been drawn for the purpose of maintaining racial inequality." *Norwalk Core* v. *Norwalk Redevelopment Agency*, 395 F. 2d 920, 931–932 (CA2 1968) (footnote omitted). But where race is considered "for the purpose of achieving equality," *id.*, at 932, no automatic proscription is in order. For, as insightfully explained: "The Constitution is both colorblind and color conscious. To avoid conflict with the equal protection clause, a classification that denies a benefit, causes harm, or imposes a burden must not be based on race. In that sense, the Constitution is color blind. But the Constitution is color conscious to prevent discrimination being perpetuated and to undo the effects of past discrimination." *United States* v. *Jefferson County Bd. of Ed.*, 372 F. 2d 836, 876 (CA5 1966) (Wisdom, J.); see Wechsler, The Nationalization of Civil Liberties and Civil Rights, Supp. to 12 Tex. Q. 10, 23 (1968) (*Brown* may be seen as disallowing racial classifications that "impl[y] an invidious assessment" while allowing such classifications when "not invidious in implication" but advanced to "correct inequalities"). Contemporary human rights documents draw just this line; they distinguish between policies of oppression and measures designed to accelerate *de facto* equality. See *Grutter, post*, at 344 (GINSBURG, J., concurring) (citing the United Nations–initiated Conventions on the Elimination of All Forms of Racial Discrimination and on the Elimination of All Forms of Discrimination against Women).

The mere assertion of a laudable governmental purpose, of course, should not immunize a race-conscious measure from careful judicial inspection. See *Jefferson County*, 372 F. 2d, at 876 ("The criterion is the relevancy of color to a legitimate governmental purpose."). Close review is needed "to ferret out classifications in reality malign, but masquerading as benign," *Adarand*, 515 U.S., at 275 (GINSBURG, J., dissenting), and to "ensure that preferences are not so large as to trammel unduly upon the opportunities of others or interfere too harshly with legitimate expectations of persons in once-preferred groups," *id.*, at 276.

II

Examining in this light the admissions policy employed by the University of Michigan's College of Literature, Science, and the Arts (College), and for the reasons well stated by JUSTICE SOUTER, I see no constitutional infirmity. See *ante*, at 293–298 (dissenting opinion). Like other top-ranking institutions, the College has many more applicants for admission than it can accommodate in an entering class. App. to Pet. for Cert. 108a. Every applicant admitted under the current plan, petitioners do not here dispute, is qualified to attend the College. *Id.*, at 111a. The racial and ethnic groups to which the College accords special consideration (African-Americans, Hispanics, and Native-Americans) historically have been relegated to inferior status by law and social practice; their members continue to experience class-based discrimination to this day, see *supra*, at 298–301. There is no suggestion that the College adopted its current policy in order to limit or decrease enrollment by any particular racial or ethnic group, and no seats are reserved on the basis of race. See Brief for Respondent Bollinger et al. 10; Tr. of Oral Arg. 41–42 (in the range between 75 and 100 points, the review committee may look at applications individually and ignore the points). Nor has there been any demonstration that the College's program unduly constricts admissions opportunities for students who do not receive special consideration based on race. Cf. Liu, The Causation Fallacy: *Bakke* and the Basic Arithmetic of Selective Admissions, 100 Mich. L. Rev. 1045, 1049 (2002) ("In any admissions process where applicants greatly outnumber admittees, and where white applicants greatly outnumber minority applicants, substantial preferences for minority applicants will not significantly diminish the odds of admission facing white applicants.").[10]

---

10 The United States points to the "percentage plans" used in California, Florida, and Texas as one example of a "race-neutral alternativ[e]" that would permit the College to enroll meaningful numbers of minority students. Brief for United States as *Amicus Curiae* 14; see U.S. Commission on Civil Rights, Beyond Percentage Plans: The Challenge of Equal Opportunity in Higher Education 1 (Nov. 2002), http://www.usccr.gov/pubs/percent2/percent2.pdf (percentage plans guarantee admission to state universities for a fixed percentage of the top students from high schools in the State). Calling such 10% or 20% plans "race-neutral" seems to me disingenuous, for they "unquestionably were adopted with the specific purpose of increasing representation of African-Americans and Hispanics in the public higher education system." Brief for Respondent Bollinger et al. 44; see C. Horn & S. Flores, Percent Plans in College Admissions: A Comparative Analysis of Three States' Experiences 14–19 (2003), http://www.civilrightsproject.harvard.edu/research/affirmativeaction/tristate.pdf. Percentage plans depend for their effectiveness on continued racial segregation at the secondary school level: They can ensure significant minority enrollment in universities only if the majority-minority high school population is large enough to guarantee that, in many schools, most of the students in the top 10% or 20% are minorities. Moreover, because such plans link college admission to a single criterion—high school class rank—they create perverse incentives. They encourage parents to keep their children in low-performing segregated schools, and discourage students from taking challenging classes that might lower their grade point averages. See Selingo, What States Aren't Saying About the 'X-Percent Solution,' Chronicle of Higher Education, June 2, 2000, p. A31. And even if percentage plans could boost the sheer numbers of minority enrollees at the undergraduate level, they do not touch enrollment in graduate and professional schools.

The stain of generations of racial oppression is still visible in our society, see Krieger, 86 Calif. L. Rev., at 1253, and the determination to hasten its removal remains vital. One can reasonably anticipate, therefore, that colleges and universities will seek to maintain their minority enrollment—and the networks and opportunities thereby opened to minority graduates—whether or not they can do so in full candor through adoption of affirmative action plans of the kind here at issue. Without recourse to such plans, institutions of higher education may resort to camouflage. For example, schools may encourage applicants to write of their cultural traditions in the essays they submit, or to indicate whether English is their second language. Seeking to improve their chances for admission, applicants may highlight the minority group associations to which they belong, or the Hispanic surnames of their mothers or grandparents. In turn, teachers' recommendations may emphasize who a student is as much as what he or she has accomplished. See, *e.g.*, Steinberg, Using Synonyms for Race, College Strives for Diversity, N. Y. Times, Dec. 8, 2002, section 1, p. 1, col. 3 (describing admissions process at Rice University); cf. Brief for United States as *Amicus Curiae* 14–15 (suggesting institutions could consider, *inter alia*, "a history of overcoming disadvantage," "reputation and location of high school," and "individual outlook as reflected by essays"). If honesty is the best policy, surely Michigan's accurately described, fully disclosed College affirmative action program is preferable to achieving similar numbers through winks, nods, and disguises.[11]

* * *

For the reasons stated, I would affirm the judgment of the District Court.

---

11 Contrary to the Court's contention, I do not suggest "changing the Constitution so that it conforms to the conduct of the universities." *Ante*, at 275, n. 22. In my view, the Constitution, properly interpreted, permits government officials to respond openly to the continuing importance of race. See *supra*, at 301–302. Among constitutionally permissible options, those that candidly disclose their consideration of race seem to me preferable to those that conceal it.

Gonzales v. Carhart, 550 U.S. 124 (2007)

Dissenting Opinion

*C*ongress's 2003 Partial-Birth Abortion Ban outlawed the controversial late-term abortion practice of "intact D&E" ("dilation and evacuation"), in which the death of the fetus occurs when "the entire fetal head . . . or . . . any part of the fetal trunk past the navel is outside the body of the mother." Dr. Leroy Carhart, and other physicians who performed such procedures, sued to stop the act from going into effect, arguing that it infringed on personal liberty protections the court had previously upheld in Planned Parenthood v. Casey, and that it lacked an exception for protecting the health of the mother, which would be considered unconstitutional in light of the Court's decision in Stenberg v. Carhart.

The Court had to determine whether the ban on partial-birth abortion represented a violation of personal liberty protected by the Fifth Amendment of the Constitution because it lacked an exception for partial-birth abortions when necessary to protect the mother's health. In a 5–4 ruling written by Justice Anthony Kennedy, the Court upheld the ban, stating that it did not impose an undue burden on the right to an abortion and was not constitutionally vague. In her dissent, Justice Ginsburg argued that the ruling was not consistent with the precedents set in Casey and Stenberg, and staunchly defends her views on the right to abortion.

Nos. 05-380 and 05-1382
ALBERTO R. GONZALES, ATTORNEY GENERAL,
PETITIONER
05-380 v.
LEROY CARHART et al.
ON WRIT OF CERTIORARI TO THE UNITED STATES
COURT OF APPEALS FOR THE EIGHTH CIRCUIT

ALBERTO R. GONZALES, ATTORNEY GENERAL,
PETITIONER
05-1382 v.
PLANNED PARENTHOOD FEDERATION OF
AMERICA, INC., et al.
ON WRIT OF CERTIORARI TO THE UNITED STATES
COURT OF APPEALS FOR THE NINTH CIRCUIT
[April 18, 2007]

Justice Ginsburg, with whom Justice Stevens, Justice Souter, and Justice Breyer join, dissenting.

In *Planned Parenthood of Southeastern Pa.* v. *Casey*, 505 U.S. 833, 844 (1992), the Court declared that "[l]iberty finds no refuge in a jurisprudence of doubt." There was, the Court said, an "imperative" need to dispel doubt as to "the meaning and reach" of the Court's 7-to-2 judgment, rendered nearly two decades earlier in *Roe* v. *Wade*, 410 U.S. 113 (1973). 505 U.S., at 845. Responsive to that need, the Court endeavored to provide secure guidance to "[s]tate and federal courts as well as legislatures throughout the Union," by defining "the rights of the woman and the legitimate authority of the State respecting the termination of pregnancies by abortion procedures." *Ibid.*

Taking care to speak plainly, the *Casey* Court restated and reaffirmed *Roe*'s essential holding. 505 U.S., at 845–846. First, the Court addressed the type of abortion regulation permissible prior to fetal viability. It recognized "the right of the woman to choose to have an abortion before viability and to obtain it

176

without undue interference from the State." *Id.*, at 846. Second, the Court acknowledged "the State's power to restrict abortions *after fetal viability*, if the law contains exceptions for pregnancies which endanger the woman's life or *health*." *Ibid.* (emphasis added). Third, the Court confirmed that "the State has legitimate interests from the outset of the pregnancy in protecting the health of the woman and the life of the fetus that may become a child." *Ibid.* (emphasis added).

In reaffirming *Roe*, the *Casey* Court described the centrality of "the decision whether to bear . . . a child," *Eisenstadt* v. *Baird*, 405 U.S. 438, 453 (1972), to a woman's "dignity and autonomy," her "personhood" and "destiny," her "conception of . . . her place in society." 505 U.S., at 851–852. Of signal importance here, the *Casey* Court stated with unmistakable clarity that state regulation of access to abortion procedures, even after viability, must protect "the health of the woman." *Id.*, at 846.

Seven years ago, in *Stenberg* v. *Carhart*, 530 U.S. 914 (2000), the Court invalidated a Nebraska statute criminalizing the performance of a medical procedure that, in the political arena, has been dubbed "partial-birth abortion."[1] With fidelity to the *Roe-Casey* line of precedent, the Court held the Nebraska statute unconstitutional in part because it lacked the requisite protection for the preservation of a woman's health. *Stenberg*, 530 U.S., at 930; cf. *Ayotte* v. *Planned Parenthood of Northern New Eng.*, 546 U.S. 320, 327 (2006).

Today's decision is alarming. It refuses to take *Casey* and *Stenberg* seriously. It tolerates, indeed applauds, federal intervention to ban nationwide a procedure found necessary and proper in certain cases by the American College of Obstetricians and Gynecologists (ACOG). It blurs the line, firmly drawn in *Casey*, between previability and postviability abortions. And, for the

---

1 The term "partial-birth abortion" is neither recognized in the medical literature nor used by physicians who perform second-trimester abortions. See *Planned Parenthood Federation of Am.* v. *Ashcroft*, 320 F. Supp. 2d 957, 964 (ND Cal. 2004), aff'd, 435 F. 3d 1163 (CA9 2006). The medical community refers to the procedure as either dilation & extraction (D&X) or intact dilation and evacuation (intact D&E). See, *e.g.*, *ante*, at 136; *Stenberg* v. *Carhart*, 530 U.S. 914, 927 (2000).

first time since *Roe*, the Court blesses a prohibition with no exception safeguarding a woman's health.

I dissent from the Court's disposition. Retreating from prior rulings that abortion restrictions cannot be imposed absent an exception safeguarding a woman's health, the Court upholds an Act that surely would not survive under the close scrutiny that previously attended state-decreed limitations on a woman's reproductive choices.

I

A

As *Casey* comprehended, at stake in cases challenging abortion restrictions is a woman's "control over her [own] destiny." 505 U.S., at 869 (plurality opinion). See also *id.*, at 852 (majority opinion).[2] "There was a time, not so long ago," when women were "regarded as the center of home and family life, with attendant special responsibilities that precluded full and independent legal status under the Constitution." *Id.*, at 896–897 (quoting *Hoyt* v. *Florida*, 368 U.S. 57, 62 (1961)). Those views, this Court made clear in *Casey*, "are no longer consistent with our understanding of the family, the individual, or the Constitution." 505 U.S., at 897. Women, it is now acknowledged, have the talent, capacity, and right "to participate equally in the economic and social life of the Nation." *Id.*, at 856. Their ability to realize their full potential, the Court recognized, is intimately connected to "their ability to control their reproductive lives." *Ibid.* Thus, legal challenges to undue restrictions on abortion procedures do not seek to vindicate some generalized notion of privacy; rather, they center on a woman's autonomy to determine her life's course, and thus to enjoy equal citizenship stature. See, *e.g.*, Siegel, Reasoning from the Body: A Historical Perspective on Abortion Regulation and Questions of Equal Protection, 44 Stan. L. Rev. 261 (1992);

---

2 *Planned Parenthood of Southeastern Pa.* v. *Casey*, 505 U.S. 833, 851–852 (1992), described more precisely than did *Roe* v. *Wade*, 410 U.S. 113 (1973), the impact of abortion restrictions on women's liberty. *Roe*'s focus was in considerable measure on "vindicat[ing] the right of the physician to administer medical treatment according to his professional judgment." *Id.*, at 165.

Law, Rethinking Sex and the Constitution, 132 U. Pa. L. Rev. 955, 1002–1028 (1984).

In keeping with this comprehension of the right to reproductive choice, the Court has consistently required that laws regulating abortion, at any stage of pregnancy and in all cases, safeguard a woman's health. See, *e.g.*, *Ayotte*, 546 U.S., at 327–328 ("[O]ur precedents hold . . . that a State may not restrict access to abortions that are necessary, in appropriate medical judgment, for the preservation of the life or health of the [woman]." (quoting Casey, 505 U.S., at 879 (plurality opinion))); *Stenberg*, 530 U.S., at 930 ("Since the law requires a health exception in order to validate even a postviability abortion regulation, it at a minimum requires the same in respect to previability regulation."). See also *Thornburgh* v. *American College of Obstetricians and Gynecologists*, 476 U.S. 747, 768–769 (1986) (invalidating a post-viability abortion regulation for "fail[ure] to require that [a pregnant woman's] health be the physician's paramount consideration").

We have thus ruled that a State must avoid subjecting women to health risks not only where the pregnancy itself creates danger, but also where state regulation forces women to resort to less safe methods of abortion. See *Planned Parenthood of Central Mo.* v. *Danforth*, 428 U.S. 52, 79 (1976) (holding unconstitutional a ban on a method of abortion that "force[d] a woman . . . to terminate her pregnancy by methods more dangerous to her health"). See also *Stenberg*, 530 U.S., at 931 ("[Our cases] make clear that a risk to . . . women's health is the same whether it happens to arise from regulating a particular method of abortion, or from barring abortion entirely."). Indeed, we have applied the rule that abortion regulation must safeguard a woman's health to the particular procedure at issue here—intact dilation and evacuation (intact D&E).[3]

---

3 Dilation and evacuation (D&E) is the most frequently used abortion procedure during the second trimester of pregnancy; intact D&E is a variant of the D&E procedure. See *ante*, at 135, 137; *Stenberg*, 530 U.S., at 924, 927; *Planned Parenthood*, 320 F. Supp. 2d, at 966. Second-trimester abortions (i.e., midpregnancy, previability abortions) are, however, relatively

In *Stenberg*, we expressly held that a statute banning intact
D&E was unconstitutional in part because it lacked a health
exception. 530 U.S., at 930, 937. We noted that there existed a
"division of medical opinion" about the relative safety of intact
D&E, *id.*, at 937, but we made clear that as long as "substantial
medical authority supports the proposition that banning a particular abortion procedure could endanger women's health," a
health exception is required, *id.*, at 938. We explained:

> "The word 'necessary' in *Casey*'s phrase 'necessary, in
> appropriate medical judgment, for the preservation
> of the life or health of the [pregnant woman],'
> cannot refer to an absolute necessity or to absolute
> proof. Medical treatments and procedures are often
> considered appropriate (or inappropriate) in light
> of estimated comparative health risks (and health
> benefits) in particular cases. Neither can that phrase
> require unanimity of medical opinion. Doctors
> often differ in their estimation of comparative health
> risks and appropriate treatment. And *Casey*'s words
> 'appropriate medical judgment' must embody the

uncommon. Between 85 and 90 percent of all abortions performed in the United States take
place during the first three months of pregnancy. See *ante*, at 134. See also *Stenberg*, 530 U.S.,
at 923–927; *National Abortion Federation* v. *Ashcroft*, 330 F. Supp. 2d 436, 464 (SDNY 2004),
aff'd sub nom. *National Abortion Federation* v. *Gonzales*, 437 F. 3d 278 (CA2 2006); *Planned
Parenthood*, 320 F. Supp. 2d, at 960, and n. 4.

Adolescents and indigent women, research suggests, are more likely than other women to
have difficulty obtaining an abortion during the first trimester of pregnancy. Minors may be
unaware they are pregnant until relatively late in pregnancy, while poor women's financial
constraints are an obstacle to timely receipt of services. See Finer, Frohwirth, Dauphinee, Singh,
& Moore, Timing of Steps and Reasons for Delays in Obtaining Abortions in the United
States, 74 Contraception 334, 341–343 (2006). See also Drey et al., Risk Factors Associated
with Presenting for Abortion in the Second Trimester, 107 Obstetrics & Gynecology 128, 133
(Jan. 2006) (concluding that women who have second-trimester abortions typically discover
relatively late that they are pregnant). Severe fetal anomalies and health problems confronting
the pregnant woman are also causes of second-trimester abortions; many such conditions
cannot be diagnosed or do not develop until the second trimester. See, *e.g.*, Finer, *supra*,
at 344; F. Cunningham et al., Williams Obstetrics 242, 290, 328–329 (22d ed. 2005); cf.
Schechtman, Gray, Baty, & Rothman, Decision-Making for Termination of Pregnancies with
Fetal Anomalies: Analysis of 53,000 Pregnancies, 99 Obstetrics & Gynecology 216, 220–221
(Feb. 2002) (nearly all women carrying fetuses with the most serious central nervous system
anomalies chose to abort their pregnancies).

judicial need to tolerate responsible differences of medical opinion . . . ." *Id.*, at 937 (citation omitted).

Thus, we reasoned, division in medical opinion "at most means uncertainty, a factor that signals the presence of risk, not its absence." *Ibid.* "[A] statute that altogether forbids [intact D&E] . . . consequently must contain a health exception." *Id.*, at 938. See also *id.*, at 948 (O'Connor, J., concurring) ("Th[e] lack of a health exception necessarily renders the statute unconstitutional.").

B

In 2003, a few years after our ruling in *Stenberg*, Congress passed the Partial-Birth Abortion Ban Act—without an exception for women's health. See 18 U. S. C. § 1531(a) (2000 ed., Supp. IV).[4] The congressional findings on which the Partial-Birth Abortion Ban Act rests do not withstand inspection, as the lower courts have determined and this Court is obliged to concede. *Ante*, at 165–166. See *National Abortion Federation* v. *Ashcroft*, 330 F. Supp. 2d 436, 482 (SDNY 2004) ("Congress did not . . . carefully consider the evidence before arriving at its findings."), aff'd *sub nom. National Abortion Federation* v. *Gonzales*, 437 F. 3d 278 (CA2 2006). See also *Planned Parenthood Federation of Am.* v. *Ashcroft*, 320 F. Supp. 2d 957, 1019 (ND Cal. 2004) ("[N]one of the six physicians who testified before Congress had ever performed an intact D&E. Several did not provide abortion services at all; and one was not even an obgyn. . . . [T]he oral testimony before Congress was not only unbalanced, but intentionally polemic."), aff'd, 435 F. 3d 1163 (CA9 2006); *Carhart* v. *Ashcroft*, 331 F. Supp. 2d 805, 1011 (Neb. 2004) ("Congress arbitrarily relied upon the opinions of doctors who claimed to have no (or very little) recent and relevant experience with

4 The Act's sponsors left no doubt that their intention was to nullify our ruling in *Stenberg*, 530 U.S. 914. See, *e.g.*, 149 Cong. Rec. 5731 (2003) (statement of Sen. Santorum) ("Why are we here? We are here because the Supreme Court defended the indefensible. . . . We have responded to the Supreme Court."). See also 148 Cong. Rec. 14273 (2002) (statement of Rep. Linder) (rejecting proposition that Congress has "no right to legislate a ban on this horrible practice because the Supreme Court says [it] cannot").

surgical abortions, and disregarded the views of doctors who had significant and relevant experience with those procedures."), aff'd, 413 F. 3d 791 (CA8 2005).

Many of the Act's recitations are incorrect. See *ante*, at 165–166. For example, Congress determined that no medical schools provide instruction on intact D&E. § 2(14)(B), 117 Stat. 1204, notes following 18 U. S. C. § 1531 (2000 ed., Supp. IV), p. 769, ¶ (14)(B) (Congressional Findings). But in fact, numerous leading medical schools teach the procedure. See *Planned Parenthood*, 320 F. Supp. 2d, at 1029; *National Abortion Federation*, 330 F. Supp. 2d, at 479. See also Brief for ACOG as *Amicus Curiae* 18 ("Among the schools that now teach the intact variant are Columbia, Cornell, Yale, New York University, Northwestern, University of Pittsburgh, University of Pennsylvania, University of Rochester, and University of Chicago.").

More important, Congress claimed there was a medical consensus that the banned procedure is never necessary. Congressional Findings ¶ (1). But the evidence "very clearly demonstrate[d] the opposite." *Planned Parenthood*, 320 F. Supp. 2d, at 1025. See also *Carhart*, 331 F. Supp. 2d, at 1008–1009 ("[T]here was no evident consensus in the record that Congress compiled. There was, however, a substantial body of medical opinion presented to Congress in opposition. If anything . . . the congressional record establishes that there was a 'consensus' in favor of the banned procedure."); *National Abortion Federation*, 330 F. Supp. 2d, at 488 ("The congressional record itself undermines [Congress'] finding" that there is a medical consensus that intact D&E "is never medically necessary and should be prohibited." (internal quotation marks omitted)).

Similarly, Congress found that "[t]here is no credible medical evidence that partial-birth abortions are safe or are safer than other abortion procedures." Congressional Findings (14)(B), in notes following 18 U. S. C. § 1531 (2000 ed., Supp. IV), p. 769. But the congressional record includes letters from numerous individual physicians stating that pregnant women's health would be jeopardized under the Act, as well as statements from nine professional associations, including ACOG, the American Public Health Association, and the California Medical Association, attesting that intact D&E carries meaningful safety advantages over other methods. See *National Abortion Federation*, 330 F. Supp. 2d, at 490. See also *Planned Parenthood*, 320 F. Supp. 2d, at 1021 ("Congress in its findings . . . chose to disregard the statements by ACOG and other medical organizations."). No comparable medical groups supported the ban. In fact, "all of the government's own witnesses disagreed with many of the specific congressional findings." *Id.*, at 1024.

C

In contrast to Congress, the District Courts made findings after full trials at which all parties had the opportunity to present their best evidence. The courts had the benefit of "much more extensive medical and scientific evidence . . . concerning the safety and necessity of intact D&Es." *Planned Parenthood*, 320 F. Supp. 2d, at 1014; cf. *National Abortion Federation*, 330 F. Supp. 2d, at 482 (District Court "heard more evidence during its trial than Congress heard over the span of eight years.").

During the District Court trials, "numerous" "extraordinarily accomplished" and "very experienced" medical experts explained that, in certain circumstances and for certain women, intact D&E is safer than alternative procedures and necessary to protect women's health. *Carhart*, 331 F. Supp. 2d, at 1024–1027; see *Planned Parenthood*, 320 F. Supp. 2d, at 1001 ("[A]ll of the doctors who actually perform intact D&Es concluded that in their opinion and clinical judgment, intact D&Es remain the safest option for certain individual women under certain individual health circumstances, and are significantly safer for these women than other abortion techniques, and are thus medically necessary."); cf. *ante*, at 161 ("Respondents presented evidence that intact D&E may be the safest method of abortion, for reasons similar to those adduced in *Stenberg*.").

According to the expert testimony plaintiffs introduced, the safety advantages of intact D&E are marked for women with certain medical conditions, for example, uterine scarring, bleeding disorders, heart disease, or compromised immune systems. See *Carhart*, 331 F. Supp. 2d, at 924–929, 1026–1027; *National Abortion Federation*, 330 F. Supp. 2d, at 472–473; *Planned Parenthood*, 320 F. Supp. 2d, at 992–994, 1001. Further, plaintiffs' experts testified that intact D&E is significantly safer for women with certain pregnancy-related conditions, such as placenta previa and accreta, and for women carrying fetuses with certain abnormalities, such as severe hydrocephalus. See *Carhart*, 331 F. Supp. 2d, at 924, 1026–1027; *National Abortion Federation*, 330 F. Supp. 2d, at 473–474; *Planned Parenthood*, 320 F. Supp. 2d, at 992–994, 1001. See also *Stenberg*, 530 U.S., at 929; Brief for ACOG as *Amicus Curiae* 2, 13–16.

Intact D&E, plaintiffs' experts explained, provides safety benefits over D&E by dismemberment for several reasons: First, intact D&E minimizes the number of times a physician must insert instruments through the cervix and into the uterus, and thereby reduces the risk of trauma to, and perforation of, the cervix and uterus—the most serious complication associated with nonintact D&E. See *Carhart*, 331 F. Supp. 2d, at 923–928, 1025; *National Abortion Federation*, 330 F. Supp. 2d, at 471; *Planned Parenthood*, 320 F. Supp. 2d, at 982, 1001. Second, removing the fetus intact, instead of dismembering it in utero, decreases the likelihood that fetal tissue will be retained in the uterus, a condition that can cause infection, hemorrhage, and infertility. See *Carhart*, 331 F. Supp. 2d, at 923–928, 1025–1026; *National Abortion Federation*, 330 F. Supp. 2d, at 472; *Planned Parenthood*, 320 F. Supp. 2d, at 1001. Third, intact D&E diminishes the chances of exposing the patient's tissues to sharp bony fragments sometimes resulting from dismemberment of the fetus. See *Carhart*, 331 F. Supp. 2d, at 923–928, 1026; *National Abortion Federation*, 330 F. Supp. 2d, at 471; *Planned Parenthood*, 320 F. Supp. 2d, at 1001. Fourth, intact

D&E takes less operating time than D&E by dismemberment, and thus may reduce bleeding, the risk of infection, and complications relating to anesthesia. See *Carhart*, 331 F. Supp. 2d, at 923–928, 1026; *National Abortion Federation*, 330 F. Supp. 2d, at 472; *Planned Parenthood*, 320 F. Supp. 2d, at 1001. See also *Stenberg*, 530 U.S., at 928–929, 932; Brief for ACOG as *Amicus Curiae* 2, 11–13.

Based on thoroughgoing review of the trial evidence and the congressional record, each of the District Courts to consider the issue rejected Congress' findings as unreasonable—and not supported by the evidence. See *Carhart*, 331 F. Supp. 2d, at 1008–1027; *National Abortion Federation*, 330 F. Supp. 2d, at 482, 488–491; *Planned Parenthood*, 320 F. Supp. 2d, at 1032. The trial courts concluded, in contrast to Congress' findings, that "significant medical authority supports the proposition that in some circumstances, [intact D&E] is the safest procedure." *Id.*, at 1033 (quoting *Stenberg*, 530 U.S., at 932); accord *Carhart*, 331 F. Supp. 2d, at 1008–1009, 1017–1018; *National Abortion Federation*, 330 F. Supp. 2d, at 480–482;[5] cf. *Stenberg*, 530 U.S., at 932 ("[T]he record shows that significant medical authority supports the proposition that in some circumstances, [intact D&E] would be the safest procedure.").

The District Courts' findings merit this Court's respect. See, *e.g.*, Fed. Rule Civ. Proc. 52(a); *Salve Regina College* v. *Russell*, 499 U.S. 225, 233 (1991). Today's opinion supplies no reason to reject those findings. Nevertheless, despite the District Courts' appraisal of the weight of the evidence, and in undisguised conflict with *Stenberg*, the Court asserts that the Partial-Birth Abortion Ban Act can survive "when . . . medical uncertainty

---

5 Even the District Court for the Southern District of New York, which was more skeptical of the health benefits of intact D&E, see *ante*, at 162, recognized: "[T]he Government's own experts disagreed with almost all of Congress's factual findings"; a "significant body of medical opinion" holds that intact D&E has safety advantages over nonintact D&E; "[p]rofessional medical associations have also expressed their view that [intact D&E] may be the safest procedure for some women"; and "[t]he evidence indicates that the same disagreement among experts found by the Supreme Court in *Stenberg* existed throughout the time that Congress was considering the legislation, despite Congress's findings to the contrary." *National Abortion Federation*, 330 F. Supp. 2d, at 480–482.

persists." *Ante*, at 163. This assertion is bewildering. Not only does it defy the Court's longstanding precedent affirming the necessity of a health exception, with no carve-out for circumstances of medical uncertainty, see *supra*, at 172–173; it gives short shrift to the records before us, carefully canvassed by the District Courts. Those records indicate that "the majority of highly-qualified experts on the subject believe intact D&E to be the safest, most appropriate procedure under certain circumstances." *Planned Parenthood*, 320 F. Supp. 2d, at 1034. See *supra*, at 177.

The Court acknowledges some of this evidence, *ante*, at 161, but insists that, because some witnesses disagreed with ACOG and other experts' assessment of risk, the Act can stand. *Ante*, at 162, 166–167. In this insistence, the Court brushes under the rug the District Courts' well-supported findings that the physicians who testified that intact D&E is never necessary to preserve the health of a woman had slim authority for their opinions. They had no training for, or personal experience with, the intact D&E procedure, and many performed abortions only on rare occasions. See *Planned Parenthood*, 320 F. Supp. 2d, at 980; *Carhart*, 331 F. Supp. 2d, at 1025; cf. *National Abortion Federation*, 330 F. Supp. 2d, at 462–464. Even indulging the assumption that the Government witnesses were equally qualified to evaluate the relative risks of abortion procedures, their testimony could not erase the "significant medical authority support[ing] the proposition that in some circumstances, [intact D&E] would be the safest procedure." *Stenberg*, 530 U.S., at 932.[6]

---

6 The majority contends that "[i]f the intact D&E procedure is truly necessary in some circumstances, it appears likely an injection that kills the fetus is an alternative under the Act that allows the doctor to perform the procedure." *Ante*, at 164. But a "significant body of medical opinion believes that inducing fetal death by injection is almost always inappropriate to the preservation of the health of women undergoing abortion because it poses tangible risk and provides no benefit to the woman." *Carhart* v. *Ashcroft*, 331 F. Supp. 2d 805, 1028 (Neb. 2004) (internal quotation marks omitted), aff'd, 413 F. 3d 791 (CA8 2005). In some circumstances, injections are "absolutely [medically] contraindicated." 331 F. Supp. 2d, at 1027. See also *id.*, at 907–912; *National Abortion Federation*, 330 F. Supp. 2d, at 474–475; *Planned Parenthood*, 320 F. Supp. 2d, at 995–997. The Court also identifies medical induction

II

A

The Court offers flimsy and transparent justifications for upholding a nationwide ban on intact D&E *sans* any exception to safeguard a woman's health. Today's ruling, the Court declares, advances "a premise central to [*Casey's*] conclusion"—*i.e.*, the Government's "legitimate and substantial interest in preserving and promoting fetal life." *Ante*, at 145. See also *ante*, at 146 ("[W]e must determine whether the Act furthers the legitimate interest of the Government in protecting the life of the fetus that may become a child."). But the Act scarcely furthers that interest: The law saves not a single fetus from destruction, for it targets only a *method* of performing abortion. See *Stenberg*, 530 U.S., at 930. And surely the statute was not designed to protect the lives or health of pregnant women. *Id.*, at 951 (GINSBURG, J., concurring); cf. *Casey*, 505 U.S., at 846 (recognizing along with the State's legitimate interest in the life of the fetus, its "legitimate interes[t] . . . in protecting the *health of the woman*" (emphasis added)). In short, the Court upholds a law that, while doing nothing to "preserv[e] . . . fetal life," *ante*, at 145, bars a woman from choosing intact D&E although her doctor "reasonably believes [that procedure] will best protect [her]," *Stenberg*, 530 U.S., at 946 (STEVENS, J., concurring).

As another reason for upholding the ban, the Court emphasizes that the Act does not proscribe the nonintact D&E procedure. See *ante*, at 164. But why not, one might ask. Nonintact D&E could equally be characterized as "brutal," *ante*, at 157, involving as it does "tear[ing] [a fetus] apart" and "ripp[ing] off" its limbs, *ante*, at 135. "[T]he notion that either of these two equally gruesome procedures . . . is more akin to infanticide than the other, or that the State furthers any legitimate interest by banning one

---

of labor as an alternative. See *ante*, at 140. That procedure, however, requires a hospital stay, *ibid.*, rendering it inaccessible to patients who lack financial resources, and it too is considered less safe for many women, and impermissible for others. See *Carhart*, 331 F. Supp. 2d, at 940–949, 1017; *National Abortion Federation*, 330 F. Supp. 2d, at 468–470; *Planned Parenthood*, 320 F. Supp. 2d, at 961, n. 5, 992–994, 1000–1002.

but not the other, is simply irrational." *Stenberg*, 530 U.S., at 946–947 (STEVENS, J., concurring).

Delivery of an intact, albeit nonviable, fetus warrants special condemnation, the Court maintains, because a fetus that is not dismembered resembles an infant. *Ante*, at 158. But so, too, does a fetus delivered intact after it is terminated by injection a day or two before the surgical evacuation, *ante*, at 136, 164, or a fetus delivered through medical induction or cesarean, *ante*, at 140. Yet, the availability of those procedures—along with D&E by dismemberment—the Court says, saves the ban on intact D&E from a declaration of unconstitutionality. *Ante*, at 164–165. Never mind that the procedures deemed acceptable might put a woman's health at greater risk. See *supra*, at 180, and n. 6; cf. *ante*, at 136, 161–162.

Ultimately, the Court admits that "moral concerns" are at work, concerns that could yield prohibitions on any abortion. See *ante*, at 158 ("Congress could . . . conclude that the type of abortion proscribed by the Act requires specific regulation because it implicates additional ethical and moral concerns that justify a special prohibition."). Notably, the concerns expressed are untethered to any ground genuinely serving the Government's interest in preserving life. By allowing such concerns to carry the day and case, overriding fundamental rights, the Court dishonors our precedent. See, *e.g.*, *Casey*, 505 U.S., at 850 ("Some of us as individuals find abortion offensive to our most basic principles of morality, but that cannot control our decision. Our obligation is to define the liberty of all, not to mandate our own moral code."); *Lawrence* v. *Texas*, 539 U.S. 558, 571 (2003) (Though "[f]or many persons [objections to homosexual conduct] are not trivial concerns but profound and deep convictions accepted as ethical and moral principles," the power of the State may not be used "to enforce these views on the whole society through operation of the criminal law." (citing *Casey*, 505 U.S., at 850)).

Revealing in this regard, the Court invokes an antiabortion

shibboleth for which it concededly has no reliable evidence: Women who have abortions come to regret their choices, and consequently suffer from "[s]evere depression and loss of esteem." *Ante*, at 159.[7] Because of women's fragile emotional state and because of the "bond of love the mother has for her child," the Court worries, doctors may withhold information about the nature of the intact D&E procedure. *Ante*, at 159.[8] The solution the Court approves, then, is not to require doctors

---

7 The Court is surely correct that, for most women, abortion is a painfully difficult decision. See *ante*, at 159. But "neither the weight of the scientific evidence to date nor the observable reality of 33 years of legal abortion in the United States comports with the idea that having an abortion is any more dangerous to a woman's long-term mental health than delivering and parenting a child that she did not intend to have . . . ." Cohen, Abortion and Mental Health: Myths and Realities, 9 Guttmacher Policy Rev. 8 (2006); see generally Bazelon, Is There a Post-Abortion Syndrome? N. Y. Times Magazine, Jan. 21, 2007, p. 40. See also, *e.g.*, American Psychological Association, APA Briefing Paper on the Impact of Abortion (2005) (rejecting theory of a postabortion syndrome and stating that "[a]ccess to legal abortion to terminate an unwanted pregnancy is vital to safeguard both the physical and mental health of women"); Schmiege & Russo, Depression and Unwanted First Pregnancy: Longitudinal Cohort Study, 331 British Medical J. 1303 (2005) (finding no credible evidence that choosing to terminate an unwanted first pregnancy contributes to risk of subsequent depression); Gilchrist, Hannaford, Frank, & Kay, Termination of Pregnancy and Psychiatric Morbidity, 167 British J. of Psychiatry 243, 247–248 (1995) (finding, in a cohort of more than 13,000 women, that the rate of psychiatric disorder was no higher among women who terminated pregnancy than among those who carried pregnancy to term); Stotland, The Myth of the Abortion Trauma Syndrome, 268 JAMA 2078, 2079 (1992) ("Scientific studies indicate that legal abortion results in fewer deleterious sequelae for women compared with other possible outcomes of unwanted pregnancy. There is no evidence of an abortion trauma syndrome."); American Psychological Association, Council Policy Manual: (N)(I)(3), Public Interest (1989) (declaring assertions about widespread severe negative psychological effects of abortion to be "without fact"). But see Cougle, Reardon, & Coleman, Generalized Anxiety Following Unintended Pregnancies Resolved Through Childbirth and Abortion: A Cohort Study of the 1995 National Survey of Family Growth, 19 J. Anxiety Disorders 137, 142 (2005) (advancing theory of a postabortion syndrome but acknowledging that "no causal relationship between pregnancy outcome and anxiety could be determined" from study); Reardon et al., Psychiatric Admissions of Low-Income Women Following Abortion and Childbirth, 168 Canadian Medical Assn. J. 1253, 1255–1256 (May 13, 2003) (concluding that psychiatric admission rates were higher for women who had an abortion compared with women who delivered); cf. Major, Psychological Implications of Abortion—Highly Charged and Rife with Misleading Research, 168 Canadian Medical Assn. J. 1257, 1258 (May 13, 2003) (critiquing Reardon study for failing to control for a host of differences between women in the delivery and abortion samples).

8 Notwithstanding the "bond of love" women often have with their children, see *ante*, at 159, not all pregnancies, this Court has recognized, are wanted, or even the product of consensual activity. See *Casey*, 505 U.S., at 891 ("[O]n an average day in the United States, nearly 11,000 women are severely assaulted by their male partners. Many of these incidents involve sexual assault."). See also Glander, Moore, Michielutte, & Parsons, The Prevalence of Domestic Violence Among Women Seeking Abortion, 91 Obstetrics & Gynecology 1002 (1998); Holmes, Resnick, Kilpatrick, & Best, Rape-Related Pregnancy: Estimates and Descriptive Characteristics from a National Sample of Women, 175 Am. J. Obstetrics & Gynecology 320 (Aug. 1996).

to inform women, accurately and adequately, of the different procedures and their attendant risks. Cf. *Casey*, 505 U.S., at 873 (plurality opinion) ("States are free to enact laws to provide a reasonable framework for a woman to make a decision that has such profound and lasting meaning."). Instead, the Court deprives women of the right to make an autonomous choice, even at the expense of their safety.[9]

This way of thinking reflects ancient notions about women's place in the family and under the Constitution—ideas that have long since been discredited. Compare, *e.g.*, *Muller* v. *Oregon*, 208 U.S. 412, 422–423 (1908) ("protective" legislation imposing hours-of-work limitations on women only held permissible in view of women's "physical structure and a proper discharge of her maternal functio[n]"); *Bradwell* v. *State*, 16 Wall. 130, 141 (1873) (Bradley, J., concurring) ("Man is, or should be, woman's protector and defender. The natural and proper timidity and delicacy which belongs to the female sex evidently unfits it for many of the occupations of civil life. . . . The paramount destiny and mission of woman are to fulfil[l] the noble and benign offices of wife and mother."), with *United States* v. *Virginia*, 518 U.S. 515, 533, 542, n. 12 (1996) (State may not rely on "overbroad generalizations" about the "talents, capacities, or preferences" of women; "[s]uch judgments have . . . impeded . . . women's progress toward full citizenship stature throughout our Nation's history"); *Califano* v. *Goldfarb*, 430 U.S. 199, 207 (1977) (gender-based Social Security classification rejected because it rested on "archaic and

---

9 Eliminating or reducing women's reproductive choices is manifestly *not* a means of protecting them. When safe abortion procedures cease to be an option, many women seek other means to end unwanted or coerced pregnancies. See, *e.g.*, World Health Organization, Unsafe Abortion: Global and Regional Estimates of the Incidence of Unsafe Abortion and Associated Mortality in 2000, pp. 3, 16 (4th ed. 2004) ("Restrictive legislation is associated with a high incidence of unsafe abortion" worldwide; unsafe abortion represents 13 percent of all "maternal" deaths); Henshaw, Unintended Pregnancy and Abortion: A Public Health Perspective, in A Clinician's Guide to Medical and Surgical Abortion 11, 19 (M. Paul, E. Lichtenberg, L. Borgatta, D. Grimes, & P. Stubblefield eds. 1999) ("Before legalization, large numbers of women in the United States died from unsafe abortions."); H. Boonstra, R. Gold, C. Richards, & L. Finer, Abortion in Women's Lives 13, and fig. 2.2 (2006) ("as late as 1965, illegal abortion still accounted for an estimated . . . 17% of all officially reported pregnancy-related deaths"; "[d]eaths from abortion declined dramatically after legalization").

overbroad generalizations'" "such as assumptions as to [women's] dependency" (internal quotation marks omitted)).

Though today's majority may regard women's feelings on the matter as "self-evident," *ante*, at 159, this Court has repeatedly confirmed that "[t]he destiny of the woman must be shaped . . . on her own conception of her spiritual imperatives and her place in society," *Casey*, 505 U.S., at 852. See also *id.*, at 877 (plurality opinion) ("[M]eans chosen by the State to further the interest in potential life must be calculated to inform the woman's free choice, not hinder it."); *supra*, at 171–172.

B

In cases on a "woman's liberty to determine whether to [continue] her pregnancy," this Court has identified viability as a critical consideration. See *Casey*, 505 U.S., at 869–870 (plurality opinion). "[T]here is no line [more workable] than viability," the Court explained in *Casey*, for viability is "the time at which there is a realistic possibility of maintaining and nourishing a life outside the womb, so that the independent existence of the second life can in reason and all fairness be the object of state protection that now overrides the rights of the woman. . . . In some broad sense it might be said that a woman who fails to act before viability has consented to the State's intervention on behalf of the developing child." *Id.*, at 870.

Today, the Court blurs that line, maintaining that "[t]he Act [legitimately] appl[ies] both previability and postviability because . . . a fetus is a living organism while within the womb, whether or not it is viable outside the womb." *Ante*, at 147. Instead of drawing the line at viability, the Court refers to Congress' purpose to differentiate "abortion and infanticide" based not on whether a fetus can survive outside the womb, but on where a fetus is anatomically located when a particular medical procedure is performed. See *ante*, at 158 (quoting Congressional Findings ¶ (14)(G)).

One wonders how long a line that saves no fetus from destruction will hold in face of the Court's "moral concerns." See *supra*, at 182; cf. *ante*, at 147 (noting that "[i]n this litigation" the Attorney General "does not dispute that the Act would impose an undue burden if it covered standard D&E"). The Court's hostility to the right *Roe* and *Casey* secured is not concealed. Throughout, the opinion refers to obstetrician-gynecologists and surgeons who perform abortions not by the titles of their medical specialties, but by the pejorative label "abortion doctor." *Ante*, at 144, 154, 155, 161, 163. A fetus is described as an "unborn child," and as a "baby," *ante*, at 134, 138; second-trimester, previability abortions are referred to as "late-term," *ante*, at 156; and the reasoned medical judgments of highly trained doctors are dismissed as "preferences" motivated by "mere convenience," *ante*, at 134, 166. Instead of the heightened scrutiny we have previously applied, the Court determines that a "rational" ground is enough to uphold the Act, *ante*, at 158, 166. And, most troubling, *Casey's* principles, confirming the continuing vitality of "the essential holding of *Roe*," are merely "assume[d]" for the moment, *ante*, at 146, 161, rather than "retained" or "reaffirmed," *Casey*, 505 U.S., at 846.

III

A

The Court further confuses our jurisprudence when it declares that "facial attacks" are not permissible in "these circumstances," *i.e.*, where medical uncertainty exists. *Ante*, at 167; see *ibid*. ("In an as-applied challenge the nature of the medical risk can be better quantified and balanced than in a facial attack."). This holding is perplexing given that, in materially identical circumstances we held that a statute lacking a health exception was unconstitutional on its face. *Stenberg*, 530 U.S., at 930; see *id.*, at 937 (in facial challenge, law held unconstitutional because "significant body of medical opinion believes [the] procedure may bring with it greater safety for *some patients*" (emphasis added)). See also *Sabri* v. *United States*, 541 U.S. 600, 609–610 (2004) (identifying abortion as one setting in which we have recognized the validity of facial challenges); Fallon, Making Sense of Overbreadth, 100 Yale L. J. 853, 859, n. 29 (1991) ("[V]irtu-ally all of the abortion cases reaching the Supreme Court since *Roe* v. *Wade*, 410 U.S. 113 (1973), have involved facial attacks on state statutes, and the Court, whether accepting or rejecting the challenges on the merits, has typically accepted this fram-ing of the question presented."). Accord Fallon, As-Applied and Facial Challenges and Third-Party Standing, 113 Harv. L. Rev. 1321, 1356 (2000); Dorf, Facial Challenges to State and Federal Statutes, 46 Stan. L. Rev. 235, 271–276 (1994).

Without attempting to distinguish Stenberg and earlier deci-sions, the majority asserts that the Act survives review because respondents have not shown that the ban on intact D&E would be unconstitutional "in a large fraction of [relevant] cases." *Ante*, at 167 (citing *Casey*, 505 U.S., at 895). But *Casey* makes clear that, in determining whether any restriction poses an undue burden on a "large fraction" of women, the relevant class is *not* "all women," nor "all pregnant women," nor even all women "seeking abortions." *Ibid*. Rather, a provision restricting access to abortion "must be judged by reference to those [women] for whom it is an actual rather than an irrelevant restriction." *Ibid*. Thus the absence of a health exception burdens *all* women for whom it is relevant—women who, in the judgment of their doc-tors, require an intact D&E because other procedures would place their health at risk.[10] Cf. *Stenberg*, 530 U.S., at 934 (accept-ing the "relative rarity" of medically indicated intact D&Es as true but not "highly relevant"— for "the health exception ques-tion is whether protecting women's health requires an exception for those infrequent occasions"); *Ayotte*, 546 U.S., at 328 (facial challenge entertained where "[i]n some very small percentage of cases . . . women . . . need immediate abortions to avert serious and often irreversible damage to their health"). It makes no sense to conclude that this facial challenge fails because respondents

---

10 There is, in short, no fraction because the numerator and denominator are the same: The health exception reaches only those cases where a woman's health is at risk. Perhaps for this reason, in mandating safeguards for women's health, we have never before invoked the "large fraction" test.

have not shown that a health exception is necessary for a large fraction of second-trimester abortions, including those for which a health exception is unnecessary: The very purpose of a health *exception* is to protect women in *exceptional* cases.

B

If there is anything at all redemptive to be said of today's opinion, it is that the Court is not willing to foreclose entirely a constitutional challenge to the Act. "The Act is open," the Court states, "to a proper as-applied challenge in a discrete case." *Ante*, at 168; see *ante*, at 167 ("The Government has acknowledged that preenforcement, as-applied challenges to the Act can be maintained."). But the Court offers no clue on what a "proper" lawsuit might look like. See *ante*, at 167–168. Nor does the Court explain why the injunctions ordered by the District Courts should not remain in place, trimmed only to exclude instances in which another procedure would safeguard a woman's health at least equally well. Surely the Court cannot mean that no suit may be brought until a woman's health is immediately jeopardized by the ban on intact D&E. A woman "suffer[ing] from medical complications," *ante*, at 168, needs access to the medical procedure at once and cannot wait for the judicial process to unfold. See *Ayotte*, 546 U.S., at 328.

The Court appears, then, to contemplate another lawsuit by the initiators of the instant actions. In such a second round, the Court suggests, the challengers could succeed upon demonstrating that "in discrete and well-defined instances a particular condition has or is likely to occur in which the procedure prohibited by the Act must be used." *Ante*, at 167. One may anticipate that such a preenforcement challenge will be mounted swiftly, to ward off serious, sometimes irremediable harm, to women whose health would be endangered by the intact D&E prohibition.

The Court envisions that in an as-applied challenge, "the nature of the medical risk can be better quantified and balanced." *Ibid*. But it should not escape notice that the record already includes hundreds and hundreds of pages of testimony identifying "discrete and well-defined instances" in which recourse to an intact D&E would better protect the health of women with particular conditions. See *supra*, at 177–179. Record evidence also documents that medical exigencies, unpredictable in advance, may indicate to a well-trained doctor that intact D&E is the safest procedure. See *ibid.* In light of this evidence, our unanimous decision just one year ago in *Ayotte* counsels against reversal. See 546 U.S., at 331 (remanding for reconsideration of the remedy for the absence of a health exception, suggesting that an injunction prohibiting unconstitutional applications might suffice).

The Court's allowance only of an "as-applied challenge in a discrete case," *ante*, at 168—jeopardizes women's health and places doctors in an untenable position. Even if courts were able to carve out exceptions through piecemeal litigation for "discrete and well-defined instances," *ante*, at 167, women whose circumstances have not been anticipated by prior litigation could well be left unprotected. In treating those women, physicians would risk criminal prosecution, conviction, and imprisonment if they exercise their best judgment as to the safest medical procedure for their patients. The Court is thus gravely mistaken to conclude that narrow as-applied challenges are "the proper manner to protect the health of the woman." Cf. *ibid.*

IV

As the Court wrote in *Casey,* "overruling *Roe*'s central holding would not only reach an unjustifiable result under principles of *stare decisis,* but would seriously weaken the Court's capacity to exercise the judicial power and to function as the Supreme Court of a Nation dedicated to the rule of law." 505 U.S., at 865. "[T]he very concept of the rule of law underlying our own Constitution requires such continuity over time that a respect for precedent is, by definition, indispensable." *Id.,* at 854. See also *id.,* at 867 ("[T]o overrule under fire in the absence of the most compelling reason to reexamine a watershed decision would subvert the Court's legitimacy beyond any serious question.").

Though today's opinion does not go so far as to discard *Roe* or *Casey*, the Court, differently composed than it was when we last considered a restrictive abortion regulation, is hardly faithful to our earlier invocations of "the rule of law" and the "principles of *stare decisis*." Congress imposed a ban despite our clear prior holdings that the State cannot proscribe an abortion procedure when its use is necessary to protect a woman's health. See *supra*, at 174–175, n. 4. Although Congress' findings could not withstand the crucible of trial, the Court defers to the legislative override of our Constitution-based rulings. See *supra*, at 174–176. A decision so at odds with our jurisprudence should not have staying power.

In sum, the notion that the Partial-Birth Abortion Ban Act furthers any legitimate governmental interest is, quite simply, irrational. The Court's defense of the statute provides no saving explanation. In candor, the Act, and the Court's defense of it, cannot be understood as anything other than an effort to chip away at a right declared again and again by this Court—and with increasing comprehension of its centrality to women's lives. See *supra*, at 171, n. 2; *supra*, at 174–175, n. 4. When "a statute burdens constitutional rights and all that can be said on its behalf is that it is the vehicle that legislators have chosen for expressing their hostility to those rights, the burden is undue." *Stenberg*, 530 U.S., at 952 (GINSBURG, J., concurring) (quoting *Hope Clinic* v. *Ryan*, 195 F. 3d 857, 881 (CA7 1999) (POSNER, C. J., dissenting)).

* * *

For the reasons stated, I dissent from the Court's disposition and would affirm the judgments before us for review.

Ledbetter v. Goodyear Tire & Rubber Co., 550 U.S. 618 (2007)

Dissenting Opinion

Title VII of the Civil Rights Act of 1964 outlawed employer discrimination based on gender, but included a provision requiring complaints of discrimination to be filed within 180 days of an employer's discriminatory conduct. Lilly Ledbetter, employed by Goodyear Tire for 19 years, had a history of receiving poor annual performance-and-salary reviews and raises that were lower than her peers; she sued Goodyear, claiming that her low salary was a result of the company's gender discrimination. The lawsuit was settled in her favor, but Goodyear successfully appealed.

When the case reached the Supreme Court, the Justices had to determine whether Title VII allowed a plaintiff to sue for salary discrimination if the salary is received during the 180-day period, but is the result of actions taken by the employer prior to that period. In his 5-4 majority opinion, Justice Samuel Alito said no, arguing that the discriminatory intent must take place within the 180-day charging period—though the intent behind the salary decisions may have been discriminatory, the issuing of the paychecks themselves held no discriminatory intent and therefore did not constitute discriminatory action. Justice Ginsburg, in her dissent, argued that the employer had been "knowingly carrying past pay discrimination forward" during the 180-day charging period, and that the 180-day statutory limit should not be applied to pay discrimination given that such discrimination can happen incrementally over time rather than in a single instance.

No. 05-1074
LILLY M. LEDBETTER, PETITIONER
v.
THE GOODYEAR TIRE & RUBBER COMPANY, INC.
ON WRIT OF CERTIORARI TO THE
UNITED STATES COURT OF APPEALS FOR
THE ELEVENTH CIRCUIT

[MAY 29, 2007]

JUSTICE GINSBURG, with whom JUSTICE STEVENS, JUSTICE SOUTER, and JUSTICE BREYER join, dissenting.

Lilly Ledbetter was a supervisor at Goodyear Tire & Rubber's plant in Gadsden, Alabama, from 1979 until her retirement in 1998. For most of those years, she worked as an area manager, a position largely occupied by men. Initially, Ledbetter's salary was in line with the salaries of men performing substantially similar work. Over time, however, her pay slipped in comparison to the pay of male area managers with equal or less seniority. By the end of 1997, Ledbetter was the only woman working as an area manager and the pay discrepancy between Ledbetter and her 15 male counterparts was stark: Ledbetter was paid $3,727 per month; the lowest paid male area manager received $4,286 per month, the highest paid, $5,236. See 421 F. 3d 1169, 1174 (CA11 2005); Brief for Petitioner 4.

Ledbetter launched charges of discrimination before the Equal Employment Opportunity Commission (EEOC) in March 1998. Her formal administrative complaint specified that, in violation of Title VII, Goodyear paid her a discriminatorily low salary because of her sex. See 42 U. S. C. § 2000e–2(a)(1) (rendering it unlawful for an employer "to discriminate against any individual with respect to [her] compensation . . . because of such individual's . . . sex"). That charge was eventually tried to a jury, which found it "more likely than not that [Goodyear] paid [Ledbetter] a[n] unequal salary because of her sex." App. 102. In accord with the jury's liability determination, the District Court entered judgment for Ledbetter for backpay and damages, plus counsel fees and costs.

The Court of Appeals for the Eleventh Circuit reversed. Relying on Goodyear's system of annual merit-based raises, the court held that Ledbetter's claim, in relevant part, was time barred. 421 F. 3d, at 1171, 1182–1183. Title VII provides that a charge of discrimination "shall be filed within [180] days after the alleged unlawful employment practice occurred." 42 U. S. C. § 2000e–5(e)(1).[1] Ledbetter charged, and proved at trial, that within the 180-day period, her pay was substantially less than the pay of men doing the same work. Further, she introduced evidence sufficient to establish that discrimination against female managers at the Gadsden plant, not performance inadequacies on her part, accounted for the pay differential. See, e.g., App. 36–47, 51–68, 82–87, 90–98, 112–113. That evidence was unavailing, the Eleventh Circuit held, and the Court today agrees, because it was incumbent on Ledbetter to file charges year by year, each time Goodyear failed to increase her salary commensurate with the salaries of male peers. Any annual pay decision not contested immediately (within 180 days), the Court affirms, becomes grandfathered, a *fait accompli* beyond the province of Title VII ever to repair.

The Court's insistence on immediate contest overlooks common characteristics of pay discrimination. Pay disparities often occur, as they did in Ledbetter's case, in small increments; cause to suspect that discrimination is at work develops only over time. Comparative pay information, moreover, is often hidden from the employee's view. Employers may keep under wraps the pay differentials maintained among supervisors, no less the reasons for those differentials. Small initial discrepancies may not be seen as meet for a federal case, particularly when the employee,

---

1 If the complainant has first instituted proceedings with a state or local agency, the filing period is extended to 300 days or 30 days after the denial of relief by the agency. 42 U. S. C. § 2000e–5(e)(1). Because the 180-day period applies to Ledbetter's case, that figure will be used throughout. See *ante*, at 622, 624.

trying to succeed in a nontraditional environment, is averse to making waves.

Pay disparities are thus significantly different from adverse actions "such as termination, failure to promote, . . . or refusal to hire," all involving fully communicated discrete acts, "easy to identify" as discriminatory. See *National Railroad Passenger Corporation* v. *Morgan*, 536 U.S. 101, 114 (2002). It is only when the disparity becomes apparent and sizable, *e.g.*, through future raises calculated as a percentage of current salaries, that an employee in Ledbetter's situation is likely to comprehend her plight and, therefore, to complain. Her initial readiness to give her employer the benefit of the doubt should not preclude her from later challenging the then current and continuing payment of a wage depressed on account of her sex.

On questions of time under Title VII, we have identified as the critical inquiries: "What constitutes an 'unlawful employment practice' and when has that practice 'occurred'?" *Id.*, at 110. Our precedent suggests, and lower courts have overwhelmingly held, that the unlawful practice is the current payment of salaries infected by gender-based (or race-based) discrimination—a practice that occurs whenever a paycheck delivers less to a woman than to a similarly situated man. See *Bazemore* v. *Friday*, 478 U.S. 385, 395 (1986) (Brennan, J., joined by all other Members of the Court, concurring in part).

Title VII proscribes as an "unlawful employment practice" discrimination "against any individual with respect to his compensation . . . because of such individual's race, color, religion, sex, or national origin." 42 U. S. C. § 2000e–2(a)(1). An individual seeking to challenge an employment practice under this proscription must file a charge with the EEOC within 180 days "after the alleged unlawful employment practice occurred." § 2000e–5(e)(1). See *ante*, at 624; *supra*, at 644, n. 1.

Ledbetter's petition presents a question important to the sound application of Title VII: What activity qualifies as an unlawful employment practice in cases of discrimination with respect to compensation. One answer identifies the pay-setting decision, and that decision alone, as the unlawful practice. Under this view, each particular salary-setting decision is discrete from prior and subsequent decisions, and must be challenged within 180 days on pain of forfeiture. Another response counts both the pay-setting decision and the actual payment of a discriminatory wage as unlawful practices. Under this approach, each payment of a wage or salary infected by sex-based discrimination constitutes an unlawful employment practice; prior decisions, outside the 180-day charge-filing period, are not themselves actionable, but they are relevant in determining the lawfulness of conduct within the period. The Court adopts the first view, see *ante*, at 621, 624, 628–629, but the second is more faithful to precedent, more in tune with the realities of the workplace, and more respectful of Title VII's remedial purpose.

A

In *Bazemore*, we unanimously held that an employer, the North Carolina Agricultural Extension Service, committed an unlawful employment practice each time it paid black employees less than similarly situated white employees. 478 U.S., at 395 (opinion of Brennan, J.). Before 1965, the Extension Service was divided into two branches: a white branch and a "Negro branch." *Id.*, at 390. Employees in the "Negro branch" were paid less than their white counterparts. In response to the Civil Rights Act of 1964, which included Title VII, the State merged the two branches into a single organization, made adjustments to reduce the salary disparity, and began giving annual raises based on nondiscriminatory factors. *Id.*, at 390–391, 394–395. Nonetheless, "some pre-existing salary disparities continued to linger on." *Id.*, at 394 (internal quotation marks omitted). We rejected the Court of Appeals' conclusion that the plaintiffs could not prevail because the lingering disparities were simply a continuing effect of a decision lawfully made prior to the effective date of Title VII. See *id.*, at 395–396. Rather, we reasoned, "[e]ach week's paycheck that delivers less to a black than to a similarly situated white is a wrong actionable under Title VII." *Id.*, at 395. Paychecks perpetuating past discrimination, we thus recognized, are actionable not simply because they are "related" to a decision made outside the charge-filing period, cf. *ante*, at 636, but because they discriminate anew each time they issue, see *Bazemore*, 478 U.S., at 395–396, and n. 6; *Morgan*, 536 U.S., at 111–112.

Subsequently, in *Morgan*, we set apart, for purposes of Title VII's timely filing requirement, unlawful employment actions of two kinds: "discrete acts" that are "easy to identify" as discriminatory, and acts that recur and are cumulative in impact. See *id.*, at 110, 113–115. "[A] [d]iscrete ac[t] such as termination, failure to promote, denial of transfer, or refusal to hire," *id.*, at 114, we explained, "'occur[s]' on the day that it 'happen[s].' A party, therefore, must file a charge within . . . 180 . . . days of the date of the act or lose the ability to recover for it." *Id.*, at 110; see *id.*, at 113 ("[D]iscrete discriminatory acts are not actionable if time barred, even when they are related to acts alleged in timely filed charges. Each discrete discriminatory act starts a new clock for filing charges alleging that act.").

"[D]ifferent in kind from discrete acts," we made clear, are "claims . . . based on the cumulative effect of individual acts." *Id.*, at 115. The *Morgan* decision placed hostile work environment claims in that category. "Their very nature involves repeated conduct." *Ibid.* "The unlawful employment practice" in hostile work environment claims "cannot be said to occur on any particular day. It occurs over a series of days or perhaps years and, in direct contrast to discrete acts, a single act of harassment may not be actionable on its own." *Ibid.* (internal quotation marks omitted). The persistence of the discriminatory conduct both indicates that management should have known of its existence and produces a cognizable harm. *Ibid.* Because the very nature of the hostile work environment claim involves repeated conduct, "[i]t does not matter, for purposes of the statute, that some of the component acts of the hostile work environment fall outside the statutory time period. Provided that an act contributing to the claim occurs within the filing period, the entire time period of the hostile environment may be considered by a court for the purposes of determining liability." *Id.*, at 117.

Consequently, although the unlawful conduct began in the past, "a charge may be filed at a later date and still encompass the whole." *Ibid.*

Pay disparities, of the kind Ledbetter experienced, have a closer kinship to hostile work environment claims than to charges of a single episode of discrimination. Ledbetter's claim, resembling Morgan's, rested not on one particular paycheck, but on "the cumulative effect of individual acts." See *id.*, at 115. See also Brief for Petitioner 13, 15–17, and n. 9 (analogizing Ledbetter's claim to the recurring and cumulative harm at issue in *Morgan*); Reply Brief for Petitioner 13 (distinguishing pay discrimination from "easy to identify" discrete acts (internal quotation marks omitted)). She charged insidious discrimination building up slowly but steadily. See Brief for Petitioner 5–8. Initially in line with the salaries of men performing substantially the same work, Ledbetter's salary fell 15 to 40 percent behind her male counterparts only after successive evaluations and percentage-based pay adjustments. See *supra*, at 643–644. Over time, she alleged and proved, the repetition of pay decisions undervaluing her work gave rise to the current discrimination of which she complained. Though component acts fell outside the charge-filing period, with each new paycheck, Goodyear contributed incrementally to the accumulating harm. See *Morgan*, 536 U.S., at 117; *Bazemore*, 478 U.S., at 395–396; cf. *Hanover Shoe, Inc.* v. *United Shoe Machinery Corp.*, 392 U.S. 481, 502, n. 15 (1968).[2]

---

2 *National Railroad Passenger Corporation* v. *Morgan*, 536 U.S. 101, 117 (2002), the Court emphasizes, required that "an act contributing to the claim occu[r] within the [charge-]filing

B

The realities of the workplace reveal why the discrimination with respect to compensation that Ledbetter suffered does not fit within the category of singular discrete acts "easy to identify." A worker knows immediately if she is denied a promotion or transfer, if she is fired or refused employment. And promotions, transfers, hirings, and firings are generally public events, known to co-workers. When an employer makes a decision of such open and definitive character, an employee can immediately seek out an explanation and evaluate it for pretext. Compensation disparities, in contrast, are often hidden from sight. It is not unusual, decisions in point illustrate, for management to decline to publish employee pay levels, or for employees to keep private their own salaries. See, *e.g.*, *Goodwin* v. *General Motors Corp.*, 275 F. 3d 1005, 1008–1009 (CA10 2002) (plaintiff did not know what her colleagues earned until a printout listing of salaries appeared on her desk, seven years after her starting salary was set lower than her co-workers' salaries); *McMillan* v. *Massachusetts Soc. For Prevention of Cruelty to Animals*, 140 F. 3d 288, 296 (CA1 1998) (plaintiff worked for employer for years before learning of salary disparity published in a newspaper).[3] Tellingly, as the record in this case bears out, Goodyear kept salaries confidential; employees had only limited access to information regarding their colleagues' earnings. App. 56–57, 89.

The problem of concealed pay discrimination is particularly acute where the disparity arises not because the female employee is flatly denied a raise but because male counterparts are given larger raises. Having received a pay increase, the female employee is unlikely to discern at once that she has experienced an adverse

---

period." *Ante*, at 638, and n. 7 (emphasis deleted; internal quotation marks omitted). Here, each paycheck within the filing period compounded the discrimination Ledbetter encountered, and thus contributed to the "actionable wrong," *i.e.*, the succession of acts composing the pattern of discriminatory pay, of which she complained.

3 See also Bierman & Gely, "Love, Sex and Politics? Sure. Salary? No Way": Workplace Social Norms and the Law, 25 Berkeley J. Emp. & Lab. L. 167, 168, 171 (2004) (one-third of private sector employers have adopted specific rules prohibiting employees from discussing their wages with co-workers; only one in ten employers has adopted a pay openness policy).

employment decision. She may have little reason even to suspect discrimination until a pattern develops incrementally and she ultimately becomes aware of the disparity. Even if an employee suspects that the reason for a comparatively low raise is not performance but sex (or another protected ground), the amount involved may seem too small, or the employer's intent too ambiguous, to make the issue immediately actionable—or winnable.

Further separating pay claims from the discrete employment actions identified in *Morgan*, an employer gains from sex-based pay disparities in a way it does not from a discriminatory denial of promotion, hiring, or transfer. When a male employee is selected over a female for a higher level position, someone still gets the promotion and is paid a higher salary; the employer is not enriched. But when a woman is paid less than a similarly situated man, the employer reduces its costs each time the pay differential is implemented. Furthermore, decisions on promotions, like decisions installing seniority systems, often implicate the interests of third-party employees in a way that pay differentials do not. Cf. *Teamsters* v. *United States*, 431 U.S. 324, 352–353 (1977) (recognizing that seniority systems involve "vested . . . rights of employees" and concluding that Title VII was not intended to "destroy or water down" those rights). Disparate pay, by contrast, can be remedied at any time solely at the expense of the employer who acts in a discriminatory fashion.

C

In light of the significant differences between pay disparities and discrete employment decisions of the type identified in *Morgan*, the cases on which the Court relies hold no sway. See *ante*, at 625–629 (discussing *United Air Lines, Inc.* v. *Evans*, 431 U.S. 553 (1977), *Delaware State College* v. *Ricks*, 449 U.S. 250 (1980), and *Lorance* v. *AT&T Technologies, Inc.*, 490 U.S. 900 (1989)). *Evans* and *Ricks* both involved a single, immediately identifiable act of discrimination: in *Evans*, a constructive discharge, 431 U.S., at 554; in *Ricks*, a denial of tenure, 449 U.S., at 252. In each case, the employee filed charges well after the discrete discriminatory act occurred: When United Airlines forced Evans to resign because of its policy barring married female flight attendants, she filed no charge; only four years later, when Evans was rehired, did she allege that the airline's former no-marriage rule was unlawful and therefore should not operate to deny her seniority credit for her prior service. See *Evans*, 431 U.S., at 554–557. Similarly, when Delaware State College denied Ricks tenure, he did not object until his terminal contract came to an end, one year later. *Ricks*, 449 U.S., at 253–254, 257–258. No repetitive, cumulative discriminatory employment practice was at issue in either case. See *Evans*, 431 U.S., at 557–558; *Ricks*, 449 U.S., at 258.[4]

Lorance is also inapposite, for, in this Court's view, it too involved a one-time discrete act: the adoption of a new seniority system that "had its genesis in sex discrimination." See 490 U.S., at 902, 905 (internal quotation marks omitted). The Court's extensive reliance on *Lorance*, *ante*, at 626–629, 633, 636–637, moreover, is perplexing for that decision is no longer effective: In the 1991 Civil Rights Act, Congress superseded *Lorance*'s holding. § 112, 105 Stat. 1079 (codified as amended at 42 U. S. C. § 2000e–5(e)(2)). Repudiating our judgment that a facially neutral seniority system adopted with discriminatory intent must be challenged immediately, Congress provided:

> "For purposes of this section, an unlawful employment practice occurs . . . when the seniority system is adopted, when an individual becomes subject to the seniority system, or when a person aggrieved is injured

---

4 The Court also relies on *Machinists* v. *NLRB*, 362 U.S. 411 (1960), which like *Evans* and *Ricks*, concerned a discrete act: the execution of a collective-bargaining agreement containing a union security clause. 362 U.S., at 412, 417. In *Machinists*, it was undisputed that under the National Labor Relations Act (NLRA), a union and an employer may not agree to a union security clause "if at the time of original execution the union does not represent a majority of the employees in the [bargaining] unit." *Id.*, at 412–414, 417. The complainants, however, failed to file a charge within the NLRA's six-month charge-filing period; instead, they filed charges 10 and 12 months after the execution of the agreement, objecting to its subsequent enforcement. See *id.*, at 412, 414. Thus, as in *Evans* and *Ricks*, but in contrast to Ledbetter's case, the employment decision at issue was easily identifiable and occurred on a single day.

by the application of the seniority system or provision of the system." *Ibid.*

Congress thus agreed with the dissenters in *Lorance* that "the harsh reality of [that] decision" was "glaringly at odds with the purposes of Title VII." 490 U.S., at 914 (opinion of Marshall, J.). See also § 3, 105 Stat. 1071 (1991 Civil Rights Act was designed "to respond to recent decisions of the Supreme Court by expanding the scope of relevant civil rights statutes in order to provide adequate protection to victims of discrimination").

True, § 112 of the 1991 Civil Rights Act directly addressed only seniority systems. See *ante*, at 627, and n. 2. But Congress made clear (1) its view that this Court had unduly contracted the scope of protection afforded by Title VII and other civil rights statutes, and (2) its aim to generalize the ruling in *Bazemore*. As the Senate Report accompanying the proposed Civil Rights Act of 1990, the precursor to the 1991 Act, explained:

> "Where, as was alleged in *Lorance*, an employer adopts a rule or decision with an unlawful discriminatory motive, each application of that rule or decision is a new violation of the law. In *Bazemore* . . . , for example, . . . the Supreme Court properly held that each application of th[e] racially motivated salary structure, *i.e.*, each new paycheck, constituted a distinct violation of Title VII. Section 7(a)(2) generalizes the result correctly reached in *Bazemore*." Civil Rights Act of 1990, S. Rep. No. 101–315, p. 54 (1990).[5]

See also 137 Cong. Rec. 29046, 29047 (1991) (Sponsors' Interpretative Memorandum) ("This legislation should be interpreted as disapproving the extension of [*Lorance*] to contexts outside of seniority systems."). But cf. *ante*, at 637 (relying on

---

5 No Senate Report was submitted with the Civil Rights Act of 1991, which was in all material respects identical to the proposed 1990 Act.

Lorance to conclude that "when an employer issues paychecks pursuant to a system that is facially nondiscriminatory and neutrally applied" a new Title VII violation does not occur (internal quotation marks omitted)).

Until today, in the more than 15 years since Congress amended Title VII, the Court had not once relied upon *Lorance*. It is mistaken to do so now. Just as Congress' "goals in enacting Title VII . . . never included conferring absolute immunity on discriminatorily adopted seniority systems that survive their first [180] days," 490 U.S., at 914 (Marshall, J., dissenting), Congress never intended to immunize forever discriminatory pay differentials unchallenged within 180 days of their adoption. This assessment gains weight when one comprehends that even a relatively minor pay disparity will expand exponentially over an employee's working life if raises are set as a percentage of prior pay.

A clue to congressional intent can be found in Title VII's backpay provision. The statute expressly provides that backpay may be awarded for a period of up to two years before the discrimination charge is filed. 42 U. S. C. § 2000e–5(g)(1) ("Back pay liability shall not accrue from a date more than two years prior to the filing of a charge with the Commission."). This prescription indicates that Congress contemplated challenges to pay discrimination commencing before, but continuing into, the 180-day filing period. See *Morgan*, 536 U.S., at 119 ("If Congress intended to limit liability to conduct occurring in the period within which the party must file the charge, it seems unlikely that Congress would have allowed recovery for two years of backpay."). As we recognized in *Morgan*, "the fact that Congress expressly limited the amount of recoverable damages elsewhere to a particular time period [*i.e.*, two years] indicates that the [180-day] timely filing provision was not meant to serve as a specific limitation . . . [on] the conduct that may be considered." *Ibid.*

D

In tune with the realities of wage discrimination, the Courts of Appeals have overwhelmingly judged as a present violation the payment of wages infected by discrimination: Each paycheck less than the amount payable had the employer adhered to a nondiscriminatory compensation regime, courts have held, constitutes a cognizable harm. See, *e.g.*, *Forsyth* v. *Federation Employment and Guidance Serv.*, 409 F. 3d 565, 573 (CA2 2005) ("Any paycheck given within the [charge-filing] period . . . would be actionable, even if based on a discriminatory pay scale set up outside of the statutory period."); *Shea* v. *Rice*, 409 F. 3d 448, 452–453 (CADC 2005) ("[An] employer commit[s] a separate unlawful employment practice each time he pa[ys] one employee less than another for a discriminatory reason" (citing *Bazemore*, 478 U.S., at 396)); *Goodwin*, 275 F. 3d, at 1009–1010 ("[*Bazemore*] has taught a crucial distinction with respect to discriminatory disparities in pay, establishing that a discriminatory salary is not merely a lingering effect of past discrimination—instead it is itself a continually recurring violation. . . . [E]ach race-based discriminatory salary payment constitutes a fresh violation of Title VII." (footnote omitted)); *Anderson* v. *Zubieta*, 180 F. 3d 329, 335 (CADC 1999) ("The Courts of Appeals have repeatedly reached the . . . conclusion" that pay discrimination is "actionable upon receipt of each paycheck."); accord *Hildebrandt* v. *Illinois Dept. of Natural Resources*, 347 F. 3d 1014, 1025–1029 (CA7 2003); *Cardenas* v. *Massey*, 269 F. 3d 251, 257 (CA3 2001); *Ashley* v. *Boyle's Famous Corned Beef Co.*, 66 F. 3d 164, 167–168 (CA8 1995) (en banc); *Brinkley-Obu* v. *Hughes Training, Inc.*, 36 F. 3d 336, 347–349 (CA4 1994); *Gibbs* v. *Pierce Cty. Law Enforcement Support Agcy.*, 785 F. 2d 1396, 1399–1400 (CA9 1986).

Similarly in line with the real-world characteristics of pay discrimination, the EEOC—the federal agency responsible for enforcing Title VII, see, *e.g.*, 42 U. S. C. §§ 2000e–5(f), 2000e–12(a)—has interpreted the Act to permit employees to challenge disparate pay each time it is received. The EEOC's Compliance Manual provides that "[r]epeated occurrences of the same discriminatory employment action, such as discriminatory paychecks, can be challenged as long as one discriminatory act occurred within the charge filing period." 2 EEOC Compliance Manual § 2–IV–C(1)(a), p. 605:0024, and n. 183 (2006); cf. *id.*, § 10–III, p. 633:0002 (Title VII requires an employer to eliminate pay disparities attributable to a discriminatory system, even if that system has been discontinued).

The EEOC has given effect to its interpretation in a series of administrative decisions. See *Albritton* v. *Potter*, No. 01A44063, 2004 WL 2983682, *2 (EEOC Office of Fed. Operations, Dec. 17, 2004) (although disparity arose and employee became aware of the disparity outside the charge filing period, claim was not time barred because "[e]ach paycheck that complainant receives which is less than that of similarly situated employees outside of her protected classes could support a claim under Title VII if discrimination is found to be the reason for the pay discrepancy." (citing *Bazemore*, 478 U.S., at 396)). See also *Bynum-Doles* v. *Winter*, No. 01A53973, 2006 WL 2096290 (EEOC Office of Fed. Operations, July 18, 2006); *Ward* v. *Potter*, No. 01A60047, 2006 WL 721992 (EEOC Office of Fed. Operations, Mar. 10, 2006). And in this very case, the EEOC urged the Eleventh Circuit to recognize that Ledbetter's failure to challenge any particular pay-setting decision when that decision was made "does not deprive her of the right to seek relief for discriminatory paychecks she received in 1997 and 1998." Brief of EEOC in Support of Petition for Rehearing and Suggestion for Rehearing En Banc, in No. 03–15264–GG (CA11), p. 14 (hereinafter EEOC Brief) (citing *Morgan*, 536 U.S., at 113).[6]

---

6 The Court dismisses the EEOC's considerable "experience and informed judgment," *Firefighters* v. *Cleveland*, 478 U.S. 501, 518 (1986) (internal quotation marks omitted), as unworthy of any deference in this case, see *ante*, at 642–643, n. 11. But the EEOC's interpretations mirror workplace realities and merit at least respectful attention. In any event, the level of deference due the EEOC here is an academic question, for the agency's conclusion that Ledbetter's claim is not time barred is the best reading of the statute even if the Court "were interpreting [Title VII] from scratch." See *Edelman* v. *Lynchburg* College, 535 U.S. 106, 114 (2002); see *supra*, at 646–655 and this page.

II

The Court asserts that treating pay discrimination as a discrete act, limited to each particular pay-setting decision, is necessary to "protec[t] employers from the burden of defending claims arising from employment decisions that are long past." *Ante*, at 630 (quoting *Ricks*, 449 U.S., at 256–257). But the discrimination of which Ledbetter complained is not long past. As she alleged, and as the jury found, Goodyear continued to treat Ledbetter differently because of sex each pay period, with mounting harm. Allowing employees to challenge discrimination "that extend[s] over long periods of time," into the charge-filing period, we have previously explained, "does not leave employers defenseless" against unreasonable or prejudicial delay. *Morgan*, 536 U.S., at 121. Employers disadvantaged by such delay may raise various defenses. *Id.*, at 122. Doctrines such as "waiver, estoppel, and equitable tolling" "allow us to honor Title VII's remedial purpose without negating the particular purpose of the filing requirement, to give prompt notice to the employer." *Id.*, at 121 (quoting *Zipes* v. *Trans World Airlines, Inc.*, 455 U.S. 385, 398 (1982)); see 536 U.S., at 121 (defense of laches may be invoked to block an employee's suit "if he unreasonably delays in filing [charges] and as a result harms the defendant"); EEOC Brief 15 ("[I]f Ledbetter unreasonably delayed challenging an earlier decision, and that delay significantly impaired Goodyear's ability to defend itself . . . Goodyear can raise a defense of laches. . . .").[7]

In a last-ditch argument, the Court asserts that this dissent would allow a plaintiff to sue on a single decision made 20 years ago "even if the employee had full knowledge of all the circumstances relating to the . . . decision at the time it was made." *Ante*, at 639. It suffices to point out that the defenses just noted would make such a suit foolhardy. No sensible judge would tolerate

---

7 Further, as the EEOC appropriately recognized in its brief to the Eleventh Circuit, Ledbetter's failure to challenge particular pay raises within the charge-filing period "significantly limit[s] the relief she can seek. By waiting to file a charge, Ledbetter lost her opportunity to seek relief for any discriminatory paychecks she received between 1979 and late 1997." EEOC Brief 14. See also *supra*, at 654–656.

such inexcusable neglect. See *Morgan*, 536 U.S., at 121 ("In such cases, the federal courts have the discretionary power . . . to locate a just result in light of the circumstances peculiar to the case." (internal quotation marks omitted)).

Ledbetter, the Court observes, *ante*, at 640–641, n. 9, dropped an alternative remedy she could have pursued: Had she persisted in pressing her claim under the Equal Pay Act of 1963 (EPA), 29 U. S. C. § 206(d), she would not have encountered a time bar.[8] See *ante*, at 640 ("If Ledbetter had pursued her EPA claim, she would not face the Title VII obstacles that she now confronts."); cf. *Corning Glass Works* v. *Brennan*, 417 U.S. 188, 208–210 (1974). Notably, the EPA provides no relief when the pay discrimination charged is based on race, religion, national origin, age, or disability. Thus, in truncating the Title VII rule this Court announced in *Bazemore*, the Court does not disarm female workers from achieving redress for unequal pay, but it does impede racial and other minorities from gaining similar relief.[9]

Furthermore, the difference between the EPA's prohibition against paying unequal wages and Title VII's ban on discrimination with regard to compensation is not as large as the Court's opinion might suggest. See *ante*, at 640. The key distinction is that Title VII requires a showing of intent. In practical effect, "if the trier of fact is in equipoise about whether the wage differential is motivated by gender discrimination," Title VII compels a verdict for the employer, while the EPA compels a verdict for the plaintiff. 2 C. Sullivan, M. Zimmer, & R. White, Employment Discrimination: Law and Practice § 7.08[F][3], p. 532 (3d ed.

---

8 Under the EPA, 29 U. S. C. § 206(d), which is subject to the Fair Labor Standards Act's time prescriptions, a claim charging denial of equal pay accrues anew with each paycheck. 1 B. Lindemann & P. Grossman, Employment Discrimination Law 529 (3d ed. 1996); cf. 29 U. S. C. § 255(a) (prescribing a two-year statute of limitations for violations generally, but a three-year limitation period for willful violations).

9 For example, under today's decision, if a black supervisor initially received the same salary as his white colleagues, but annually received smaller raises, there would be no right to sue under Title VII outside the 180-day window following each annual salary change, however strong the cumulative evidence of discrimination might be. The Court would thus force plaintiffs, in many cases, to sue too soon to prevail, while cutting them off as time barred once the pay differential is large enough to enable them to mount a winnable case.

2002). In this case, Ledbetter carried the burden of persuading the jury that the pay disparity she suffered was attributable to intentional sex discrimination. See *supra*, at 643–644; *infra* this page and 660.

III

To show how far the Court has strayed from interpretation of Title VII with fidelity to the Act's core purpose, I return to the evidence Ledbetter presented at trial. Ledbetter proved to the jury the following: She was a member of a protected class; she performed work substantially equal to work of the dominant class (men); she was compensated less for that work; and the disparity was attributable to gender-based discrimination. See *supra*, at 643–644.

Specifically, Ledbetter's evidence demonstrated that her current pay was discriminatorily low due to a long series of decisions reflecting Goodyear's pervasive discrimination against women managers in general and Ledbetter in particular. Ledbetter's former supervisor, for example, admitted to the jury that Ledbetter's pay, during a particular one-year period, fell below Goodyear's minimum threshold for her position. App. 93–97. Although Goodyear claimed the pay disparity was due to poor performance, the supervisor acknowledged that Ledbetter received a "Top Performance Award" in 1996. *Id.*, at 90–93. The jury also heard testimony that another supervisor—who evaluated Ledbetter in 1997 and whose evaluation led to her most recent raise denial—was openly biased against women. *Id.*, at 46, 77–82. And two women who had previously worked as managers at the plant told the jury they had been subject to pervasive discrimination and were paid less than their male counterparts. One was paid less than the men she supervised. *Id.*, at 51–68. Ledbetter herself testified about the discriminatory animus conveyed to her by plant officials. Toward the end of her career, for instance, the plant manager told Ledbetter that the "plant did not need women, that [women] didn't help it, [and] caused problems." *Id.*, at 36.[10] After weighing all the evidence, the jury found for Ledbetter, concluding that the pay disparity was due to intentional discrimination.

Yet, under the Court's decision, the discrimination Ledbetter proved is not redressable under Title VII. Each and every pay decision she did not immediately challenge wiped the slate clean. Consideration may not be given to the cumulative effect of a series of decisions that, together, set her pay well below that of every male area manager. Knowingly carrying past pay discrimination forward must be treated as lawful conduct. Ledbetter may not be compensated for the lower pay she was in fact receiving when she complained to the EEOC. Nor, were she still employed by Goodyear, could she gain, on the proof she presented at trial, injunctive relief requiring, prospectively, her receipt of the same compensation men receive for substantially similar work. The Court's approbation of these consequences is totally at odds with the robust protection against workplace discrimination Congress intended Title VII to secure. See, *e.g.*, *Teamsters* v. *United States*, 431 U.S., at 348 ("The primary purpose of Title VII was to assure equality of employment opportunities and to eliminate . . . discriminatory practices and devices . . . ." (internal quotation marks omitted)); *Albemarle Paper Co.* v. *Moody*, 422 U.S. 405, 418 (1975) ("It is . . . the purpose of Title VII to make persons whole for injuries suffered on account of unlawful employment discrimination."). This is not the first time the Court has ordered a cramped interpretation of Title VII, incompatible with the statute's broad remedial purpose. See *supra*, at 652–654. See also *Wards Cove Packing Co.* v. *Atonio*, 490 U.S. 642 (1989) (superseded in part by the Civil Rights Act of 1991); *Price Waterhouse* v. *Hopkins*, 490 U.S. 228 (1989) (plurality opinion) (same); 1 B. Lindemann & P. Grossman, Employment Discrimination Law 2 (3d ed. 1996) ("A spate of Court decisions in the late 1980s drew congressional fire and

---

10 Given this abundant evidence, the Court cannot tenably maintain that Ledbetter's case "turned principally on the misconduct of a single Goodyear supervisor." See *ante*, at 632, n. 4.

resulted in demands for legislative change[,]" culminating in the 1991 Civil Rights Act (footnote omitted)). Once again, the ball is in Congress' court. As in 1991, the Legislature may act to correct this Court's parsimonious reading of Title VII.

* * *

For the reasons stated, I would hold that Ledbetter's claim is not time barred and would reverse the Eleventh Circuit's judgment.

Ricci v. DeStefano,
557 U.S. 557
(2009)

Dissenting Opinion

Twenty firefighters—nineteen White and one Hispanic—from the New Haven Fire Department in Connecticut brought a lawsuit claiming discrimination under Title VII of the Civil Rights Act of 1964, and alleging violation of the Fourteenth Amendment's Equal Protection Clause, when they were refused promotion after successfully passing necessary civil service exams. No Black firefighters who took the test scored high enough to qualify for promotion. City officials claimed they refused to certify the results of the tests because they feared that the disproportionate promotion of White candidates would invite a lawsuit based on "disparate impact."

The Court held 5–4 that discarding the exams was indeed a violation of Title VII of the Civil Rights Act of 1964. Justice John G. Roberts, in his majority opinion, stated that an employer must have a "strong basis in evidence" for believing it will be at risk for liability before it engages in intentional discrimination under the auspices of avoiding "disparate impact"; the city of New Haven had failed to prove their discriminatory actions were necessary. In a separate concurring opinion, Justice Antonin G. Scalia noted that the Court avoided addressing the matter of the plaintiffs' Equal Protection Clause claim. In her dissent, Justice Ginsburg not only argued that New Haven's fears were legitimate, but that the tests themselves were flawed.

RICCI ET AL.

v.

DeSTEFANO ET AL.

CERTIORARI TO THE UNITED STATES COURT OF
APPEALS FOR THE SECOND CIRCUIT
[June 29, 2009]

JUSTICE GINSBURG, with whom JUSTICE STEVENS joins, and with
whom JUSTICE SOUTER and JUSTICE BREYER join, dissenting.

In assessing claims of race discrimination, "[c]ontext matters." *Grutter* v. *Bollinger*, 539 U.S. 306, 327 (2003). In 1972,
Congress extended Title VII of the Civil Rights Act of 1964 to
cover public employment. At that time, municipal fire departments across the country, including New Haven's, pervasively
discriminated against minorities. The extension of Title VII to
cover jobs in firefighting effected no overnight change. It took
decades of persistent effort, advanced by Title VII litigation, to
open firefighting posts to members of racial minorities.

The white firefighters who scored high on New Haven's promotional exams understandably attract this Court's sympathy.
But they had no vested right to promotion. Nor have other persons received promotions in preference to them. New Haven
maintains that it refused to certify the test results because it
believed, for good cause, that it would be vulnerable to a Title
VII disparate-impact suit if it relied on those results. The Court
today holds that New Haven has not demonstrated "a strong
basis in evidence" for its plea. *Ante*, at 563. In so holding, the
Court pretends that "[t]he City rejected the test results solely
because the higher scoring candidates were white." *Ante*, at 580.
That pretension, essential to the Court's disposition, ignores substantial evidence of multiple flaws in the tests New Haven used.
The Court similarly fails to acknowledge the better tests used in
other cities, which have yielded less racially skewed outcomes.[1]

1 Never mind the flawed tests New Haven used and the better selection methods used

By order of this Court, New Haven, a city in which African-Americans and Hispanics account for nearly 60 percent of the population, must today be served—as it was in the days of undisguised discrimination—by a fire department in which members of racial and ethnic minorities are rarely seen in command positions. In arriving at its order, the Court barely acknowledges the pathmarking decision in *Griggs* v. *Duke Power Co.*, 401 U.S. 424 (1971), which explained the centrality of the disparate-impact concept to effective enforcement of Title VII. The Court's order and opinion, I anticipate, will not have staying power.

I

A

The Court's recitation of the facts leaves out important parts of the story. Firefighting is a profession in which the legacy of racial discrimination casts an especially long shadow. In extending Title VII to state and local government employers in 1972, Congress took note of a U.S. Commission on Civil Rights (USCCR) report finding racial discrimination in municipal employment even "more pervasive than in the private sector." H. R. Rep. No. 92–238, p. 17 (1971). According to the report, overt racism was partly to blame, but so too was a failure on the part of municipal employers to apply merit-based employment principles. In making hiring and promotion decisions, public employers often "rel[ied] on criteria unrelated to job performance," including nepotism or political patronage. 118 Cong. Rec. 1817 (1972). Such flawed selection methods served to entrench preexisting racial hierarchies. The USCCR report singled out police and fire departments for having "[b]arriers to equal employment . . . greater . . . than in any other area of State or local government," with African-Americans "hold[ing] almost no positions in the officer ranks." *Ibid.* See also National

---

elsewhere, JUSTICE ALITO's concurring opinion urges. Overriding all else, racial politics, fired up by a strident African-American pastor, were at work in New Haven. See *ante*, at 599–604. Even a detached and disinterested observer, however, would have every reason to ask: Why did such racially skewed results occur in New Haven, when better tests likely would have produced less disproportionate results?

Commission on Fire Prevention and Control, America Burning 5 (1973) ("Racial minorities are under-represented in the fire departments in nearly every community in which they live.").

The city of New Haven (City) was no exception. In the early 1970's, African-Americans and Hispanics composed 30 percent of New Haven's population, but only 3.6 percent of the City's 502 firefighters. The racial disparity in the officer ranks was even more pronounced: "[O]f the 107 officers in the Department only one was black, and he held the lowest rank above private." *Firebird Soc. Of New Haven, Inc.* v. *New Haven Bd. Of Fire Comm'rs*, 66 F. R. D. 457, 460 (Conn. 1975).

Following a lawsuit and settlement agreement, see *ibid.*, the City initiated efforts to increase minority representation in the New Haven Fire Department (Department). Those litigation-induced efforts produced some positive change. New Haven's population includes a greater proportion of minorities today than it did in the 1970's: Nearly 40 percent of the City's residents are African-American and more than 20 percent are Hispanic. Among entry-level firefighters, minorities are still underrepresented, but not starkly so. As of 2003, African-Americans and Hispanics constituted 30 percent and 16 percent of the City's firefighters, respectively. In supervisory positions, however, significant disparities remain. Overall, the senior officer ranks (captain and higher) are nine percent African-American and nine percent Hispanic. Only one of the Department's 21 fire captains is African-American. See App. in No. 06–4996–cv (CA2), p. A1588 (hereinafter CA2 App.). It is against this backdrop of entrenched inequality that the promotion process at issue in this litigation should be assessed.

B

By order of its charter, New Haven must use competitive examinations to fill vacancies in fire-officer and other civil service positions. Such examinations, the City's civil service rules specify, "shall be practical in nature, shall relate to matters which fairly measure the relative fitness and capacity of the applicants to discharge the duties of the position which they seek, and shall take into account character, training, experience, physical and mental fitness." *Id.*, at A331. The City may choose among a variety of testing methods, including written and oral exams and "[p]erformance tests to demonstrate skill and ability in performing actual work." *Id.*, at A332.

New Haven, the record indicates, did not closely consider what sort of "practical" examination would "fairly measure the relative fitness and capacity of the applicants to discharge the duties" of a fire officer. Instead, the City simply adhered to the testing regime outlined in its two-decades-old contract with the local firefighters' union: a written exam, which would account for 60 percent of an applicant's total score, and an oral exam, which would account for the remaining 40 percent. *Id.*, at A1045. In soliciting bids from exam development companies, New Haven made clear that it would entertain only "proposals that include a written component that will be weighted at 60%, and an oral component that will be weighted at 40%." *Id.*, at A342. Chad Legel, a representative of the winning bidder, Industrial/Organizational Solutions, Inc. (IOS), testified during his deposition that the City never asked whether alternative methods might better measure the qualities of a successful fire officer, including leadership skills and command presence. See *id.*, at A522 ("I was under contract and had responsibility only to create the oral interview and the written exam.").

Pursuant to New Haven's specifications, IOS developed and administered the oral and written exams. The results showed significant racial disparities. On the lieutenant exam, the pass rate for African-American candidates was about one-half the rate for Caucasian candidates; the pass rate for Hispanic candidates was even lower. On the captain exam, both African-American and Hispanic candidates passed at about half the rate of their Caucasian counterparts. See App. 225–226. More striking still, although nearly half of the 77 lieutenant candidates were African-American or Hispanic, none would have been eligible for promotion to the eight positions then vacant. The highest scoring African-American candidate ranked 13th; the top Hispanic candidate was 26th. As for the seven then-vacant captain positions, two Hispanic candidates would have been eligible, but no African-Americans. The highest scoring African-American candidate ranked 15th. See *id.*, at 218–219.

These stark disparities, the Court acknowledges, sufficed to state a prima facie case under Title VII's disparate-impact provision. See *ante*, at 586 ("The pass rates of minorities . . . f[e]ll well below the 80-percent standard set by the [Equal Employment Opportunity Commission (EEOC)] to implement the disparate-impact provision of Title VII."). New Haven thus had cause for concern about the prospect of Title VII litigation and liability. City officials referred the matter to the New Haven Civil Service Board (CSB), the entity responsible for certifying the results of employment exams.

Between January and March 2004, the CSB held five public meetings to consider the proper course. At the first meeting, New Haven's Corporation Counsel, Thomas Ude, described the legal standard governing Title VII disparate impact claims. Statistical imbalances alone, Ude correctly recognized, do not give rise to liability. Instead, presented with a disparity, an employer "has the opportunity and the burden of proving that the test is job-related and consistent with business necessity." CA2 App. A724. A Title VII plaintiff may attempt to rebut an employer's showing of job relatedness and necessity by identifying alternative selection methods that would have been at least as valid but with "less of an adverse or disparate or discriminatory effect." *Ibid.* See also *id.*, at A738. Accordingly, the CSB commissioners understood, their principal task was to decide whether they were confident about the reliability of the exams: Had the exams fairly measured the qualities of a successful fire officer despite their disparate results? Might an alternative examination process have identified the most qualified candidates without creating such significant racial imbalances?

Seeking a range of input on these questions, the CSB heard

from test takers, the test designer, subject-matter experts, City officials, union leaders, and community members. Several candidates for promotion, who did not yet know their exam results, spoke at the CSB's first two meetings. Some candidates favored certification. The exams, they emphasized, had closely tracked the assigned study materials. Having invested substantial time and money to prepare themselves for the test, they felt it would be unfair to scrap the results. See, *e.g., id.*, at A772–A773, A785–A789.

Other firefighters had a different view. A number of the exam questions, they pointed out, were not germane to New Haven's practices and procedures. See, *e.g., id.*, at A774–A784. At least two candidates opposed to certification noted unequal access to study materials. Some individuals, they asserted, had the necessary books even before the syllabus was issued. Others had to invest substantial sums to purchase the materials and "wait a month and a half for some of the books because they were on back-order." *Id.*, at A858. These disparities, it was suggested, fell at least in part along racial lines. While many Caucasian applicants could obtain materials and assistance from relatives in the fire service, the overwhelming majority of minority applicants were "first-generation firefighters" without such support networks. See *id.*, at A857–A861, A886–A887.

A representative of the Northeast Region of the International Association of Black Professional Firefighters, Donald Day, also spoke at the second meeting. Statistical disparities, he told the CSB, had been present in the Department's previous promotional exams. On earlier tests, however, a few minority candidates had fared well enough to earn promotions. *Id.*, at A828. See also App. 218–219. Day contrasted New Haven's experience with that of nearby Bridgeport, where minority firefighters held one-third of lieutenant and captain positions. Bridgeport, Day observed, had once used a testing process similar to New Haven's, with a written exam accounting for 70 percent of an applicant's score, an oral exam for 25 percent, and seniority for the remaining five percent. CA2 App. A830. Bridgeport recognized, however, that the oral component, more so than the written component, addressed the sort of "real-life scenarios" fire officers encounter on the job. *Id.*, at A832. Accordingly, that city "changed the relative weights" to give primacy to the oral exam. *Ibid.* Since that time, Day reported, Bridgeport had seen minorities "fairly represented" in its exam results. *Ibid.*

The CSB's third meeting featured IOS representative Legel, the leader of the team that had designed and administered the exams for New Haven. Several City officials also participated in the discussion. Legel described the exam development process in detail. The City, he recounted, had set the "parameters" for the exams, specifically, the requirement of written and oral components with a 60/40 weighting. *Id.*, at A923, A974. For security reasons, Department officials had not been permitted to check the content of the questions prior to their administration. Instead, IOS retained a senior fire officer from Georgia to review the exams "for content and fidelity to the source material." *Id.*, at A936. Legel defended the exams as "facially neutral," and stated that he "would stand by the[ir] validity." *Id.*, at A962. City officials did not dispute the neutrality of IOS's work. But, they cautioned, even if individual exam questions had no intrinsic bias, the selection process as a whole may nevertheless have been deficient. The officials urged the CSB to consult with experts about the "larger picture." *Id.*, at A1012.

At its fourth meeting, CSB solicited the views of three individuals with testing-related expertise. Dr. Christopher Hornick, an industrial/organizational psychology consultant with 25 years' experience with police and firefighter testing, described the exam results as having "relatively high adverse impact." *Id.*, at A1028. Most of the tests he had developed, Hornick stated, exhibited "significantly and dramatically less adverse impact." *Id.*, at A1029. Hornick downplayed the notion of "facial neutrality." It was more important, he advised the CSB, to consider "the broader issue of how your procedures and your rules and the types of tests that you are using are contributing to the adverse impact." *Id.*, at A1038.

Specifically, Hornick questioned New Haven's union-prompted 60/40 written/oral examination structure, noting the availability of "different types of testing procedures that are much more valid in terms of identifying the best potential supervisors in [the] fire department." *Id.*, at A1032. He suggested, for example, "an assessment center process, which is essentially an opportunity for candidates . . . to demonstrate how they would address a particular problem as opposed to just verbally saying it or identifying the correct option on a written test." *Id.*, at A1039–A1040. Such selection processes, Hornick said, better "identif[y] the best possible people" and "demonstrate dramatically less adverse impacts." *Ibid.* Hornick added:

> "I've spoken to at least 10,000, maybe 15,000,
> firefighters in group settings in my consulting practice
> and I have never one time ever had anyone in the fire
> service say to me, 'Well, the person who answers—gets
> the highest score on a written job knowledge, multiple
> guess test makes the best company officer.' We know
> that it's not as valid as other procedures that exist." *Id.*,
> at A1033.

See also *id.*, at A1042–A1043 ("I think a person's leadership skills, their command presence, their interpersonal skills, their management skills, their tactical skills could have been identified and evaluated in a much more appropriate way.").

Hornick described the written test itself as "reasonably good," *id.*, at A1041, but he criticized the decision not to allow Department officials to check the content. According to Hornick, this "inevitably" led to "test[ing] for processes and procedures that don't necessarily match up into the department." *Id.*, at A1034–A1035. He preferred "experts from within the department who have signed confidentiality agreements . . .

to make sure that the terminology and equipment that's being identified from standardized reading sources apply to the department." *Id.*, at A1035.

Asked whether he thought the City should certify the results, Hornick hedged: "There is adverse impact in the test. That will be identified in any proceeding that you have. You will have industrial psychology experts, if it goes to court, on both sides. And it will not be a pretty or comfortable position for anyone to be in." *Id.*, at A1040–A1041. Perhaps, he suggested, New Haven might certify the results but immediately begin exploring "alternative ways to deal with these issues" in the future. *Id.*, at A1041.

The two other witnesses made relatively brief appearances. Vincent Lewis, a specialist with the Department of Homeland Security and former fire officer in Michigan, believed the exams had generally tested relevant material, although he noted a relatively heavy emphasis on questions pertaining to being an "apparatus driver." He suggested that this may have disadvantaged test takers "who had not had the training or had not had an opportunity to drive the apparatus." *Id.*, at A1051. He also urged the CSB to consider whether candidates had, in fact, enjoyed equal access to the study materials. *Ibid.* Cf. *supra*, at 613–614.

Janet Helms, a professor of counseling psychology at Boston College, observed that two-thirds of the incumbent fire officers who submitted job analyses to IOS during the exam-design phase were Caucasian. Members of different racial groups, Helms told the CSB, sometimes do their jobs in different ways, "often because the experiences that are open to white male firefighters are not open to members of these other under-represented groups." CA2 App. A1063–A1064. The heavy reliance on job analyses from white firefighters, she suggested, may thus have introduced an element of bias. *Id.*, at A1063.

The CSB's fifth and final meeting began with statements from City officials recommending against certification. Ude, New Haven's counsel, repeated the applicable disparate-impact standard:

"[A] finding of adverse impact is the beginning, not the end, of a review of testing procedures. Where a procedure demonstrates adverse impact, you look to how closely it is related to the job that you're looking to fill and you also look at whether there are other ways to test for those qualities, those traits, those positions that are equally valid with less adverse impact." *Id.*, at A1100–A1101.

New Haven, Ude and other officials asserted, would be vulnerable to Title VII liability under this standard. Even if the exams were "facially neutral," significant doubts had been raised about whether they properly assessed the key attributes of a successful fire officer. *Id.*, at A1103. See also *id.*, at A1125 ("Upon close reading of the exams, the questions themselves would appear to test a candidate's ability to memorize textbooks but not necessarily to identify solutions to real problems on the fire ground."). Moreover, City officials reminded the CSB, Hornick and others had identified better, less discriminatory selection methods—such as assessment centers or exams with a more heavily weighted oral component. *Id.*, at A1108–A1109, A1129–A1130.

After giving members of the public a final chance to weigh in, the CSB voted on certification, dividing 2 to 2. By rule, the result was noncertification. Voting no, Commissioner Webber stated, "I originally was going to vote to certify. . . . But I've heard enough testimony here to give me great doubts about the test itself and . . . some of the procedures. And I believe we can do better." *Id.*, at A1157. Commissioner Tirado likewise concluded that the "flawed" testing process counseled against certification. *Id.*, at A1158. Chairman Segaloff and Commissioner Caplan voted to certify. According to Segaloff, the testimony had not "compelled [him] to say this exam was not job-related," and he was unconvinced that alternative selection processes would be "less discriminatory." *Id.*, at A1159–A1160. Both Segaloff and Caplan, however, urged the City to undertake civil-service reform. *Id.*, at A1150–A1154.

C

Following the CSB's vote, petitioners—17 white firefighters and one Hispanic firefighter, all of whom had high marks on the exams—filed suit in the United States District Court for the District of Connecticut. They named as defendants—respondents here—the City, several City officials, a local political activist, and the two CSB members who voted against certifying the results. By opposing certification, petitioners alleged, respondents had discriminated against them in violation of Title VII's disparate-treatment provision and the Fourteenth Amendment's Equal Protection Clause. The decision not to certify, respondents answered, was a lawful effort to comply with Title VII's disparate-impact provision and thus could not have run afoul of Title VII's prohibition of disparate treatment. Characterizing respondents' stated rationale as a mere pretext, petitioners insisted that New Haven would have had a solid defense to any disparate-impact suit.

In a decision summarily affirmed by the Court of Appeals, the District Court granted summary judgment for respondents. 554 F. Supp. 2d 142 (Conn. 2006), aff'd, 530 F. 3d 87 (CA2 2008) (*per curiam*). Under Second Circuit precedent, the District Court explained, "the intent to remedy the disparate impact" of a promotional exam "is not equivalent to an intent to discriminate against non-minority applicants." 554 F. Supp. 2d, at 157 (quoting *Hayden* v. *County of Nassau*, 180 F. 3d 42, 51 (CA2 1999)). Rejecting petitioners' pretext argument, the court observed that the exam results were sufficiently skewed "to make out a prima facie case of discrimination" under Title VII's disparate-impact provision. 554 F. Supp. 2d, at 158. Had New Haven gone forward with certification and been sued by aggrieved minority test takers, the City would have been forced to defend tests that were presumptively invalid. And, as the CSB testimony of Hornick and others indicated, overcoming that presumption would have been no easy task. *Id.*, at 153–156. Given Title VII's preference for voluntary compliance, the court held, New Haven could lawfully discard the disputed exams even if the City had not definitively "pinpoint[ed]" the source of the disparity and "ha[d] not yet formulated a better selection method." *Id.*, at 156.

Respondents were no doubt conscious of race during their decision-making process, the court acknowledged, but this did not mean they had engaged in racially disparate treatment. The conclusion they had reached and the action thereupon taken were race neutral in this sense: "[A]ll the test results were discarded, no one was promoted, and firefighters of every race will have to participate in another selection process to be considered for promotion." *Id.*, at 158. New Haven's action, which gave no individual a preference, "was 'simply not analogous to a quota system or a minority set-aside where candidates, on the basis of their race, are not treated uniformly.'" *Id.*, at 157 (quoting Hayden, 180 F. 3d, at 50). For these and other reasons, the court also rejected petitioners' equal protection claim.

II

A

Title VII became effective in July 1965. Employers responded to the law by eliminating rules and practices that explicitly barred racial minorities from "white" jobs. But removing overtly race-based job classifications did not usher in genuinely equal opportunity. More subtle—and sometimes unconscious—forms of discrimination replaced once undisguised restrictions.

In *Griggs* v. *Duke Power Co.*, 401 U.S. 424 (1971), this Court responded to that reality and supplied important guidance on Title VII's mission and scope. Congress, the landmark decision recognized, aimed beyond "disparate treatment"; it targeted "disparate impact" as well. Title VII's original text, it was plain to the Court, "proscribe[d] not only overt discrimination but also practices that are fair in form, but discriminatory in operation."

Id., at 431.[2] Only by ignoring Griggs could one maintain that intentionally disparate treatment alone was Title VII's "original, foundational prohibition," and disparate impact a mere afterthought. Cf. *ante*, at 581.

Griggs addressed Duke Power Company's policy that applicants for positions, save in the company's labor department, be high school graduates and score satisfactorily on two professionally prepared aptitude tests. "[T]here was no showing of a discriminatory purpose in the adoption of the diploma and test requirements." 401 U.S., at 428. The policy, however, "operated to render ineligible a markedly disproportionate number of [African-Americans]." *Id.*, at 429. At the time of the litigation, in North Carolina, where the Duke Power plant was located, 34 percent of white males, but only 12 percent of African-American males, had high school diplomas. *Id.*, at 430, n. 6. African-Americans also failed the aptitude tests at a significantly higher rate than whites. *Ibid.* Neither requirement had been "shown to bear a demonstrable relationship to successful performance of the jobs for which it was used." *Id.*, at 431.

The Court unanimously held that the company's diploma and test requirements violated Title VII. "[T]o achieve equality of employment opportunities," the Court comprehended, Congress "directed the thrust of the Act to the consequences of employment practices, not simply the motivation." *Id.*, at 429, 432. That meant "unnecessary barriers to employment" must fall, even if "neutral on their face" and "neutral in terms of intent." *Id.*, at 430, 431. "The touchstone" for determining whether a

---

2 The Court's disparate-impact analysis rested on two provisions of Title VII: § 703(a)(2), which made it unlawful for an employer "to limit, segregate, or classify his employees in any way which would deprive or tend to deprive any individual of employment opportunities or otherwise adversely affect his status as an employee, because of such individual's race, color, religion, sex, or national origin"; and § 703(h), which permitted employers "to act upon the results of any professionally developed ability test provided that such test, its administration or action upon the results is not designed, intended or used to discriminate because of race, color, religion, sex or national origin." *Griggs* v. *Duke Power Co.*, 401 U.S. 424, 426, n. 1 (1971) (quoting 78 Stat. 255, 42 U. S. C. § 2000e–2(a)(2), (h) (1964 ed.)). See also 401 U.S., at 433–436 (explaining that § 703(h) authorizes only tests that are "demonstrably a reasonable measure of job performance").

test or qualification meets Title VII's measure, the Court said, is not "good intent or the absence of discriminatory intent"; it is "business necessity." *Id.*, at 431, 432. Matching procedure to substance, the *Griggs* Court observed, Congress "placed on the employer the burden of showing that any given requirement . . . ha[s] a manifest relationship to the employment in question." *Id.*, at 432.

In *Albemarle Paper Co.* v. *Moody*, 422 U.S. 405 (1975), the Court, again without dissent, elaborated on *Griggs*. When an employment test "select[s] applicants for hire or promotion in a racial pattern significantly different from the pool of applicants," the Court reiterated, the employer must demonstrate a "manifest relationship" between test and job. 422 U.S., at 425. Such a showing, the Court cautioned, does not necessarily mean the employer prevails: "[I]t remains open to the complaining party to show that other tests or selection devices, without a similarly undesirable racial effect, would also serve the employer's legitimate interest in 'efficient and trustworthy workmanship.' " *Ibid.*

Federal trial and appellate courts applied *Griggs* and *Albemarle* to disallow a host of hiring and promotion practices that "operate[d] as 'built in headwinds' for minority groups." *Griggs*, 401 U.S., at 432. Practices discriminatory in effect, courts repeatedly emphasized, could be maintained only upon an employer's showing of "an overriding and compelling business purpose." *Chrisner* v. *Complete Auto Transit, Inc.*, 645 F. 2d 1251, 1261, n. 9 (CA6 1981).[3] That a practice served "legitimate management

---

3 See also *Dothard* v. *Rawlinson*, 433 U.S. 321, 332, n. 14 (1977) ("a discriminatory employment practice must be shown to be necessary to safe and efficient job performance to survive a Title VII challenge"); *Williams* v. *Colorado Springs, Colo., School Dist.*, 641 F. 2d 835, 840–841 (CA10 1981) ("The term 'necessity' connotes that the exclusionary practice must be shown to be of great importance to job performance."); *Kirby* v. *Colony Furniture Co.*, 613 F. 2d 696, 705, n. 6 (CA8 1980) ("the proper standard for determining whether 'business necessity' justifies a practice which has a racially discriminatory result is not whether it is justified by routine business considerations but whether there is a compelling need for the employer to maintain that practice and whether the employer can prove there is no alternative to the challenged practice"); *Pettway* v. *American Cast Iron Pipe Co.*, 494 F. 2d 211, 244, n. 87 (CA5 1974) ("this doctrine of business necessity . . . connotes an irresistible demand" (internal quotation marks omitted)); *United States* v. *Bethlehem Steel Corp.*, 446 F. 2d 652, 662 (CA2 1971) (an exclusionary practice "must not only directly foster safety and efficiency of a plant, but also be essential to those goals"); *Robinson* v. *Lorillard Corp.*, 444 F. 2d 791, 798 (CA4

functions" did not, it was generally understood, suffice to estab-lish business necessity. *Williams* v. *Colorado Springs, Colo., School Dist.*, 641 F. 2d 835, 840–841 (CA10 1981) (internal quotation marks omitted). Among selection methods cast aside for lack of a "manifest relationship" to job performance were a number of written hiring and promotional examinations for firefighters.[4]

Moving in a different direction, in *Wards Cove Packing Co.* v. *Atonio*, 490 U.S. 642 (1989), a bare majority of this Court significantly modified the *Griggs-Albemarle* delineation of Title VII's disparate-impact proscription. As to business necessity for a practice that disproportionately excludes members of minority groups, *Wards Cove* held, the employer bears only the burden of production, not the burden of persuasion. 490 U.S., at 659–660. And in place of the instruction that the challenged practice "must have a manifest relationship to the employment in question," *Griggs*, 401 U.S., at 432, *Wards Cove* said that the practice would be permissible as long as it "serve[d], in a signif-icant way, the legitimate employment goals of the employer," 490 U.S., at 659.

In response to *Wards Cove* and "a number of [other] recent decisions by the United States Supreme Court that sharply cut back on the scope and effectiveness of [civil rights] laws," Congress enacted the Civil Rights Act of 1991. H. R. Rep. No. 102–40, pt. 2, p. 2 (1991). Among the 1991 alterations, Congress formally codified the disparate-impact component of Title VII. In so amending the statute, Congress made plain its intention to restore "the concepts of 'business necessity' and 'job related' enunciated by the Supreme Court in *Griggs* v. *Duke Power Co.* . . . and in other Supreme Court decisions

---

1971) ("The test is whether there exists an overriding legitimate business purpose such that the practice is necessary to the safe and efficient operation of the business.").

4 See, *e.g.*, *Nash* v. *Jacksonville*, 837 F. 2d 1534 (CA11 1988), vacated, 490 U.S. 1103 (1989), opinion reinstated, 905 F. 2d 355 (1990); *Vulcan Pioneers, Inc.* v. *New Jersey Dept. of Civil Serv.*, 832 F. 2d 811 (CA3 1987); *Guardians Assn. of N. Y. City Police Dept.* v. *Civil Serv. Comm'n*, 630 F. 2d 79 (CA2 1980); *Ensley Branch of NAACP* v. *Seibels*, 616 F. 2d 812 (CA5 1980); *Firefighters Inst. for Racial Equality* v. *St. Louis*, 616 F. 2d 350 (CA8 1980); *Boston Chapter, NAACP, Inc.* v. *Beecher*, 504 F. 2d 1017 (CA1 1974).

prior to *Wards Cove Packing Co.* v. *Atonio.*" § 3(2), 105 Stat. 1071. Once a complaining party demonstrates that an employment practice causes a disparate impact, amended Title VII states, the burden is on the employer "to demonstrate that the challenged practice is job related for the position in question and consistent with business necessity." 42 U. S. C. § 2000e–2(k)(1)(A)(i). If the employer carries that substantial burden, the complainant may respond by identifying "an alternative employment practice" which the employer "refuses to adopt." § 2000e–2(k)(1)(A)(ii), (C).

B

Neither Congress' enactments nor this Court's Title VII precedents (including the now-discredited decision in *Wards Cove*) offer even a hint of "conflict" between an employer's obligations under the statute's disparate-treatment and disparate-impact provisions. Cf. *ante*, at 580. Standing on an equal footing, these twin pillars of Title VII advance the same objectives: ending workplace discrimination and promoting genuinely equal opportunity. See *McDonnell Douglas Corp.* v. *Green*, 411 U.S. 792, 800 (1973).

Yet the Court today sets at odds the statute's core directives. When an employer changes an employment practice in an effort to comply with Title VII's disparate-impact provision, the Court reasons, it acts "because of race"—something Title VII's disparate-treatment provision, see § 2000e–2(a)(1), generally forbids. *Ante*, at 579–580. This characterization of an employer's compliance-directed action shows little attention to Congress' design or to the Griggs line of cases Congress recognized as pathmarking.

"[O]ur task in interpreting separate provisions of a single Act is to give the Act the most harmonious, comprehensive meaning possible in light of the legislative policy and purpose." *Weinberger* v. *Hynson, Westcott & Dunning, Inc.*, 412 U.S. 609, 631–632 (1973) (internal quotation marks omitted). A particular phrase need not "extend to the outer limits of its definitional possibilities" if an incongruity would result. *Dolan* v. *Postal Service*, 546

U.S. 481, 486 (2006). Here, Title VII's disparate-treatment and disparate-impact proscriptions must be read as complementary.

In codifying the *Griggs* and *Albemarle* instructions, Congress declared unambiguously that selection criteria operating to the disadvantage of minority group members can be retained only if justified by business necessity.[5] In keeping with Congress' design, employers who reject such criteria due to reasonable doubts about their reliability can hardly be held to have engaged in discrimination "because of" race. A reasonable endeavor to comply with the law and to ensure that qualified candidates of all races have a fair opportunity to compete is simply not what Congress meant to interdict. I would therefore hold that an employer who jettisons a selection device when its dispropor-tionate racial impact becomes apparent does not violate Title VII's disparate-treatment bar automatically or at all, subject to this key condition: The employer must have good cause to believe the device would not withstand examination for busi-ness necessity. Cf. *Faragher* v. *Boca Raton*, 524 U.S. 775, 806 (1998) (observing that it accords with "clear statutory policy" for employers "to prevent violations" and "make reasonable efforts to discharge their duty" under Title VII).

EEOC's interpretative guidelines are corroborative. "[B]y the enactment of title VII," the guidelines state, "Congress did not intend to expose those who comply with the Act to charges that they are violating the very statute they are seeking to implement." 29 CFR § 1608.1(a) (2008). Recognizing EEOC's "enforcement responsibility" under Title VII, we have previously accorded the Commission's position respectful consideration. See, *e.g.*, *Albemarle*, 422 U.S., at 431; *Griggs*, 401 U.S., at 434. Yet the Court today does not so much as mention EEOC's counsel.

Our precedents defining the contours of Title VII's disparate-treatment prohibition further confirm the absence of any

---

5 What was the "business necessity" for the tests New Haven used? How could one justify, *e.g.*, the 60/40 written/oral ratio, see *supra*, at 611–612, 614–615, under that standard? Neither the Court nor the concurring opinions attempt to defend the ratio.

intrastatutory discord. In *Johnson* v. *Transportation Agency, Santa Clara Cty.*, 480 U.S. 616 (1987), we upheld a municipal employer's voluntary affirmative-action plan against a disparate-treatment challenge. Pursuant to the plan, the employer selected a woman for a road-dispatcher position, a job category traditionally regarded as "male." A male applicant who had a slightly higher interview score brought suit under Title VII. This Court rejected his claim and approved the plan, which allowed consideration of gender as "one of numerous factors." *Id.*, at 638. Such consideration, we said, is "fully consistent with Title VII" because plans of that order can aid "in eliminating the vestiges of discrimination in the workplace." *Id.*, at 642.

This litigation does not involve affirmative action. But if the voluntary affirmative action at issue in *Johnson* does not discriminate within the meaning of Title VII, neither does an employer's reasonable effort to comply with Title VII's disparate-impact provision by refraining from action of doubtful consistency with business necessity.

C

To "reconcile" the supposed "conflict" between disparate treatment and disparate impact, the Court offers an enigmatic standard. *Ante*, at 580. Employers may attempt to comply with Title VII's disparate-impact provision, the Court declares, only where there is a "strong basis in evidence" documenting the necessity of their action. *Ante*, at 583. The Court's standard, drawn from inapposite equal protection precedents, is not elaborated. One is left to wonder what cases would meet the standard and why the Court is so sure cases of this genre do not.

1

In construing Title VII, I note preliminarily, equal protection doctrine is of limited utility. The Equal Protection Clause, this Court has held, prohibits only intentional discrimination; it does not have a disparate-impact component. See *Personnel Administrator of Mass.* v. *Feeney*, 442 U.S. 256, 272 (1979); *Washington* v. *Davis*, 426 U.S. 229, 239 (1976). Title VII, in contrast, aims to eliminate all forms of employment discrimination, unintentional as well as deliberate. Until today, cf. *ante*, at 584; *ante*, p. 594 (Scalia, J., concurring), this Court has never questioned the constitutionality of the disparate-impact component of Title VII, and for good reason. By instructing employers to avoid needlessly exclusionary selection processes, Title VII's disparate-impact provision calls for a "race-neutral means to increase minority . . . participation"—something this Court's equal protection precedents also encourage. See *Adarand Constructors, Inc.* v. *Peña*, 515 U.S. 200, 238 (1995) (quoting *Richmond* v. *J. A. Croson Co.*, 488 U.S. 469, 507 (1989)). "The very radicalism of holding disparate impact doctrine unconstitutional as a matter of equal protection," moreover, "suggests that only a very uncompromising court would issue such a decision." Primus, Equal Protection and Disparate Impact: Round Three, 117 Harv. L. Rev. 493, 585 (2003).

The cases from which the Court draws its strong-basis-in-evidence standard are particularly inapt; they concern the constitutionality of absolute racial preferences. See *Wygant* v. *Jackson Bd. of Ed.*, 476 U.S. 267, 277 (1986) (plurality opinion) (invalidating a school district's plan to lay off nonminority teachers while retaining minority teachers with less seniority); *Croson*, 488 U.S., at 499–500 (rejecting a set-aside program for minority contractors that operated as "an unyielding racial quota"). An employer's effort to avoid Title VII liability by repudiating a suspect selection method scarcely resembles those cases. Race was not merely a relevant consideration in *Wygant* and *Croson*; it was the decisive factor. Observance of Title VII's disparate-impact provision, in contrast, calls for no racial preference, absolute or otherwise. The very purpose of the provision is to ensure that individuals are hired and promoted based on qualifications manifestly necessary to successful performance of the job in question, qualifications that do not screen out members of any race.[6]

---

6 Even in Title VII cases involving race-conscious (or gender-conscious) affirmative-

2

The Court's decision in this litigation underplays a dominant Title VII theme. This Court has repeatedly emphasized that the statute "should not be read to thwart" efforts at voluntary compliance. *Johnson*, 480 U.S., at 630. Such compliance, we have explained, is "the preferred means of achieving [Title VII's] objectives." *Firefighters* v. *Cleveland*, 478 U.S. 501, 515 (1986). See also *Kolstad* v. *American Dental Assn.*, 527 U.S. 526, 545 (1999) ("Dissuading employers from [taking voluntary action] to prevent discrimination in the workplace is directly contrary to the purposes underlying Title VII."); 29 CFR § 1608.1(c). The strong-basis-in-evidence standard, however, as barely described in general, and cavalierly applied in this litigation, makes voluntary compliance a hazardous venture.

As a result of today's decision, an employer who discards a dubious selection process can anticipate costly disparate-treatment litigation in which its chances for success—even for surviving a summary-judgment motion—are highly problematic. Concern about exposure to disparate-impact liability, however well grounded, is insufficient to insulate an employer from attack. Instead, the employer must make a "strong" showing that (1) its selection method was "not job related and consistent with business necessity," or (2) that it refused to adopt "an equally valid, less discriminatory alternative." *Ante*, at 587. It is hard to see how these requirements differ from demanding that an employer establish "a provable, actual violation" against itself. Cf. *ante*, at 583. There is indeed a sharp conflict here, but it is not the false one the Court describes between Title VII's core provisions. It is, instead, the discordance of the Court's opinion

---

action plans, the Court has never proposed a strong-basis-in-evidence standard. In *Johnson* v. *Transportation Agency, Santa Clara Cty.*, 480 U.S. 616 (1987), the Court simply examined the municipal employer's action for reasonableness: "Given the obvious imbalance in the Skilled Craft category, and given the Agency's commitment to eliminating such imbalances, it was plainly not unreasonable for the Agency . . . to consider as one factor the sex of [applicants] in making its decision." *Id.*, at 637. See also *Firefighters* v. *Cleveland*, 478 U.S. 501, 516 (1986) ("Title VII permits employers and unions voluntarily to make use of reasonable race-conscious affirmative action.").

with the voluntary compliance ideal. Cf. *Wygant*, 476 U.S., at 290 (O'Connor, J., concurring in part and concurring in judgment) ("The imposition of a requirement that public employers make findings that they have engaged in illegal discrimination before they [act] would severely undermine public employers' incentive to meet voluntarily their civil rights obligations.").[7]

3

The Court's additional justifications for announcing a strong-basis-in-evidence standard are unimpressive. First, discarding the results of tests, the Court suggests, calls for a heightened standard because it "upset[s] an employee's legitimate expectation." *Ante*, at 585. This rationale puts the cart before the horse. The legitimacy of an employee's expectation depends on the legitimacy of the selection method. If an employer reasonably concludes that an exam fails to identify the most qualified individuals and needlessly shuts out a segment of the applicant pool, Title VII surely does not compel the employer to hire or promote based on the test, however unreliable it may be. Indeed, the statute's prime objective is to prevent exclusionary practices from "operat[ing] to 'freeze' the status quo." *Griggs*, 401 U.S., at 430.

Second, the Court suggests, anything less than a strong basis-in-evidence standard risks creating "a de facto quota system, in which . . . an employer could discard test results . . . with the intent of obtaining the employer's preferred racial balance." *Ante*, at 581–582. Under a reasonableness standard, however, an employer could not cast aside a selection method based on a statistical disparity alone.[8] The employer must have good cause

---

7 Notably, prior decisions applying a strong-basis-in-evidence standard have not imposed a burden as heavy as the one the Court imposes today. In *Croson*, the Court found no strong basis in evidence because the city had offered "nothing approaching a prima facie case." *Richmond* v. *J. A. Croson Co.*, 488 U.S. 469, 500 (1989). The Court did not suggest that anything beyond a prima facie case would have been required. In the context of race-based electoral districting, the Court has indicated that a "strong basis" exists when the "threshold conditions" for liability are present. *Bush* v. *Vera*, 517 U.S. 952, 978 (1996) (plurality opinion).

8 Infecting the Court's entire analysis is its insistence that the City rejected the test results "in sole reliance upon race-based statistics." *Ante*, at 584. See also *ante*, at 580, 587. But as the part of the story the Court leaves out, see *supra*, at 609–618, so plainly shows—the long

to believe that the method screens out qualified applicants and would be difficult to justify as grounded in business necessity. Should an employer repeatedly reject test results, it would be fair, I agree, to infer that the employer is simply seeking a racially balanced outcome and is not genuinely endeavoring to comply with Title VII.

D

The Court stacks the deck further by denying respondents any chance to satisfy the newly announced strong-basis-in-evidence standard. When this Court formulates a new legal rule, the ordinary course is to remand and allow the lower courts to apply the rule in the first instance. See, *e.g.*, *Johnson* v. *California*, 543 U.S. 499, 515 (2005); *Pullman-Standard* v. *Swint*, 456 U.S. 273, 291 (1982). I see no good reason why the Court fails to follow that course today. Indeed, the sole basis for the Court's peremptory ruling is the demonstrably false pretension that respondents showed "nothing more" than "a significant statistical disparity." *Ante*, at 587; see *supra*, at 630, n. 8.[9]

III

A

Applying what I view as the proper standard to the record thus far made, I would hold that New Haven had ample cause

---

history of rank discrimination against African-Americans in the firefighting profession, the multiple flaws in New Haven's test for promotions—"sole reliance" on statistics certainly is not descriptive of the CSB's decision.

9 The Court's refusal to remand for further proceedings also deprives respondents of an opportunity to invoke 42 U. S. C. § 2000e–12(b) as a shield to liability. Section 2000e–12(b) provides:

"In any action or proceeding based on any alleged unlawful employment practice, no person shall be subject to any liability or punishment for or on account of (1) the commission by such person of an unlawful employment practice if he pleads and proves that the act or omission complained of was in good faith, in conformity with, and in reliance on any written interpretation or opinion of the [EEOC] . . . . Such a defense, if established, shall be a bar to the action or proceeding, notwithstanding that (A) after such act or omission, such interpretation or opinion is modified or rescinded or is determined by judicial authority to be invalid or of no legal effect . . . ."

Specifically, given the chance, respondents might have called attention to the EEOC guidelines set out in 29 CFR §§ 1608.3 and 1608.4 (2008). The guidelines recognize that employers may "take affirmative action based on an analysis which reveals facts constituting actual or potential adverse impact." § 1608.3(a). If "affirmative action" is in order, so is the lesser step of discarding a dubious selection device.

to believe its selection process was flawed and not justified by business necessity. Judged by that standard, petitioners have not shown that New Haven's failure to certify the exam results violated Title VII's disparate-treatment provision.[10]

The City, all agree, "was faced with a prima facie case of disparate-impact liability," *ante*, at 586 (majority opinion): The pass rate for minority candidates was half the rate for nonminority candidates, and virtually no minority candidates would have been eligible for promotion had the exam results been certified. Alerted to this stark disparity, the CSB heard expert and lay testimony, presented at public hearings, in an endeavor to ascertain whether the exams were fair and consistent with business necessity. Its investigation revealed grave cause for concern about the exam process itself and the City's failure to consider alternative selection devices.

Chief among the City's problems was the very nature of the tests for promotion. In choosing to use written and oral exams with a 60/40 weighting, the City simply adhered to the union's preference and apparently gave no consideration to whether the weighting was likely to identify the most qualified fire-officer candidates.[11] There is strong reason to think it was not.

10 The lower courts focused on respondents' "intent" rather than on whether respondents in fact had good cause to act. See 554 F. Supp. 2d 142, 157 (Conn. 2006). Ordinarily, a remand for fresh consideration would be in order. But the Court has seen fit to preclude further proceedings. I therefore explain why, if final adjudication by this Court is indeed appropriate, New Haven should be the prevailing party.

11 This alone would have posed a substantial problem for New Haven in a disparate-impact suit, particularly in light of the disparate results the City's scheme had produced in the past. See *supra*, at 614. Under the Uniform Guidelines on Employee Selection Procedures (Uniform Guidelines), employers must conduct "an investigation of suitable alternative selection procedures." 29 CFR § 1607.3(B). See also *Officers for Justice* v. *Civil Serv. Comm'n*, 979 F. 2d 721, 728 (CA9 1992) ("before utilizing a procedure that has an adverse impact on minorities, the City has an *obligation* pursuant to the *Uniform Guidelines* to explore alternative procedures and to implement them if they have less adverse impact and are substantially equally valid"). It is no answer to "presume" that the two-decades-old 60/40 formula was adopted for a "rational reason" because it "was the result of a union-negotiated collective-bargaining agreement." Cf. *ante*, at 589. That the parties may have been "rational" says nothing about whether their agreed-upon selection process was consistent with business necessity. It is not at all unusual for agreements negotiated between employers and unions to run afoul of Title VII. See, *e.g.*, *Peters* v. *Missouri-Pacific R. Co.*, 483 F. 2d 490, 497 (CA5 1973) (an employment practice "is not shielded [from the requirements of Title VII] by the facts that it is the product of collective bargaining and meets the standards of fair representation").

Relying heavily on written tests to select fire officers is a questionable practice, to say the least. Successful fire officers, the City's description of the position makes clear, must have the "[a]bility to lead personnel effectively, maintain discipline, promote harmony, exercise sound judgment, and cooperate with other officials." CA2 App. A432. These qualities are not well measured by written tests. Testifying before the CSB, Christopher Hornick, an exam-design expert with more than two decades of relevant experience, was emphatic on this point: Leadership skills, command presence, and the like "could have been identified and evaluated in a much more appropriate way." *Id.*, at A1042–A1043.

Hornick's commonsense observation is mirrored in case law and in Title VII's administrative guidelines. Courts have long criticized written firefighter promotion exams for being "more probative of the test taker's ability to recall what a particular text stated on a given topic than of his firefighting or supervisory knowledge and abilities." *Vulcan Pioneers, Inc.* v. *New Jersey Dept. of Civil Serv.*, 625 F. Supp. 527, 539 (NJ 1985). A fire officer's job, courts have observed, "involves complex behaviors, good interpersonal skills, the ability to make decisions under tremendous pressure, and a host of other abilities—none of which is easily measured by a written, multiple choice test." *Firefighters Inst. for Racial Equality* v. *St. Louis*, 616 F. 2d 350, 359 (CA8 1980).[12] Interpreting the Uniform Guidelines, EEOC and other federal agencies responsible for enforcing equal opportunity employment laws have similarly recognized that, as measures of "interpersonal relations" or "ability to function under danger (*e.g.*, firefighters)," "[p]encil-and-paper tests . . . generally are not close enough approximations of work behaviors to show

---

12 See also *Nash*, 837 F. 2d, at 1538 ("the examination did not test the one aspect of job performance that differentiated the job of firefighter engineer from fire lieutenant (combat): supervisory skills"); *Firefighters Inst. for Racial Equality* v. *St. Louis*, 549 F. 2d 506, 512 (CA8 1977) ("there is no good pen and paper test for evaluating supervisory skills"); *Boston Chapter, NAACP*, 504 F. 2d, at 1023 ("[T]here is a difference between memorizing . . . fire fighting terminology and being a good fire fighter. If the Boston Red Sox recruited players on the basis of their knowledge of baseball history and vocabulary, the team might acquire [players] who could not bat, pitch or catch.").

content validity." 44 Fed. Reg. 12007 (1979). See also 29 CFR § 1607.15(C)(4).[13]

Given these unfavorable appraisals, it is unsurprising that most municipal employers do not evaluate their fire-officer candidates as New Haven does. Although comprehensive statistics are scarce, a 1996 study found that nearly two-thirds of surveyed municipalities used assessment centers ("simulations of the real world of work") as part of their promotion processes. P. Lowry, A Survey of the Assessment Center Process in the Public Sector, 25 Public Personnel Management 307, 315 (1996). That figure represented a marked increase over the previous decade, see *ibid.*, so the percentage today may well be even higher. Among municipalities still relying in part on written exams, the median weight assigned to them was 30 percent—half the weight given to New Haven's written exam. *Id.*, at 309.

Testimony before the CSB indicated that these alternative methods were both more reliable and notably less discriminatory in operation. According to Donald Day of the International Association of Black Professional Firefighters, nearby Bridgeport saw less skewed results after switching to a selection process that placed primary weight on an oral exam. CA2 App. A830–A832; see *supra*, at 614. And Hornick described assessment centers as "demonstrat[ing] dramatically less adverse impacts" than written exams. CA2 App. A1040.[14] Considering the prevalence of these proven alternatives, New Haven was poorly positioned to

---

13 Cf. *Gillespie* v. *Wisconsin*, 771 F. 2d 1035, 1043 (CA7 1985) (courts must evaluate "the degree to which the nature of the examination procedure approximates the job conditions"). In addition to "content validity," the Uniform Guidelines discuss "construct validity" and "criterion validity" as means by which an employer might establish the reliability of a selection method. See 29 CFR § 1607.14(B)–(D). Content validity, however, is the only type of validity addressed by the parties and "the only feasible type of validation in these circumstances." Brief for Industrial-Organizational Psychologists as *Amicus Curiae* 7, n. 2 (hereinafter I–O Psychologists Brief).

14 See also G. Thornton & D. Rupp, Assessment Centers in Human Resource Management 15 (2006) ("Assessment centers predict future success, do not cause adverse impact, and are seen as fair by participants."); W. Cascio & H. Aguinis, Applied Psychology in Human Resource Management 372 (6th ed. 2005) ("research has demonstrated that adverse impact is less of a problem in an [assessment center] as compared to an aptitude test"). Cf. *Firefighters Inst. for Racial Equality*, 549 F. 2d, at 513 (recommending assessment centers as an alternative to written exams).

argue that promotions based on its outmoded and exclusionary selection process qualified as a business necessity. Cf. *Robinson* v. *Lorillard Corp.*, 444 F. 2d 791, 798, n. 7 (CA4 1971) ("It should go without saying that a practice is hardly 'necessary' if an alternative practice better effectuates its intended purpose or is equally effective but less discriminatory.")[15]

Ignoring the conceptual and other defects in New Haven's selection process, the Court describes the exams as "painstaking[ly]" developed to test "relevant" material and on that basis finds no substantial risk of disparate-impact liability. See *ante*, at 588. Perhaps such reasoning would have sufficed under *Wards Cove*, which permitted exclusionary practices as long as they advanced an employer's "legitimate" goals. 490 U.S., at 659. But Congress repudiated *Wards Cove* and reinstated the "business necessity" rule attended by a "manifest relationship" requirement. See *Griggs*, 401 U.S., at 431–432. See also *supra*, at 624. Like the chess player who tries to win by sweeping the opponent's pieces off the table, the Court simply shuts from its sight the formidable obstacles New Haven would have faced in defending against a disparate-impact suit. See *Lanning* v. *Southeastern Pa. Transp. Auth.*, 181 F. 3d 478, 489 (CA3 1999) ("Judicial application of a standard focusing solely on whether the qualities measured by an . . . exam bear some relationship to the job in question would impermissibly write out the business necessity prong of the Act's chosen standard.").

That IOS representative Chad Legel and his team may have

---

15 Finding the evidence concerning these alternatives insufficiently developed to "create a genuine issue of fact," *ante*, at 591, the Court effectively confirms that an employer cannot prevail under its strong-basis-in-evidence standard unless the employer decisively proves a disparate-impact violation against itself. The Court's specific arguments are unavailing. First, the Court suggests, changing the oral/written weighting may have violated Title VII's prohibition on altering test scores. *Ante*, at 590. No one is arguing, however, that the results of the exams given should have been altered. Rather, the argument is that the City could have availed itself of a better option when it initially decided what selection process to use. Second, with respect to assessment centers, the Court identifies "statements to the CSB indicat[ing] that the Department could not have used [them] for the 2003 examinations." *Ante*, at 591. The Court comes up with only a single statement on this subject—an offhand remark made by petitioner Ricci, who hardly qualifies as an expert in testing methods. See *ante*, at 574. Given the large number of municipalities that regularly use assessment centers, it is impossible to fathom why the City, with proper planning, could not have done so as well.

been diligent in designing the exams says little about the exams' suitability for selecting fire officers. IOS worked within the City's constraints. Legel never discussed with the City the propriety of the 60/40 weighting and "was not asked to consider the possibility of an assessment center." CA2 App. A522. See also *id.*, at A467. The IOS exams, Legel admitted, had not even attempted to assess "command presence": "[Y]ou would probably be better off with an assessment center if you cared to measure that." *Id.*, at A521. Cf. *Boston Chapter, NAACP, Inc.* v. *Beecher*, 504 F. 2d 1017, 1021–1022 (CA1 1974) ("A test fashioned from materials pertaining to the job . . . superficially may seem job-related. But what is at issue is whether it demonstrably selects people who will perform better the required on-the-job behaviors.").

In addition to the highly questionable character of the exams and the neglect of available alternatives, the City had other reasons to worry about its vulnerability to disparate-impact liability. Under the City's ground rules, IOS was not allowed to show the exams to anyone in the New Haven Fire Department prior to their administration. This "precluded [IOS] from being able to engage in [its] normal subject matter expert review process"— something Legel described as "very critical." CA2 App. A477, A506. As a result, some of the exam questions were confusing or irrelevant, and the exams may have overtested some subject-matter areas while missing others. See, *e.g.*, *id.*, at A1034–A1035, A1051. Testimony before the CSB also raised questions concerning unequal access to study materials, see *id.*, at A857–A861, and the potential bias introduced by relying principally on job analyses from nonminority fire officers to develop the exams, see *id.*, at A1063–A1064.[16] See also *supra*, at 613–614, 617.

---

16 The I–O Psychologists Brief identifies still other, more technical flaws in the exams that may well have precluded the City from prevailing in a disparate-impact suit. Notably, the exams were never shown to be suitably precise to allow strict rank ordering of candidates. A difference of one or two points on a multiple-choice exam should not be decisive of an applicant's promotion chances if that difference bears little relationship to the applicant's qualifications for the job. Relatedly, it appears that the line between a passing and failing score did not accurately differentiate between qualified and unqualified candidates. A number of fire-officer promotional exams have been invalidated on these bases. See, *e.g.*, *Guardians Assn.*, 630 F. 2d, at 105 ("When a cutoff score unrelated to job performance produces disparate

The Court criticizes New Haven for failing to obtain a "technical report" from IOS, which, the Court maintains, would have provided "detailed information to establish the validity of the exams." *Ante*, at 589. The record does not substantiate this assertion. As Legel testified during his deposition, the technical report merely summarized "the steps that [IOS] took methodologically speaking," and would not have established the exams' reliability. CA2 App. A461. See also *id.*, at A462 (the report "doesn't say anything that other documents that already existed wouldn't say").

In sum, the record solidly establishes that the City had good cause to fear disparate-impact liability. Moreover, the Court supplies no tenable explanation why the evidence of the tests' multiple deficiencies does not create at least a triable issue under a strong-basis-in-evidence standard.

B

Concurring in the Court's opinion, JUSTICE ALITO asserts that summary judgment for respondents would be improper even if the City had good cause for its noncertification decision. A reasonable jury, he maintains, could have found that respondents were not actually motivated by concern about disparate-impact litigation, but instead sought only "to placate a politically important [African-American] constituency." *Ante*, at 597. As earlier noted, I would not oppose a remand for further proceedings fair to both sides. See *supra*, at 632, n. 10. It is the Court that has chosen to short circuit this litigation based on its pretension that the City has shown, and can show, nothing more than a statistical disparity. See *supra*, at 630, n. 8, 631. JUSTICE ALITO compounds the Court's error.

Offering a truncated synopsis of the many hours of deliberations undertaken by the CSB, JUSTICE ALITO finds evidence suggesting that respondents' stated desire to comply with Title

---

racial results, Title VII is violated."); *Vulcan Pioneers, Inc.* v. *New Jersey Dept. of Civil Serv.*, 625 F. Supp. 527, 538 (NJ 1985) ("[T]he tests here at issue are not appropriate for ranking candidates.").

VII was insincere, a mere "pretext" for discrimination against white firefighters. *Ante*, at 596–597. In support of his assertion, JUSTICE ALITO recounts at length the alleged machinations of Rev. Boise Kimber (a local political activist), Mayor John DeStefano, and certain members of the mayor's staff. See *ante*, at 598–604.

Most of the allegations JUSTICE ALITO repeats are drawn from petitioners' statement of facts they deem undisputed, a statement displaying an adversarial zeal not uncommonly found in such presentations.[17] What cannot credibly be denied, however, is that the decision against certification of the exams was made neither by Kimber nor by the mayor and his staff. The relevant decision was made by the CSB, an unelected, politically insulated body. It is striking that JUSTICE ALITO's concurrence says hardly a word about the CSB itself, perhaps because there is scant evidence that its motivation was anything other than to comply with Title VII's disparate-impact provision. Notably, petitioners did not even seek to take depositions of the two commissioners who voted against certification. Both submitted uncontested affidavits declaring unequivocally that their votes were "based solely on [their] good faith belief that certification" would have discriminated against minority candidates in violation of federal law. CA2 App. A1605, A1611.

JUSTICE ALITO discounts these sworn statements, suggesting

---

17 Some of petitioners' so-called facts find little support in the record, and many others can scarcely be deemed material. Petitioners allege, for example, that City officials prevented New Haven's fire chief and assistant chief from sharing their views about the exams with the CSB. App. to Pet. for Cert. in No. 07–1428, p. 228a. None of the materials petitioners cite, however, "suggests" that this proposition is accurate. Cf. *ante*, at 600. In her deposition testimony, City official Karen Dubois-Walton specifically denied that she or her colleagues directed the chief and assistant chief not to appear. App. to Pet. for Cert. in No. 07–1428, p. 850a. Moreover, contrary to the insinuations of petitioners and JUSTICE ALITO, the statements made by City officials before the CSB did not emphasize allegations of cheating by test takers. Cf. *ante*, at 602–603. In her deposition, Dubois-Walton acknowledged sharing the cheating allegations not with the CSB, but with a different City commission. App. to Pet. for Cert. in No. 07–1428, p. 837a. JUSTICE ALITO also reports that the City's attorney advised the mayor's team that the way to convince the CSB not to certify was "to focus on something other than 'a big discussion re: adverse impact' law." *Ante*, at 603 (quoting App. to Pet. for Cert. in No. 07–1428, p. 458a). This is a misleading abbreviation of the attorney's advice. Focusing on the exams' defects and on disparate-impact law is precisely what he recommended. See *id.*, at 458a–459a.

that the CSB's deliberations were tainted by the preferences of Kimber and City officials, whether or not the CSB itself was aware of the taint. Kimber and City officials, JUSTICE ALITO speculates, decided early on to oppose certification and then "engineered" a skewed presentation to the CSB to achieve their preferred outcome. *Ante*, at 606.

As an initial matter, JUSTICE ALITO exaggerates the influence of these actors. The CSB, the record reveals, designed and conducted an inclusive decision-making process, in which it heard from numerous individuals on both sides of the certification question. See, *e.g.*, CA2 App. A1090. Kimber and others no doubt used strong words to urge the CSB not to certify the exam results, but the CSB received "pressure" from supporters of certification as well as opponents. Cf. *ante*, at 600. Petitioners, for example, engaged counsel to speak on their behalf before the CSB. Their counsel did not mince words: "[I]f you discard these results," she warned, "you will get sued. You will force the taxpayers of the city of New Haven into protracted litigation." CA2 App. A816. See also *id.*, at A788.

The local firefighters union—an organization required by law to represent all the City's firefighters—was similarly outspoken in favor of certification. Discarding the test results, the union's president told the CSB, would be "totally ridiculous." *Id.*, at A806. He insisted, inaccurately, that the City was not at risk of disparate-impact liability because the exams were administered pursuant to "a collective bargaining agreement." *Id.*, at A1137. Cf. *supra*, at 632–633, n. 11. Never mentioned by JUSTICE ALITO in his attempt to show testing expert Christopher Hornick's alliance with the City, *ante*, at 603–604, the CSB solicited Hornick's testimony at the union's suggestion, not the City's. CA2 App. A1128. Hornick's cogent testimony raised substantial doubts about the exams' reliability. See *supra*, at 615–616.[18]

---

18 City officials, JUSTICE ALITO reports, sent Hornick newspaper accounts and other material about the exams prior to his testimony. *Ante*, at 603. Some of these materials, JUSTICE ALITO intimates, may have given Hornick an inaccurate portrait of the exams. But Hornick's testimony before the CSB, viewed in full, indicates that Hornick had an accurate understanding

There is scant cause to suspect that maneuvering or overheated rhetoric, from either side, prevented the CSB from evenhandedly assessing the reliability of the exams and rendering an independent, good-faith decision on certification. JUSTICE ALITO acknowledges that the CSB had little patience for Kimber's antics. *Ante*, at 600–602.[19] As to petitioners, Chairman Segaloff—who voted to certify the exam results—dismissed the threats made by their counsel as unhelpful and needlessly "inflammatory." CA2 App. A821. Regarding the views expressed by City officials, the CSB made clear that they were entitled to no special weight. *Id.*, at A1080.[20]

In any event, JUSTICE ALITO's analysis contains a more fundamental flaw: It equates political considerations with unlawful discrimination. As JUSTICE ALITO sees it, if the mayor and his staff were motivated by their desire "to placate a . . . racial constituency," *ante*, at 597, then they engaged in unlawful discrimination against petitioners. But JUSTICE ALITO fails to ask a vital question: "[P]lacate" how? That political officials would have politics in mind is hardly extraordinary, and there are many ways in which a politician can attempt to win over a constituency—including a racial constituency—without engaging in unlawful discrimination. As courts have recognized, "[p]oliticians routinely respond to bad press . . . , but it is not a violation of Title VII to take advantage of a situation to gain political favor." *Henry* v. *Jones*, 507 F. 3d 558, 567 (CA7 2007).

---

of the exam process. Much of Hornick's analysis focused on the 60/40 weighting of the written and oral exams, something that neither the Court nor the concurrences even attempt to defend. It is, moreover, entirely misleading to say that the City later hired union-proposed Hornick as a "rewar[d]" for his testimony. Cf. *ibid.*

19 To be clear, the board of fire commissioners on which Kimber served is an entity separate from the CSB. Kimber was not a member of the CSB. Kimber, JUSTICE ALITO states, requested a private meeting with the CSB. *Ante*, at 601. There is not a shred of evidence that a private meeting with Kimber or anyone else took place.

20 JUSTICE ALITO points to evidence that the mayor had decided not to make promotions based on the exams even if the CSB voted to certify the results, going so far as to prepare a press release to that effect. *Ante*, at 604. If anything, this evidence reinforces the conclusion that the CSB—which made the noncertification decision—remained independent and above the political fray. The mayor and his staff needed a contingency plan precisely because they did not control the CSB.

The real issue, then, is not whether the mayor and his staff were politically motivated; it is whether their attempt to score political points was legitimate (*i.e.*, nondiscriminatory). Were they seeking to exclude white firefighters from promotion (unlikely, as a fair test would undoubtedly result in the addition of white firefighters to the officer ranks), or did they realize, at least belatedly, that their tests could be toppled in a disparate-impact suit? In the latter case, there is no disparate-treatment violation. JUSTICE ALITO, I recognize, would disagree. In his view, an employer's action to avoid Title VII disparate-impact liability qualifies as a presumptively improper race-based employment decision. See *ante*, at 597. I reject that construction of Title VII. See *supra*, at 625–627. As I see it, when employers endeavor to avoid exposure to disparate-impact liability, they do not thereby encounter liability for disparate treatment.

Applying this understanding of Title VII, supported by *Griggs* and the long line of decisions following *Griggs*, see *supra*, at 623–624, and nn. 3–4, the District Court found no genuine dispute of material fact. That court noted, particularly, the guidance furnished by Second Circuit precedent. See *supra*, at 619. Petitioners' allegations that City officials took account of politics, the District Court determined, simply "d[id] not suffice" to create an inference of unlawful discrimination. 554 F. Supp. 2d, at 160, n. 12. The noncertification decision, even if undertaken "in a political context," reflected a legitimate "intent not to implement a promotional process based on testing results that had an adverse impact." *Id.*, at 158, 160. Indeed, the District Court perceived "a total absence of any evidence of discriminatory animus towards [petitioners]." *Id.*, at 158. See also *id.*, at 162 ("Nothing in the record in this case suggests that the City defendants or CSB acted 'because of' discriminatory animus toward [petitioners] or other nonminority applicants for promotion."). Perhaps the District Court could have been more expansive in its discussion of these issues, but its conclusions appear entirely consistent with the record before it.[21]

It is indeed regrettable that the City's noncertification decision would have required all candidates to go through another selection process. But it would have been more regrettable to rely on flawed exams to shut out candidates who may well have the command presence and other qualities needed to excel as fire officers. Yet that is the choice the Court makes today. It is a choice that breaks the promise of *Griggs* that groups long denied equal opportunity would not be held back by tests "fair in form, but discriminatory in operation." 401 U.S., at 431.

* * *

These cases present an unfortunate situation, one New Haven might well have avoided had it utilized a better selection process in the first place. But what this litigation does not present is race-based discrimination in violation of Title VII. I dissent from the Court's judgment, which rests on the false premise that respondents showed "a significant statistical disparity," but "nothing more." See *ante*, at 587.

---

21 The District Court, JUSTICE ALITO writes, "all but conceded that a jury could find that the City's asserted justification was pretextual" by "admitt[ing] that 'a jury could rationally infer that city officials worked behind the scenes to sabotage the promotional examinations because they knew that, were the exams certified, the Mayor would incur the wrath of [Rev. Boise] Kimber and other influential leaders of New Haven's African-American community.'" *Ante*, at 598, 608 (quoting 554 F. Supp. 2d, at 162). The District Court drew the quoted passage from petitioners' lower court brief, and used it in reference to a First Amendment claim not before this Court. In any event, it is not apparent why these alleged political maneuvers suggest an intent to discriminate against petitioners. That City officials may have wanted to please political supporters is entirely consistent with their stated desire to avoid a disparate-impact violation. Cf. *Ashcroft* v. *Iqbal*, 556 U.S. 662, 682 (2009) (allegations that senior Government officials condoned the arrest and detention of thousands of Arab Muslim men following the September 11 attacks failed to establish even a "plausible inference" of unlawful discrimination sufficient to survive a motion to dismiss).

Shelby County v. Holder, 570 U.S. 529 (2013)

Dissenting Opinion

*I*n this landmark voting-rights case, the Court ruled on the constitutionality of two provisions of the Voting Rights Act of 1965—
*legislation that was enacted with the intent of correcting a long
history of voting discrimination. Section 5 of the Act requires eligible
districts to obtain official authorization before making changes to
election laws or procedures. Section 4(b) defines eligible districts according to parameters established in the 1964 presidential election.
Section 5 was originally intended to last for five years, but had been
continually renewed since being enacted. Shelby County, Alabama,
filed suit, claiming that the renewal of Section 5 of the Act, due
to the restraints of Section 4(b), violated the Constitution's Tenth
Amendment (which ensures that all rights not granted to the federal
government belong to the states) and Article Four (which guarantees
the states' right to self-government).*

*Justice John G. Roberts, in his majority opinion, argued that
yes, Section 4(b) is unconstitutional: it imposes burdens upon the
states based on outdated models no longer relevant to current conditions, and it exceeds Congress's powers to uphold the Fourteenth
Amendment (which ensures the right to due process) and Fifteenth
Amendment (which protects citizens from having their voting rights
infringed because of "race, color, or previous condition of servitude").
Justice Ginsburg dissented, acknowledging that voting discrimination had eased since the passage of the Voting Rights Act, but arguing
that the decrease in discrimination was due to the Act itself and
likening the elimination of provisions in the Act because they've been
successful to "throwing away your umbrella in a rainstorm because
you are not getting wet."*

SHELBY COUNTY, ALABAMA
v.
HOLDER, ATTORNEY GENERAL, ET AL.

CERTIORARI TO THE UNITED STATES COURT
OF APPEALS FOR THE DISTRICT OF COLUMBIA
CIRCUIT
[June 25, 2013]

Justice Ginsburg, with whom Justice Breyer, Justice Sotomayor, and Justice Kagan join, dissenting.

In the Court's view, the very success of §5 of the Voting Rights Act demands its dormancy. Congress was of another mind. Recognizing that large progress has been made, Congress determined, based on a voluminous record, that the scourge of discrimination was not yet extirpated. The question this case presents is who decides whether, as currently operative, §5 remains justifiable,[1] this Court, or a Congress charged with the obligation to enforce the post-Civil War Amendments "by appropriate legislation." With overwhelming support in both Houses, Congress concluded that, for two prime reasons, §5 should continue in force, unabated. First, continuance would facilitate completion of the impressive gains thus far made; and second, continuance would guard against backsliding. Those assessments were well within Congress' province to make and should elicit this Court's unstinting approbation.

I

"[V]oting discrimination still exists; no one doubts that." *Ante*, at 2. But the Court today terminates the remedy that proved to be best suited to block that discrimination. The Voting Rights Act of 1965 (VRA) has worked to combat voting discrimination where other remedies had been tried and failed. Particularly effective is the VRA's requirement of federal preclearance for all

1 The Court purports to declare unconstitutional only the coverage formula set out in §4(b). See *ante*, at 24. But without that formula, §5 is immobilized.

changes to voting laws in the regions of the country with the most aggravated records of rank discrimination against minority voting rights.

A century after the Fourteenth and Fifteenth Amendments guaranteed citizens the right to vote free of discrimination on the basis of race, the "blight of racial discrimination in voting" continued to "infec[t] the electoral process in parts of our country." *South Carolina* v. *Katzenbach*, 383 U.S. 301, 308 (1966). Early attempts to cope with this vile infection resembled battling the Hydra. Whenever one form of voting discrimination was identified and prohibited, others sprang up in its place. This Court repeatedly encountered the remarkable "variety and persistence" of laws disenfranchising minority citizens. *Id.*, at 311. To take just one example, the Court, in 1927, held unconstitutional a Texas law barring black voters from participating in primary elections, *Nixon* v. *Herndon*, 273 U.S. 536, 541; in 1944, the Court struck down a "reenacted" and slightly altered version of the same law, *Smith* v. *Allwright*, 321 U.S. 649, 658; and in 1953, the Court once again confronted an attempt by Texas to "circumven[t]" the Fifteenth Amendment by adopting yet another variant of the all-white primary, *Terry* v. *Adams*, 345 U.S. 461, 469.

During this era, the Court recognized that discrimination against minority voters was a quintessentially political problem requiring a political solution. As Justice Holmes explained: If "the great mass of the white population intends to keep the blacks from voting," "relief from [that] great political wrong, if done, as alleged, by the people of a State and the State itself, must be given by them or by the legislative and political department of the government of the United States." *Giles* v. *Harris*, 189 U.S. 475, 488 (1903).

Congress learned from experience that laws targeting particular electoral practices or enabling case-by-case litigation were inadequate to the task. In the Civil Rights Acts of 1957, 1960, and 1964, Congress authorized and then expanded the power of "the Attorney General to seek injunctions against public and private interference with the right to vote on racial grounds." *Katzenbach*, 383 U.S., at 313. But circumstances reduced the ameliorative potential of these legislative Acts:

> "Voting suits are unusually onerous to prepare, sometimes requiring as many as 6,000 man-hours spent combing through registration records in preparation for trial. Litigation has been exceedingly slow, in part because of the ample opportunities for delay afforded voting officials and others involved in the proceedings. Even when favorable decisions have finally been obtained, some of the States affected have merely switched to discriminatory devices not covered by the federal decrees or have enacted difficult new tests designed to prolong the existing disparity between white and Negro registration. Alternatively, certain local officials have defied and evaded court orders or have simply closed their registration offices to freeze the voting rolls." *Id.*, at 314 (footnote omitted).

Patently, a new approach was needed.

Answering that need, the Voting Rights Act became one of the most consequential, efficacious, and amply justified exercises of federal legislative power in our Nation's history. Requiring federal preclearance of changes in voting laws in the covered jurisdictions—those States and localities where opposition to the Constitution's commands were most virulent—the VRA provided a fit solution for minority voters as well as for States. Under the preclearance regime established by §5 of the VRA, covered jurisdictions must submit proposed changes in voting laws or procedures to the Department of Justice (DOJ), which has 60 days to respond to the changes. 79 Stat. 439, codified at 42 U. S. C. §1973c(a). A change will be approved unless DOJ finds it has "the purpose [or] . . . the effect of denying or abridging the right to vote on account of race or color." *Ibid.* In the alternative, the covered jurisdiction may seek approval by a three-judge District Court in the District of Columbia.

After a century's failure to fulfill the promise of the Fourteenth and Fifteenth Amendments, passage of the VRA finally led to signal improvement on this front. "The Justice Department estimated that in the five years after [the VRA's] passage, almost as many blacks registered [to vote] in Alabama, Mississippi, Georgia, Louisiana, North Carolina, and South Carolina as in the entire century before 1965." Davidson, The Voting Rights Act: A Brief History, in Controversies in Minority Voting 7, 21 (B. Grofman & C. Davidson eds. 1992). And in assessing the overall effects of the VRA in 2006, Congress found that "[s]ignificant progress has been made in eliminating first generation barriers experienced by minority voters, including increased numbers of registered minority voters, minority voter turnout, and minority representation in Congress, State legislatures, and local elected offices. This progress is the direct result of the Voting Rights Act of 1965." Fannie Lou Hamer, Rosa Parks, and Coretta Scott King Voting Rights Act Reauthorization and Amendments Act of 2006 (hereinafter 2006 Reauthorization), §2(b)(1), 120 Stat. 577. On that matter of cause and effects there can be no genuine doubt.

Although the VRA wrought dramatic changes in the realization of minority voting rights, the Act, to date, surely has not eliminated all vestiges of discrimination against the exercise of the franchise by minority citizens. Jurisdictions covered by the preclearance requirement continued to submit, in large numbers, proposed changes to voting laws that the Attorney General declined to approve, auguring that barriers to minority voting would quickly resurface were the preclearance remedy eliminated. *City of Rome* v. *United States*, 446 U.S. 156, 181 (1980). Congress also found that as "registration and voting of minority citizens increas[ed], other measures may be resorted to which would dilute increasing minority voting strength." *Ibid.* (quoting

H. R. Rep. No. 94–196, p. 10 (1975)). See also *Shaw* v. *Reno*, 509 U.S. 630, 640 (1993) ("[I]t soon became apparent that guaranteeing equal access to the polls would not suffice to root out other racially discriminatory voting practices" such as voting dilution). Efforts to reduce the impact of minority votes, in contrast to direct attempts to block access to the ballot, are aptly described as "second-generation barriers" to minority voting.

Second-generation barriers come in various forms. One of the blockages is racial gerrymandering, the redrawing of legislative districts in an "effort to segregate the races for purposes of voting." *Id.*, at 642. Another is adoption of a system of at-large voting in lieu of district-by-district voting in a city with a sizable black minority. By switching to at-large voting, the overall majority could control the election of each city council member, effectively eliminating the potency of the minority's votes. Grofman & Davidson, The Effect of Municipal Election Structure on Black Representation in Eight Southern States, in Quiet Revolution in the South 301, 319 (C. Davidson & B. Grofman eds. 1994) (hereinafter Quiet Revolution). A similar effect could be achieved if the city engaged in discriminatory annexation by incorporating majority-white areas into city limits, thereby decreasing the effect of VRA-occasioned increases in black voting. Whatever the device employed, this Court has long recognized that vote dilution, when adopted with a discriminatory purpose, cuts down the right to vote as certainly as denial of access to the ballot. *Shaw*, 509 U.S., at 640–641; *Allen* v. *State Bd. of Elections*, 393 U.S. 544, 569 (1969); *Reynolds* v. *Sims*, 377 U.S. 533, 555 (1964). See also H. R. Rep. No. 109–478, p. 6 (2006) (although "[d]iscrimination today is more subtle than the visible methods used in 1965," "the effect and results are the same, namely a diminishing of the minority community's ability to fully participate in the electoral process and to elect their preferred candidates").

In response to evidence of these substituted barriers, Congress reauthorized the VRA for five years in 1970, for seven years in

1975, and for 25 years in 1982. *Ante*, at 4–5. Each time, this Court upheld the reauthorization as a valid exercise of congressional power. *Ante*, at 5. As the 1982 reauthorization approached its 2007 expiration date, Congress again considered whether the VRA's preclearance mechanism remained an appropriate response to the problem of voting discrimination in covered jurisdictions.

Congress did not take this task lightly. Quite the opposite. The 109th Congress that took responsibility for the renewal started early and conscientiously. In October 2005, the House began extensive hearings, which continued into November and resumed in March 2006. S. Rep. No. 109–295, p. 2 (2006). In April 2006, the Senate followed suit, with hearings of its own. *Ibid.* In May 2006, the bills that became the VRA's reauthorization were introduced in both Houses. *Ibid.* The House held further hearings of considerable length, as did the Senate, which continued to hold hearings into June and July. H. R. Rep. 109–478, at 5; S. Rep. 109–295, at 3–4. In mid-July, the House considered and rejected four amendments, then passed the reauthorization by a vote of 390 yeas to 33 nays. 152 Cong. Rec. H5207 (July 13, 2006); Persily, The Promise and Pitfalls of the New Voting Rights Act, 117 Yale L. J. 174, 182–183 (2007) (hereinafter Persily). The bill was read and debated in the Senate, where it passed by a vote of 98 to 0. 152 Cong. Rec. S8012 (July 20, 2006). President Bush signed it a week later, on July 27, 2006, recognizing the need for "further work . . . in the fight against injustice," and calling the reauthorization "an example of our continued commitment to a united America where every person is valued and treated with dignity and respect." 152 Cong. Rec. S8781 (Aug. 3, 2006).

In the long course of the legislative process, Congress "amassed a sizable record." *Northwest Austin Municipal Util. Dist. No. One v. Holder*, 557 U.S. 193, 205 (2009). See also 679 F. 3d 848, 865–873 (CADC 2012) (describing the "extensive record" supporting Congress' determination that "serious and widespread intentional discrimination persisted in covered jurisdictions"). The House and Senate Judiciary Committees held 21 hearings, heard from scores of witnesses, received a number of investigative reports and other written documentation of continuing discrimination in covered jurisdictions. In all, the legislative record Congress compiled filled more than 15,000 pages. H. R. Rep. 109–478, at 5, 11–12; S. Rep. 109–295, at 2–4, 15. The compilation presents countless "examples of flagrant racial discrimination" since the last reauthorization; Congress also brought to light systematic evidence that "intentional racial discrimination in voting remains so serious and widespread in covered jurisdictions that section 5 preclearance is still needed." 679 F. 3d, at 866.

After considering the full legislative record, Congress made the following findings: The VRA has directly caused significant progress in eliminating first-generation barriers to ballot access, leading to a marked increase in minority voter registration and turnout and the number of minority elected officials. 2006 Reauthorization §2(b)(1). But despite this progress, "second generation barriers constructed to prevent minority voters from fully participating in the electoral process" continued to exist, as well as racially polarized voting in the covered jurisdictions, which increased the political vulnerability of racial and language minorities in those jurisdictions. §§2(b)(2)–(3), 120 Stat. 577. Extensive "[e]vidence of continued discrimination," Congress concluded, "clearly show[ed] the continued need for Federal oversight" in covered jurisdictions. §§2(b)(4)–(5), *id.*, at 577–578. The overall record demonstrated to the federal lawmakers that, "without the continuation of the Voting Rights Act of 1965 protections, racial and language minority citizens will be deprived of the opportunity to exercise their right to vote, or will have their votes diluted, undermining the significant gains made by minorities in the last 40 years." §2(b)(9), *id.*, at 578.

Based on these findings, Congress reauthorized preclearance for another 25 years, while also undertaking to reconsider the extension after 15 years to ensure that the provision was still necessary and effective. 42 U. S. C. §1973b(a)(7), (8) (2006 ed., Supp. V). The question before the Court is whether Congress had the authority under the Constitution to act as it did.

II

In answering this question, the Court does not write on a clean slate. It is well established that Congress' judgment regarding exercise of its power to enforce the Fourteenth and Fifteenth Amendments warrants substantial deference. The VRA addresses the combination of race discrimination and the right to vote, which is "preservative of all rights." *Yick Wo* v. *Hopkins*, 118 U.S. 356, 370 (1886). When confronting the most constitutionally invidious form of discrimination, and the most fundamental right in our democratic system, Congress' power to act is at its height.

The basis for this deference is firmly rooted in both constitutional text and precedent. The Fifteenth Amendment, which targets precisely and only racial discrimination in voting rights, states that, in this domain, "Congress shall have power to enforce this article by appropriate legislation."[2] In choosing this language, the Amendment's framers invoked Chief Justice Marshall's formulation of the scope of Congress' powers under the Necessary and Proper Clause:

> "Let the end be legitimate, let it be within the scope of the constitution, and *all means which are appropriate, which are plainly adapted to that end*, which are not prohibited, but consist with the letter and spirit of

---

2 The Constitution uses the words "right to vote" in five separate places: the Fourteenth, Fifteenth, Nineteenth, Twenty-Fourth, and Twenty-Sixth Amendments. Each of these Amendments contains the same broad empowerment of Congress to enact "appropriate legislation" to enforce the protected right. The implication is unmistakable: Under our constitutional structure, Congress holds the lead rein in making the right to vote equally real for all U.S. citizens. These Amendments are in line with the special role assigned to Congress in protecting the integrity of the democratic process in federal elections. U.S. Const., Art. I, §4 ("[T]he Congress may at any time by Law make or alter" regulations concerning the "Times, Places and Manner of holding Elections for Senators and Representatives."); *Arizona* v. *Inter Tribal Council of Ariz., Inc., ante*, at 5–6.

the constitution, are constitutional." *McCulloch* v. *Maryland*, 4 Wheat. 316, 421 (1819) (emphasis added).

It cannot tenably be maintained that the VRA, an Act of Congress adopted to shield the right to vote from racial discrimination, is inconsistent with the letter or spirit of the Fifteenth Amendment, or any provision of the Constitution read in light of the Civil War Amendments. Nowhere in today's opinion, or in *Northwest Austin*,[3] is there clear recognition of the transformative effect the Fifteenth Amendment aimed to achieve. Notably, "the Founders' first successful amendment told Congress that it could 'make no law' over a certain domain"; in contrast, the Civil War Amendments used "language [that] authorized transformative new federal statutes to uproot all vestiges of unfreedom and inequality" and provided "sweeping enforcement powers . . . to enact 'appropriate' legislation targeting state abuses." A. Amar, America's Constitution: A Biography 361, 363, 399 (2005). See also McConnell, Institutions and Interpretation: A Critique of *City of Boerne* v. *Flores*, 111 Harv. L. Rev. 153, 182 (1997) (quoting Civil War–era framer that "the remedy for the violation of the fourteenth and fifteenth amendments was expressly not left to the courts. The remedy was legislative.").

The stated purpose of the Civil War Amendments was to arm Congress with the power and authority to protect all persons within the Nation from violations of their rights by the States. In exercising that power, then, Congress may use "all means which are appropriate, which are plainly adapted" to the constitutional ends declared by these Amendments. *McCulloch*, 4 Wheat., at 421. So when Congress acts to enforce the right to vote free from racial discrimination, we ask not whether Congress has chosen the means most wise, but whether Congress has rationally selected means appropriate to a legitimate end. "It is not

---

3 Acknowledging the existence of "serious constitutional questions," see *ante*, at 22 (internal quotation marks omitted), does not suggest how those questions should be answered.

for us to review the congressional resolution of [the need for its chosen remedy]. It is enough that we be able to perceive a basis upon which the Congress might resolve the conflict as it did." *Katzenbach* v. *Morgan*, 384 U.S. 641, 653 (1966).

Until today, in considering the constitutionality of the VRA, the Court has accorded Congress the full measure of respect its judgments in this domain should garner. *South Carolina* v. *Katzenbach* supplies the standard of review: "As against the reserved powers of the States, Congress may use any rational means to effectuate the constitutional prohibition of racial discrimination in voting." 383 U.S., at 324. Faced with subsequent reauthorizations of the VRA, the Court has reaffirmed this standard. *E.g.*, *City of Rome*, 446 U.S., at 178. Today's Court does not purport to alter settled precedent establishing that the dispositive question is whether Congress has employed "rational means."

For three reasons, legislation *re*authorizing an existing statute is especially likely to satisfy the minimal requirements of the rational-basis test. First, when reauthorization is at issue, Congress has already assembled a legislative record justifying the initial legislation. Congress is entitled to consider that preexisting record as well as the record before it at the time of the vote on reauthorization. This is especially true where, as here, the Court has repeatedly affirmed the statute's constitutionality and Congress has adhered to the very model the Court has upheld. See *id.*, at 174 ("The appellants are asking us to do nothing less than overrule our decision in *South Carolina* v. *Katzenbach* . . . , in which we upheld the constitutionality of the Act."); *Lopez* v. *Monterey County*, 525 U.S. 266, 283 (1999) (similar).

Second, the very fact that reauthorization is necessary arises because Congress has built a temporal limitation into the Act. It has pledged to review, after a span of years (first 15, then 25) and in light of contemporary evidence, the continued need for the VRA. Cf. *Grutter* v. *Bollinger*, 539 U.S. 306, 343 (2003) (anticipating, but not guaranteeing, that, in 25 years, "the use of racial preferences [in higher education] will no longer be necessary").

Third, a reviewing court should expect the record supporting reauthorization to be less stark than the record originally made. Demand for a record of violations equivalent to the one earlier made would expose Congress to a catch-22. If the statute was working, there would be less evidence of discrimination, so opponents might argue that Congress should not be allowed to renew the statute. In contrast, if the statute was not working, there would be plenty of evidence of discrimination, but scant reason to renew a failed regulatory regime. See Persily 193–194.

This is not to suggest that congressional power in this area is limitless. It is this Court's responsibility to ensure that Congress has used appropriate means. The question meet for judicial review is whether the chosen means are "adapted to carry out the objects the amendments have in view." *Ex parte Virginia*, 100 U.S. 339, 346 (1880). The Court's role, then, is not to substitute its judgment for that of Congress, but to determine whether the legislative record sufficed to show that "Congress could rationally have determined that [its chosen] provisions were appropriate methods." *City of Rome*, 446 U.S., at 176–177.

In summary, the Constitution vests broad power in Congress to protect the right to vote, and in particular to combat racial discrimination in voting. This Court has repeatedly reaffirmed Congress' prerogative to use any rational means in exercise of its power in this area. And both precedent and logic dictate that the rational-means test should be easier to satisfy, and the burden on the statute's challenger should be higher, when what is at issue is the reauthorization of a remedy that the Court has previously affirmed, and that Congress found, from contemporary evidence, to be working to advance the legislature's legitimate objective.

III

The 2006 reauthorization of the Voting Rights Act fully satisfies the standard stated in *McCulloch*, 4 Wheat., at 421: Congress may choose any means "appropriate" and "plainly adapted to" a legitimate constitutional end. As we shall see, it is implausible to suggest otherwise.

A

I begin with the evidence on which Congress based its decision to continue the preclearance remedy. The surest way to evaluate whether that remedy remains in order is to see if preclearance is still effectively preventing discriminatory changes to voting laws. See *City of Rome*, 446 U.S., at 181 (identifying "information on the number and types of submissions made by covered jurisdictions and the number and nature of objections interposed by the Attorney General" as a primary basis for upholding the 1975 reauthorization). On that score, the record before Congress was huge. In fact, Congress found there were *more* DOJ objections between 1982 and 2004 (626) than there were between 1965 and the 1982 reauthorization (490). 1 Voting Rights Act: Evidence of Continued Need, Hearing before the Subcommittee on the Constitution of the House Committee on the Judiciary, 109th Cong., 2d Sess., p. 172 (2006) (hereinafter Evidence of Continued Need).

All told, between 1982 and 2006, DOJ objections blocked over 700 voting changes based on a determination that the changes were discriminatory. H. R. Rep. No. 109–478, at 21. Congress found that the majority of DOJ objections included findings of discriminatory intent, see 679 F. 3d, at 867, and that the changes blocked by preclearance were "calculated decisions to keep minority voters from fully participating in the political process." H. R. Rep. 109–478, at 21. On top of that, over the same time period the DOJ and private plaintiffs succeeded in more than 100 actions to enforce the §5 preclearance requirements. 1 Evidence of Continued Need 186, 250.

In addition to blocking proposed voting changes through preclearance, DOJ may request more information from a jurisdiction proposing a change. In turn, the jurisdiction may modify or withdraw the proposed change. The number of such modifications or withdrawals provides an indication of how many discriminatory proposals are deterred without need for formal objection. Congress received evidence that more than

800 proposed changes were altered or withdrawn since the last reauthorization in 1982. H. R. Rep. No. 109–478, at 40–41.[4] Congress also received empirical studies finding that DOJ's requests for more information had a significant effect on the degree to which covered jurisdictions "compl[ied] with their obligatio[n]" to protect minority voting rights. 2 Evidence of Continued Need 2555.

Congress also received evidence that litigation under §2 of the VRA was an inadequate substitute for preclearance in the covered jurisdictions. Litigation occurs only after the fact, when the illegal voting scheme has already been put in place and individuals have been elected pursuant to it, thereby gaining the advantages of incumbency. 1 Evidence of Continued Need 97. An illegal scheme might be in place for several election cycles before a §2 plaintiff can gather sufficient evidence to challenge it. 1 Voting Rights Act: Section 5 of the Act—History, Scope, and Purpose: Hearing before the Subcommittee on the Constitution of the House Committee on the Judiciary, 109th Cong., 1st Sess., p. 92 (2005) (hereinafter Section 5 Hearing). And litigation places a heavy financial burden on minority voters. See *id.*, at 84. Congress also received evidence that preclearance lessened the litigation burden on covered jurisdictions themselves, because the preclearance process is far less costly than defending against a §2 claim, and clearance by DOJ substantially reduces the likelihood that a §2 claim will be mounted. Reauthorizing the Voting Rights Act's Temporary Provisions: Policy Perspectives and Views From the Field: Hearing before the Subcommittee on the Constitution, Civil Rights and Property Rights of the Senate Committee on the Judiciary, 109th Cong., 2d Sess.,

---

4 This number includes only changes actually proposed. Congress also received evidence that many covered jurisdictions engaged in an "informal consultation process" with DOJ before formally submitting a proposal, so that the deterrent effect of preclearance was far broader than the formal submissions alone suggest. The Continuing Need for Section 5 Pre-Clearance: Hearing before the Senate Committee on the Judiciary, 109th Cong., 2d Sess., pp. 53–54 (2006). All agree that an unsupported assertion about "deterrence" would not be sufficient to justify keeping a remedy in place in perpetuity. See *ante*, at 17. But it was certainly reasonable for Congress to consider the testimony of witnesses who had worked with officials in covered jurisdictions and observed a real-world deterrent effect.

pp. 13, 120–121 (2006). See also Brief for States of New York, California, Mississippi, and North Carolina as *Amici Curiae* 8–9 (Section 5 "reduc[es] the likelihood that a jurisdiction will face costly and protracted Section 2 litigation").

The number of discriminatory changes blocked or deterred by the preclearance requirement suggests that the state of voting rights in the covered jurisdictions would have been significantly different absent this remedy. Surveying the type of changes stopped by the preclearance procedure conveys a sense of the extent to which §5 continues to protect minority voting rights. Set out below are characteristic examples of changes blocked in the years leading up to the 2006 reauthorization:

- In 1995, Mississippi sought to reenact a dual voter registration system, "which was initially enacted in 1892 to disenfranchise Black voters," and for that reason, was struck down by a federal court in 1987. H. R. Rep. No. 109–478, at 39.

- Following the 2000 census, the City of Albany, Georgia, proposed a redistricting plan that DOJ found to be "designed with the purpose to limit and retrogress the increased black voting strength . . . in the city as a whole." *Id.*, at 37 (internal quotation marks omitted).

- In 2001, the mayor and all-white five-member Board of Aldermen of Kilmichael, Mississippi, abruptly canceled the town's election after "an unprecedented number" of African-American candidates announced they were running for office. DOJ required an election, and the town elected its first black mayor and three black aldermen. *Id.*, at 36–37.

- In 2006, this Court found that Texas' attempt to redraw a congressional district to reduce the strength of Latino voters bore "the mark of intentional discrimination that could give rise to an equal protection violation," and ordered the district redrawn in compliance with the

VRA. *League of United Latin American Citizens* v. *Perry*, 548 U.S. 399, 440 (2006). In response, Texas sought to undermine this Court's order by curtailing early voting in the district, but was blocked by an action to enforce the §5 preclearance requirement. See Order in *League of United Latin American Citizens* v. *Texas*, No. 06–cv–1046 (WD Tex.), Doc. 8.

- In 2003, after African-Americans won a majority of the seats on the school board for the first time in history, Charleston County, South Carolina, proposed an at-large voting mechanism for the board. The proposal, made without consulting any of the African-American members of the school board, was found to be an " 'exact replica' " of an earlier voting scheme that, a federal court had determined, violated the VRA. 811 F. Supp. 2d 424, 483 (DDC 2011). See also S. Rep. No. 109–295, at 309. DOJ invoked §5 to block the proposal.

- In 1993, the City of Millen, Georgia, proposed to delay the election in a majority-black district by two years, leaving that district without representation on the city council while the neighboring majority-white district would have three representatives. 1 Section 5 Hearing 744. DOJ blocked the proposal. The county then sought to move a polling place from a predominantly black neighborhood in the city to an inaccessible location in a predominantly white neighborhood outside city limits. *Id.*, at 816.

- In 2004, Waller County, Texas, threatened to prosecute two black students after they announced their intention to run for office. The county then attempted to reduce the availability of early voting in that election at polling places near a historically black university. 679 F. 3d, at 865–866.

- In 1990, Dallas County, Alabama, whose county seat is the City of Selma, sought to purge its voter rolls of many black voters. DOJ rejected the purge as discriminatory, noting that it would have disqualified many citizens from voting "simply because they failed to pick up or return a voter update form, when there was no valid requirement that they do so." 1 Section 5 Hearing 356.

These examples, and scores more like them, fill the pages of the legislative record. The evidence was indeed sufficient to support Congress' conclusion that "racial discrimination in voting in covered jurisdictions [remained] serious and pervasive." 679 F. 3d, at 865.[5]

Congress further received evidence indicating that formal requests of the kind set out above represented only the tip of the iceberg. There was what one commentator described as an "avalanche of case studies of voting rights violations in the covered jurisdictions," ranging from "outright intimidation and violence against minority voters" to "more subtle forms of voting rights deprivations." Persily 202 (footnote omitted). This evidence gave Congress ever more reason to conclude that the time had not yet come for relaxed vigilance against the scourge of race discrimination in voting.

True, conditions in the South have impressively improved since passage of the Voting Rights Act. Congress noted this improvement and found that the VRA was the driving force behind it. 2006 Reauthorization §2(b)(1). But Congress also found that voting discrimination had evolved into subtler second-generation barriers, and that eliminating preclearance would risk loss of the gains that had been made. §§2(b)(2), (9). Concerns of this order, the Court previously found, gave

---

5 For an illustration postdating the 2006 reauthorization, see *South Carolina* v. *United States*, 898 F. Supp. 2d 30 (DC 2012), which involved a South Carolina voter-identification law enacted in 2011. Concerned that the law would burden minority voters, DOJ brought a §5 enforcement action to block the law's implementation. In the course of the litigation, South Carolina officials agreed to binding interpretations that made it "far easier than some might have expected or feared" for South Carolina citizens to vote. *Id.*, at 37. A three-judge panel precleared the law after adopting both interpretations as an express "condition of preclearance." *Id.*, at 37–38. Two of the judges commented that the case demonstrated "the continuing utility of Section 5 of the Voting Rights Act in deterring problematic, and hence encouraging non-discriminatory, changes in state and local voting laws." *Id.*, at 54 (opinion of Bates, J.).

Congress adequate cause to reauthorize the VRA. *City of Rome*, 446 U.S., at 180–182 (congressional reauthorization of the pre-clearance requirement was justified based on "the number and nature of objections interposed by the Attorney General" since the prior reauthorization; extension was "necessary to preserve the limited and fragile achievements of the Act and to promote further amelioration of voting discrimination") (internal quotation marks omitted). Facing such evidence then, the Court expressly rejected the argument that disparities in voter turnout and number of elected officials were the only metrics capable of justifying reauthorization of the VRA. *Ibid.*

B

I turn next to the evidence on which Congress based its decision to reauthorize the coverage formula in §4(b). Because Congress did not alter the coverage formula, the same jurisdictions previously subject to preclearance continue to be covered by this remedy. The evidence just described, of preclearance's continuing efficacy in blocking constitutional violations in the covered jurisdictions, itself grounded Congress' conclusion that the remedy should be retained for those jurisdictions.

There is no question, moreover, that the covered jurisdictions have a unique history of problems with racial discrimination in voting. *Ante*, at 12–13. Consideration of this long history, still in living memory, was altogether appropriate. The Court criticizes Congress for failing to recognize that "history did not end in 1965." *Ante*, at 20. But the Court ignores that "what's past is prologue." W. Shakespeare, The Tempest, act 2, sc. 1. And "[t]hose who cannot remember the past are condemned to repeat it." 1 G. Santayana, The Life of Reason 284 (1905). Congress was especially mindful of the need to reinforce the gains already made and to prevent backsliding. 2006 Reauthorization §2(b)(9).

Of particular importance, even after 40 years and thousands of discriminatory changes blocked by preclearance, conditions in the covered jurisdictions demonstrated that the formula was still justified by "current needs." *Northwest Austin*, 557 U.S., at 203.

Congress learned of these conditions through a report, known as the Katz study, that looked at §2 suits between 1982 and 2004. To Examine the Impact and Effectiveness of the Voting Rights Act: Hearing before the Subcommittee on the Constitution of the House Committee on the Judiciary, 109th Cong., 1st Sess., pp. 964–1124 (2005) (hereinafter Impact and Effectiveness). Because the private right of action authorized by §2 of the VRA applies nationwide, a comparison of §2 lawsuits in covered and noncovered jurisdictions provides an appropriate yardstick for measuring differences between covered and noncovered jurisdictions. If differences in the risk of voting discrimination between covered and noncovered jurisdictions had disappeared, one would expect that the rate of successful §2 lawsuits would be roughly the same in both areas.[6] The study's findings, however, indicated that racial discrimination in voting remains "concentrated in the jurisdictions singled out for preclearance." *Northwest Austin*, 557 U.S., at 203.

Although covered jurisdictions account for less than 25 percent of the country's population, the Katz study revealed that they accounted for 56 percent of successful §2 litigation since 1982. Impact and Effectiveness 974. Controlling for population, there were nearly *four* times as many successful §2 cases in covered jurisdictions as there were in noncovered jurisdictions. 679 F. 3d, at 874. The Katz study further found that §2 lawsuits are more likely to succeed when they are filed in covered jurisdictions than in noncovered jurisdictions. Impact and Effectiveness 974. From these findings—ignored by the Court—Congress reasonably concluded that the coverage formula continues to identify the jurisdictions of greatest concern.

The evidence before Congress, furthermore, indicated that voting in the covered jurisdictions was more racially polarized than elsewhere in the country. H. R. Rep. No. 109–478, at

---

6 Because preclearance occurs only in covered jurisdictions and can be expected to stop the most obviously objectionable measures, one would expect a *lower* rate of successful §2 lawsuits in those jurisdictions if the risk of voting discrimination there were the same as elsewhere in the country.

34–35. While racially polarized voting alone does not signal a constitutional violation, it is a factor that increases the vulnerability of racial minorities to discriminatory changes in voting law. The reason is twofold. First, racial polarization means that racial minorities are at risk of being systematically outvoted and having their interests underrepresented in legislatures. Second, "when political preferences fall along racial lines, the natural inclinations of incumbents and ruling parties to entrench themselves have predictable racial effects. Under circumstances of severe racial polarization, efforts to gain political advantage translate into race-specific disadvantages." Ansolabehere, Persily, & Stewart, Regional Differences in Racial Polarization in the 2012 Presidential Election: Implications for the Constitutionality of Section 5 of the Voting Rights Act, 126 Harv. L. Rev. Forum 205, 209 (2013).

In other words, a governing political coalition has an incentive to prevent changes in the existing balance of voting power. When voting is racially polarized, efforts by the ruling party to pursue that incentive "will inevitably discriminate against a racial group." *Ibid.* Just as buildings in California have a greater need to be earthquake-proofed, places where there is greater racial polarization in voting have a greater need for prophylactic measures to prevent purposeful race discrimination. This point was understood by Congress and is well recognized in the academic literature. See 2006 Reauthorization §2(b)(3), 120 Stat. 577 ("The continued evidence of racially polarized voting in each of the jurisdictions covered by the [preclearance requirement] demonstrates that racial and language minorities remain politically vulnerable"); H. R. Rep. No. 109–478, at 35; Davidson, The Recent Evolution of Voting Rights Law Affecting Racial and Language Minorities, in Quiet Revolution 21, 22.

The case for retaining a coverage formula that met needs on the ground was therefore solid. Congress might have been charged with rigidity had it afforded covered jurisdictions no way out or ignored jurisdictions that needed superintendence.

Congress, however, responded to this concern. Critical components of the congressional design are the statutory provisions allowing jurisdictions to "bail out" of preclearance, and for court-ordered "bail ins." See *Northwest Austin*, 557 U.S., at 199. The VRA permits a jurisdiction to bail out by showing that it has complied with the Act for ten years, and has engaged in efforts to eliminate intimidation and harassment of voters. 42 U. S. C. §1973b(a) (2006 ed. and Supp. V). It also authorizes a court to subject a noncovered jurisdiction to federal preclearance upon finding that violations of the Fourteenth and Fifteenth Amendments have occurred there. §1973a(c) (2006 ed.).

Congress was satisfied that the VRA's bailout mechanism provided an effective means of adjusting the VRA's coverage over time. H. R. Rep. No. 109–478, at 25 (the success of bailout "illustrates that: (1) covered status is neither permanent nor over-broad; and (2) covered status has been and continues to be within the control of the jurisdiction such that those jurisdictions that have a genuinely clean record and want to terminate coverage have the ability to do so"). Nearly 200 jurisdictions have successfully bailed out of the preclearance requirement, and DOJ has consented to every bailout application filed by an eligible jurisdiction since the current bailout procedure became effective in 1984. Brief for Federal Respondent 54. The bail-in mechanism has also worked. Several jurisdictions have been subject to federal preclearance by court orders, including the States of New Mexico and Arkansas. App. to Brief for Federal Respondent 1a–3a.

This experience exposes the inaccuracy of the Court's portrayal of the Act as static, unchanged since 1965. Congress designed the VRA to be a dynamic statute, capable of adjusting to changing conditions. True, many covered jurisdictions have not been able to bail out due to recent acts of noncompliance with the VRA, but that truth reinforces the congressional judgment that these jurisdictions were rightfully subject to preclearance, and ought to remain under that regime.

IV

Congress approached the 2006 reauthorization of the VRA with great care and seriousness. The same cannot be said of the Court's opinion today. The Court makes no genuine attempt to engage with the massive legislative record that Congress assembled. Instead, it relies on increases in voter registration and turnout as if that were the whole story. See *supra*, at 18–19. Without even identifying a standard of review, the Court dismissively brushes off arguments based on "data from the record," and declines to enter the "debat[e about] what [the] record shows." *Ante*, at 20–21. One would expect more from an opinion striking at the heart of the Nation's signal piece of civil-rights legislation.

I note the most disturbing lapses. First, by what right, given its usual restraint, does the Court even address Shelby County's facial challenge to the VRA? Second, the Court veers away from controlling precedent regarding the "equal sovereignty" doctrine without even acknowledging that it is doing so. Third, hardly showing the respect ordinarily paid when Congress acts to implement the Civil War Amendments, and as just stressed, the Court does not even deign to grapple with the legislative record.

A

Shelby County launched a purely facial challenge to the VRA's 2006 reauthorization. "A facial challenge to a legislative Act," the Court has other times said, "is, of course, the most difficult challenge to mount successfully, since the challenger must establish that no set of circumstances exists under which the Act would be valid." *United States* v. *Salerno*, 481 U.S. 739, 745 (1987).

"[U]nder our constitutional system[,] courts are not roving commissions assigned to pass judgment on the validity of the Nation's laws." *Broadrick* v. *Oklahoma*, 413 U.S. 601, 610–611 (1973). Instead, the "judicial Power" is limited to deciding particular "Cases" and "Controversies." U.S. Const., Art. III, §2. "Embedded in the traditional rules governing constitutional adjudication is the principle that a person to whom a statute may constitutionally be applied will not be heard to challenge that statute on the ground that it may conceivably be applied unconstitutionally to others, in other situations not before the Court." *Broadrick*, 413 U.S., at 610. Yet the Court's opinion in this case contains not a word explaining why Congress lacks the power to subject to preclearance the particular plaintiff that initiated this lawsuit—Shelby County, Alabama. The reason for the Court's silence is apparent, for as applied to Shelby County, the VRA's preclearance requirement is hardly contestable.

Alabama is home to Selma, site of the "Bloody Sunday" beatings of civil-rights demonstrators that served as the catalyst for the VRA's enactment. Following those events, Martin Luther King, Jr., led a march from Selma to Montgomery, Alabama's capital, where he called for passage of the VRA. If the Act passed, he foresaw, progress could be made even in Alabama, but there had to be a steadfast national commitment to see the task through to completion. In King's words, "the arc of the moral universe is long, but it bends toward justice." G. May, Bending Toward Justice: The Voting Rights Act and the Transformation of American Democracy 144 (2013).

History has proved King right. Although circumstances in Alabama have changed, serious concerns remain. Between 1982 and 2005, Alabama had one of the highest rates of successful §2 suits, second only to its VRA-covered neighbor Mississippi. 679 F. 3d, at 897 (Williams, J., dissenting). In other words, even while subject to the restraining effect of §5, Alabama was found to have "deni[ed] or abridge[d]" voting rights "on account of race or color" more frequently than nearly all other States in the Union. 42 U. S. C. §1973(a). This fact prompted the dissenting judge below to concede that "a more narrowly tailored coverage formula" capturing Alabama and a handful of other jurisdictions with an established track record of racial discrimination in voting "might be defensible." 679 F. 3d, at 897 (opinion of Williams, J.). That is an understatement. Alabama's sorry history of §2 violations alone provides sufficient justification for

Congress' determination in 2006 that the State should remain subject to §5's preclearance requirement.[7]

A few examples suffice to demonstrate that, at least in Alabama, the "current burdens" imposed by §5's preclearance requirement are "justified by current needs." *Northwest Austin*, 557 U.S., at 203. In the interim between the VRA's 1982 and 2006 reauthorizations, this Court twice confronted purposeful racial discrimination in Alabama. In *Pleasant Grove* v. *United States*, 479 U.S. 462 (1987), the Court held that Pleasant Grove—a city in Jefferson County, Shelby County's neighbor—engaged in purposeful discrimination by annexing all-white areas while rejecting the annexation request of an adjacent black neighborhood. The city had "shown unambiguous opposition to racial integration, both before and after the passage of the federal civil rights laws," and its strategic annexations appeared to be an attempt "to provide for the growth of a monolithic white voting block" for "the impermissible purpose of minimizing future black voting strength." *Id.*, at 465, 471–472.

Two years before *Pleasant Grove*, the Court in *Hunter* v. *Underwood*, 471 U.S. 222 (1985), struck down a provision of the Alabama Constitution that prohibited individuals convicted of misdemeanor offenses "involving moral turpitude" from voting. *Id.*, at 223 (internal quotation marks omitted). The provision violated the Fourteenth Amendment's Equal Protection Clause, the Court unanimously concluded, because "its original enactment was motivated by a desire to discriminate against blacks on account of race[,] and the [provision] continues to this day to have that effect." *Id.*, at 233.

Pleasant Grove and Hunter were not anomalies. In 1986, a Federal District Judge concluded that the at-large election

---

7 This lawsuit was filed by Shelby County, a political subdivision of Alabama, rather than by the State itself. Nevertheless, it is appropriate to judge Shelby County's constitutional challenge in light of instances of discrimination statewide because Shelby County is subject to §5's preclearance requirement by virtue of Alabama's designation as a covered jurisdiction under §4(b) of the VRA. See *ante*, at 7. In any event, Shelby County's recent record of employing an at-large electoral system tainted by intentional racial discrimination is by itself sufficient to justify subjecting the county to §5's preclearance mandate. See *infra*, at 26.

systems in several Alabama counties violated §2. *Dillard* v. *Crenshaw Cty.*, 640 F. Supp. 1347, 1354–1363 (MD Ala. 1986). Summarizing its findings, the court stated that "[f]rom the late 1800's through the present, [Alabama] has consistently erected barriers to keep black persons from full and equal participation in the social, economic, and political life of the state." *Id.*, at 1360.

The Dillard litigation ultimately expanded to include 183 cities, counties, and school boards employing discriminatory at-large election systems. *Dillard* v. *Baldwin Cty. Bd. of Ed.*, 686 F. Supp. 1459, 1461 (MD Ala. 1988). One of those defendants was Shelby County, which eventually signed a consent decree to resolve the claims against it. See *Dillard* v. *Crenshaw Cty.*, 748 F. Supp. 819 (MD Ala. 1990).

Although the Dillard litigation resulted in overhauls of numerous electoral systems tainted by racial discrimination, concerns about backsliding persist. In 2008, for example, the city of Calera, located in Shelby County, requested preclearance of a redistricting plan that "would have eliminated the city's sole majority-black district, which had been created pursuant to the consent decree in *Dillard*." 811 F. Supp. 2d 424, 443 (DC 2011). Although DOJ objected to the plan, Calera forged ahead with elections based on the unprecleared voting changes, resulting in the defeat of the incumbent African-American councilman who represented the former majority-black district. *Ibid.* The city's defiance required DOJ to bring a §5 enforcement action that ultimately yielded appropriate redress, including restoration of the majority-black district. *Ibid.*; Brief for Respondent-Intervenors Earl Cunningham et al. 20.

A recent FBI investigation provides a further window into the persistence of racial discrimination in state politics. See *United States* v. *McGregor*, 824 F. Supp. 2d 1339, 1344–1348 (MD Ala. 2011). Recording devices worn by state legislators cooperating with the FBI's investigation captured conversations between members of the state legislature and their political allies. The recorded conversations are shocking. Members of the state Senate derisively refer to African-Americans as "Aborigines" and talk openly of their aim to quash a particular gambling-related referendum because the referendum, if placed on the ballot, might increase African-American voter turnout. *Id.*, at 1345–1346 (internal quotation marks omitted). See also *id.*, at 1345 (legislators and their allies expressed concern that if the referendum were placed on the ballot, "'[e]very black, every illiterate' would be 'bused [to the polls] on HUD financed buses'"). These conversations occurred not in the 1870's, or even in the 1960's, they took place in 2010. *Id.*, at 1344–1345. The District Judge presiding over the criminal trial at which the recorded conversations were introduced commented that the "recordings represent compelling evidence that political exclusion through racism remains a real and enduring problem" in Alabama. *Id.*, at 1347. Racist sentiments, the judge observed, "remain regrettably entrenched in the high echelons of state government." *Ibid.*

These recent episodes forcefully demonstrate that §5's preclearance requirement is constitutional as applied to Alabama and its political subdivisions.[8] And under our case law, that conclusion should suffice to resolve this case. See *United States* v. *Raines*, 362 U.S. 17, 24–25 (1960) ("[I]f the complaint here called for an application of the statute clearly constitutional under the Fifteenth Amendment, that should have been an end to the question of constitutionality."). See also *Nevada Dept. of Human Resources* v. *Hibbs*, 538 U.S. 721, 743 (2003) (Scalia, J., dissenting) (where, as here, a state or local government raises a facial challenge to a federal statute on the ground that it exceeds Congress' enforcement powers under the Civil War Amendments, the challenge fails if the opposing party is able to show that the statute "could constitutionally be applied to some jurisdictions").

---

8 Congress continued preclearance over Alabama, including Shelby County, *after* considering evidence of current barriers there to minority voting clout. Shelby County, thus, is no "redhead" caught up in an arbitrary scheme. See *ante*, at 22.

This Court has consistently rejected constitutional challenges to legislation enacted pursuant to Congress' enforcement powers under the Civil War Amendments upon finding that the legislation was constitutional as applied to the particular set of circumstances before the Court. See *United States* v. *Georgia*, 546 U.S. 151, 159 (2006) (Title II of the Americans with Disabilities Act of 1990 (ADA) validly abrogates state sovereign immunity "insofar as [it] creates a private cause of action . . . for conduct that actually violates the Fourteenth Amendment"); *Tennessee* v. *Lane*, 541 U.S. 509, 530–534 (2004) (Title II of the ADA is constitutional "as it applies to the class of cases implicating the fundamental right of access to the courts"); *Raines*, 362 U.S., at 24–26 (federal statute proscribing deprivations of the right to vote based on race was constitutional as applied to the state officials before the Court, even if it could not constitutionally be applied to other parties). A similar approach is warranted here.[9]

The VRA's exceptionally broad severability provision makes it particularly inappropriate for the Court to allow Shelby County to mount a facial challenge to §§4(b) and 5 of the VRA, even though application of those provisions to the county falls well within the bounds of Congress' legislative authority. The severability provision states:

> "If any provision of [this Act] or the application thereof to any person or circumstances is held invalid, the remainder of [the Act] and the application of the provision to other persons not similarly situated or to other circumstances shall not be affected thereby." 42 U. S. C. §1973p.

---

9 The Court does not contest that Alabama's history of racial discrimination provides a sufficient basis for Congress to require Alabama and its political subdivisions to preclear electoral changes. Nevertheless, the Court asserts that Shelby County may prevail on its facial challenge to §4's coverage formula because it is subject to §5's preclearance requirement by virtue of that formula. See *ante*, at 22 ("The county was selected [for preclearance] based on th[e] [coverage] formula."). This misses the reality that Congress decided to subject Alabama to preclearance based on evidence of continuing constitutional violations in that State. See *supra*, at 28, n. 8.

In other words, even if the VRA could not constitutionally be applied to certain States—*e.g.*, Arizona and Alaska, see *ante*, at 8—§1973p calls for those unconstitutional applications to be severed, leaving the Act in place for jurisdictions as to which its application does not transgress constitutional limits.

Nevertheless, the Court suggests that limiting the jurisdictional scope of the VRA in an appropriate case would be "to try our hand at updating the statute." *Ante*, at 22. Just last Term, however, the Court rejected this very argument when addressing a materially identical severability provision, explaining that such a provision is "Congress' explicit textual instruction to leave unaffected the remainder of [the Act]" if any particular "application is unconstitutional." *National Federation of Independent Business* v. *Sebelius*, 567 U.S. __, __ (2012) (plurality opinion) (slip op., at 56) (internal quotation marks omitted); *id.*, at __ (GINSBURG, J., concurring in part, concurring in judgment in part, and dissenting in part) (slip op., at 60) (agreeing with the plurality's severability analysis). See also *Raines*, 362 U.S., at 23 (a statute capable of some constitutional applications may nonetheless be susceptible to a facial challenge only in "that rarest of cases where this Court can justifiably think itself able confidently to discern that Congress would not have desired its legislation to stand at all unless it could validly stand in its every application"). Leaping to resolve Shelby County's facial challenge without considering whether application of the VRA to Shelby County is constitutional, or even addressing the VRA's severability provision, the Court's opinion can hardly be described as an exemplar of restrained and moderate decision making. Quite the opposite. Hubris is a fit word for today's demolition of the VRA.

B

The Court stops any application of §5 by holding that §4(b)'s coverage formula is unconstitutional. It pins this result, in large measure, to "the fundamental principle of equal sovereignty." *Ante*, at 10–11, 23. In *Katzenbach*, however, the Court held, in no uncertain terms, that the principle *"applies only to the terms upon which States are admitted to the Union*, and not to the remedies for local evils which have subsequently appeared." 383 U.S., at 328–329 (emphasis added).

Katzenbach, the Court acknowledges, "rejected the notion that the [equal sovereignty] principle operate[s] as a bar on differential treatment outside [the] context [of the admission of new States]." *Ante*, at 11 (citing 383 U.S., at 328–329) (emphasis omitted). But the Court clouds that once clear understanding by citing dictum from *Northwest Austin* to convey that the principle of equal sovereignty "remains highly pertinent in assessing subsequent disparate treatment of States." *Ante*, at 11 (citing 557 U.S., at 203). See also *ante*, at 23 (relying on *Northwest Austin*'s "emphasis on [the] significance" of the equal-sovereignty principle). If the Court is suggesting that dictum in *Northwest Austin* silently overruled *Katzenbach*'s limitation of the equal sovereignty doctrine to "the admission of new States," the suggestion is untenable. *Northwest Austin* cited *Katzenbach*'s holding in the course of declining to decide whether the VRA was constitutional or even what standard of review applied to the question. 557 U.S., at 203–204. In today's decision, the Court ratchets up what was pure dictum in *Northwest Austin*, attributing breadth to the equal sovereignty principle in flat contradiction of *Katzenbach*. The Court does so with nary an explanation of why it finds *Katzenbach* wrong, let alone any discussion of whether stare decisis nonetheless counsels adherence to *Katzenbach*'s ruling on the limited "significance" of the equal sovereignty principle.

Today's unprecedented extension of the equal sovereignty principle outside its proper domain—the admission of new States—is capable of much mischief. Federal statutes that treat States disparately are hardly novelties. See, *e.g.*, 28 U. S. C. §3704 (no State may operate or permit a sports-related gambling scheme, unless that State conducted such a scheme "at any time during the period beginning January 1, 1976, and ending August 31, 1990"); 26 U. S. C. §142(l) (EPA required to locate green building project in a State meeting specified population criteria); 42 U. S. C. §3796bb (at least 50 percent of rural drug enforcement assistance funding must be allocated to States with "a population density of fifty-two or fewer persons per square mile or a State in which the largest county has fewer than one hundred and fifty thousand people, based on the decennial census of 1990 through fiscal year 1997"); §§13925, 13971 (similar population criteria for funding to combat rural domestic violence); §10136 (specifying rules applicable to Nevada's Yucca Mountain nuclear waste site, and providing that "[n]o State, other than the State of Nevada, may receive financial assistance under this subsection after December 22, 1987"). Do such provisions remain safe given the Court's expansion of equal sovereignty's sway?

Of gravest concern, Congress relied on our pathmarking *Katzenbach* decision in each reauthorization of the VRA. It had every reason to believe that the Act's limited geographical scope would weigh in favor of, not against, the Act's constitutionality. See, *e.g.*, *United States* v. *Morrison*, 529 U.S. 598, 626–627 (2000) (confining preclearance regime to States with a record of discrimination bolstered the VRA's constitutionality). Congress could hardly have foreseen that the VRA's limited geographic reach would render the Act constitutionally suspect. See Persily 195 ("[S]upporters of the Act sought to develop an evidentiary record for the principal purpose of explaining why the covered jurisdictions should remain covered, rather than justifying the coverage of certain jurisdictions but not others.").

In the Court's conception, it appears, defenders of the VRA could not prevail upon showing what the record overwhelmingly bears out, *i.e.*, that there is a need for continuing the preclearance regime in covered States. In addition, the defenders would have to disprove the existence of a comparable need elsewhere. See Tr. of Oral Arg. 61–62 (suggesting that proof of egregious episodes of racial discrimination in covered jurisdictions would not suffice to carry the day for the VRA, unless such episodes are shown to be absent elsewhere). I am aware of no precedent for imposing such a double burden on defenders of legislation.

C

The Court has time and again declined to upset legislation of this genre unless there was no or almost no evidence of unconstitutional action by States. See, *e.g.*, *City of Boerne* v. *Flores*, 521 U.S. 507, 530 (1997) (legislative record "mention[ed] no episodes [of the kind the legislation aimed to check] occurring in the past 40 years"). No such claim can be made about the congressional record for the 2006 VRA reauthorization. Given a record replete with examples of denial or abridgment of a paramount federal right, the Court should have left the matter where it belongs: in Congress' bailiwick.

Instead, the Court strikes §4(b)'s coverage provision because, in its view, the provision is not based on "current conditions." *Ante*, at 17. It discounts, however, that one such condition was the preclearance remedy in place in the covered jurisdictions, a remedy Congress designed both to catch discrimination before it causes harm, and to guard against return to old ways. 2006 Reauthorization §2(b)(3), (9). Volumes of evidence supported Congress' determination that the prospect of retrogression was real. Throwing out preclearance when it has worked and is continuing to work to stop discriminatory changes is like throwing away your umbrella in a rainstorm because you are not getting wet.

But, the Court insists, the coverage formula is no good; it is based on "decades-old data and eradicated practices." *Ante*, at 18. Even if the legislative record shows, as engaging with it would reveal, that the formula accurately identifies the jurisdictions with the worst conditions of voting discrimination, that is of no moment, as the Court sees it. Congress, the Court decrees, must "star[t] from scratch." *Ante*, at 23. I do not see why that should be so.

Congress' chore was different in 1965 than it was in 2006. In 1965, there were a "small number of States . . . which in most instances were familiar to Congress by name," on which Congress fixed its attention. *Katzenbach*, 383 U.S., at 328. In drafting the coverage formula, "Congress began work with reliable evidence of actual voting discrimination in a great majority of the States" it sought to target. *Id.*, at 329. "The formula [Congress] eventually evolved to describe these areas" also captured a few States that had not been the subject of congressional factfinding. *Ibid.* Nevertheless, the Court upheld the formula in its entirety, finding it fair "to infer a significant danger of the evil" in all places the formula covered. *Ibid.*

The situation Congress faced in 2006, when it took up *re*authorization of the coverage formula, was not the same. By then, the formula had been in effect for many years, and all of the jurisdictions covered by it were "familiar to Congress by name." *Id.*, at 328. The question before Congress: Was there still a sufficient basis to support continued application of the preclearance remedy in each of those already-identified places? There was at that point no chance that the formula might inadvertently sweep in new areas that were not the subject of congressional findings. And Congress could determine from the record whether the jurisdictions captured by the coverage formula still belonged under the preclearance regime. If they did, there was no need to alter the formula. That is why the Court, in addressing prior reauthorizations of the VRA, did not question the continuing "relevance" of the formula.

Consider once again the components of the record before Congress in 2006. The coverage provision identified a known list of places with an undisputed history of serious problems with racial discrimination in voting. Recent evidence relating to Alabama and its counties was there for all to see. Multiple Supreme Court decisions had upheld the coverage provision, most recently in 1999. There was extensive evidence that, due to the preclearance mechanism, conditions in the covered jurisdictions had notably improved. And there was evidence that preclearance was still having a substantial real-world effect, having stopped hundreds of discriminatory voting changes in the covered jurisdictions since the last reauthorization. In addition, there was evidence that racial polarization in voting was higher in covered jurisdictions than elsewhere, increasing the vulnerability of minority citizens in those jurisdictions. And countless witnesses, reports, and case studies documented continuing problems with voting discrimination in those jurisdictions. In light of this record, Congress had more than a reasonable basis to conclude that the existing coverage formula was not out of sync with conditions on the ground in covered areas. And certainly Shelby County was no candidate for release through the mechanism Congress provided. See *supra*, at 22–23, 26–28.

The Court holds §4(b) invalid on the ground that it is "irrational to base coverage on the use of voting tests 40 years ago, when such tests have been illegal since that time." *Ante*, at 23. But the Court disregards what Congress set about to do in enacting the VRA. That extraordinary legislation scarcely stopped at the particular tests and devices that happened to exist in 1965. The grand aim of the Act is to secure to all in our polity equal citizenship stature, a voice in our democracy undiluted by race. As the record for the 2006 reauthorization makes abundantly clear, second-generation barriers to minority voting rights have emerged in the covered jurisdictions as attempted *substitutes* for the first-generation barriers that originally triggered preclearance in those jurisdictions. See *supra*, at 5–6, 8, 15–17.

The sad irony of today's decision lies in its utter failure to grasp why the VRA has proven effective. The Court appears to believe that the VRA's success in eliminating the specific devices extant in 1965 means that preclearance is no longer needed. *Ante*, at 21–22, 23–24. With that belief, and the argument derived from it, history repeats itself. The same assumption—that the problem could be solved when particular methods of voting discrimination are identified and eliminated—was indulged and proved wrong repeatedly prior to the VRA's enactment. Unlike prior statutes, which singled out particular tests or devices, the VRA is grounded in Congress' recognition of the "variety and persistence" of measures designed to impair minority voting rights. *Katzenbach*, 383 U.S., at 311; *supra*, at 2. In truth, the evolution of voting discrimination into more subtle second-generation barriers is powerful evidence that a remedy as effective as preclearance remains vital to protect minority voting rights and prevent backsliding.

Beyond question, the VRA is no ordinary legislation. It is extraordinary because Congress embarked on a mission long delayed and of extraordinary importance: to realize the purpose and promise of the Fifteenth Amendment. For a half century, a concerted effort has been made to end racial discrimination in voting. Thanks to the Voting Rights Act, progress once the subject of a dream has been achieved and continues to be made.

The record supporting the 2006 reauthorization of the VRA is also extraordinary. It was described by the Chairman of the House Judiciary Committee as "one of the most extensive considerations of any piece of legislation that the United States Congress has dealt with in the 27½ years" he had served in the House. 152 Cong. Rec. H5143 (July 13, 2006) (statement of Rep. Sensenbrenner). After exhaustive evidence-gathering and deliberative process, Congress reauthorized the VRA, including the coverage provision, with overwhelming bipartisan support. It was the judgment of Congress that "40 years has not been a sufficient amount of time to eliminate the vestiges of discrimination following nearly 100 years of disregard for the dictates of the 15th amendment and to ensure that the right of all citizens to vote is protected as guaranteed by the Constitution." 2006 Reauthorization §2(b)(7), 120 Stat. 577. That determination of the body empowered to enforce the Civil War Amendments "by appropriate legislation" merits this Court's utmost respect. In my judgment, the Court errs egregiously by overriding Congress' decision.

*   *   *

For the reasons stated, I would affirm the judgment of the Court of Appeals.

Vance v. Ball State Univ.,
570 U.S. 421
(2013)

Dissenting Opinion

*M*aetta Vance filed a lawsuit against Ball State University, where she was the only Black employee in the dining services department, because of harassment from another employee, including the use of racial epithets, taking away her ability to work overtime, and other unjust discipline. Per Title VII of the Civil Rights Act of 1964, an employer is liable if it has been negligent in responding to harassment claims; however, a harassment claim brought against a supervisor, not an employer, does not require proving negligence because the behavior of a supervisor is attributed to the employer. Vance claimed that Davis was her supervisor, while Ball State claimed Davis was a coworker, and the lower federal district court found insufficient evidence to prove a hostile work environment.

Because of Title VII's distinctions between coworkers and supervisors for the purposes of employer liability, the question before the Court was whether a coworker who has authority to oversee another employee's work is considered a supervisor. In a majority opinion authored by Justice Samuel A. Alito, Jr., the Court established a narrow interpretation of "supervisor": one who can take tangible employment action against an employee. Justice Clarence Thomas, in his concurring opinion, called this the "narrowest and most workable rule" for determining an employer's liability. Justice Ginsburg argued in her dissent that a more suitable definition of "supervisor" would be anyone who has authority over an employee's day-to-day activities.

No. 11–556
MAETTA VANCE, PETITIONER
v.
BALL STATE UNIVERSITY
ON WRIT OF CERTIORARI TO THE
UNITED STATES COURT OF APPEALS
FOR THE SEVENTH CIRCUIT
[June 24, 2013]

JUSTICE GINSBURG, with whom JUSTICE BREYER, JUSTICE SOTOMAYOR, and JUSTICE KAGAN join, dissenting.

In *Faragher* v. *Boca Raton*, 524 U.S. 775 (1998), and *Burlington Industries, Inc.* v. *Ellerth*, 524 U.S. 742 (1998), this Court held that an employer can be vicariously liable under Title VII of the Civil Rights Act of 1964 for harassment by an employee given supervisory authority over subordinates. In line with those decisions, in 1999, the Equal Employment Opportunity Commission (EEOC) provided enforcement guidance "regarding employer liability for harassment by supervisors based on sex, race, color, religion, national origin, age, disability, or protected activity." EEOC, Guidance on Vicarious Employer Liability For Unlawful Harassment by Supervisors, 8 BNA FEP Manual 405:7651 (Feb. 2003) (hereinafter EEOC Guidance). Addressing who qualifies as a supervisor, the EEOC answered: (1) an individual authorized "to undertake or recommend tangible employment decisions affecting the employee," including "hiring, firing, promoting, demoting, and reassigning the employee"; or (2) an individual authorized "to direct the employee's daily work activities." *Id.*, at 405:7654.

The Court today strikes from the supervisory category employees who control the day-to-day schedules and assignments of others, confining the category to those formally empowered to take tangible employment actions. The limitation the Court decrees diminishes the force of *Faragher* and *Ellerth*, ignores the conditions under which members of the work force

labor, and disserves the objective of Title VII to prevent discrimination from infecting the Nation's workplaces. I would follow
the EEOC's Guidance and hold that the authority to direct an
employee's daily activities establishes supervisory status under
Title VII.

I

A

Title VII makes it "an unlawful employment practice for an
employer" to "discriminate against any individual with respect
to" the "terms, conditions, or privileges of employment, because
of such individual's race, color, religion, sex, or national origin."
42 U. S. C. §2000e–2(a). The creation of a hostile work environment through harassment, this Court has long recognized, is a
form of proscribed discrimination. *Oncale* v. *Sundowner Offshore
Services, Inc.*, 523 U.S. 75, 78 (1998); *Meritor Savings Bank, FSB*
v. *Vinson*, 477 U.S. 57, 64–65 (1986).

What qualifies as harassment? Title VII imposes no "general
civility code." *Oncale*, 523 U.S., at 81. It does not reach "the ordinary tribulations of the workplace," for example, "sporadic use of
abusive language" or generally boorish conduct. B. Lindemann
& D. Kadue, Sexual Harassment in Employment Law 175
(1992). See also 1 B. Lindemann & P. Grossman, Employment
Discrimination Law 1335–1343 (4th ed. 2007) (hereinafter
Lindemann & Grossman). To be actionable, charged behavior
need not drive the victim from her job, but it must be of such
severity or pervasiveness as to pollute the working environment,
thereby "alter[ing] the conditions of the victim's employment."
Harris v. *Forklift Systems, Inc.*, 510 U.S. 17, 21–22 (1993).

In *Faragher* and *Ellerth*, this Court established a framework
for determining when an employer may be held liable for its
employees' creation of a hostile work environment. Recognizing
that Title VII's definition of "employer" includes an employer's
"agent[s]," 42 U. S. C. §2000e(b), the Court looked to agency
law for guidance in formulating liability standards. *Faragher*, 524
U.S., at 791, 801; *Ellerth*, 524 U.S., at 755–760. In particular,

the Court drew upon §219(2)(d) of the Restatement (Second) of Agency (1957), which makes an employer liable for the conduct of an employee, even when that employee acts beyond the scope of her employment, if the employee is "aided in accomplishing" a tort "by the existence of the agency relation." See *Faragher*, 524 U.S., at 801; *Ellerth*, 524 U.S., at 758.

Stemming from that guide, *Faragher* and *Ellerth* distinguished between harassment perpetrated by supervisors, which is often enabled by the supervisor's agency relationship with the employer, and harassment perpetrated by co-workers, which is not similarly facilitated. *Faragher*, 524 U.S., at 801–803; *Ellerth*, 524 U.S., at 763–765. If the harassing employee is a supervisor, the Court held, the employer is vicariously liable whenever the harassment culminates in a tangible employment action. *Faragher*, 524 U.S., at 807–808; *Ellerth*, 524 U.S., at 764–765. The term "tangible employment action," *Ellerth* observed, "constitutes a significant change in employment status, such as hiring, firing, failing to promote, reassignment with significantly different responsibilities, or a decision causing a significant change in benefits." *Id.*, at 761. Such an action, the Court explained, provides "assurance the injury could not have been inflicted absent the agency relation." *Id.*, at 761–762.

An employer may also be held vicariously liable for a supervisor's harassment that does not culminate in a tangible employment action, the Court next determined. In such a case, however, the employer may avoid liability by showing that (1) it exercised reasonable care to prevent and promptly correct harassing behavior, and (2) the complainant unreasonably failed to take advantage of preventative or corrective measures made available to her. *Faragher*, 524 U.S., at 807; *Ellerth*, 524 U.S., at 765. The employer bears the burden of establishing this affirmative defense by a preponderance of the evidence. *Faragher*, 524 U.S., at 807; *Ellerth*, 524 U.S., at 765.

In contrast, if the harassing employee is a co-worker, a negligence standard applies. To satisfy that standard, the complainant must show that the employer knew or should have known of the offensive conduct but failed to take appropriate corrective action. See *Faragher*, 524 U.S., at 799; *Ellerth*, 524 U.S., at 758–759. See also 29 CFR §1604.11(d) (2012); EEOC Guidance 405:7652.

B

The distinction *Faragher* and *Ellerth* drew between supervisors and co-workers corresponds to the realities of the workplace. Exposed to a fellow employee's harassment, one can walk away or tell the offender to "buzz off." A supervisor's slings and arrows, however, are not so easily avoided. An employee who confronts her harassing supervisor risks, for example, receiving an undesirable or unsafe work assignment or an unwanted transfer. She may be saddled with an excessive workload or with placement on a shift spanning hours disruptive of her family life. And she may be demoted or fired. Facing such dangers, she may be reluctant to blow the whistle on her superior, whose "power and authority invests his or her harassing conduct with a particular threatening character." *Ellerth*, 524 U.S., at 763. See also *Faragher*, 524 U.S., at 803; Brief for Respondent 23 ("The potential threat to one's livelihood or working conditions will make the victim think twice before resisting harassment or fighting back."). In short, as *Faragher* and *Ellerth* recognized, harassment by supervisors is more likely to cause palpable harm and to persist unabated than similar conduct by fellow employees.

II

While *Faragher* and *Ellerth* differentiated harassment by supervisors from harassment by co-workers, neither decision gave a definitive answer to the question: Who qualifies as a supervisor? Two views have emerged. One view, in line with the EEOC's Guidance, counts as a supervisor anyone with authority to take tangible employment actions or to direct an employee's daily work activities. *E.g.*, *Mack* v. *Otis Elevator Co.*, 326 F. 3d 116, 127 (CA2 2003); *Whitten* v. *Fred's, Inc.*, 601 F. 3d 231, 246 (CA4 2010); EEOC Guidance 405:7654. The other view ranks as supervisors only those authorized to take tangible employment actions. *E.g.*, *Noviello* v. *Boston*, 398 F. 3d 76, 96 (CA1 2005); *Parkins* v. *Civil Constructors of Ill., Inc.*, 163 F. 3d 1027, 1034 (CA7 1998); *Joens* v. *John Morrell & Co.*, 354 F. 3d 938, 940–941 (CA8 2004).

Notably, respondent Ball State University agreed with petitioner Vance and the United States, as *amicus curiae*, that the tangible-employment-action-only test "does not necessarily capture all employees who may qualify as supervisors." Brief for Respondent 1. "[V]icarious liability," Ball State acknowledged, "also may be triggered when the harassing employee has the authority to control the victim's daily work activities in a way that materially enables the harassment." *Id.*, at 1–2.

The different view taken by the Court today is out of accord with the agency principles that, *Faragher* and *Ellerth* affirmed, govern Title VII. See *supra*, at 3–4. It is blind to the realities of the workplace, and it discounts the guidance of the EEOC, the agency Congress established to interpret, and superintend the enforcement of, Title VII. Under that guidance, the appropriate question is: Has the employer given the alleged harasser authority to take tangible employment actions or to control the conditions under which subordinates do their daily work? If the answer to either inquiry is yes, vicarious liability is in order, for the superior-subordinate working arrangement facilitating the harassment is of the employer's making.

A

Until today, our decisions have assumed that employees who direct subordinates' daily work are supervisors. In *Faragher*, the city of Boca Raton, Florida, employed Bill Terry and David Silverman to oversee the city's corps of ocean lifeguards. 524 U.S., at 780. Terry and Silverman "repeatedly subject[ed] Faragher and other female lifeguards to uninvited and offensive touching," and they regularly "ma[de] lewd remarks, and [spoke] of women in offensive terms." *Ibid.* (internal quotation marks omitted). Terry told a job applicant that "female lifeguards had sex with their male counterparts," and then "asked whether she would do the same." *Id.*, at 782. Silverman threatened to assign Faragher to toilet-cleaning duties for a year if she refused to date him. *Id.*, at 780. In words and conduct, Silverman and Terry made the beach a hostile place for women to work.

As Chief of Boca Raton's Marine Safety Division, Terry had authority to "hire new lifeguards (subject to the approval of higher management), to supervise all aspects of the lifeguards' work assignments, to engage in counseling, to deliver oral reprimands, and to make a record of any such discipline." *Id.*, at 781. Silverman's duties as a Marine Safety lieutenant included "making the lifeguards' daily assignments, and . . . supervising their work and fitness training." *Ibid.* Both men "were granted virtually unchecked authority over their subordinates, directly controlling and supervising all aspects of Faragher's day-to-day activities." *Id.*, at 808 (internal quotation marks and brackets omitted).

We may assume that Terry would fall within the definition of supervisor the Court adopts today. See *ante*, at 9.[1] But nothing in the *Faragher* record shows that Silverman would. Silverman had oversight and assignment responsibilities—he could punish lifeguards who would not date him with full-time toilet-cleaning duty—but there was no evidence that he had authority to take tangible employment actions. See *Faragher*, 524 U.S., at 780–781. Holding that Boca Raton was vicariously liable for Silverman's harassment, *id.*, at 808–809, the Court characterized him as Faragher's supervisor, see *id.*, at 780, and there was no dissent on that point, see *id.*, at 810 (THOMAS, J., dissenting).

---

1 It is not altogether evident that Terry would qualify under the Court's test. His authority to hire was subject to approval by higher management, *Faragher* v. *Boca Raton*, 524 U.S. 775, 781 (1998), and there is scant indication that he possessed other powers on the Court's list. The Court observes that Terry was able to "recommen[d]," and "initiat[e]" tangible employment actions. *Ante*, at 15, n. 8 (internal quotation marks omitted). Nothing in the *Faragher* record, however, shows that Terry had authority to take such actions himself. Faragher's complaint alleged that Terry said he would never promote a female lifeguard to the rank of lieutenant, 524 U.S., at 780, but that statement hardly suffices to establish that he had ultimate promotional authority. Had Boca Raton anticipated the position the Court today announces, the city might have urged classification of Terry as Faragher's superior, but not her "supervisor."

Subsequent decisions reinforced *Faragher's* use of the term "supervisor" to encompass employees with authority to direct the daily work of their victims. In *Pennsylvania State Police* v. *Suders*, 542 U.S. 129, 140 (2004), for example, the Court considered whether a constructive discharge occasioned by supervisor harassment ranks as a tangible employment action. The harassing employees lacked authority to discharge or demote the complainant, but they were "responsible for the day-to-day supervision" of the workplace and for overseeing employee shifts. *Suders* v. *Easton*, 325 F. 3d 432, 450, n. 11 (CA3 2003). Describing the harassing employees as the complainant's "supervisors," the Court proceeded to evaluate the complainant's constructive discharge claim under the *Ellerth* and *Faragher* framework. *Suders*, 542 U.S., at 134, 140–141.

It is true, as the Court says, *ante*, at 15–17, and n. 11, that *Faragher* and later cases did not squarely resolve whether an employee without power to take tangible employment actions may nonetheless qualify as a supervisor. But in laboring to establish that Silverman's supervisor status, undisputed in *Faragher*, is not dispositive here, the Court misses the forest for the trees. *Faragher* illustrates an all-too-plain reality: A supervisor with authority to control subordinates' daily work is no less aided in his harassment than is a supervisor with authority to fire, demote, or transfer. That Silverman could threaten Faragher with toilet-cleaning duties while Terry could orally reprimand her was inconsequential in *Faragher*, and properly so. What mattered was that both men took advantage of the power vested in them as agents of Boca Raton to facilitate their abuse. See *Faragher*, 524 U.S., at 801 (Silverman and Terry "implicitly threaten[ed] to misuse their supervisory powers to deter any resistance or complaint."). And when, assisted by an agency relationship, in-charge superiors like Silverman perpetuate a discriminatory work environment, our decisions have appropriately held the employer vicariously liable, subject to the above-described affirmative defense. See *supra*, at 3–4.

B

Workplace realities fortify my conclusion that harassment by an employee with power to direct subordinates' day-to-day work activities should trigger vicarious employer liability. The following illustrations, none of them hypothetical, involve in-charge employees of the kind the Court today excludes from supervisory status.[2]

Yasharay Mack: Yasharay Mack, an African-American woman, worked for the Otis Elevator Company as an elevator mechanic's helper at the Metropolitan Life Building in New York City. James Connolly, the "mechanic in charge" and the senior employee at the site, targeted Mack for abuse. He commented frequently on her "fantastic ass," "luscious lips," and "beautiful eyes," and, using deplorable racial epithets, opined that minorities and women did not "belong in the business." Once, he pulled her on his lap, touched her buttocks, and tried to kiss her while others looked on. Connolly lacked authority to take tangible employment actions against mechanic's helpers, but he did assign their work, control their schedules, and direct the particulars of their workdays. When he became angry with Mack, for example, he denied her overtime hours. And when she complained about the mistreatment, he scoffed, "I get away with everything." See *Mack*, 326 F. 3d, at 120–121, 125–126 (internal quotation marks omitted).

Donna Rhodes: Donna Rhodes, a seasonal highway maintainer for the Illinois Department of Transportation, was responsible for plowing snow during winter months. Michael Poladian was a "Lead Lead Worker" and Matt Mara, a "Technician" at the maintenance yard where Rhodes worked. Both men assembled plow crews and managed the work assignments of employees in Rhodes's position, but neither had authority to hire, fire, promote, demote, transfer, or discipline employees. In her third season working at the yard, Rhodes

---

2 The illustrative cases reached the appellate level after grants of summary judgment in favor of the employer. Like the Courts of Appeals in each case, I recount the facts in the light most favorable to the employee, the nonmoving party.

was verbally assaulted with sex-based invectives and a pornographic image was taped to her locker. Poladian forced her to wash her truck in sub-zero temperatures, assigned her undesirable yard work instead of road crew work, and prohibited another employee from fixing the malfunctioning heating system in her truck. Conceding that Rhodes had been subjected to a sex-based hostile work environment, the Department of Transportation argued successfully in the District Court and Court of Appeals that Poladian and Mara were not Rhodes's supervisors because they lacked authority to take tangible employment actions against her. See *Rhodes* v. *Illinois Dept. of Transp.*, 359 F. 3d 498, 501–503, 506–507 (CA7 2004).

Clara Whitten: Clara Whitten worked at a discount retail store in Belton, South Carolina. On Whitten's first day of work, the manager, Matt Green, told her to "give [him] what [he] want[ed]" in order to obtain approval for long weekends off from work. Later, fearing what might transpire, Whitten ignored Green's order to join him in an isolated storeroom. Angered, Green instructed Whitten to stay late and clean the store. He demanded that she work over the weekend despite her scheduled day off. Dismissing her as "dumb and stupid," Green threatened to make her life a "living hell." Green lacked authority to fire, promote, demote, or otherwise make decisions affecting Whitten's pocketbook. But he directed her activities, gave her tasks to accomplish, burdened her with undesirable work assignments, and controlled her schedule. He was usually the highest ranking employee in the store, and both Whitten and Green considered him the supervisor. See *Whitten*, 601 F. 3d, at 236, 244–247 (internal quotation marks omitted).

Monika Starke: CRST Van Expedited, Inc., an interstate transit company, ran a training program for newly hired truckdrivers requiring a 28-day on-the-road trip. Monika Starke participated in the program. Trainees like Starke were paired in a truck cabin with a single "lead driver" who lacked authority to hire, fire, promote, or demote, but who exercised control over the work environment for the duration of the trip. Lead drivers were responsible for providing instruction on CRST's driving method, assigning specific tasks, and scheduling rest stops. At the end of the trip, lead drivers evaluated trainees' performance with a nonbinding pass or fail recommendation that could lead to full driver status. Over the course of Starke's training trip, her first lead driver, Bob Smith, filled the cabin with vulgar sexual remarks, commenting on her breast size and comparing the gear stick to genitalia. A second lead driver, David Goodman, later forced her into unwanted sex with him, an outrage to which she submitted, believing it necessary to gain a passing grade. See *EEOC* v. *CRST Van Expedited, Inc.*, 679 F. 3d 657, 665–666, 684–685 (CA8 2012).

In each of these cases, a person vested with authority to control the conditions of a subordinate's daily work life used his position to aid his harassment. But in none of them would the Court's severely confined definition of supervisor yield vicarious liability for the employer. The senior elevator mechanic in charge, the Court today tells us, was Mack's co-worker, not her supervisor. So was the store manager who punished Whitten with long hours for refusing to give him what he wanted. So were the lead drivers who controlled all aspects of Starke's working environment, and the yard worker who kept other employees from helping Rhodes to control the heat in her truck.

As anyone with work experience would immediately grasp, James Connolly, Michael Poladian, Matt Mara, Matt Green, Bob Smith, and David Goodman wielded employer-conferred supervisory authority over their victims. Each man's discriminatory harassment derived force from, and was facilitated by, the control reins he held. Cf. *Burlington N. & S. F. R. Co.* v. *White*, 548 U.S. 53, 70–71 (2006) ("Common sense suggests that one good way to discourage an employee . . . from bringing discrimination charges would be to insist that she spend more time performing the more arduous duties and less time performing those that are easier or more agreeable."). Under any fair reading of Title VII, in each of the illustrative cases, the superior employee should have been classified a supervisor whose conduct would trigger vicarious liability.[3]

C

Within a year after the Court's decisions in *Faragher* and *Ellerth*, the EEOC defined "supervisor" to include any employee with "authority to undertake or recommend tangible employment decisions," or with "authority to direct [another] employee's daily work activities." EEOC Guidance 405:7654. That definition should garner "respect proportional to its 'power to persuade.'" *United States* v. *Mead Corp.*, 533 U.S. 218, 235 (2001) (quoting *Skidmore* v. *Swift & Co.*, 323 U.S. 134, 140 (1944)). See also *Crawford* v. *Metropolitan Government of Nashville and Davidson Cty.*, 555 U.S. 271, 276 (2009) (EEOC guidelines merited *Skidmore* deference); *Federal Express Corp.* v. *Holowecki*, 552 U.S. 389, 399–403 (2008) (same); *Meritor*, 477 U.S., at 65 (same).[4]

The EEOC's definition of supervisor reflects the agency's "informed judgment" and "body of experience" in enforcing Title VII. *Id.*, at 65 (internal quotation marks omitted). For 14 years, in enforcement actions and litigation, the EEOC has firmly adhered to its definition. See Brief for United States as *Amicus Curiae* 28 (citing numerous briefs in the Courts of Appeals setting forth the EEOC's understanding).

3 The Court misses the point of the illustrations. See *ante*, at 26–28, and nn. 15–16. Even under a vicarious liability rule, the Court points out, employers might escape liability for reasons other than the harasser's status as supervisor. For example, Rhodes might have avoided summary judgment in favor of her employer; even so, it would have been open to the employer to raise and prove to a jury the *Faragher/Ellerth* affirmative defense, see *supra*, at 3–4. No doubt other barriers also might impede an employee from prevailing, for example, Whitten's and Starke's intervening bankruptcies, see *Whitten* v. *Fred's Inc.*, No. 8:08–0218–HMH–BHH, 2010 WL 2757005 (D. SC, July 12, 2010); *EEOC* v. *CRST Van Expedited, Inc.*, 679 F. 3d 657, 678, and n. 14 (CA8 2012), or Mack's withdrawal of her complaint for reasons not apparent from the record, see *ante*, at 27–28, n. 16. That, however, is no reason to restrict the definition of supervisor in a way that leaves out those genuinely in charge.

4 Respondent's *amici* maintain that the EEOC Guidance is ineligible for deference under *Skidmore* v. *Swift & Co.*, 323 U.S. 134 (1944), because it interprets *Faragher* and *Burlington Industries, Inc.* v. *Ellerth*, 524 U.S. 742 (1998), not the text of Title VII. See Brief for Society for Human Resource Management et al. 11–16. They are mistaken. The EEOC Guidance rests on the employer liability framework set forth in *Faragher* and *Ellerth*, but both the framework and EEOC Guidance construe the term "agent" in 42 U. S. C. §2000e(b).

In developing its definition of supervisor, the EEOC paid close attention to the *Faragher* and *Ellerth* framework. An employer is vicariously liable only when the authority it has delegated enables actionable harassment, the EEOC recognized. EEOC Guidance 405:7654. For that reason, a supervisor's authority must be "of a sufficient magnitude so as to assist the harasser . . . in carrying out the harassment." *Ibid.* Determining whether an employee wields sufficient authority is not a mechanical inquiry, the EEOC explained; instead, specific facts about the employee's job function are critical. *Id.*, at 405:7653 to 405:7654. Thus, an employee with authority to increase another's workload or assign undesirable tasks may rank as a supervisor, for those powers can enable harassment. *Id.*, at 405:7654. On the other hand, an employee "who directs only a limited number of tasks or assignments" ordinarily would not qualify as a supervisor, for her harassing conduct is not likely to be aided materially by the agency relationship. *Id.*, at 405:7655.

In my view, the EEOC's definition, which the Court puts down as "a study in ambiguity," *ante*, at 21, has the ring of truth and, therefore, powerfully persuasive force. As a precondition to vicarious employer liability, the EEOC explained, the harassing supervisor must wield authority of sufficient magnitude to enable the harassment. In other words, the aided-in-accomplishment standard requires "something more than the employment relation itself." *Ellerth*, 524 U.S., at 760. Furthermore, as the EEOC perceived, in assessing an employee's qualification as a supervisor, context is often key. See *infra*, at 16–17. I would accord the agency's judgment due respect.

III

Exhibiting remarkable resistance to the thrust of our prior decisions, workplace realities, and the EEOC's Guidance, the Court embraces a position that relieves scores of employers of responsibility for the behavior of the supervisors they employ. Trumpeting the virtues of simplicity and administrability, the Court restricts supervisor status to those with power to take tangible employment actions. In so restricting the definition of supervisor, the Court once again shuts from sight the "robust protection against workplace discrimination Congress intended Title VII to secure." *Ledbetter* v. *Goodyear Tire & Rubber Co.*, 550 U.S. 618, 660 (2007) (GINSBURG, J., dissenting).

A

The Court purports to rely on the *Ellerth* and *Faragher* framework to limit supervisor status to those capable of taking tangible employment actions. *Ante*, at 10, 18. That framework, we are told, presupposes "a sharp line between co-workers and supervisors." *Ante*, at 18. The definition of supervisor decreed today, the Court insists, is "clear," "readily applied," and "easily workable," *ante*, at 10, 20, when compared to the EEOC's vague standard, *ante*, at 22.

There is reason to doubt just how "clear" and "workable" the Court's definition is. A supervisor, the Court holds, is someone empowered to "take tangible employment actions against the victim, *i.e.*, to effect a 'significant change in employment status, such as hiring, firing, failing to promote, reassignment with significantly different responsibilities, or a decision causing a significant change in benefits.'" *Ante*, at 9 (quoting *Ellerth*, 524 U.S., at 761). Whether reassignment authority makes someone a supervisor might depend on whether the reassignment carries economic consequences. *Ante*, at 16, n. 9. The power to discipline other employees, when the discipline has economic consequences, might count, too. *Ibid.* So might the power to initiate or make recommendations about tangible employment actions. *Ante*, at 15, n. 8. And when an employer "concentrates all decision making authority in a few individuals" who rely on information from "other workers who actually interact with the affected employee," the other workers may rank as supervisors (or maybe not; the Court does not commit one way or the other). *Ante*, at 26.

Someone in search of a bright line might well ask, what counts as "significantly different responsibilities"? Can any economic consequence make a reassignment or disciplinary action "significant," or is there a minimum threshold? How concentrated must the decisionmaking authority be to deem those not formally endowed with that authority nevertheless "supervisors"? The Court leaves these questions unanswered, and its liberal use of "mights" and "mays," *ante*, at 15, n. 8, 16, n. 9, 26, dims the light it casts.[5]

That the Court has adopted a standard, rather than a clear rule, is not surprising, for no crisp definition of supervisor could supply the unwavering line the Court desires. Supervisors, like the workplaces they manage, come in all shapes and sizes. Whether a pitching coach supervises his pitchers (can he demote them?), or an artistic director supervises her opera star (can she impose significantly different responsibilities?), or a law firm associate supervises the firm's paralegals (can she fire them?) are matters not susceptible to mechanical rules and on-off switches. One cannot know whether an employer has vested supervisory authority in an employee, and whether harassment is aided by that authority, without looking to the particular working relationship between the harasser and the victim. That is why *Faragher* and *Ellerth* crafted an employer liability standard embracive of all whose authority significantly aids in the creation and perpetuation of harassment.

The Court's focus on finding a definition of supervisor capable of instant application is at odds with the Court's ordinary emphasis on the importance of particular circumstances in Title VII cases. See, *e.g.*, *Burlington Northern*, 548 U.S., at 69 ("[T]he significance of any given act of retaliation will often depend upon the particular circumstances."); *Harris*, 510 U.S., at 23 ("[W]hether

---

5 Even the Seventh Circuit, whose definition of supervisor the Court adopts in large measure, has candidly acknowledged that, under its definition, supervisor status is not a clear and certain thing. See *Doe v. Oberweis Dairy*, 456 F. 3d 704, 717 (2006) ("The difficulty of classification in this case arises from the fact that Nayman, the shift supervisor, was in between the paradigmatic classes [of supervisor and co-worker]. He had supervisory responsibility in the sense of authority to direct the work of the [ice-cream] scoopers, and he was even authorized to issue disciplinary write-ups, but he had no authority to fire them. He was either an elevated coworker or a diminished supervisor.").

an environment is 'hostile' or 'abusive' can be determined only by looking at all the circumstances.").[6] The question of supervisory status, no less than the question whether retaliation or harassment has occurred, "depends on a constellation of surrounding circumstances, expectations, and relationships." *Oncale*, 523 U.S., at 81–82. The EEOC's Guidance so perceives.

B

As a consequence of the Court's truncated conception of supervisory authority, the *Faragher* and *Ellerth* framework has shifted in a decidedly employer-friendly direction. This realignment will leave many harassment victims without an effective remedy and undermine Title VII's capacity to prevent workplace harassment.

The negligence standard allowed by the Court, see *ante*, at 24, scarcely affords the protection the *Faragher* and *Ellerth* framework gave victims harassed by those in control of their lives at work. Recall that an employer is negligent with regard to harassment only if it knew or should have known of the conduct but failed to take appropriate corrective action. See 29 CFR §1604.11(d); EEOC Guidance 405:7652 to 405:7653. It is not uncommon for employers to lack actual or constructive notice of a harassing employee's conduct. See Lindemann & Grossman 1378–1379. An employee may have a reputation as a harasser among those in his vicinity, but if no complaint makes its way up to management, the employer will escape liability under a negligence standard. *Id.*, at 1378.

Faragher is illustrative. After enduring unrelenting harassment, Faragher reported Terry's and Silverman's conduct informally to Robert Gordon, another immediate supervisor. 524 U.S., at 782–783. But the lifeguards were "completely isolated from the

---

6 The Court worries that the EEOC's definition of supervisor will confound jurors who must first determine whether the harasser is a supervisor and second apply the correct employer liability standard. *Ante*, at 22–24, and nn. 13, 14. But the Court can point to no evidence that jury instructions on supervisor status in jurisdictions following the EEOC Guidance have in fact proved unworkable or confusing to jurors. Moreover, under the Court's definition of supervisor, jurors in many cases will be obliged to determine, as a threshold question, whether the alleged harasser possessed supervisory authority. See *supra*, at 15–16.

City's higher management," and it did not occur to Faragher to pursue the matter with higher ranking city officials distant from the beach. *Id.*, at 783, 808 (internal quotation marks omitted). Applying a negligence standard, the Eleventh Circuit held that, despite the pervasiveness of the harassment, and despite Gordon's awareness of it, Boca Raton lacked constructive notice and therefore escaped liability. *Id.*, at 784–785. Under the vicarious liability standard, however, Boca Raton could not make out the affirmative defense, for it had failed to disseminate a policy against sexual harassment. *Id.*, at 808–809.

On top of the substantive differences in the negligence and vicarious liability standards, harassment victims, under today's decision, are saddled with the burden of proving the employer's negligence whenever the harasser lacks the power to take tangible employment actions. *Faragher* and *Ellerth*, by contrast, placed the burden squarely on the employer to make out the affirmative defense. See *Suders*, 542 U.S., at 146 (citing *Ellerth*, 524 U.S., at 765; *Faragher*, 524 U.S., at 807). This allocation of the burden was both sensible and deliberate: An employer has superior access to evidence bearing on whether it acted reasonably to prevent or correct harassing behavior, and superior resources to marshal that evidence. See 542 U.S., at 146, n. 7 ("The employer is in the best position to know what remedial procedures it offers to employees and how those procedures operate.").

Faced with a steeper substantive and procedural hill to climb, victims like Yasharay Mack, Donna Rhodes, Clara Whitten, and Monika Starke likely will find it impossible to obtain redress. We can expect that, as a consequence of restricting the supervisor category to those formally empowered to take tangible employment actions, victims of workplace harassment with meritorious Title VII claims will find suit a hazardous endeavor.[7]

Inevitably, the Court's definition of supervisor will hinder

---

7 Nor is the Court's confinement of supervisor status needed to deter insubstantial claims. Under the EEOC Guidance, a plaintiff must meet the threshold requirement of actionable harassment and then show that her supervisor's authority was of "sufficient magnitude" to assist in the harassment. See EEOC Guidance 405:7652, 405:7654.

efforts to stamp out discrimination in the workplace. Because supervisors are comparatively few, and employees are many, "the employer has a greater opportunity to guard against misconduct by supervisors than by common workers," and a greater incentive to "screen [supervisors], train them, and monitor their performance." *Faragher*, 524 U.S., at 803. Vicarious liability for employers serves this end. When employers know they will be answerable for the injuries a harassing jobsite boss inflicts, their incentive to provide preventative instruction is heightened. If vicarious liability is confined to supervisors formally empowered to take tangible employment actions, however, employers will have a diminished incentive to train those who control their subordinates' work activities and schedules, *i.e.*, the supervisors who "actually interact" with employees. *Ante*, at 26.

IV

I turn now to the case before us. Maetta Vance worked as substitute server and part-time catering assistant for Ball State University's Banquet and Catering Division. During the period in question, she alleged, Saundra Davis, a catering specialist, and other Ball State employees subjected her to a racially hostile work environment. Applying controlling Circuit precedent, the District Court and Seventh Circuit concluded that Davis was not Vance's supervisor, and reviewed Ball State's liability for her conduct under a negligence standard. 646 F. 3d 461, 470–471 (2011); App. to Pet. for Cert. 53a–55a, 59a–60a. Because I would hold that the Seventh Circuit erred in restricting supervisor status to employees formally empowered to take tangible employment actions, I would remand for application of the proper standard to Vance's claim. On this record, however, there is cause to anticipate that Davis would not qualify as Vance's supervisor.[8]

---

8 In addition to concluding that Davis was not Vance's supervisor, the District Court held that the conduct Vance alleged was "neither sufficiently severe nor pervasive to be considered objectively hostile for the purposes of Title VII." App. to Pet. for Cert. 66a. The Seventh Circuit declined to address this issue. See 646 F. 3d 461, 471 (2011). If the case were remanded, the Court of Appeals could resolve the hostile environment issue first, and then, if necessary, Davis' status as supervisor or co-worker.

Supervisor status is based on "job function rather than job title," and depends on "specific facts" about the working relationship. EEOC Guidance 405:7654. See *supra*, at 13. Vance has adduced scant evidence that Davis controlled the conditions of her daily work. Vance stated in an affidavit that the general manager of the Catering Division, Bill Kimes, was charged with "overall supervision in the kitchen," including "reassign[ing] people to perform different tasks," and "control[ling] the schedule." App. 431. The chef, Shannon Fultz, assigned tasks by preparing "prep lists" of daily duties. *Id.*, at 277–279, 427. There is no allegation that Davis had a hand in creating these prep lists, nor is there any indication that, in fact, Davis otherwise controlled the particulars of Vance's workday. Vance herself testified that she did not know whether Davis was her supervisor. *Id.*, at 198.

True, Davis' job description listed among her responsibilities "[l]ead[ing] and direct[ing] kitchen part-time, substitute, and student employee helpers via demonstration, coaching, and overseeing their work." *Id.*, at 13. And another employee testified to believing that Davis was "a supervisor." *Id.*, at 386. But because the supervisor-status inquiry should focus on substance, not labels or paper descriptions, it is doubtful that this slim evidence would enable Vance to survive a motion for summary judgment. Nevertheless, I would leave it to the Seventh Circuit to decide, under the proper standard for supervisory status, what impact, if any, Davis' job description and the co-worker's statement should have on the determination of Davis' status.[9]

V

Regrettably, the Court has seized upon Vance's thin case to narrow the definition of supervisor, and thereby manifestly limit Title VII's protections against workplace harassment. Not even Ball State, the defendant-employer in this case, has advanced the

---

9 The Court agrees that Davis "would probably not qualify" as Vance's supervisor under the EEOC's definition. *Ante*, at 28–29. Then why, one might ask, does the Court nevertheless reach out to announce its restrictive standard in this case, one in which all parties, including the defendant-employer, accept the fitness for Title VII of the EEOC's Guidance? See *supra*, at 5.

restrictive definition the Court adopts. See *supra*, at 5. Yet the Court, insistent on constructing artificial categories where context should be key, proceeds on an immoderate and unrestrained course to corral Title VII.

Congress has, in the recent past, intervened to correct this Court's wayward interpretations of Title VII. See Lilly Ledbetter Fair Pay Act of 2009, 123 Stat. 5, superseding *Ledbetter* v. *Goodyear Tire & Rubber Co.*, 550 U.S. 618 (2007). See also Civil Rights Act of 1991, 105 Stat. 1071, superseding in part, *Lorance* v. *AT&T Technologies, Inc.*, 490 U.S. 900 (1989); *Martin* v. *Wilks*, 490 U.S. 755 (1989); *Wards Cove Packing Co.* v. *Atonio*, 490 U.S. 642 (1989); and *Price Waterhouse* v. *Hopkins*, 490 U.S. 228 (1989). The ball is once again in Congress' court to correct the error into which this Court has fallen, and to restore the robust protections against workplace harassment the Court weakens today.

* * *

For the reasons stated, I would reverse the judgment of the Seventh Circuit and remand the case for application of the proper standard for determining who qualifies as a supervisor.

Burwell v. Hobby Lobby Stores, Inc., 573 U.S. 682 (2014)

Dissenting Opinion

*T*he *Patient Protection and Affordable Care Act (ACA), passed in 2010, required that employer-provided group health care plans must cover contraceptives. The Green family, owners of the craft-supply chain Hobby Lobby Stores, Inc., objected to this requirement because it conflicted with their belief that use of contraceptives is akin to abortion and is immoral, a belief that was grounded in their Christian faith. The Greens sued Kathleen Sebelius, then Secretary of the Department of Health and Human Services, challenging the ACA's contraceptive requirement and arguing that it violated the Free Exercise Clause of the First Amendment and the Religious Freedom Restoration Act (RFRA) of 1993.*

The question before the Supreme Court was whether the RFRA allowed for a for-profit company to deny contraceptive coverage to employees because of the religious beliefs of the company's owners. In a 5-4 opinion, Justice Samuel A. Alito, Jr., said yes, and stated that Congress, when passing the RFRA, had intended for it to apply to corporations because those corporations are composed of individuals; in addition, forcing religious corporations to either fund what they consider abortion or face significant fines creates a substantial burden that doesn't further the government's interests in the least restrictive manner. Justice Ginsburg dissented, arguing that religious beliefs may not affect the rights of third parties, which a religious-based exemption would do to Hobby Lobby's female employees seeking contraceptives.

SUPREME COURT OF THE UNITED STATES

SYLVIA BURWELL, SECRETARY OF HEALTH AND
HUMAN SERVICES, ET AL., PETITIONERS
13–354

v.

HOBBY LOBBY STORES, INC., ET AL.
ON WRIT OF CERTIORARI TO THE UNITED STATES
COURT OF APPEALS FOR THE TENTH CIRCUIT
AND
CONESTOGA WOOD SPECIALTIES CORPORATION
ET AL., PETITIONERS
13–356

v.

SYLVIA BURWELL, SECRETARY OF HEALTH AND
HUMAN SERVICES, ET AL.
ON WRIT OF CERTIORARI TO THE UNITED STATES
COURT OF APPEALS FOR THE THIRD CIRCUIT
[June 30, 2014]

Justice Ginsburg, with whom Justice Sotomayor joins, and with whom Justice Breyer and Justice Kagan join as to all but Part III–C–1, dissenting.

In a decision of startling breadth, the Court holds that commercial enterprises, including corporations, along with partnerships and sole proprietorships, can opt out of any law (saving only tax laws) they judge incompatible with their sincerely held religious beliefs. See *ante*, at 16–49. Compelling governmental interests in uniform compliance with the law, and disadvantages that religion-based opt-outs impose on others, hold no sway, the Court decides, at least when there is a "less restrictive alternative." And such an alternative, the Court suggests, there always will be whenever, in lieu of tolling an enterprise claiming a religion-based exemption, the government, *i.e.,* the general public, can pick up the tab. See *ante*, at 41–43.[1]

---

1 The Court insists it has held none of these things, for another less restrictive alternative

The Court does not pretend that the First Amendment's Free Exercise Clause demands religion-based accommodations so extreme, for our decisions leave no doubt on that score. See *infra*, at 6–8. Instead, the Court holds that Congress, in the Religious Freedom Restoration Act of 1993 (RFRA), 42 U. S. C. §2000bb *et seq.*, dictated the extraordinary religion-based exemptions today's decision endorses. In the Court's view, RFRA demands accommodation of a for-profit corporation's religious beliefs no matter the impact that accommodation may have on third parties who do not share the corporation owners' religious faith—in these cases, thousands of women employed by Hobby Lobby and Conestoga or dependents of persons those corporations employ. Persuaded that Congress enacted RFRA to serve a far less radical purpose, and mindful of the havoc the Court's judgment can introduce, I dissent.

I

"The ability of women to participate equally in the economic and social life of the Nation has been facilitated by their ability to control their reproductive lives." *Planned Parenthood of Southeastern Pa.* v. *Casey*, 505 U.S. 833, 856 (1992). Congress acted on that understanding when, as part of a nationwide insurance program intended to be comprehensive, it called for coverage of preventive care responsive to women's needs. Carrying out Congress' direction, the Department of Health and Human Services (HHS), in consultation with public health experts, promulgated regulations requiring group health plans to cover all forms of contraception approved by the Food and Drug Administration (FDA). The genesis of this coverage should enlighten the Court's resolution of these cases.

---

is at hand: extending an existing accommodation, currently limited to religious nonprofit organizations, to encompass commercial enterprises. See *ante*, at 3–4. With that accommodation extended, the Court asserts, "women would still be entitled to all [Food and Drug Administration]-approved contraceptives without cost sharing." *Ante*, at 4. In the end, however, the Court is not so sure. In stark contrast to the Court's initial emphasis on this accommodation, it ultimately declines to decide whether the highlighted accommodation is even lawful. See *ante*, at 44 ("We do not decide today whether an approach of this type complies with RFRA . . . .").

A

The Affordable Care Act (ACA), in its initial form, specified three categories of preventive care that health plans must cover at no added cost to the plan participant or beneficiary.[2] Particular services were to be recommended by the U.S. Preventive Services Task Force, an independent panel of experts. The scheme had a large gap, however; it left out preventive services that "many women's health advocates and medical professionals believe are critically important." 155 Cong. Rec. 28841 (2009) (statement of Sen. Boxer). To correct this oversight, Senator Barbara Mikulski introduced the Women's Health Amendment, which added to the ACA's minimum coverage requirements a new category of preventive services specific to women's health.

Women paid significantly more than men for preventive care, the amendment's proponents noted; in fact, cost barriers operated to block many women from obtaining needed care at all. See, e.g., id., at 29070 (statement of Sen. Feinstein) ("Women of childbearing age spend 68 percent more in out-of-pocket health care costs than men."); id., at 29302 (statement of Sen. Mikulski) ("co-payments are [often] so high that [women] avoid getting [preventive and screening services] in the first place"). And increased access to contraceptive services, the sponsors comprehended, would yield important public health gains. See, e.g., id., at 29768 (statement of Sen. Durbin) ("This bill will expand health insurance coverage to the vast majority of [the 17 million women of reproductive age in the United States who are uninsured] . . . . This expanded access will reduce unintended pregnancies.").

As altered by the Women's Health Amendment's passage, the ACA requires new insurance plans to include coverage without cost sharing of "such additional preventive care and screenings . . .

2 See 42 U. S. C. §300gg–13(a)(1)–(3) (group health plans must provide coverage, without cost sharing, for (1) certain "evidence-based items or services" recommended by the U.S. Preventive Services Task Force; (2) immunizations recommended by an advisory committee of the Centers for Disease Control and Prevention; and (3) "with respect to infants, children, and adolescents, evidence-informed preventive care and screenings provided for in the comprehensive guidelines supported by the Health Resources and Services Administration").

as provided for in comprehensive guidelines supported by the Health Resources and Services Administration [(HRSA)]," a unit of HHS. 42 U. S. C. §300gg–13(a)(4). Thus charged, the HRSA developed recommendations in consultation with the Institute of Medicine (IOM). See 77 Fed. Reg. 8725–8726 (2012).[3] The IOM convened a group of independent experts, including "specialists in disease prevention [and] women's health"; those experts prepared a report evaluating the efficacy of a number of preventive services. IOM, Clinical Prevention Services for Women: Closing the Gaps 2 (2011) (hereinafter IOM Report). Consistent with the findings of "[n]umerous health professional associations" and other organizations, the IOM experts determined that preventive coverage should include the "full range" of FDA-approved contraceptive methods. *Id.*, at 10. See also *id.*, at 102–110.

In making that recommendation, the IOM's report expressed concerns similar to those voiced by congressional proponents of the Women's Health Amendment. The report noted the disproportionate burden women carried for comprehensive health services and the adverse health consequences of excluding contraception from preventive care available to employees without cost sharing. See, *e.g.*, *id.*, at 19 ("[W]omen are consistently more likely than men to report a wide range of cost-related barriers to receiving . . . medical tests and treatments and to filling prescriptions for themselves and their families."); *id.*, at 103–104, 107 (pregnancy may be contraindicated for women with certain medical conditions, for example, some congenital heart diseases, pulmonary hypertension, and Marfan syndrome, and contraceptives may be used to reduce risk of endometrial cancer, among other serious medical conditions); *id.*, at 103 (women with unintended pregnancies are more likely to experience depression and anxiety, and their children face "increased odds of preterm birth and low birth weight").

---

3 The IOM is an arm of the National Academy of Sciences, an organization Congress established "for the explicit purpose of furnishing advice to the Government." *Public Citizen* v. *Department of Justice*, 491 U.S. 440, 460, n. 11 (1989) (internal quotation marks omitted).

In line with the IOM's suggestions, the HRSA adopted guidelines recommending coverage of "[a]ll [FDA-]approved contraceptive methods, sterilization procedures, and patient education and counseling for all women with reproductive capacity."[4] Thereafter, HHS, the Department of Labor, and the Department of Treasury promulgated regulations requiring group health plans to include coverage of the contraceptive services recommended in the HRSA guidelines, subject to certain exceptions, described *infra*, at 25–27.[5] This opinion refers to these regulations as the contraceptive coverage requirement.

B

While the Women's Health Amendment succeeded, a countermove proved unavailing. The Senate voted down the so-called "conscience amendment," which would have enabled any employer or insurance provider to deny coverage based on its asserted "religious beliefs or moral convictions." 158 Cong. Rec. S539 (Feb. 9, 2012); see *id.*, at S1162–S1173 (Mar. 1, 2012) (debate and vote).[6] That amendment, Senator Mikulski observed, would have "pu[t] the personal opinion of employers and insurers over the practice of medicine." *Id.*, at S1127 (Feb. 29, 2012). Rejecting the "conscience amendment," Congress left healthcare decisions—including the choice among contraceptive methods—in the hands of women, with the aid of their health care providers.

II

Any First Amendment Free Exercise Clause claim Hobby Lobby or Conestoga[7] might assert is foreclosed by this Court's

---

4 HRSA, HHS, Women's Preventive Services Guidelines, available at http://www.hrsa.gov/womensguidelines/ (all Internet materials as visited June 27, 2014, and available in Clerk of Court's case file), reprinted in App. to Brief for Petitioners in No. 13–354, pp. 43–44a. See also 77 Fed. Reg. 8725–8726 (2012).

5 5 CFR §147.130(a)(1)(iv) (2013) (HHS); 29 CFR §2590.715–2713(a)(1)(iv) (2013) (Labor); 26 CFR §54.9815–2713(a)(1)(iv) (2013)(Treasury).

6 Separating moral convictions from religious beliefs would be of questionable legitimacy. See *Welsh* v. *United States*, 398 U.S. 333, 357–358 (1970) (Harlan, J., concurring in result).

7 As the Court explains, see *ante*, at 11–16, these cases arise from two separate lawsuits, one filed by Hobby Lobby, its affiliated business (Mardel), and the family that operates these businesses (the Greens); the other filed by Conestoga and the family that owns and controls

decision in *Employment Div., Dept. of Human Resources of Ore.* v. *Smith*, 494 U.S. 872 (1990). In *Smith*, two members of the Native American Church were dismissed from their jobs and denied unemployment benefits because they ingested peyote at, and as an essential element of, a religious ceremony. Oregon law forbade the consumption of peyote, and this Court, relying on that prohibition, rejected the employees' claim that the denial of unemployment benefits violated their free exercise rights. The First Amendment is not offended, *Smith* held, when "prohibiting the exercise of religion . . . is not the object of [governmental regulation] but merely the incidental effect of a generally applicable and otherwise valid provision." *Id.*, at 878; see *id.*, at 878–879 ("an individual's religious beliefs [do not] excuse him from compliance with an otherwise valid law prohibiting conduct that the State is free to regulate"). The ACA's contraceptive coverage requirement applies generally, it is "otherwise valid," it trains on women's well being, not on the exercise of religion, and any effect it has on such exercise is incidental.

Even if *Smith* did not control, the Free Exercise Clause would not require the exemption Hobby Lobby and Conestoga seek. Accommodations to religious beliefs or observances, the Court has clarified, must not significantly impinge on the interests of third parties.[8]

The exemption sought by Hobby Lobby and Conestoga would override significant interests of the corporations' employees and

---

that business (the Hahns). Unless otherwise specified, this opinion refers to the respective groups of plaintiffs as Hobby Lobby and Conestoga.

8 See *Wisconsin* v. *Yoder*, 406 U.S. 205, 230 (1972) ("This case, of course, is not one in which any harm to the physical or mental health of the child or to the public safety, peace, order, or welfare has been demonstrated or may be properly inferred."); *Estate of Thornton* v. *Caldor, Inc.*, 472 U.S. 703 (1985) (invalidating state statute requiring employers to accommodate an employee's Sabbath observance where that statute failed to take into account the burden such an accommodation would impose on the employer or other employees). Notably, in construing the Religious Land Use and Institutionalized Persons Act of 2000 (RLUIPA), 42 U. S. C. §2000cc *et seq.*, the Court has cautioned that "adequate account" must be taken of "the burdens a requested accommodation may impose on nonbeneficiaries." *Cutter* v. *Wilkinson*, 544 U.S. 709, 720 (2005); see *id.*, at 722 ("an accommodation must be measured so that it does not override other significant interests"). A balanced approach is all the more in order when the Free Exercise Clause itself is at stake, not a statute designed to promote accommodation to religious beliefs and practices.

covered dependents. It would deny legions of women who do not hold their employers' beliefs access to contraceptive coverage that the ACA would otherwise secure. See *Catholic Charities of Sacramento, Inc.* v. *Superior Court*, 32 Cal. 4th 527, 565, 85 P. 3d 67, 93 (2004) ("We are unaware of any decision in which . . . [the U.S. Supreme Court] has exempted a religious objector from the operation of a neutral, generally applicable law despite the recognition that the requested exemption would detrimentally affect the rights of third parties."). In sum, with respect to free exercise claims no less than free speech claims, " '[y]our right to swing your arms ends just where the other man's nose begins.' " Chafee, Freedom of Speech in War Time, 32 Harv. L. Rev. 932, 957 (1919).

III

A

Lacking a tenable claim under the Free Exercise Clause, Hobby Lobby and Conestoga rely on RFRA, a statute instructing that "[g]overnment shall not substantially burden a person's exercise of religion even if the burden results from a rule of general applicability" unless the government shows that application of the burden is "the least restrictive means" to further a "compelling governmental interest." 42 U. S. C. §2000bb–1(a), (b) (2). In RFRA, Congress "adopt[ed] a statutory rule comparable to the constitutional rule rejected in *Smith*." *Gonzales* v. *O Centro Espírita Beneficente União do Vegetal*, 546 U.S. 418, 424 (2006).

RFRA's purpose is specific and written into the statute itself. The Act was crafted to "restore the compelling interest test as set forth in *Sherbert* v. *Verner*, 374 U.S. 398 (1963) and *Wisconsin* v. *Yoder*, 406 U.S. 205 (1972) and to guarantee its application in all cases where free exercise of religion is substantially burdened." §2000bb(b)(1).[9] See also §2000bb(a)(5) ("[T]he compelling interest test as set forth in prior Federal court rulings

---

9 Under *Sherbert* and *Yoder*, the Court "requir[ed] the government to justify any substantial burden on religiously motivated conduct by a compelling state interest and by means narrowly tailored to achieve that interest." *Employment Div., Dept. of Human Resources of Ore.* v. *Smith*, 494 U.S. 872, 894 (1990) (O'CONNOR, J., concurring in judgment).

is a workable test for striking sensible balances between religious liberty and competing prior governmental interests."); *ante*, at 48 (agreeing that the pre-*Smith* compelling interest test is "workable" and "strike[s] sensible balances").

The legislative history is correspondingly emphatic on RFRA's aim. See, *e.g.*, S. Rep. No. 103–111, p. 12 (1993) (hereinafter Senate Report) (RFRA's purpose was "only to overturn the Supreme Court's decision in *Smith*," not to "unsettle other areas of the law."); 139 Cong. Rec. 26178 (1993) (statement of Sen. Kennedy) (RFRA was "designed to restore the compelling interest test for deciding free exercise claims."). In line with this restorative purpose, Congress expected courts considering RFRA claims to "look to free exercise cases decided prior to *Smith* for guidance." Senate Report 8. See also H. R. Rep. No. 103–88, pp. 6–7 (1993) (hereinafter House Report) (same). In short, the Act reinstates the law as it was prior to *Smith*, without "creat[ing] . . . new rights for any religious practice or for any potential litigant." 139 Cong. Rec. 26178 (statement of Sen. Kennedy). Given the Act's moderate purpose, it is hardly surprising that RFRA's enactment in 1993 provoked little controversy. See Brief for Senator Murray et al. as *Amici Curiae* 8 (hereinafter Senators Brief) (RFRA was approved by a 97-to-3 vote in the Senate and a voice vote in the House of Representatives).

B

Despite these authoritative indications, the Court sees RFRA as a bold initiative departing from, rather than restoring, pre-*Smith* jurisprudence. See *ante*, at 6, n. 3, 7, 17, 25–27. To support its conception of RFRA as a measure detached from this Court's decisions, one that sets a new course, the Court points first to the Religious Land Use and Institutionalized Persons Act of 2000 (RLUIPA), 42 U. S. C. §2000cc *et seq.*, which altered RFRA's definition of the term "exercise of religion." RFRA, as originally enacted, defined that term to mean "the exercise of religion under the First Amendment to the Constitution." §2000bb–2(4) (1994 ed.). See *ante*, at 6–7. As amended by

RLUIPA, RFRA's definition now includes "any exercise of religion, whether or not compelled by, or central to, a system of religious belief." §2000bb–2(4) (2012 ed.) (cross-referencing §2000cc–5). That definitional change, according to the Court, reflects "an obvious effort to effect a complete separation from First Amendment case law." *Ante*, at 7.

The Court's reading is not plausible. RLUIPA's alteration clarifies that courts should not question the centrality of a particular religious exercise. But the amendment in no way suggests that Congress meant to expand the class of entities qualified to mount religious accommodation claims, nor does it relieve courts of the obligation to inquire whether a government action substantially burdens a religious exercise. See *Rasul* v. *Myers*, 563 F. 3d 527, 535 (CADC 2009) (Brown, J., concurring) ("There is no doubt that RLUIPA's drafters, in changing the definition of 'exercise of religion,' wanted to broaden the scope of the kinds of practices protected by RFRA, not increase the universe of individuals protected by RFRA."); H. R. Rep. No. 106–219, p. 30 (1999). See also *Gilardi* v. *United States Dept. of Health and Human Servs.*, 733 F. 3d 1208, 1211 (CADC 2013) (RFRA, as amended, "provides us with no helpful definition of 'exercise of religion.'"); *Henderson* v. *Kennedy*, 265 F. 3d 1072, 1073 (CADC 2001) ("The [RLUIPA] amendments did not alter RFRA's basic prohibition that the '[g]overnment shall not substantially burden a person's exercise of religion.'")[10]

Next, the Court highlights RFRA's requirement that the government, if its action substantially burdens a person's religious observance, must demonstrate that it chose the least restrictive means for furthering a compelling interest. "[B]y imposing a least-restrictive-means test," the Court suggests, RFRA "went beyond what was required by our pre-*Smith* decisions." *Ante*, at

---

10 RLUIPA, the Court notes, includes a provision directing that "[t]his chapter [*i.e.,* RLUIPA] shall be construed in favor of a broad protection of religious exercise, to the maximum extent permitted by the terms of [the Act] and the Constitution." 42 U. S. C. §2000cc–3(g); see *ante*, at 6–7, 26. RFRA incorporates RLUIPA's definition of "exercise of religion," as RLUIPA does, but contains no omnibus rule of construction governing the statute in its entirety.

17, n. 18 (citing *City of Boerne* v. *Flores*, 521 U.S. 507 (1997)). See also *ante*, at 6, n. 3. But as RFRA's statements of purpose and legislative history make clear, Congress intended only to restore, not to scrap or alter, the balancing test as this Court had applied it pre-*Smith*. See *supra*, at 8–9. See also Senate Report 9 (RFRA's "compelling interest test generally should not be construed more stringently or more leniently than it was prior to *Smith*."); House Report 7 (same).

The Congress that passed RFRA correctly read this Court's pre-*Smith* case law as including within the "compelling interest test" a "least restrictive means" requirement. See, *e.g.*, Senate Report 5 ("Where [a substantial] burden is placed upon the free exercise of religion, the Court ruled [in *Sherbert*], the Government must demonstrate that it is the least restrictive means to achieve a compelling governmental interest."). And the view that the pre-*Smith* test included a "least restrictive means" requirement had been aired in testimony before the Senate Judiciary Committee by experts on religious freedom. See, *e.g.*, Hearing on S. 2969 before the Senate Committee on the Judiciary, 102d Cong., 2d Sess., 78–79 (1993) (statement of Prof. Douglas Laycock).

Our decision in *City of Boerne*, it is true, states that the least restrictive means requirement "was not used in the pre-*Smith* jurisprudence RFRA purported to codify." See *ante*, at 6, n. 3, 17, n. 18. As just indicated, however, that statement does not accurately convey the Court's pre-*Smith* jurisprudence. See *Sherbert*, 374 U.S., at 407 ("[I]t would plainly be incumbent upon the [government] to demonstrate that no alternative forms of regulation would combat [the problem] without infringing First Amendment rights."); *Thomas* v. *Review Bd. of Indiana Employment Security Div.*, 450 U.S. 707, 718 (1981) ("The state may justify an inroad on religious liberty by showing that it is the least restrictive means of achieving some compelling state interest."). See also Berg, The New Attacks on Religious Freedom Legislation and Why They Are Wrong, 21 Cardozo L.

Rev. 415, 424 (1999) ("In *Boerne*, the Court erroneously said that the least restrictive means test 'was not used in the pre-*Smith* jurisprudence.'").[11]

C

With RFRA's restorative purpose in mind, I turn to the Act's application to the instant lawsuits. That task, in view of the positions taken by the Court, requires consideration of several questions, each potentially dispositive of Hobby Lobby's and Conestoga's claims: Do for-profit corporations rank among "person[s]" who "exercise . . . religion"? Assuming that they do, does the contraceptive coverage requirement "substantially burden" their religious exercise? If so, is the requirement "in furtherance of a compelling government interest"? And last, does the requirement represent the least restrictive means for furthering that interest?

Misguided by its errant premise that RFRA moved beyond the pre-*Smith* case law, the Court falters at each step of its analysis.

1

RFRA's compelling interest test, as noted, see *supra*, at 8, applies to government actions that "substantially burden *a person's exercise of religion*." 42 U. S. C. §2000bb–1(a) (emphasis added). This reference, the Court submits, incorporates the definition of "person" found in the Dictionary Act, 1 U. S. C. §1, which extends to "corporations, companies, associations, firms, partnerships, societies, and joint stock companies, as well as individuals." See *ante*, at 19–20. The Dictionary Act's definition, however, controls only where "context" does not "indicat[e] otherwise." §1. Here, context does so indicate. RFRA speaks of "a person's *exercise of religion*." 42 U. S. C. §2000bb–1(a) (emphasis added). See also §§2000bb–2(4), 2000cc–5(7)(a).[12] Whether a

---

11 The Court points out that I joined the majority opinion in *City of Boerne* and did not then question the statement that "least restrictive means . . . was not used [pre-*Smith*]." *Ante*, at 17, n. 18. Concerning that observation, I remind my colleagues of Justice Jackson's sage comment: "I see no reason why I should be consciously wrong today because I was unconsciously wrong yesterday." *Massachusetts* v. *United States*, 333 U.S. 611, 639–640 (1948) (dissenting opinion).

12 As earlier explained, see *supra*, at 10–11, RLUIPA's amendment of the definition of

corporation qualifies as a "person" capable of exercising religion is an inquiry one cannot answer without reference to the "full body" of pre-*Smith* "free-exercise caselaw." *Gilardi*, 733 F. 3d, at 1212. There is in that case law no support for the notion that free exercise rights pertain to for-profit corporations.

Until this litigation, no decision of this Court recognized a for-profit corporation's qualification for a religious exemption from a generally applicable law, whether under the Free Exercise Clause or RFRA.[13] The absence of such precedent is just what one would expect, for the exercise of religion is characteristic of natural persons, not artificial legal entities. As Chief Justice Marshall observed nearly two centuries ago, a corporation is "an artificial being, invisible, intangible, and existing only in contemplation of law." *Trustees of Dartmouth College* v. *Woodward*, 4 Wheat. 518, 636 (1819). Corporations, JUSTICE STEVENS more recently reminded, "have no consciences, no beliefs, no feelings, no thoughts, no desires." *Citizens United* v. *Federal Election Comm'n*, 558 U.S. 310, 466 (2010) (opinion concurring in part and dissenting in part).

The First Amendment's free exercise protections, the Court has indeed recognized, shelter churches and other nonprofit religion-based organizations.[14] "For many individuals, religious

"exercise of religion" does not bear the weight the Court places on it. Moreover, it is passing strange to attribute to RLUIPA any purpose to cover entities other than "religious assembl[ies] or institution[s]." 42 U. S. C. §2000cc(a)(1). But cf. *ante*, at 26. That law applies to land-use regulation. §2000cc(a)(1). To permit commercial enterprises to challenge zoning and other land-use regulations under RLUIPA would "dramatically expand the statute's reach" and deeply intrude on local prerogatives, contrary to Congress' intent. Brief for National League of Cities et al. as *Amici Curiae* 26.

13 The Court regards *Gallagher* v. *Crown Kosher Super Market of Mass., Inc.*, 366 U.S. 617 (1961), as "suggest[ing] . . . that for-profit corporations possess [free-exercise] rights." *Ante*, at 26–27. See also *ante*, at 21, n. 21. The suggestion is barely there. True, one of the five challengers to the Sunday closing law assailed in *Gallagher* was a corporation owned by four Orthodox Jews. The other challengers were human individuals, not artificial, law-created entities, so there was no need to determine whether the corporation could institute the litigation. Accordingly, the plurality stated it could pretermit the question "whether appellees ha[d] standing" because *Braunfeld* v. *Brown*, 366 U.S. 599 (1961), which upheld a similar closing law, was fatal to their claim on the merits. 366 U.S., at 631.

14 See, *e.g.*, *Hosanna-Tabor Evangelical Lutheran Church and School* v. *EEO*, 565 U.S. ___ (2012); *Gonzales* v. *O Centro Espírita Beneficente União do Vegetal*, 546 U.S. 418 (2006); *Church of Lukumi Babalu Aye, Inc.* v. *Hialeah*, 508 U.S. 520 (1993); *Jimmy Swaggart Ministries* v. *Board of Equalization of Cal.*, 493 U.S. 378 (1990).

activity derives meaning in large measure from participation in a larger religious community," and "furtherance of the autonomy of religious organizations often furthers individual religious freedom as well." *Corporation of Presiding Bishop of Church of Jesus Christ of Latter-day Saints* v. *Amos*, 483 U.S. 327, 342 (1987) (Brennan, J., concurring in judgment). The Court's "special solicitude to the rights of religious organizations," *Hosanna-Tabor Evangelical Lutheran Church and School* v. *EEOC*, 565 U.S. ___, ___ (2012) (slip op., at 14), however, is just that. No such solicitude is traditional for commercial organizations.[15] Indeed, until today, religious exemptions had never been extended to any entity operating in "the commercial, profit-making world." *Amos*, 483 U.S., at 337.[16]

---

15 Typically, Congress has accorded to organizations religious in character religion-based exemptions from statutes of general application. *E.g.*, 42 U. S. C. §2000e–1(a) (Title VII exemption from prohibition against employment discrimination based on religion for "a religious corporation, association, educational institution, or society with respect to the employment of individuals of a particular religion to perform work connected with the carrying on . . . of its activities"); 42 U. S. C. §12113(d)(1) (parallel exemption in Americans With Disabilities Act of 1990). It can scarcely be maintained that RFRA enlarges these exemptions to allow Hobby Lobby and Conestoga to hire only persons who share the religious beliefs of the Greens or Hahns. Nor does the Court suggest otherwise. Cf. *ante*, at 28.

The Court does identify two statutory exemptions it reads to cover for-profit corporations, 42 U. S. C. §§300a–7(b)(2) and 238n(a), and infers from them that "Congress speaks with specificity when it intends a religious accommodation not to extend to for-profit corporations," *ante*, at 28. The Court's inference is unwarranted. The exemptions the Court cites cover certain medical personnel who object to performing or assisting with abortions. Cf. *ante*, at 28, n. 27 ("the protection provided by §238n(a) differs significantly from the protection provided by RFRA"). Notably, the Court does not assert that these exemptions have in fact been afforded to for-profit corporations. See §238n(c) ("health care entity" covered by exemption is a term defined to include "an individual physician, a postgraduate physician training program, and a participant in a program of training in the health professions"); Tozzi, Whither Free Exercise: *Employment Division* v. *Smith* and the Rebirth of State Constitutional Free Exercise Clause Jurisprudence?, 48 J. Catholic Legal Studies 269, 296, n. 133 (2009) ("Catholic physicians, but not necessarily hospitals, . . . may be able to invoke [§238n(a)]. . . ."); cf. S. 137, 113th Cong., 1st Sess. (2013) (as introduced) (Abortion Non-Discrimination Act of 2013, which would amend the definition of "health care entity" in §238n to include "hospital[s]," "health insurance plan[s]," and other health care facilities). These provisions are revealing in a way that detracts from one of the Court's main arguments. They show that Congress is not content to rest on the Dictionary Act when it wishes to ensure that particular entities are among those eligible for a religious accommodation.

Moreover, the exemption codified in §238n(a) was not enacted until three years after RFRA's passage. See Omnibus Consolidated Rescissions and Appropriations Act of 1996, §515, 110 Stat. 1321–245. If, as the Court believes, RFRA opened all statutory schemes to religion-based challenges by for-profit corporations, there would be no need for a statute-specific, post-RFRA exemption of this sort.

16 That is not to say that a category of plaintiffs, such as resident aliens, may bring RFRA

The reason why is hardly obscure. Religious organizations exist to foster the interests of persons subscribing to the same religious faith. Not so of for-profit corporations. Workers who sustain the operations of those corporations commonly are not drawn from one religious community. Indeed, by law, no religion-based criterion can restrict the work force of for-profit corporations. See 42 U. S. C. §§2000e(b), 2000e–1(a), 2000e–2(a); cf. *Trans World Airlines, Inc.* v. *Hardison*, 432 U.S. 63, 80–81 (1977) (Title VII requires reasonable accommodation of an employee's religious exercise, but such accommodation must not come "at the expense of other [employees]"). The distinction between a community made up of believers in the same religion and one embracing persons of diverse beliefs, clear as it is, constantly escapes the Court's attention.[17] One can only wonder why the Court shuts this key difference from sight.

Reading RFRA, as the Court does, to require extension of religion-based exemptions to for-profit corporations surely is not grounded in the pre-*Smith* precedent Congress sought to preserve. Had Congress intended RFRA to initiate a change so huge, a clarion statement to that effect likely would have been made in the legislation. See *Whitman* v. *American Trucking Assns., Inc.*, 531 U.S. 457, 468 (2001) (Congress does not "hide elephants in mouseholes"). The text of RFRA makes no such statement and the legislative history does not so much as mention for-profit corporations. See *Hobby Lobby Stores, Inc.* v. *Sebelius*, 723 F. 3d 1114, 1169 (CA10 2013) (Briscoe, C. J., concurring in part and dissenting in part) (legislative record lacks "any suggestion that

claims only if this Court expressly "addressed their [free-exercise] rights before *Smith*." *Ante*, at 27. Continuing with the Court's example, resident aliens, unlike corporations, are flesh-and-blood individuals who plainly count as persons sheltered by the First Amendment, see *United States* v. *Verdugo-Urquidez*, 494 U.S. 259, 271 (1990) (citing *Bridges* v. *Wixon*, 326 U.S. 135, 148 (1945)), and *a fortiori*, RFRA.

17 I part ways with JUSTICE KENNEDY on the context relevant here. He sees it as the employers' "exercise [of] their religious beliefs within the context of their own closely held, for-profit corporations." *Ante*, at 2 (concurring opinion). See also *ante*, at 45–46 (opinion of the Court) (similarly concentrating on religious faith of employers without reference to the different beliefs and liberty interests of employees). I see as the relevant context the employers' asserted right to exercise religion within a nationwide program designed to protect against health hazards employees who do not subscribe to their employers' religious beliefs.

Congress foresaw, let alone intended that, RFRA would cover for-profit corporations"). See also Senators Brief 10–13 (none of the cases cited in House or Senate Judiciary Committee reports accompanying RFRA, or mentioned during floor speeches, recognized the free exercise rights of for-profit corporations).

The Court notes that for-profit corporations may support charitable causes and use their funds for religious ends, and therefore questions the distinction between such corporations and religious nonprofit organizations. See *ante*, at 20–25. See also *ante*, at 3 (KENNEDY, J., concurring) (criticizing the Government for "distinguishing between different religious believers—burdening one while accommodating the other—when it may treat both equally by offering both of them the same accommodation").[18] Again, the Court forgets that religious organizations exist to serve a community of believers. For-profit corporations do not fit that bill. Moreover, history is not on the Court's side. Recognition of the discrete characters of "ecclesiastical and lay" corporations dates back to Blackstone, see 1 W. Blackstone, Commentaries on the Laws of England 458 (1765), and was reiterated by this Court centuries before the enactment of the Internal Revenue Code. See *Terrett* v. *Taylor*, 9 Cranch 43, 49 (1815) (describing religious corporations); *Trustees of Dartmouth College*, 4 Wheat., at 645 (discussing "eleemosynary" corporations, including those "created for the promotion of religion"). To reiterate, "for-profit corporations are different from religious non-profits in that they use labor to make a profit, rather than to perpetuate [the] religious value[s] [shared by a community of believers]." *Gilardi*, 733 F. 3d, at 1242 (EDWARDS, J., concurring in part and dissenting in part) (emphasis deleted).

---

18 According to the Court, the Government "concedes" that "nonprofit corporation[s]" are protected by RFRA. *Ante*, at 19. See also *ante*, at 20, 24, 30. That is not an accurate description of the Government's position, which encompasses only "churches," "*religious* institutions," and "*religious* non-profits." Brief for Respondents in No. 13–356, p. 28 (emphasis added). See also Reply Brief in No. 13–354, p. 8 ("RFRA incorporates the longstanding and commonsense distinction between religious organizations, which sometimes have been accorded accommodations under generally applicable laws in recognition of their accepted religious character, and for-profit corporations organized to do business in the commercial world.").

Citing *Braunfeld* v. *Brown*, 366 U.S. 599 (1961), the Court questions why, if "a sole proprietorship that seeks to make a profit may assert a free-exercise claim, [Hobby Lobby and Conestoga] can't . . . do the same?" *Ante*, at 22 (footnote omitted). See also *ante*, at 16–17. But even accepting, *arguendo*, the premise that unincorporated business enterprises may gain religious accommodations under the Free Exercise Clause, the Court's conclusion is unsound. In a sole proprietorship, the business and its owner are one and the same. By incorporating a business, however, an individual separates herself from the entity and escapes personal responsibility for the entity's obligations. One might ask why the separation should hold only when it serves the interest of those who control the corporation. In any event, *Braunfeld* is hardly impressive authority for the entitlement Hobby Lobby and Conestoga seek. The free exercise claim asserted there was promptly rejected on the merits.

The Court's determination that RFRA extends to for-profit corporations is bound to have untoward effects. Although the Court attempts to cabin its language to closely held corporations, its logic extends to corporations of any size, public or private.[19] Little doubt that RFRA claims will proliferate, for the

19 The Court does not even begin to explain how one might go about ascertaining the religious scruples of a corporation where shares are sold to the public. No need to speculate on that, the Court says, for "it seems unlikely" that large corporations "will often assert RFRA claims." *Ante*, at 29. Perhaps so, but as Hobby Lobby's case demonstrates, such claims are indeed pursued by large corporations, employing thousands of persons of different faiths, whose ownership is not diffuse. "Closely held" is not synonymous with "small." Hobby Lobby is hardly the only enterprise of sizable scale that is family owned or closely held. For example, the family-owned candy giant Mars, Inc., takes in $33 billion in revenues and has some 72,000 employees, and closely held Cargill, Inc., takes in more than $136 billion in revenues and employs some 140,000 persons. See Forbes, America's Largest Private Companies 2013, available at http://www.forbes.com/largest-private-companies/.

Nor does the Court offer any instruction on how to resolve the disputes that may crop up among corporate owners over religious values and accommodations. The Court is satisfied that "[s]tate corporate law provides a ready means for resolving any conflicts," *ante*, at 30, but the authorities cited in support of that proposition are hardly helpful. See Del. Code Ann., Tit. 8, §351 (2011) (certificates of incorporation may specify how the business is managed); 1 J. Cox & T. Hazen, Treatise on the Law of Corporations §3:2 (3d ed. 2010) (section entitled "Selecting the state of incorporation"); *id.*, §14:11 (observing that "[d]espite the frequency of dissension and deadlock in close corporations, in some states neither legislatures nor courts have provided satisfactory solutions"). And even if a dispute

Court's expansive notion of corporate personhood—combined with its other errors in construing RFRA—invites for-profit entities to seek religion-based exemptions from regulations they deem offensive to their faith.

2

Even if Hobby Lobby and Conestoga were deemed RFRA "person[s]," to gain an exemption, they must demonstrate that the contraceptive coverage requirement "substantially burden[s] [their] exercise of religion." 42 U. S. C. §2000bb–1(a). Congress no doubt meant the modifier "substantially" to carry weight. In the original draft of RFRA, the word "burden" appeared unmodified. The word "substantially" was inserted pursuant to a clarifying amendment offered by Senators Kennedy and Hatch. See 139 Cong. Rec. 26180. In proposing the amendment, Senator Kennedy stated that RFRA, in accord with the Court's pre-*Smith* case law, "does not require the Government to justify every action that has some effect on religious exercise." *Ibid.*

The Court barely pauses to inquire whether any burden imposed by the contraceptive coverage requirement is substantial. Instead, it rests on the Greens' and Hahns' "belie[f] that providing the coverage demanded by the HHS regulations is connected to the destruction of an embryo in a way that is sufficient to make it immoral for them to provide the coverage." *Ante*, at 36.[20] I agree with the Court that the Green and Hahn families' religious convictions regarding contraception are sincerely held. See *Thomas*, 450 U.S., at 715 (courts are not to question where an individual "dr[aws] the line" in defining which practices run afoul of her religious beliefs). See also 42 U. S. C. §§2000bb–1(a),

settlement mechanism is in place, how is the arbiter of a religion-based intracorporate controversy to resolve the disagreement, given this Court's instruction that "courts have no business addressing [whether an asserted religious belief] is substantial," *ante*, at 36?

20 The Court dismisses the argument, advanced by some *amici*, that the $2,000-per-employee tax charged to certain employers that fail to provide health insurance is less than the average cost of offering health insurance, noting that the Government has not provided the statistics that could support such an argument. See *ante*, at 32–34. The Court overlooks, however, that it is not the Government's obligation to prove that an asserted burden is *in*substantial. Instead, it is incumbent upon plaintiffs to demonstrate, in support of a RFRA claim, the substantiality of the alleged burden.

2000bb–2(4), 2000cc–5(7)(A).[21] But those beliefs, however deeply held, do not suffice to sustain a RFRA claim. RFRA, properly understood, distinguishes between "factual allegations that [plaintiffs'] beliefs are sincere and of a religious nature," which a court must accept as true, and the "legal conclusion . . . that [plaintiffs'] religious exercise is substantially burdened," an inquiry the court must undertake. *Kaemmerling* v. *Lappin*, 553 F. 3d 669, 679 (CADC 2008).

That distinction is a facet of the pre-*Smith* jurisprudence RFRA incorporates. *Bowen* v. *Roy*, 476 U.S. 693 (1986), is instructive. There, the Court rejected a free exercise challenge to the Government's use of a Native American child's Social Security number for purposes of administering benefit programs. Without questioning the sincerity of the father's religious belief that "use of [his daughter's Social Security] number may harm [her] spirit," the Court concluded that the Government's internal uses of that number "place[d] [no] restriction on what [the father] may believe or what he may do." *Id.*, at 699. Recognizing that the father's "religious views may not accept" the position that the challenged uses concerned only the Government's internal affairs, the Court explained that "for the adjudication of a constitutional claim, the Constitution, rather than an individual's religion, must supply the frame of reference." *Id.*, at 700–701, n. 6. See also *Hernandez* v. *Commissioner*, 490 U.S. 680, 699 (1989) (distinguishing between, on the one hand, "question[s] [of] the centrality of particular beliefs or practices to a faith, or the validity of particular litigants' interpretations of those creeds," and, on the other, "whether the alleged burden imposed [by the challenged government action] is a substantial one"). Inattentive to this guidance, today's decision elides entirely

21 The Court levels a criticism that is as wrongheaded as can be. In no way does the dissent "tell the plaintiffs that their beliefs are flawed." *Ante*, at 37. Right or wrong in this domain is a judgment no Member of this Court, or any civil court, is authorized or equipped to make. What the Court must decide is not "the plausibility of a religious claim," *ante*, at 37 (internal quotation marks omitted), but whether accommodating that claim risks depriving others of rights accorded them by the laws of the United States. See *supra*, at 7–8; *infra*, at 27.

the distinction between the sincerity of a challenger's religious belief and the substantiality of the burden placed on the challenger.

Undertaking the inquiry that the Court forgoes, I would conclude that the connection between the families' religious objections and the contraceptive coverage requirement is too attenuated to rank as substantial. The requirement carries no command that Hobby Lobby or Conestoga purchase or provide the contraceptives they find objectionable. Instead, it calls on the companies covered by the requirement to direct money into undifferentiated funds that finance a wide variety of benefits under comprehensive health plans. Those plans, in order to comply with the ACA, see *supra*, at 3–6, must offer contraceptive coverage without cost sharing, just as they must cover an array of other preventive services.

Importantly, the decisions whether to claim benefits under the plans are made not by Hobby Lobby or Conestoga, but by the covered employees and dependents, in consultation with their health care providers. Should an employee of Hobby Lobby or Conestoga share the religious beliefs of the Greens and Hahns, she is of course under no compulsion to use the contraceptives in question. But "[n]o individual decision by an employee and her physician—be it to use contraception, treat an infection, or have a hip replaced—is in any meaningful sense [her employer's] decision or action." *Grote* v. *Sebelius*, 708 F. 3d 850, 865 (CA7 2013) (Rovner, J., dissenting). It is doubtful that Congress, when it specified that burdens must be "substantia[l]," had in mind a linkage thus interrupted by independent decisionmakers (the woman and her health counselor) standing between the challenged government action and the religious exercise claimed to be infringed. Any decision to use contraceptives made by a woman covered under Hobby Lobby's or Conestoga's plan will not be propelled by the Government, it will be the woman's autonomous choice, informed by the physician she consults.

3

Even if one were to conclude that Hobby Lobby and Conestoga meet the substantial burden requirement, the Government has shown that the contraceptive coverage for which the ACA provides furthers compelling interests in public health and women's well being. Those interests are concrete, specific, and demonstrated by a wealth of empirical evidence. To recapitulate, the mandated contraception coverage enables women to avoid the health problems unintended pregnancies may visit on them and their children. See IOM Report 102–107. The coverage helps safeguard the health of women for whom pregnancy may be hazardous, even life threatening. See Brief for American College of Obstetricians and Gynecologists et al. as *Amici Curiae* 14–15. And the mandate secures benefits wholly unrelated to pregnancy, preventing certain cancers, menstrual disorders, and pelvic pain. Brief for Ovarian Cancer National Alliance et al. as *Amici Curiae* 4, 6–7, 15–16; 78 Fed. Reg. 39872 (2013); IOM Report 107.

That Hobby Lobby and Conestoga resist coverage for only 4 of the 20 FDA-approved contraceptives does not lessen these compelling interests. Notably, the corporations exclude intrauterine devices (IUDs), devices significantly more effective, and significantly more expensive than other contraceptive methods. See *id.*, at 105.[22] Moreover, the Court's reasoning appears to permit commercial enterprises like Hobby Lobby and Conestoga to exclude from their group health plans all forms of contraceptives. See Tr. of Oral Arg. 38–39 (counsel for Hobby Lobby acknowledged that his "argument . . . would apply just as well if the employer said 'no contraceptives'" (internal quotation marks added)).

Perhaps the gravity of the interests at stake has led the Court to assume, for purposes of its RFRA analysis, that the

---

22 IUDs, which are among the most reliable forms of contraception, generally cost women more than $1,000 when the expenses of the office visit and insertion procedure are taken into account. See Eisenberg, McNicholas, & Peipert, Cost as a Barrier to Long-Acting Reversible Contraceptive (LARC) Use in Adolescents, 52 J. Adolescent Health S59, S60 (2013). See also Winner et al., Effectiveness of Long-Acting Reversible Contraception, 366 New Eng. J. Medicine 1998, 1999 (2012).

compelling interest criterion is met in these cases. See *ante*, at 40.[23] It bears note in this regard that the cost of an IUD is nearly equivalent to a month's full-time pay for workers earning the minimum wage, Brief for Guttmacher Institute et al. as *Amici Curiae* 16; that almost one-third of women would change their contraceptive method if costs were not a factor, Frost & Darroch, Factors Associated With Contraceptive Choice and Inconsistent Method Use, United States, 2004, 40 Perspectives on Sexual & Reproductive Health 94, 98 (2008); and that only one-fourth of women who request an IUD actually have one inserted after finding out how expensive it would be, Gariepy, Simon, Patel, Creinin, & Schwarz, The Impact of Out-of-Pocket Expense on IUD Utilization Among Women With Private Insurance, 84 Contraception e39, e40 (2011). See also Eisenberg, *supra*, at S60 (recent study found that women who face out-of-pocket IUD costs in excess of $50 were "11-times less likely to obtain an IUD than women who had to pay less than $50"); Postlethwaite, Trussell, Zoolakis, Shabear, & Petitti, A Comparison of Contraceptive Procurement Pre- and Post-Benefit Change, 76 Contraception 360, 361–362 (2007) (when one health system eliminated patient cost sharing for IUDs, use of this form of contraception more than doubled).

Stepping back from its assumption that compelling interests support the contraceptive coverage requirement, the Court notes that small employers and grandfathered plans are not subject to the requirement. If there is a compelling interest in contraceptive coverage, the Court suggests, Congress would not have created these exclusions. See *ante*, at 39–40.

Federal statutes often include exemptions for small employers, and such provisions have never been held to undermine the interests served by these statutes. See, *e.g.*, Family and Medical Leave Act of 1993, 29 U. S. C. §2611(4)(A)(i) (applicable to

---

23 Although the Court's opinion makes this assumption grudgingly, see *ante*, at 39–40, one Member of the majority recognizes, without reservation, that "the [contraceptive coverage] mandate serves the Government's compelling interest in providing insurance coverage that is necessary to protect the health of female employees." *Ante*, at 2 (opinion of KENNEDY, J.)

employers with 50 or more employees); Age Discrimination in Employment Act of 1967, 29 U. S. C. §630(b) (originally exempting employers with fewer than 50 employees, 81 Stat. 605, the statute now governs employers with 20 or more employees); Americans With Disabilities Act, 42 U. S. C. §12111(5)(A) (applicable to employers with 15 or more employees); Title VII, 42 U. S. C. §2000e(b) (originally exempting employers with fewer than 25 employees, see *Arbaugh* v. *Y & H Corp.*, 546 U.S. 500, 505, n. 2 (2006), the statute now governs employers with 15 or more employees).

The ACA's grandfathering provision, 42 U. S. C. §18011, allows a phasing-in period for compliance with a number of the Act's requirements (not just the contraceptive coverage or other preventive services provisions). Once specified changes are made, grandfathered status ceases. See 45 CFR §147.140(g). Hobby Lobby's own situation is illustrative. By the time this litigation commenced, Hobby Lobby did not have grandfathered status. Asked why by the District Court, Hobby Lobby's counsel explained that the "grandfathering requirements mean that you can't make a whole menu of changes to your plan that involve things like the amount of co-pays, the amount of co-insurance, deductibles, that sort of thing." App. in No. 13–354, pp. 39–40. Counsel acknowledged that, "just because of economic realities, our plan has to shift over time. I mean, insurance plans, as everyone knows, shif[t] over time." *Id.*, at 40.[24] The percentage of employees in grandfathered plans is steadily declining, having dropped from 56% in 2011 to 48% in 2012 to 36% in 2013. Kaiser Family Foundation & Health Research & Educ. Trust, Employer Benefits 2013 Annual Survey 7, 196. In short, far from ranking as a categorical exemption, the grandfathering provision is "temporary, intended to be a means for gradually

---

24 Hobby Lobby's *amicus* National Religious Broadcasters similarly states that, "[g]iven the nature of employers' needs to meet changing economic and staffing circumstances, and to adjust insurance coverage accordingly, the actual benefit of the 'grandfather' exclusion is *de minimis* and transitory at best." Brief for National Religious Broadcasters as *Amicus Curiae* in No. 13–354, p. 28.

transitioning employers into mandatory coverage." *Gilardi*, 733 F. 3d, at 1241 (EDWARDS, J., concurring in part and dissenting in part).

The Court ultimately acknowledges a critical point: RFRA's application "*must* take adequate account of the burdens a requested accommodation may impose on non-beneficiaries." *Ante*, at 42, n. 37 (quoting *Cutter* v. *Wilkinson*, 544 U.S. 709, 720 (2005); emphasis added). No tradition, and no prior decision under RFRA, allows a religion-based exemption when the accommodation would be harmful to others—here, the very persons the contraceptive coverage requirement was designed to protect. Cf. *supra*, at 7–8; *Prince* v. *Massachusetts*, 321 U.S. 158, 177 (1944) (Jackson, J., dissenting) ("[The] limitations which of necessity bound religious freedom . . . begin to operate whenever activities begin to affect or collide with liberties of others or of the public.").

4

After assuming the existence of compelling government interests, the Court holds that the contraceptive coverage requirement fails to satisfy RFRA's least restrictive means test. But the Government has shown that there is no less restrictive, equally effective means that would both (1) satisfy the challengers' religious objections to providing insurance coverage for certain contraceptives (which they believe cause abortions); and (2) carry out the objective of the ACA's contraceptive coverage requirement, to ensure that women employees receive, at no cost to them, the preventive care needed to safeguard their health and well being. A "least restrictive means" cannot require employees to relinquish benefits accorded them by federal law in order to ensure that their commercial employers can adhere unreservedly to their religious tenets. See *supra*, at 7–8, 27.[25]

25 As the Court made clear in *Cutter*, the government's license to grant religion-based exemptions from generally applicable laws is constrained by the Establishment Clause. 544 U.S., at 720–722. "[W]e are a cosmopolitan nation made up of people of almost every conceivable religious preference," *Braunfeld*, 366 U.S., at 606, a "rich mosaic of religious faiths," *Town of Greece* v. *Galloway*, 572 U.S. ___, ___ (2014) (KAGAN, J., dissenting) (slip op., at 15). Consequently, one person's right to free exercise must be kept in harmony with the

Then let the government pay (rather than the employees who do not share their employer's faith), the Court suggests. "The most straightforward [alternative]," the Court asserts, "would be for the Government to assume the cost of providing . . . contraceptives . . . to any women who are unable to obtain them under their health-insurance policies due to their employers' religious objections." *Ante*, at 41. The ACA, however, requires coverage of preventive services through the existing employer-based system of health insurance "so that [employees] face minimal logistical and administrative obstacles." 78 Fed. Reg. 39888. Impeding women's receipt of benefits "by requiring them to take steps to learn about, and to sign up for, a new [government funded and administered] health benefit" was scarcely what Congress contemplated. *Ibid*. Moreover, Title X of the Public Health Service Act, 42 U. S. C. §300 *et seq.*, "is the nation's only dedicated source of federal funding for safety net family planning services." Brief for National Health Law Program et al. as *Amici Curiae* 23. "Safety net programs like Title X are not designed to absorb the unmet needs of . . . insured individuals." *Id.*, at 24. Note, too, that Congress declined to write into law the preferential treatment Hobby Lobby and Conestoga describe as a less restrictive alternative. See *supra*, at 6.

And where is the stopping point to the "let the government pay" alternative? Suppose an employer's sincerely held religious belief is offended by health coverage of vaccines, or paying the minimum wage, see *Tony and Susan Alamo Foundation* v. *Secretary of Labor*, 471 U.S. 290, 303 (1985), or according women equal pay for substantially similar work, see *Dole* v. *Shenandoah Baptist Church*, 899 F. 2d 1389, 1392 (CA4 1990)? Does it rank as a less restrictive alternative to require the government to provide the money or benefit to which the employer has a religion-based objection?[26] Because the Court cannot easily answer that

---

rights of her fellow citizens, and "some religious practices [must] yield to the common good." *United States* v. *Lee*, 455 U.S. 252, 259 (1982).

26 Cf. *Ashcroft* v. *American Civil Liberties Union*, 542 U.S. 656, 666 (2004) (in context of

question, it proposes something else: Extension to commercial enterprises of the accommodation already afforded to nonprofit religion-based organizations. See *ante*, at 3–4, 9–10, 43–45. "At a minimum," according to the Court, such an approach would not "impinge on [Hobby Lobby's and Conestoga's] religious belief." *Ante*, at 44. I have already discussed the "special solicitude" generally accorded nonprofit religion-based organizations that exist to serve a community of believers, solicitude never before accorded to commercial enterprises comprising employees of diverse faiths. See *supra*, at 14–17.

Ultimately, the Court hedges on its proposal to align for-profit enterprises with nonprofit religion-based organizations. "We do not decide today whether [the] approach [the opinion advances] complies with RFRA for purposes of all religious claims." *Ante*, at 44. Counsel for Hobby Lobby was similarly noncommittal. Asked at oral argument whether the Court-proposed alternative was acceptable,[27] counsel responded: "We haven't been offered that accommodation, so we haven't had to decide what kind of objection, if any, we would make to that." Tr. of Oral Arg. 86–87.

Conestoga suggests that, if its employees had to acquire and pay for the contraceptives (to which the corporation objects) on their own, a tax credit would qualify as a less restrictive alternative. See Brief for Petitioners in No. 13–356, p. 64. A tax credit, of course, is one variety of "let the government pay." In addition

First Amendment Speech Clause challenge to a content-based speech restriction, courts must determine "whether the challenged regulation is the least restrictive means among *available*, effective alternatives" (emphasis added)).

27 On brief, Hobby Lobby and Conestoga barely addressed the extension solution, which would bracket commercial enterprises with non-profit religion-based organizations for religious accommodations purposes. The hesitation is understandable, for challenges to the adequacy of the accommodation accorded religious nonprofit organizations are currently *sub judice*. See, *e.g.*, *Little Sisters of the Poor Home for the Aged* v. *Sebelius*, ___ F. Supp. 2d ___, 2013 WL 6839900 (Colo., Dec. 27, 2013), injunction pending appeal granted, 571 U.S. ___ (2014). At another point in today's decision, the Court refuses to consider an argument neither "raised below [nor] advanced in this Court by any party," giving Hobby Lobby and Conestoga "[no] opportunity to respond to [that] novel claim." *Ante*, at 33. Yet the Court is content to decide this case (and this case only) on the ground that HHS could make an accommodation never suggested in the parties' presentations. RFRA cannot sensibly be read to "requir[e] the government to . . . refute each and every conceivable alternative regulation," *United States* v. *Wilgus*, 638 F. 3d 1274, 1289 (CA10 2011), especially where the alternative on which the Court seizes was not pressed by any challenger.

to departing from the existing employer-based system of health insurance, Conestoga's alternative would require a woman to reach into her own pocket in the first instance, and it would do nothing for the woman too poor to be aided by a tax credit.

In sum, in view of what Congress sought to accomplish, *i.e.*, comprehensive preventive care for women furnished through employer-based health plans, none of the proffered alternatives would satisfactorily serve the compelling interests to which Congress responded.

IV

Among the pathmarking pre-*Smith* decisions RFRA preserved is *United States* v. *Lee*, 455 U.S. 252 (1982). Lee, a sole proprietor engaged in farming and carpentry, was a member of the Old Order Amish. He sincerely believed that withholding Social Security taxes from his employees or paying the employer's share of such taxes would violate the Amish faith. This Court held that, although the obligations imposed by the Social Security system conflicted with Lee's religious beliefs, the burden was not unconstitutional. *Id.*, at 260–261. See also *id.*, at 258 (recognizing the important governmental interest in providing a "nationwide . . . comprehensive insurance system with a variety of benefits available to all participants, with costs shared by employers and employees").[28] The Government urges that *Lee* should control the challenges brought by Hobby Lobby and Conestoga. See Brief for Respondents in No. 13–356, p. 18. In contrast, today's Court dismisses *Lee* as a tax case. See *ante*, at 46–47. Indeed, it was a tax case and the Court in *Lee* homed in on "[t]he difficulty in attempting to accommodate religious beliefs in the area of taxation." 455 U.S., at 259.

But the *Lee* Court made two key points one cannot confine to tax cases. "When followers of a particular sect enter into commercial activity as a matter of choice," the Court observed, "the

---

28 As a sole proprietor, Lee was subject to personal liability for violating the law of general application he opposed. His claim to a religion-based exemption would have been even thinner had he conducted his business as a corporation, thus avoiding personal liability.

limits they accept on their own conduct as a matter of conscience and faith are not to be superimposed on statutory schemes which are binding on others in that activity." *Id.*, at 261. The statutory scheme of employer-based comprehensive health coverage involved in these cases is surely binding on others engaged in the same trade or business as the corporate challengers here, Hobby Lobby and Conestoga. Further, the Court recognized in *Lee* that allowing a religion-based exemption to a commercial employer would "operat[e] to impose the employer's religious faith on the employees." *Ibid.*[29] No doubt the Greens and Hahns and all who share their beliefs may decline to acquire for themselves the contraceptives in question. But that choice may not be imposed on employees who hold other beliefs. Working for Hobby Lobby or Conestoga, in other words, should not deprive employees of the preventive care available to workers at the shop next door,[30] at least in the absence of directions from the Legislature or Administration to do so.

Why should decisions of this order be made by Congress or the regulatory authority, and not this Court? Hobby Lobby and Conestoga surely do not stand alone as commercial enterprises seeking exemptions from generally applicable laws on the basis of their religious beliefs. See, *e.g., Newman* v. *Piggie Park Enterprises, Inc.*, 256 F. Supp. 941, 945 (SC 1966) (owner of restaurant chain refused to serve black patrons based on his religious beliefs opposing racial integration), aff'd in relevant part and rev'd in part on other grounds, 377 F. 2d 433 (CA4 1967), aff'd and modified on other grounds, 390 U.S. 400 (1968); *In re*

---

29 Congress amended the Social Security Act in response to *Lee.* The amended statute permits Amish sole proprietors and partnerships (but not Amish-owned corporations) to obtain an exemption from the obligation to pay Social Security taxes only for employees who are co-religionists and who likewise seek an exemption and agree to give up their Social Security benefits. See 26 U. S. C. §3127(a)(2), (b)(1). Thus, employers with sincere religious beliefs have no right to a religion-based exemption that would deprive employees of Social Security benefits without the employee's consent—an exemption analogous to the one Hobby Lobby and Conestoga seek here.

30 Cf. *Tony and Susan Alamo Foundation* v. *Secretary of Labor*, 471 U.S. 290, 299 (1985) (disallowing religion-based exemption that "would undoubtedly give [the commercial enterprise seeking the exemption] and similar organizations an advantage over their competitors").

Minnesota ex rel. McClure, 370 N. W. 2d 844, 847 (Minn. 1985) (born-again Christians who owned closely held, for-profit health clubs believed that the Bible proscribed hiring or retaining an "individua[l] living with but not married to a person of the opposite sex," "a young, single woman working without her father's consent or a married woman working without her husband's consent," and any person "antagonistic to the Bible," including "fornicators and homosexuals" (internal quotation marks omitted)), appeal dismissed, 478 U.S. 1015 (1986); *Elane Photography, LLC* v. *Willock*, 2013–NMSC–040, ___ N. M. ___, 309 P. 3d 53 (for-profit photography business owned by a husband and wife refused to photograph a lesbian couple's commitment ceremony based on the religious beliefs of the company's owners), cert. denied, 572 U.S. ___ (2014). Would RFRA require exemptions in cases of this ilk? And if not, how does the Court divine which religious beliefs are worthy of accommodation, and which are not? Isn't the Court disarmed from making such a judgment given its recognition that "courts must not presume to determine . . . the plausibility of a religious claim"? *Ante*, at 37.

Would the exemption the Court holds RFRA demands for employers with religiously grounded objections to the use of certain contraceptives extend to employers with religiously grounded objections to blood transfusions (Jehovah's Witnesses); antidepressants (Scientologists); medications derived from pigs, including anesthesia, intravenous fluids, and pills coated with gelatin (certain Muslims, Jews, and Hindus); and vaccinations (Christian Scientists, among others)?[31] According to counsel for Hobby Lobby, "each one of these cases . . . would have to be evaluated on its own . . . apply[ing] the compelling interest-least restrictive alternative test." Tr. of Oral Arg. 6. Not much help there for the lower courts bound by today's decision.

---

31 Religious objections to immunization programs are not hypothetical. See *Phillips* v. *New York*, ___ F. Supp. 2d ___, 2014 WL 2547584 (EDNY, June 5, 2014) (dismissing free exercise challenges to New York's vaccination practices); Liberty Counsel, Compulsory Vaccinations Threaten Religious Freedom (2007), available at http://www.lc.org/media/9980/attachments/memo_vaccination.pdf.

The Court, however, sees nothing to worry about. Today's cases, the Court concludes, are "concerned solely with the contraceptive mandate. Our decision should not be understood to hold that an insurance-coverage mandate must necessarily fall if it conflicts with an employer's religious beliefs. Other coverage requirements, such as immunizations, may be supported by different interests (for example, the need to combat the spread of infectious diseases) and may involve different arguments about the least restrictive means of providing them." *Ante*, at 46. But the Court has assumed, for RFRA purposes, that the interest in women's health and well being is compelling and has come up with no means adequate to serve that interest, the one motivating Congress to adopt the Women's Health Amendment.

There is an overriding interest, I believe, in keeping the courts "out of the business of evaluating the relative merits of differing religious claims," *Lee*, 455 U.S., at 263, n. 2 (STEVENS, J., concurring in judgment), or the sincerity with which an asserted religious belief is held. Indeed, approving some religious claims while deeming others unworthy of accommodation could be "perceived as favoring one religion over another," the very "risk the Establishment Clause was designed to preclude." *Ibid.* The Court, I fear, has ventured into a minefield, cf. *Spencer* v. *World Vision, Inc.*, 633 F. 3d 723, 730 (CA9 2010) (O'Scannlain, J., concurring), by its immoderate reading of RFRA. I would confine religious exemptions under that Act to organizations formed "for a religious purpose," "engage[d] primarily in carrying out that religious purpose," and not "engaged . . . substantially in the exchange of goods or services for money beyond nominal amounts." See *id.*, at 748 (Kleinfeld, J., concurring).

* * *

For the reasons stated, I would reverse the judgment of the Court of Appeals for the Tenth Circuit and affirm the judgment of the Court of Appeals for the Third Circuit.

Whole Woman's Health v. Hellerstedt, 579 U.S. ⸺ (2016)

Concurring Opinion

A 2013 Texas law, H.B. 2, included a number of provisions regarding abortion services in the state. One of the requirements in the provisions was that any doctor providing abortion services must have admitting privileges at a hospital within 30 miles of the location where the abortion is performed; another required that all abortion clinics meet the same standards as ambulatory surgical centers. A group of abortion providers sued the state, arguing in part that H.B. 2 denied equal protection by placing an undue burden on women in more rural areas who were unable to gain access to abortion because local clinics, unable to comply with the new regulations, were closing down.

In a 5-3 majority, the Court agreed that a "substantial burden" analysis should consider whether the laws restricting abortion were truly intended to protect women's health, and that the law in question did in fact create an undue burden—rendering the sections of H.B. 2 in question to be invalid. In his majority opinion, Justice Stephen G. Breyer argued that the restrictions represented undue burden because they were of no medical value, adding no further protections than regulations already in place. In her concurring opinion, Justice Ginsburg stated that modern abortions are so safe in comparison to so many other medical procedures that a law passed in the name of safety that ends up making abortions more difficult to obtain "cannot survive judicial inspection."

WHOLE WOMEN'S HEALTH, ET AL.
v.
HELLERSTEDT, COMMISSIONER, TEXAS DEPARTMENT OF STATE HEALTH SERVICES, ET AL. CERTIORARI TO THE UNITED STATES COURT OF APPEALS FOR THE FIFTH CIRCUIT

[June 27, 2016]

JUSTICE GINSBURG, concurring.

The Texas law called H. B. 2 inevitably will reduce the number of clinics and doctors allowed to provide abortion services. Texas argues that H. B. 2's restrictions are constitutional because they protect the health of women who experience complications from abortions. In truth, "complications from an abortion are both rare and rarely dangerous." *Planned Parenthood of Wis., Inc.* v. *Schimel*, 806 F. 3d 908, 912 (CA7 2015). See Brief for American College of Obstetricians and Gynecologists et al. as *Amici Curiae* 6–10 (collecting studies and concluding "[a]bortion is one of the safest medical procedures performed in the United States"); Brief for Social Science Researchers as *Amici Curiae* 5–9 (compiling studies that show "[c]omplication rates from abortion are very low"). Many medical procedures, including childbirth, are far more dangerous to patients, yet are not subject to ambulatory-surgical-center or hospital admitting-privileges requirements. See *ante*, at 31; *Planned Parenthood of Wis.*, 806 F. 3d, at 921–922. See also Brief for Social Science Researchers 9–11 (comparing statistics on risks for abortion with tonsillectomy, colonoscopy, and in-office dental surgery); Brief for American Civil Liberties Union et al. as *Amici Curiae* 7 (all District Courts to consider admitting-privileges requirements found abortion "is at least as safe as other medical procedures routinely performed in outpatient settings"). Given those realities, it is beyond rational belief that H. B. 2 could genuinely protect the health of women, and certain that the law "would simply make it more difficult for them to obtain abortions."

Planned Parenthood of Wis., 806 F. 3d, at 910. When a State severely limits access to safe and legal procedures, women in desperate circumstances may resort to unlicensed rogue practitioners, *faute de mieux*, at great risk to their health and safety. See Brief for Ten Pennsylvania Abortion Care Providers as *Amici Curiae* 17–22. So long as this Court adheres to *Roe* v. *Wade*, 410 U.S. 113 (1973), and *Planned Parenthood of Southeastern Pa.* v. *Casey*, 505 U.S. 833 (1992), Targeted Regulation of Abortion Providers laws like H. B. 2 that "do little or nothing for health, but rather strew impediments to abortion," *Planned Parenthood of Wis.*, 806 F. 3d, at 921, cannot survive judicial inspection.

Little Sisters of the Poor Saints Peter and Paul Home v. Pennsylvania, 591 U.S. _____ (2020)

Dissenting Opinion

*T*he Women's Health Amendment of the Affordable Care Act *(ACA) requires health insurance coverage for women to include contraception as part of their required preventive health care; the rule also allowed for nonprofit religious employers to request exemption from the requirement if they object to providing contraceptives. In two separate cases in 2014, the Court established that closely held for-profit organizations were also exempt from the mandate, and that it was not necessary for any organization seeking an exemption to apply for one, merely for that organization to notify the Department of Health and Human Services (HHS). In 2017 HHS put into effect additional regulations granting additional entities the ability to claim an exemption, and added a "moral" exemption in addition to a religious one. Pennsylvania and New Jersey challenged these new rules on the grounds that they were unconstitutional and violated the Administrative Procedure Act (APA).*

When the case reached the Supreme Court, the Justices had to determine whether the new rulings put forth by the Department of Health and Human Services and other federal agencies had been lawful. A 7-2 Court majority held that the ACA gave authority to these federal organizations to set forth these rules, and that the rules were instituted in a manner consistent with the requirements of the Administrative Procedure Act. Justice Clarence Thomas, in his majority opinion, explained that the language of the ACA grants authority and discretion to determine what constitutes preventive care, including the ability to create exemptions. Justice Ginsburg dissented, arguing that the language of the Act determined the type of health services that must be required, but did not grant authority to provide less than those minimum required services.

Oral arguments in the case were heard via teleconference because of the COVID-19 pandemic; Justice Ginsburg, still in recovery from an emergency surgical procedure, attended remotely from her hospital room. This dissent would prove to be her last—she died on September 18, 2020.

LITTLE SISTERS OF THE POOR SAINTS PETER AND PAUL HOME, PETITIONER 19–431 v. PENNSYLVANIA, ET AL.

DONALD J. TRUMP, PRESIDENT OF THE UNITED STATES, ET AL., PETITIONERS 19–454 v. PENNSYLVANIA, ET AL.
[July 8, 2020]

JUSTICE GINSBURG, with whom JUSTICE SOTOMAYOR joins, dissenting.

In accommodating claims of religious freedom, this Court has taken a balanced approach, one that does not allow the religious beliefs of some to overwhelm the rights and interests of others who do not share those beliefs. See, *e.g., Estate of Thornton* v. *Caldor, Inc.*, 472 U.S. 703, 708–710 (1985); *United States* v. *Lee*, 455 U.S. 252, 258–260 (1982). Today, for the first time, the Court casts totally aside countervailing rights and interests in its zeal to secure religious rights to the nth degree. Specifically, in the Women's Health Amendment to the Patient Protection and Affordable Care Act (ACA), 124 Stat. 119; 155 Cong. Rec. 28841 (2009), Congress undertook to afford gainfully employed women comprehensive, seamless, no-cost insurance coverage for preventive care protective of their health and well-being. Congress delegated to a particular agency, the Health Resources and Services Administration (HRSA), authority to designate the preventive care insurance should cover. HRSA included in its designation all contraceptives approved by the Food and Drug Administration (FDA).

Destructive of the Women's Health Amendment, this Court leaves women workers to fend for themselves, to seek contraceptive coverage from sources other than their employer's insurer, and, absent another available source of funding, to pay for contraceptive services out of their own pockets. The Constitution's Free Exercise Clause, all agree, does not call for that imbalanced result.[1] Nor does the Religious Freedom Restoration Act of 1993 (RFRA), 42 U. S. C. §2000bb *et seq.*, condone harm to third parties occasioned by entire disregard of their needs. I therefore dissent from the Court's judgment, under which, as the Government estimates, between 70,500 and 126,400 women would immediately lose access to no-cost contraceptive services. On the merits, I would affirm the judgment of the U.S. Court of Appeals for the Third Circuit.

I

A

Under the ACA, an employer-sponsored "group health plan" must cover specified "preventive health services" without "cost sharing," 42 U. S. C. §300gg–13, *i.e.*, without such out-of-pocket costs as copays or deductibles.[2] Those enumerated services

---

1 In *Employment Div., Dept. of Human Resources of Ore.* v. *Smith*, 494 U.S. 872 (1990), the Court explained that "the right of free exercise does not relieve an individual of the obligation to comply with a valid and neutral law of general applicability on the ground that the law proscribes (or prescribes) conduct that his religion prescribes (or proscribes)." *Id.*, at 879 (internal quotation marks omitted). The requirement that insurers cover FDA-approved methods of contraception "applies generally, . . . trains on women's well-being, not on the exercise of religion, and any effect it has on such exercise is incidental." *Burwell* v. *Hobby Lobby Stores, Inc.*, 573 U.S. 682, 745 (2014) (GINSBURG, J., dissenting). *Smith* forecloses "[a]ny First Amendment Free Exercise Clause claim [one] might assert" in opposition to that requirement. 573 U.S., at 744.

2 This requirement does not apply to employers with fewer than 50 employees, 26 U. S. C. §4980H(c)(2), or "grandfathered health plans"—plans in existence on March 23, 2010 that have not thereafter made specified changes in coverage, 42 U. S. C. §18011(a), (e); 45 CFR §147.140(g)(2018). "Federal statutes often include exemptions for small employers, and such provisions have never been held to undermine the interests served by these statutes." *Hobby Lobby*, 573 U.S., at 763 (GINSBURG, J., dissenting). "[T]he grandfathering provision," "far from ranking as a categorical exemption, . . . is temporary, intended to be a means for

did not, in the original draft bill, include preventive care specific to women. "To correct this oversight, Senator Barbara Mikulski introduced the Women's Health Amendment," now codified at §300gg–13(a)(4). *Burwell* v. *Hobby Lobby Stores, Inc.*, 573 U.S. 682, 741 (2014) (GINSBURG, J., dissenting); see also 155 Cong. Rec. 28841. This provision was designed "to promote equality in women's access to health care," countering gender-based discrimination and disparities in such access. Brief for 186 Members of the United States Congress as *Amici Curiae* 6 (hereinafter Brief for 186 Members of Congress). Its proponents noted, *inter alia*, that "[w]omen paid significantly more than men for preventive care," and that "cost barriers operated to block many women from obtaining needed care at all." *Hobby Lobby*, 573 U.S., at 742 (GINSBURG, J., dissenting); see, *e.g.,* 155 Cong. Rec. 28844 (statement of Sen. Hagan) ("When . . . women had to choose between feeding their children, paying the rent, and meeting other financial obligations, they skipped important preventive screenings and took a chance with their personal health.").

Due to the Women's Health Amendment, the preventive health services that group health plans must cover include, "with respect to women," "preventive care and screenings . . . provided for in comprehensive guidelines supported by [HRSA]." §300gg–13(a)(4). Pursuant to this instruction, HRSA undertook, after consulting the Institute of Medicine,[3] to state "what preventive services are necessary for women's health and well-being and therefore should be considered in the development of comprehensive guidelines for preventive services for women."[4] The resulting "Women's Preventive Services Guidelines" issued in August 2011.[5] Under these guidelines, millions of women

gradually transitioning employers into mandatory coverage." *Id.*, at 764 (internal quotation marks omitted).

3 "The [Institute of Medicine] is an arm of the National Academy of Sciences, an organization Congress established for the explicit purpose of furnishing advice to the Government." *Id.*, at 742, n. 3 (internal quotation marks omitted).

4 HRSA, U.S. Dept. of Health and Human Services (HHS), Women's Preventive Services Guidelines, www.hrsa.gov/womens-guidelines/index.html.

5 77 Fed. Reg. 8725 (2012).

who previously had no, or poor quality, health insurance gained cost-free access, not only to contraceptive services but as well to, *inter alia*, annual checkups and screenings for breast cancer, cervical cancer, postpartum depression, and gestational diabetes.[6] As to contraceptive services, HRSA directed that, to implement §300gg–13(a)(4), women's preventive services encompass "all [FDA] approved contraceptive methods, sterilization procedures, and patient education and counseling for all women with reproductive capacity."[7]

Ready access to contraceptives and other preventive measures for which Congress set the stage in §300gg–13(a)(4) both safeguards women's health and enables women to chart their own life's course. Effective contraception, it bears particular emphasis, "improves health outcomes for women and [their] children," as "women with unintended pregnancies are more likely to receive delayed or no prenatal care" than women with planned pregnancies. Brief for 186 Members of Congress 5 (internal quotation marks omitted); Brief for American College of Obstetricians and Gynecologists et al. as *Amici Curiae* 10 (hereinafter ACOG Brief) (similar). Contraception is also "critical for individuals with underlying medical conditions that would be further complicated by pregnancy," "has . . . health benefits unrelated to preventing pregnancy," (*e.g.*, it can reduce the risk of endometrial and ovarian cancer), Brief for National Women's Law Center et al. as *Amici Curiae* 23–24, 26 (hereinafter NWLC Brief), and "improves women's social and economic status," by "allow[ing] [them] to invest in higher education and a career with far less risk of an unplanned pregnancy," Brief for 186 Members of Congress 5–6 (internal quotation marks omitted).

---

6 HRSA, HHS, Women's Preventive Services Guidelines, *supra.*

7 77 Fed. Reg. 8725 (alterations and internal quotation marks omitted). Proponents of the Women's Health Amendment specifically anticipated that HRSA would require coverage of family planning services. See, *e.g.*, 155 Cong. Rec. 28841 (2009) (statement of Sen. Boxer); *id.*, at 28843 (statement of Sen. Gillibrand); *id.*, at 28844 (statement of Sen. Mikulski); *id.*, at 28869 (statement of Sen. Franken); *id.*, at 28876 (statement of Sen. Cardin); *ibid.* (statement of Sen. Feinstein); *id.*, at 29307 (statement of Sen. Murray).

B

For six years, the Government took care to protect women employees' access to critical preventive health services while accommodating the diversity of religious opinion on contraception. The Internal Revenue Service (IRS), the Employee Benefits Security Administration (EBSA), and the Center for Medicare and Medicaid Services (CMS) crafted a narrow exemption relieving houses of worship, "their integrated auxiliaries," "conventions or associations of churches," and "religious order[s]" from the contraceptive-coverage requirement. 76 Fed. Reg. 46623 (2011). For other nonprofit and closely held for-profit organizations opposed to contraception on religious grounds, the agencies made available an accommodation rather than an exemption. See 78 Fed. Reg. 39874 (2013); *Hobby Lobby*, 573 U.S., at 730–731.

> "Under th[e] accommodation, [an employer] can self-certify that it opposes providing coverage for particular contraceptive services. See 45 CFR §§147.131(b) (4),(c)(1) [(2013)]; 26 CFR §§54.9815–2713A(a) (4), (b). If [an employer] makes such a certification, the [employer's] insurance issuer or third-party administrator must '[e]xpressly exclude contraceptive coverage from the group health insurance coverage provided in connection with the group health plan' and '[p]rovide separate payments for any contraceptive services required to be covered' without imposing 'any cost-sharing requirements . . . on the [employer], the group health plan, or plan participants or beneficiaries.' 45 CFR §147.131(c)(2); 26 CFR §54.9815–2713A(c) (2)." *Id.*, at 731 (some alterations in original).[8]

---

8 This opinion refers to the contraceptive-coverage accommodation made in 2013 as the "self-certification accommodation." See *ante*, at 6 (opinion of the Court). Although this arrangement "requires the issuer to bear the cost of [contraceptive] services, HHS has determined that th[e] obligation will not impose any net expense on issuers because its cost will be less than or equal to the cost savings resulting from th[ose] services." *Hobby Lobby*, 573 U.S., at 698–699.

The self-certification accommodation, the Court observed in *Hobby Lobby*, "does not impinge on [an employer's] belief that providing insurance coverage for . . . contraceptives . . . violates [its] religion." *Ibid.* It serves "a Government interest of the highest order," *i.e.*, providing women employees "with cost-free access to all FDA-approved methods of contraception." *Id.*, at 729. And "it serves [that] stated interes[t] . . . well." *Id.*, at 731; see *id.*, at 693 (Government properly accommodated employer's religion-based objection to covering contraceptives under employer's health insurance plan when the harm to women of doing so "would be precisely zero"). Since the ACA's passage, "[gainfully employed] [w]omen, particularly in lower-income groups, have reported greater affordability of coverage, access to health care, and receipt of preventive services." Brief for 186 Members of Congress 21.

C

Religious employers, including petitioner Little Sisters of the Poor Saints Peter and Paul Home (Little Sisters), nonetheless urge that the self-certification accommodation renders them "complicit in providing [contraceptive] coverage to which they sincerely object." Brief for Little Sisters 35. In 2017, responsive to the pleas of such employers, the Government abandoned its effort to both end discrimination against employed women in access to preventive services and accommodate religious exercise. Under new rules drafted not by HRSA, but by the IRS, EBSA, and CMS, any "non-governmental employer"—even a publicly traded for-profit company—can avail itself of the religious exemption previously reserved for houses of worship. 82 Fed. Reg. 47792 (2017) (interim final rule); 45 CFR §147.132(a)(1)(i)(E) (2018).[9] More than 2.9 million Americans—including approximately 580,000 women of childbearing age—receive insurance through organizations newly eligible for this blanket

---

9 Nonprofit and closely held for-profit organizations with "sincerely held moral convictions" against contraception also qualify for the exemption. 45 CFR §147.133(a)(1)(i), (a)(2). Unless otherwise noted, this opinion refers to the religious and moral exemptions together as "the exemption" or "the blanket exemption."

exemption. 83 Fed. Reg. 57577–57578 (2018). Of cardinal significance, the exemption contains no alternative mechanism to ensure affected women's continued access to contraceptive coverage. See 45 CFR §147.132.

Pennsylvania and New Jersey, respondents here, sued to enjoin the exemption. Their lawsuit posed this core question: May the Government jettison an arrangement that promotes women workers' well-being while accommodating employers' religious tenets and, instead, defer entirely to employers' religious beliefs, although that course harms women who do not share those beliefs? The District Court answered "no," and preliminarily enjoined the blanket exemption nationwide. 281 F. Supp. 3d 553, 585 (ED Pa. 2017). The Court of Appeals affirmed. 930 F. 3d 543, 576 (CA3 2019). The same question is now presented for ultimate decision by this Court.

II

Despite Congress' endeavor, in the Women's Health Amendment to the ACA, to redress discrimination against women in the provision of healthcare, the exemption the Court today approves would leave many employed women just where they were before insurance issuers were obliged to cover preventive services for them, cost free. The Government urges that the ACA itself authorizes this result, by delegating to HRSA authority to exempt employers from the contraceptive-coverage requirement. This argument gains the Court's approbation. It should not.

A

I begin with the statute's text. But see *ante*, at 17 (opinion of the Court) (overlooking my starting place). The ACA's preventive-care provision, 42 U. S. C. §300gg–13(a), reads in full:

> "A group health plan and a health insurance issuer
> offering group or individual health insurance coverage
> shall, at a minimum provide coverage for and shall not
> impose any cost sharing requirements for—

"(1) evidence-based items or services that have in effect a rating of 'A' or 'B' in the current recommendations of the United States Preventive Services Task Force;

"(2) immunizations that have in effect a recommendation from the Advisory Committee on Immunization Practices of the Centers for Disease Control and Prevention with respect to the individual involved; . . .

"(3) with respect to infants, children, and adolescents, evidence-informed preventive care and screenings provided for in the comprehensive guidelines supported by [HRSA; and]

"(4) with respect to women, such additional preventive care and screenings not described in paragraph (1) as provided for in comprehensive guidelines supported by [HRSA] for purposes of this paragraph."

At the start of this provision, Congress instructed who is to "provide coverage for" the specified preventive health services: "group health plan[s]" and "health insurance issuer[s]." §300gg–13(a). As the Court of Appeals explained, paragraph (a)(4), added by the Women's Health Amendment, granted HRSA "authority to issue 'comprehensive guidelines' concern[ing] the *type* of services" group health plans and health insurance issuers must cover with respect to women. 930 F. 3d, at 570 (emphasis added). Nothing in paragraph (a)(4) accorded HRSA "authority to undermine Congress's [initial] directive," stated in subsection (a), "concerning *who* must provide coverage for these services." *Ibid.* (emphasis added).

The Government argues otherwise, asserting that "[t]he sweeping authorization for HRSA to 'provide[] for' and 'support[]' guidelines 'for purposes of' the women's preventive-services mandate clearly grants HRSA the power not just to specify what services should be covered, but also to provide appropriate exemptions." Brief for HHS et al. 15.[10] This terse statement—the entirety of the Government's textual case—slights the language Congress employed. Most visibly, the Government does not endeavor to explain how any language in paragraph (a)(4) counteracts Congress' opening instruction in §300gg–13(a) that group health plans "shall . . . provide" specified services. See *supra*, at 8–9.

The Court embraces, and the opinion concurring in the judgment adopts, the Government's argument. The Court correctly acknowledges that HRSA has broad discretion to determine *what* preventive services insurers should provide for women. *Ante*, at 15. But it restates that HRSA's "discretion [is] equally unchecked in other areas, including the ability to identify and create exemptions from its own Guidelines." *Ante*, at 16. See also *ante*, at 2–3 (Kagan, J., concurring in judgment) (agreeing with this interpretation). Like the Government, the Court and the opinion concurring in the judgment shut from sight §300gg–13(a)'s overarching direction that group health plans and health insurance issuers "shall" cover the specified services. See *supra*, at 8–9. That " 'absent provision[s] cannot be supplied by the courts,' " *ante*, at 16 (quoting *Rotkiske* v. *Klemm*, 589 U.S. ___, ___ (2019) (slip op., at 5), militates *against* the Court's conclusion, not in favor of it. Where Congress wanted to exempt certain employers from the ACA's requirements, it said so expressly. See, *e.g.*, *supra*, at 3, n. 2. Section 300gg–13(a)(4) includes no such exemption. See *supra*, at 8–9.[11]

B

The position advocated by the Government and endorsed by the Court and the opinion concurring in the judgment encounters further obstacles. Most saliently, the language in §300gg–13(a)(4)

---

10 This opinion uses "Brief for HHS et al." to refer to the Brief for Petitioners in No. 19–454, filed on behalf of the Departments of HHS, Treasury, and Labor, the Secretaries of those Departments, and the President.

11 The only language to which the Court points in support of its contrary conclusion is the phrase "as provided for." See *ante*, at 15. This phrase modifies "additional preventive care and screenings." §300gg–13(a)(4). It therefore speaks to what services shall be provided, not who must provide them.

mirrors that in §300gg–13(a)(3), the provision addressing *children's* preventive health services. Not contesting here that HRSA lacks authority to exempt group health plans from the children's preventive-care guidelines, the Government attempts to distinguish paragraph (a)(3) from paragraph (a)(4). Brief for HHS et al. 16–17. The attempt does not withstand inspection.

The Government first observes that (a)(4), unlike (a)(3), contemplates guidelines created "*for purposes of this paragraph.*" (Emphasis added.) This language does not speak to the scope of the guidelines HRSA is charged to create. Moreover, the Government itself accounts for this textual difference: The children's preventive-care guidelines described in paragraph (a)(3) were "preexisting guidelines . . . developed for purposes unrelated to the ACA." Brief for HHS et al. 16. The guidelines on women's preventive care, by contrast, did not exist before the ACA; they had to be created "for purposes of" the preventive-care mandate. §300gg–13(a)(4). The Government next points to the modifier "evidence-informed" placed in (a)(3), but absent in (a)(4). This omission, however it may bear on the kind of preventive services for women HRSA can require group health insurance to cover, does not touch or concern *who* is required to cover those services.[12]

HRSA's role within HHS also tugs against the Government's, the Court's, and the opinion concurring in the judgment's construction of §300gg–13(a)(4). That agency was a logical choice to determine what women's preventive services should be covered, as its mission is to "improve health care access" and "eliminate health disparities."[13] First and foremost, §300gg–13(a)(4) is directed at eradicating gender-based disparities in access to preventive care. See *supra*, at 3. Overlooked by the Court, see *ante*, at 14–18, and the opinion concurring in the judgment, see *ante*, at 2–3 (opinion of Kagan, J.), HRSA's expertise does not include

---

12 The Court does not say whether, in its view, the exemption authority it claims for women's preventive care exists as well for HRSA's children's preventive-care guidelines.

13 HRSA, HHS, Organization, www.hrsa.gov/about/organization/index.html.

any proficiency in delineating religious and moral exemptions. One would not, therefore, expect Congress to delegate to HRSA the task of crafting such exemptions. See *King* v. *Burwell*, 576 U.S. 473, 486 (2015) ("It is especially unlikely that Congress would have delegated this decision to [an agency] which has no expertise in . . . policy of this sort.").[14]

In fact, HRSA *did not* craft the blanket exemption. As earlier observed, see *supra*, at 7, that task was undertaken by the IRS, EBSA, and CMS. See also 45 CFR §147.132(a)(1), 147.133(a)(1) (direction by the IRS, EBSA, and CMS that HRSA's guidelines "*must not* provide for" contraceptive coverage in the circumstances described in the blanket exemption (emphasis added)). Nowhere in 42 U. S. C. §300gg–13(a)(4) are those agencies named, as earlier observed, see *supra*, at 8–9, an absence the Government, the Court, and the opinion concurring in the judgment do not deign to acknowledge. See Brief for HHS et al. 15–20; *ante*, at 14–18 (opinion of the Court); *ante*, at 2–3 (opinion of Kagan, J.).

C

If the ACA does not authorize the blanket exemption, the Government urges, then the exemption granted to houses of worship in 2011 must also be invalid. Brief for HHS et al. 19–20. As the Court of Appeals explained, however, see 930 F. 3d, at 570, n. 26, the latter exemption is not attributable to the ACA's text; it was justified on First Amendment grounds. See *Hosanna-Tabor Evangelical Lutheran Church and School* v. *EEOC*, 565 U.S. 171, 188 (2012) (the First Amendment's "ministerial exception" protects "the internal governance of [a] church"); 80 Fed. Reg. 41325 (2015) (the exemption "recogni[zes] [the] particular sphere of autonomy [afforded to] houses of worship . . . consistent with their special status under longstanding tradition

---

14 A more logical choice would have been HHS's Office for Civil Rights (OCR), which "enforces . . . conscience and religious freedom laws" with respect to HHS programs. HHS, OCR, About Us, www.hhs.gov/ocr/about-us/index.html. Indeed, when the Senate introduced an amendment to the ACA similar in character to the blanket exemption, a measure that failed to pass, the Senate instructed that OCR administer the exemption. 158 Cong. Rec. 1415 (2012) (proposed amendment); *id.*, at 2634 (vote tabling amendment).

in our society").[15] Even if the house-of-worship exemption extends beyond what the First Amendment would require, see *ante*, at 3, n. 1 (opinion of Kagan, J.), that extension, as just explained, cannot be extracted from the ACA's text.[16]

III

Because I conclude that the blanket exemption gains no aid from the ACA, I turn to the Government's alternative argument. The *religious* exemption, if not the moral exemption, the Government urges, is necessary to protect religious freedom. The Government does not press a free exercise argument, see *supra*, at 2, and n. 1, instead invoking RFRA. Brief for HHS et al. 20–31. That statute instructs that the "Government shall not substantially burden a person's exercise of religion even if the burden results from a rule of general applicability," unless doing so "is the least restrictive means of furthering [a] compelling governmental interest." 42 U. S. C. §2000bb–1(a), (b).

A

1

The parties here agree that federal agencies may craft accommodations and exemptions to cure violations of RFRA. See, *e.g.*, Brief for Respondents 36.[17] But that authority is not unbounded. *Cutter* v. *Wilkinson*, 544 U.S. 709, 720 (2005) (construing Religious Land Use and Institutionalized Persons Act of 2000, the Court cautioned that "adequate account" must be taken of "the burdens a requested accommodation may impose on

---

15 On the broad scope the Court today attributes to the "ministerial exception," see *Our Lady of Guadalupe School* v. *Morrissey-Berru*, 591 U.S. ___ (2020).

16 The Government does not argue that my view of the limited compass of §300gg–13(a)(4) imperils the self-certification accommodation. Brief for HHS et al. 19–20. But see *ante*, at 18, n. 9 (opinion of the Court). That accommodation aligns with the Court's decisions under the Religious Freedom Restoration Act of 1993 (RFRA). See *infra*, at 14–15. It strikes a balance between women's health and religious opposition to contraception, preserving women's access to seamless, no-cost contraceptive coverage, but imposing the obligation to provide such coverage directly on insurers, rather than on the objecting employer. See *supra*, at 6; *infra*, at 18–20. The blanket exemption, in contrast, entirely disregards women employees' preventive care needs.

17 But see, e.g., Brief for Professors of Criminal Law et al. as *Amici Curiae* 8–11 (RFRA does not grant agencies independent rulemaking authority; instead, laws allegedly violating RFRA must be challenged in court). No party argues that agencies can act to cure violations of RFRA only after a court has found a RFRA violation, and this opinion does not adopt any such view.

nonbeneficiaries" of the Act); *Caldor*, 472 U.S., at 708–710 (invalidating state statute requiring employers to accommodate an employee's religious observance for failure to take into account the burden such an accommodation would impose on the employer and other employees). "[O]ne person's right to free exercise must be kept in harmony with the rights of her fellow citizens." *Hobby Lobby*, 573 U.S., at 765, n. 25 (GINSBURG, J., dissenting). See also *id.*, at 746 ("[Y]our right to swing your arms ends just where the other man's nose begins." (quoting Chafee, Freedom of Speech in War Time, 32 Harv. L. Rev. 932, 957 (1919)).

In this light, the Court has repeatedly assumed that any religious accommodation to the contraceptive-coverage requirement would preserve women's continued access to seamless, no-cost contraceptive coverage. See *Zubik* v. *Burwell*, 578 U.S. ___, ___ (2016) (*per curiam*) (slip op., at 4) ("[T]he parties on remand should be afforded an opportunity to arrive at an approach . . . that accommodates petitioners' religious exercise while . . . ensuring that women covered by petitioners' health plans receive full and equal health coverage, including contraceptive coverage." (internal quotation marks omitted)); *Wheaton College* v. *Burwell*, 573 U.S. 958, 959 (2014) ("Nothing in this interim order affects the ability of applicant's employees and students to obtain, without cost, the full range of [FDA] approved contraceptives."); *Hobby Lobby*, 573 U.S., at 692 ("There are other ways in which Congress or HHS could equally ensure that every woman has cost-free access to . . . all [FDA]-approved contraceptives. In fact, HHS has already devised and implemented a system that seeks to respect the religious liberty of religious non-profit corporations while ensuring that the employees of these entities have precisely the same access to all FDA-approved contraceptives as employees of [other] companies."). The assumption made in the above-cited cases rests on the basic principle just stated, one on which this dissent relies: While the Government may "accommodate religion beyond free exercise requirements,"

Cutter, 544 U.S., at 713, when it does so, it may not benefit religious adherents at the expense of the rights of third parties. See, *e.g., id.*, at 722 ("[A]n accommodation must be measured so that it does not override other significant interests."); *Caldor*, 472 U.S., at 710 (religious exemption was invalid for its "unyielding weighting in favor of" interests of religious adherents "over all other interests"). Holding otherwise would endorse "the regulatory equivalent of taxing non-adherents to support the faithful." Brief for Church-State Scholars as *Amici Curiae* 3.

2

The expansive religious exemption at issue here imposes significant burdens on women employees. Between 70,500 and 126,400 women of childbearing age, the Government estimates, will experience the disappearance of the contraceptive coverage formerly available to them, 83 Fed. Reg. 57578–57580; indeed, the numbers may be even higher.[18] Lacking any alternative insurance coverage mechanism, see *supra*, at 7, the exemption leaves women two options, neither satisfactory.

The first option—the one suggested by the Government in its most recent rulemaking, 82 Fed. Reg. 47803—is for women to seek contraceptive care from existing government-funded programs. Such programs, serving primarily low-income individuals, are not designed to handle an influx of tens of thousands of previously insured women.[19] Moreover, as the Government has

---

18 The Government notes that 2.9 million people were covered by the 209 plans that previously utilized the self-certification accommodation. 83 Fed. Reg. 57577. One hundred nine of those plans covering 727,000 people, the Government estimates, will use the religious exemption, while 100 plans covering more than 2.1 million people will continue to use the self-certification accommodation. *Id.*, at 57578. If more plans, or plans covering more people, use the new exemption, more women than the Government estimates will be affected.

19 Title X "is the only federal grant program dedicated solely to providing individuals with comprehensive family planning and related preventive health services." HHS, About Title X Grants, www.hhs.gov/opa/title-x-family-planning/about-title-x-grants/index.html. A recent rule makes women who lose contraceptive coverage due to the religious exemption eligible for Title X services. See 84 Fed. Reg. 7734 (2019). Expanding *eligibility*, however, "does nothing to ensure Title X providers actually have capacity to meet the expanded client population." Brief for National Women's Law Center et al. as *Amici Curiae* 22. Moreover, that same rule forced 1,041 health providers, serving more than 41% of Title X patients, out of the Title X provider network due to their affiliation with abortion providers. 84 Fed. Reg. 7714; Brief for Planned Parenthood Federation of America et al. as *Amici Curiae* 18–19.

acknowledged, requiring women "to take steps to learn about, and to sign up for, a new health benefit" imposes "additional barriers," "mak[ing] that coverage accessible to fewer women." 78 Fed. Reg. 39888. Finally, obtaining care from a government-funded program instead of one's regular care provider creates a continuity-of-care problem, "forc[ing those] who lose coverage away from trusted providers who know their medical histories." NWLC Brief 18.

The second option for women losing insurance coverage for contraceptives is to pay for contraceptive counseling and devices out of their own pockets. Notably, however, "the most effective contraception is also the most expensive." ACOG Brief 14–15. "[T]he cost of an IUD [intrauterine device]," for example, "is nearly equivalent to a month's full-time pay for workers earning the minimum wage." *Hobby Lobby*, 573 U.S., at 762 (GINSBURG, J., dissenting). Faced with high out-of-pocket costs, many women will forgo contraception, Brief for 186 Members of Congress 11, or resort to less effective contraceptive methods, 930 F. 3d, at 563.

As the foregoing indicates, the religious exemption "reintroduce[s] the very health inequities and barriers to care that Congress intended to eliminate when it enacted the women's preventive services provision of the ACA." NWLC Brief 5. "No tradition, and no prior decision under RFRA, allows a religion-based exemption when [it] would be harmful to others—here, the very persons the contraceptive coverage requirement was designed to protect." *Hobby Lobby*, 573 U.S., at 764 (GINSBURG, J., dissenting).[20] I would therefore hold the religious exemption neither required nor permitted by RFRA.[21]

---

20 Remarkably, JUSTICE ALITO maintains that stripping women of insurance coverage for contraceptive services imposes no burden. See *ante*, at 18 (concurring opinion). He reaches this conclusion because, in his view, federal law does not require the contraceptive coverage denied to women under the exemption. *Ibid.* Congress, however, called upon HRSA to specify contraceptive and other preventive services for women in order to ensure equality in women employees' access to healthcare, thus safeguarding their health and well-being. See *supra*, at 2–5.

21 As above stated, the Government does not defend the moral exemption under RFRA. See *supra*, at 13.

B

Pennsylvania and New Jersey advance an additional argument: The exemption is not authorized by RFRA, they maintain, because the self-certification accommodation it replaced was sufficient to alleviate any substantial burden on religious exercise. Brief for Respondents 36–42. That accommodation, I agree, further indicates the religious exemption's flaws.

1

For years, religious organizations have challenged the self-certification accommodation as insufficiently protective of their religious rights. See, *e.g.*, *Zubik*, 578 U.S., at ___ (slip op., at 3). While I do not doubt the sincerity of these organizations' opposition to that accommodation, *Hobby Lobby*, 573 U.S., at 758–759 (GINSBURG, J., dissenting), I agree with Pennsylvania and New Jersey that the accommodation does not substantially burden objectors' religious exercise.

As Senator Hatch observed, "[RFRA] does not require the Government to justify every action that has some effect on religious exercise." 139 Cong. Rec. 26180 (1993). *Bowen* v. *Roy*, 476 U.S. 693 (1986), is instructive in this regard. There, a Native American father asserted a sincere religious belief that his daughter's spirit would be harmed by the Government's use of her social security number. *Id.*, at 697. The Court, while casting no doubt on the sincerity of this religious belief, explained:

> "Never to our knowledge has the Court interpreted the First Amendment to require the Government *itself* to behave in ways that the individual believes will further his or her spiritual development or that of his or her family. The Free Exercise Clause simply cannot be understood to require the Government to conduct its own internal affairs in ways that comport with the religious beliefs of particular citizens." *Id.*, at 699.[22]

---

22 JUSTICE ALITO disputes the relevance of *Roy*, asserting that the religious adherent in that case faced no penalty for noncompliance with the legal requirement under consideration. See

Roy signals a critical distinction in the Court's religious exercise jurisprudence: A religious adherent may be entitled to religious accommodation with regard to her own conduct, but she is not entitled to "insist that . . . *others* must conform *their* conduct to [her] own religious necessities.'" *Caldor*, 472 U.S., at 710 (quoting *Otten* v. *Baltimore & Ohio R. Co.*, 205 F. 2d 58, 61 (CA2 1953) (Hand, J.); (emphasis added).[23] Counsel for the Little Sisters acknowledged as much when he conceded that religious "employers could [not] object at all" to a "government obligation" to provide contraceptive coverage "imposed directly on the insurers." Tr. of Oral Arg. 41.[24]

But that is precisely what the self-certification accommodation does. As the Court recognized in *Hobby Lobby*: "When a group-health-insurance issuer receives notice that [an employer opposes coverage for some or all contraceptive services for religious reasons], the issuer must then exclude [that] coverage from the employer's plan and provide separate payments for contraceptive services for plan participants." 573 U.S., at 698–699; see also *id.*, at 738 (KENNEDY, J., concurring) ("The accommodation works by requiring *insurance companies* to cover . . . contraceptive coverage for female employees who wish it." (emphasis added)). Under the self-certification accommodation, then, the objecting employer is absolved of any obligation to provide the contraceptive coverage to which it objects; that obligation is transferred to the insurer. This arrangement "furthers the Government's interest [in women's health] but does not impinge on the [employer's] religious beliefs." *Ibid.*; see *supra*, at 18–19.

---

ante, at 6, n. 5. As JUSTICE ALITO acknowledges, however, the critical inquiry has two parts. See *ante*, at 6–7. It is not enough to ask whether noncompliance entails "substantial adverse practical consequences." One must also ask whether compliance substantially burdens religious exercise. Like *Roy*, my dissent homes in on the latter question.

23   Even if RFRA sweeps more broadly than the Court's pre-*Smith* jurisprudence in some respects, see *Hobby Lobby*, 573 U.S., at 695, n. 3; but see *id.*, at 749–750 (GINSBURG, J., dissenting), there is no cause to believe that Congress jettisoned this fundamental distinction.

24   JUSTICE ALITO ignores the distinction between (1) a request for an accommodation with regard to one's own conduct, and (2) an attempt to require others to conform their conduct to one's own religious beliefs. This distinction is fatal to JUSTICE ALITO's argument that the self-certification accommodation violates RFRA. See *ante*, at 6–10.

2

The Little Sisters, adopting the arguments made by religious organizations in *Zubik*, resist this conclusion in two ways. First, they urge that contraceptive coverage provided by an insurer under the self-certification accommodation forms "part of the same plan as the coverage provided by the employer." Brief for Little Sisters 12 (internal quotation marks omitted). See also Tr. of Oral Arg. 29 (Little Sisters object "to having their plan hijacked"); *ante*, at 8 (ALITO, J., concurring) (Little Sisters object to "maintain[ing] and pay[ing] for a plan under which coverage for contraceptives would be provided"). This contention is contradicted by the plain terms of the regulation establishing that accommodation: To repeat, an insurance issuer "must . . . *[e]xpressly exclude* contraceptive coverage from the group health insurance coverage provided in connection with the group health plan." 45 CFR §147.131(c)(2)(i)(A) (2013) (emphasis added); see *supra*, at 6.[25]

Second, the Little Sisters assert that "tak[ing] affirmative steps to execute paperwork . . . necessary for the provision of 'seamless' contraceptive coverage to their employees" implicates them in providing contraceptive services to women in violation of their religious beliefs. Little Sisters Reply Brief 7. At the same time, however, they have been adamant that they do not oppose merely "register[ing] their objections" to the contraceptive-coverage requirement. *Ibid.* See also Tr. of Oral Arg. 29, 42–43 (Little Sisters have "no objection to objecting"); *ante*, at 8 (ALITO, J., concurring) (Little Sisters' "concern was not with notifying the Government that they wished to be exempted from complying with the mandate *per se*"). These statements, taken together, reveal that the Little Sisters do not object to what the self-certification accommodation asks of *them*, namely, attesting to their

---

25 Religious organizations have observed that, under the self-certification accommodation, insurers need not, and do not, provide contraceptive coverage under a separate policy number. Supp. Brief for Petitioners in *Zubik* v. *Burwell*, O. T. 2015, No. 14–1418, p. 1. This objection does not relate to a religious employer's own conduct; instead, it concerns the insurer's conduct. See *supra*, at 18–19.

religious objection to contraception. See *supra*, at 6. They object, instead, to the particular use insurance issuers make of that attestation. See *supra*, at 18–19.[26] But that use originated from the ACA and its once-implementing regulation, not from religious employers' self-certification or alternative notice.

* * *

The blanket exemption for religious and moral objectors to contraception formulated by the IRS, EBSA, and CMS is inconsistent with the text of, and Congress' intent for, both the ACA and RFRA. Neither law authorizes it.[27] The original administrative regulation accommodating religious objections to contraception appropriately implemented the ACA and RFRA consistent with Congress' staunch determination to afford women employees equal access to preventive services, thereby advancing public health and welfare and women's well-being. I would therefore affirm the judgment of the Court of Appeals.[28]

---

26 JUSTICE ALITO asserts that the Little Sisters' "situation [is] the same as that of the conscientious objector in *Thomas* [v. *Review Bd. of Ind. Employment Security Div.*, 450 U.S. 707, 715 (1981)]." *Ante*, at 9–10. I disagree. In *Thomas*, a Jehovah's Witness objected to "work[ing] on weapons," 450 U.S., at 710, which is what his employer required of him. As above stated, however, the Little Sisters have no objection to objecting, the only other action the self-certification accommodation requires of them.

27 Given this conclusion, I need not address whether the exemption is procedurally invalid. See *ante*, at 22–26 (opinion of the Court).

28 Although the Court does not reach the issue, the District Court did not abuse its discretion in issuing a nationwide injunction. The Administrative Procedure Act contemplates nationwide relief from invalid agency action. See 5 U. S. C. §706(2) (empowering courts to "hold unlawful and set aside agency action"). Moreover, the nationwide reach of the injunction "was 'necessary to provide complete relief to the plaintiffs.'" *Trump* v. *Hawaii*, 585 U.S. ___, ___, n. 15 (2018) (SOTOMAYOR, J., dissenting) (slip op., at 25, n. 13) (quoting *Madsen* v. *Women's Health Center*, Inc., 512 U.S. 753, 765 (1994)). Harm to Pennsylvania and New Jersey, the Court of Appeals explained, occurs because women who lose benefits under the exemption "will turn to state-funded services for their contraceptive needs and for the unintended pregnancies that may result from the loss of coverage." 930 F. 3d, at 562. This harm is not bounded by state lines. The Court of Appeals noted, for example, that some 800,000 residents of Pennsylvania and New Jersey work—and thus receive their health insurance—out of State. *Id.*, at 576. Similarly, many students who attend colleges and universities in Pennsylvania and New Jersey receive their health insurance from their parents' out-of-state health plans. *Ibid.*

Word Cloud Classics

Word Cloud Classics

Leaves of Grass

The Legend of Sleepy Hollow and Other Tales

Les Misérables

A Little Princess

Little Women

Love Poems

Mansfield Park

The Merry Adventures of Robin Hood

Moby-Dick

My Ántonia

Northanger Abbey

Odyssey

Peter Pan

The Phantom of the Opera

The Picture of Dorian Gray

The Poetry of Emily Dickinson

Presidential Inaugural Addresses

Pride and Prejudice

The Prince and Other Writings

The Prophet and Other Tales

The Romantic Poets

The Scarlet Letter

The Secret Garden

Selected Works of Alexander Hamilton

Selected Works of Edgar Allan Poe

Selected Works of H. G. Wells

Sense and Sensibility

Shakespeare's Sonnets and Other Poems

Strange Case of Dr. Jekyll and Mr. Hyde & Other Stories

A Tale of Two Cities

The Three Musketeers

Treasure Island

Twenty Thousand Leagues Under the Sea

The U.S. Constitution and Other Key American Writings

Walden and Civil Disobedience

William Shakespeare Comedies

William Shakespeare Tragedies

The Wind in the Willows and Other Stories

The Wizard of Oz

Wuthering Heights